The Storyteller of Jerusalem

The Storyteller of Jerusalem

The Life and Times of Wasif Jawhariyyeh, 1904–1948

Edited and introduced by
Salim Tamari and Issam Nassar

Translated by Nada Elzeer
Foreword by Rachel Beckles Willson

An imprint of Interlink Publishing Group, Inc.
www.interlinkbooks.com

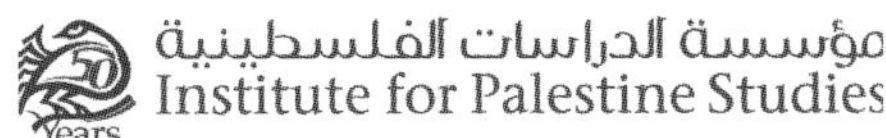

This edition first published in 2021 by

OLIVE BRANCH PRESS
An imprint of Interlink Publishing Group, Inc.
46 Crosby Street, Northampton, Massachusetts 01060
www.interlinkbooks.com

Originally published in Arabic in two volumes by the Institute for Palestine Studies, Beirut, Lebanon under the tiles: *Al-Quds al-Uthmaniyyah fi al-mudhakkirat al-jawhariyyah: al-kitab al-awwal min mudhakkirat al-musiqi Wasif Jawhariyyah, 1904–1917* [Ottoman Jerusalem in the Jawhariyyeh Memoirs: Volume One of the Memoirs of the Musician Wasif Jawhariyyeh, 1904–1917], Nassar and Tamari, eds. (2003) and *Al-Quds al-intidabiyyah fi al-mudhakkirat al-jawhariyyah: al-kitab al-thani min mudhakkirat al-musiqi Wasif Jawhariyyah, 1918–1948* [British Mandate Jerusalem in the Jawhariyyeh Memoirs: Volume Two of the Memoirs of the Musician Wasif Jawhariyyeh, 1918–1948], Nassar and Tamari, eds. (2005).

Library of Congress Cataloging-in-Publication Data

Jawhariyah, Wasif, 1897-1973.
[Quds al-'Uthmaniyah fi al-mudhakkirat al-Jawhariyah. English]
The storyteller of Jerusalem : the life and times of musician Wasif Jawhariyyeh, 1904-1948 / edited and introduced by Salim Tamari and Issam Nassar ; translated by Nada Elzeer ; with a foreword by Rachel Beckles Willson. -- First American edition.
pages cm
Translation of: al-Quds al-'Uthmaniyah fi al-mudhakkirat al-Jawhariyah.
ISBN 978-1-56656-925-5
1. Jawhariyah, Wasif, 1897-1973. 2. Musicians--Jerusalem--Biography. 3. Jerusalem--History--20th century. I. Tamari, Salim, editor. II. Nassar, Issam, editor. III. Elzeer, Nada, traslator. IV. Title.
ML420.J285A313 2013
780.92'2569442--dc23

2013000398

General Editor: Michel S. Moushabeck
Editor: John Fiscella
Proofreader: Jennifer Staltare
Cover design: James MacDonald/The Impress Group
Book design and production: Pam Fontes-May

Printed and bound in the United States of America

10 9 8 7 6 5 4 3 2

CONTENTS

NOTE ON THIS EDITION

The complete memoirs of Wasif Jawhariyyeh (b. 1897, d. 1972) are archived at the Institute for Palestine Studies (IPS) in Ramallah. The original handwritten manuscript comprises three volumes that Wasif entitled Books I, II, and III. The collection also includes seven photographic albums.

The memoirs were first published in Arabic in two volumes by IPS in Beirut.* Volume I is devoted to Ottoman Jerusalem and the time period 1904–1917. Volume II covers British Mandate Jerusalem, 1918–1948, as well as entries through 1968 from the period of Wasif's exile in Beirut.

In this English-language edition of the memoirs, entries have been selected to convey in a single volume the range and richness of the original, with an emphasis on the musical life of the times. As Salim Tamari points out, the Jawhariyyeh memoirs offer readers of history "one of the most valuable records of Palestinian urban life that exists anywhere." At the same time they offer simply one person's voice chronicling contested life in Jerusalem, a local artist and patriot telling his story of a city.

* *Al-Quds al-Uthmaniyyah fi al-mudhakkirat al-jawhariyyah: al-kitab al-awwal min mudhakkirat al-musiqi Wasif Jawhariyyah, 1904–1917* [*Ottoman Jerusalem in the Jawhariyyeh Memoirs: Volume I of the Memoirs of the Musician Wasif Jawhariyyeh, 1904–1917*], edited by Issam Nassar and Salim Tamari (Beirut: Institute for Palestine Studies, 2003).

Al-Quds al-intidabiyyah fi al-mudhakkirat al-jawhariyyah: al-kitab al-thani min mudhakkirat al-musiqi Wasif Jawhariyyah, 1918–1948 [*British Mandate Jerusalem in the Jawhariyyeh Memoirs: Volume II of the Memoirs of the Musician Wasif Jawhariyyeh, 1918–1948*], Nassar and Tamari, eds. (Beirut: IPS, 2005).

ACKNOWLEDGMENTS

Collecting, preserving, translating, editing, and publishing these memoirs, or selections of them, was an ongoing effort for close to a decade. In the process, numerous individuals helped in various ways to eventually bring the memoirs to light, first in Arabic and now in English. We would like to thank each and every one of them, but listing their names and contributions would require many pages. So our thanks go to them all, those unknown soldiers in Palestine, Lebanon, Jordan, and elsewhere.

However, without the help of the surviving children of Wasif Jawharieh, the memoirs would not have seen the light, perhaps for many more years. The support, both financial and otherwise, of George Jawharieh was crucial. Aya Jawharieh-Shaker provided us with the manuscript, photographs, and many stories about Wasif that helped us place the memoirs in historical contexts. Special thanks go to Amal Nashashibi, who first drew our attention to the memoirs. The staff at the Institute for Palestine Studies in Beirut, especially the librarians, was exceptionally helpful, in particular Mona Nsouli, when it came to the use of photographs from their collection. The staff and members of the Institute's research committee deserve our thanks for their support for this project. We are also grateful to the Music and Letters Trust for its generous financial support.

A special thank you goes to the translator, Nada Elzeer, who did a splendid job and produced a meticulous translation of the selections of the memoirs. Finally, essential to the publication of this book were the patience and enthusiasm of our publisher, Michel Moushabeck, and the contributions of this project's team at Interlink Publishing: John Fiscella (editing), Jennifer Staltare (proofreading), Leyla Moushabeck and Pam Fontes-May (production), and James McDonald (cover design).

— Issam Nassar and Salim Tamari

FOREWORD
HEARING PALESTINE
by Rachel Beckles Willson

For anyone in search of the sounds of Ottoman Palestine, the memoirs of Wasif Jawhariyyeh provide an indispensable guide. Wasif was a passionate amateur musician who was familiar with the music not only of his native Jerusalem but of neighboring towns and villages. His writings retrieve for us a sense of the beauty of the region's music, its meanings to local people, and its shifting roles under the influence of enormous regional change. We learn about Palestine's ritual music, street music, concert music, puppet show music, party music, plus music on gramophone records and the radio station, through anecdotes and invaluable historical snapshots.

As his account leads us from the Ottoman period into the era of British control, Wasif also describes the foreigners who wrote about residents such as himself, turning the lens around and offering us a panoply of musical confrontations. He seems often to have faced the most pressing political questions of his time while involved with music. Thus by following the music in his memoirs we gain more than a new appreciation of the past sounds of Palestine. At once the subject and the observer, Wasif records for us intimate glimpses of how new arrivals from abroad—pilgrims, missionaries, colonial officers, educators, Jewish settlers—perceived and sought to transform the world of Palestinian Arabs.

Musical Elevations

From a young age Wasif gathered music from people he met in fields, streets, and homes, so that he built up skills that included singing Arabic song, folk dancing, and playing the *darbuka, tanboor, rebeck, oud,* violin, and *cümbüs*. His memoirs attest that the region possessed a wide range of musical instruments and practices—Arabic, Armenian, Kurdish, Turkish, European—that multiplied during his lifetime. He enjoyed remarkable privileges through family contact with the man who would become mayor, Hussein Effendi, who supported him as a child and young adult. Without Hussein Effendi, it is questionable if any of the key reference points in his music education would be there at all—whether meeting a Moroccan man tending Husseini's fields who helped him make his first real instrument or hearing and meeting the great Egyptian musician and actor Sheikh Salama Hijazi at the age of eleven.[1] But he benefited first from a domestic background shaped by his father. A successful lawyer and powerful, if intimidating, presence who valued art and painted icons, Jiryis Jawhariyyeh encouraged his son to practice Qu'ranic recitation and fostered his love of classical music. Thus when a family friend had been persuaded to teach Wasif the oud, Jiryis was at hand to host the lessons, serving wine and delicacies to keep the teacher happy.[2]

Wasif himself was passionately committed. He could not have acquired his skills otherwise, for he learned through what he refers to as "the old method." The teacher showed the pupil where to place his fingers on the oud when playing a short melody, then passing it to the pupil to try. Back and forth they passed the instrument, continuing in hope that a piece would emerge from the fragments and be remembered.[3] This process would rapidly enable Wasif to provide music in the Palestinian community, including at the parties that he and his friends enjoyed in intense inebriation. The pleasure-loving lifestyle he describes belies foreign notions of "the holy city" and may in certain periods have been widespread. He enlivened a wide range of situations with his musicianship, not only in gatherings of friends and (later on) colonial officers, but also with colleagues at his office jobs, and in the face of what one suspects was an increasing sense of political helplessness.

One aspect of his musicianship that stands out is his pursuit of an empathetic sense of *tarab*. "Tarab" refers in part to genres of modal Arabic music associated with professional musicians in certain urban centers of the Middle East. But it also applies to the intense feeling of ecstasy sought by devotees of the tradition.[4] Wasif's references to tarab in Palestine are fascinating for a number of reasons.

For a start, his world of musical tarab is greatly at odds with the sectarian thinking of visiting commentators. It was only natural that Europeans coming with a desire to "rescue" Palestine from Islam and restore it to Christianity were attached to the perception of a sharp division between Christians and Muslims. The British systematically set about instituting separation strategies once they took control in 1917. But the embrace of tarab by Wasif (a Greek Orthodox Christian) contains within it his love of Qu'ranic recitation, a love that he absorbed not only from Muslim musicians advising him how to improve his singing but also from other Christians (in addition to his father, the renowned teacher Khalil Sakakini).[5] Although he loved and emulated styles that were less elevated (such as the popular song genre known as *taqtouqa*), he absorbed a sense of musical refinement from his father, who had corrected his singing and accused him angrily of sounding like a "handyman" when neglecting the rhyming qualities of language in verse.[6] It was primarily devotion to classical Arabic, as mediated most rigorously by the Qu'ran, which secured a sense of musical quality for Christians and Muslims alike. And tarab was one of the embodiments of that. Wasif remarked of Egyptian Sheikh Ahmed al-Tarifi that he put listeners in a state of tarab when he sang because of "a performance style which resembled Qu'ran recitation."[7]

The welcome of tarab in Palestine provides one of many examples of how residents sought paths into a more modern world distinct from colonial models. Wasif's appreciation of tarab was a product of contemporary Egyptian music making, in which the most renowned singers were Qu'ran chanters. Even when music expanded into a secular professional sphere there, Qu'ranic recitation continued to underpin the most celebrated vocal styles.[8] From 1910 onwards in Jerusalem, when gramophone records could be heard in cafés and on the street, the music of Egypt in particular held Wasif's rapt attention, whether that of Sheikh Yusuf al-Manyalawi, Muhammad Uthman, Sheikh Salama Hijazi, or others. Opportunities for hearing such repertoire were only increased by the enhanced opportunities for musicians to travel during the early years of British Mandate rule, and then the Palestine Broadcasting Station founded in 1936 became a potent attraction for Arab musicians regionally. In short, Palestinian culture was able to develop along Egyptian models—facilitated, ironically, by some of the British interpolations. Wasif's personal enthusiasm for appropriating everything new can be traced in his songbook, a compilation of song texts he wrote down for future generations.[9]

The musical experience of tarab also challenges the very architecture of Jerusalem as mapped by foreigners. From the mid-nineteenth century onwards, it was routine to consider Jerusalem's Old City as lying in confessional "quarters," and it became a colonial project to erect new buildings marking areas associated with biblical sites in order to manage Christian relics effectively. Thus, for instance, in the latter half of the nineteenth century, four very substantial Roman Catholic institutions were built shaping the Via Dolorosa, a Christian pilgrimage site.[10] But this same location figures in one of Wasif's recollections as a site in which there were experiences of tarab shared by a large number of the city's residents. When singer and oud player Muhammad al-Ashiq stayed in Jerusalem, for instance, he arranged to sit outside the so-called Hospice Café (opposite the Catholic Austrian Hospice) and make music.[11] In Wasif's recollection, the footsteps of Christian pilgrims—so central in European accounts of daytime pursuits in Jerusalem—go unmentioned. Instead, it is the mesmerizing sounds of new songs from Egypt that transfigure the surroundings. These sounds pass between the buildings and elevate themselves above them, reaching out towards homes throughout the city.

Musical Interactions

It might seem from pilgrim-versus-resident accounts of the Via Dolorosa that there was no overlap between the experiences of visitors and that of locals. But of course the opposite was the case, and Wasif's memoirs are exceptional for their accounts of such meetings. They document the fact that the military governor of Jerusalem in the early British Mandate years, Ronald Storrs, was so exasperated by the crowing of a neighborhood rooster that he ordered its execution.[12] Yet Wasif also observes that the bird belonged to translator As'ad Khodr, who found Storrs's late-night piano playing a disturbance. His account illuminates a dynamic relationship, with sounds infiltrating homes and causing substantial tension between people affected.

Such relationships are of special interest today when they reveal broad changes among and between the region's population groups. Early on in the memoirs, Wasif lists Syrian Jewish players among the "professional" musicians active in Jerusalem. He identifies their loyalty to the tradition of Arabic song known as *muwashah*, while observing (without criticism) that they altered the language and indeed content of the texts.[13] He also describes the contexts in which he heard these musicians, making clear that some of these were characterized by inter-confessional fluidity and exchange. One of the well-known *janakis* (singers) was the Jewish Sulika, who led a band with accompanying dancers. Wasif remarked, "there is not a single Arab Muslim or Christian house in Jerusalem whose celebrations had not been led by Sulika, who [...] converted to Islam."[14] Similarly, he recalls that when the famous singer and dancer Badi'a Masabni visited Jerusalem, she was accompanied by a musical band conducted by the Jewish player Shehada. Wasif admired their performance greatly, also observing that Shehada played the oud "very well indeed."[15] And he was happy to have learned an Egyptian song from Shehada himself and later teach it to the English teacher at Saint George's School, the Arab Dr. Izzat Tannous.[16]

With respect to Jews who later settled in the region, however, the picture seems much more burdened with plays of power. This evident rivalry should be seen in the context of the British government's use of the categories "Arab" and "Jewish" in support of the plan to create a "Jewish national home." Music was directly affected by the division, and the Palestine Broadcasting Service is a perfect illustration. This trilingual radio station, which divided airtime between the perceived cultural interests of Arabic, English, and Hebrew speakers, normalized, naturalized, and indeed *amplified* the boundaries between categories, cementing fault lines between people who had frequently interacted fluidly.[17] A vibrant community of musicians coalesced around the Arabic Section, which became a meeting point between local musicians (including Wasif's brother Tawfiq, composer and oud player Rowhi al-Khamash, violinist Jaleel Rakb, oud player Ramez al-Zaaa, percussionist Basil Tharwat, Armenian santur player Artin Santurji) and leading musical figures from the rest of the Arab world (such as violinist al-Shawwa, composer and oud player Jamil Aweis, buzuq player Mohammed Abdul Karim, and many others). A range of recollections indicates that the Arabic Section was highly successful and extremely popular, and enjoyed at times a high degree of autonomy in programs understood by the British as "cultural." Yet, such work was always in competition with activities at the English and Hebrew Sections, and the Arabic Section's self-definition reflected that.

For Wasif, the main culprit in this sorry state of affairs was the British government. He was, nevertheless, a complex figure in this regard. His anger did not stop him from interacting extensively with British officials. Writing of his friendship with the mandate government's director of education, W. A. Stewart, he notes that they spent time together not only in Jerusalem but also in Tel Aviv, where they played the oud in basement venues, assisting Jews learning Arabic song and folk dance.[18] He recalls that he returned home only at dawn with a member of the British establishment, with whom he had been enjoying music and dance in the company of "beautiful oriental Jewish young ladies."

On one level this could be seen as a sign that he managed to continue a lifestyle introduced to him early in his life by Hussein Effendi, who had regularly brought him into social contact with Turkish officials and visiting dignitaries from the Arab world. On another, it could be understood as signaling a broader trend, because a considerable number of Arabs considered it an honor to socialize with British officials. Some Arab nationalists saw this as a major problem, arguing that it undermined the coherence of the Arab striving for independence (and Wasif himself was even accused in one incident of being a spy for the British).[19] While keeping Stewart's company in Tel Aviv basements, he was also using the opportunity to teach Jewish pupils the Arabic traditions he knew, thereby enabling—even if inadvertently—a peculiarly Zionist project. The dabkeh was one of several local Arab genres that Zionists learned, redefined as "Jewish," and used to affirm their claim to the land.[20]

However, Wasif's access to élite company simultaneously went hand-in-hand with an "Oriental" position, not only as a colonized Arab resident but also as a musician. Wasif composed a song based on a published variant of a song by Egyptian composer Sayed Darwish.[21] Within his own version he complained that the British had appointed Herbert Samuel as Palestine's first high commissioner, a man who was for Wasif "one of the world's pioneering Zionists." The song stated that the Arabs had been "sold" and would be led by people called "Shabtai, Sholem, and Haim" who would oblige them to speak Hebrew. This expression of anger towards the British became popular, and Wasif sang it at many social gatherings.

We might set this memory alongside a story from 1927, while he was working at the Revenue Department. The Egyptian currency that had been in use was being replaced by a currency for Palestine, on which the text "the land of Israel" appeared in Hebrew.[22] One of his responses was to compose and sing a song about the situation, lamenting not only his dreary counting job but also the new currency itself, which he referred to as "the Palestinian disaster." While probably sensing that the years ahead would not be free of strife, he made music to spread among his colleagues and friends. Moreover, he ironically suggested to his boss that anyone wishing to work at the Revenue Department should be taught to learn his song, rather than take the entrance exam. Such recollections allow us to see how the region's music, while for many Arabs a source of comfort and pleasure, was also an expression of gentle subversion.

Musical Confrontations

While Wasif's social commentary provides insights into informal spheres of music making, his musical expertise touches on professional areas as well. He kept his distance somewhat, preferring to be what he called a "true artist" himself, and refraining from taking direct financial benefit from music. He passed up opportunities at the Arabic Section of the Palestine Broadcasting Service when it opened in 1936, for example.[23] He seems to have undertaken some teaching, apparently making a brief appearance as oud instructor at the Palestine Conservatory for Music and Dramatic Art, the reports and prospectuses of which list him among the staff from 1934 until 1937. Wasif's own remarks on this episode are less clear, however.[24] He may have taught briefly, or irregularly, but either way the political situation seems to have ended his formal relationship with the institution. The Conservatoire very rapidly became an institution run by and for Jews, with an explicitly Zionist curriculum.[25] It is difficult to imagine he would have had a comfortable position there.

Still, the memoirs reveal his interest in formal music education, because the matter was increasingly pressing in the region. Wasif wrote with admiration about the visiting Armenian musician he refers to as Sisaq, partly because his "ability to read music gave him a firm foundation for the mastering of the instrument."[26] He tried himself to adapt aspects of Western notation to make them useful to oud players.[27] Most worrying, perhaps, was the fact that Western music was being disseminated effectively within the Arab community itself, thanks in part to notation; and a middle class was emerging that had learned European music but had no taste for Arabic music. Wasif reports, for instance, that one of his teachers at Saint George's School had himself loathed Arabic music until Wasif led him to it.[28]

The teacher was apparently a product of an effective Anglicization and the scarcity of formal training in Arabic styles.

Institutional attempts to counter the problem were not always successful. When a founder of the nationalist Independence Party, Ajaj Nuwayhid, took over the Arabic Section of the Palestine Broadcasting Service in 1940, he argued that it was "unacceptable that Arab musicians should continue to resist learning to read and write musical transcription."[29] He arranged for the classically trained Palestinian Youssef Batrouni to teach them, and offered financial reward to those who excelled. But several of the musicians working at the station were not educated beyond an elementary level so there was a high price to pay: the much celebrated *buzuq* player Mohammed Abdul Karim refused to learn and was fired. Nuwayhid later discovered that Abdul Karim was completely illiterate, and he greatly regretted the fact that he could not find him to offer employment again.[30] This loss to the Arabic Section, a woeful consequence of a blanket decision made by an Arab director seeking progress, can be read as a symbol of the fragility of a musical practice falling outside the dominant, colonial scheme for social advancement.

A particular section of Wasif's memoirs alerts us to one of the most poignant dimensions of this situation. The occasion was an event in which he was on stage with the German researcher Robert Lachmann (1892–1939), illustrating one of Lachmann's lectures. Lachmann had been trained by the celebrated music scholars Curt Sachs and Erich von Hornbostel, but rather unusually for his time, he was critical of commentators who were disparaging of Arab musics.[31] He took an exceptional position, stating that the European notion that Oriental music was "on a low stage of development" was a product of Europeans' ignorance of such musical practices themselves.[32] He was, then, interested in Arabic music to a rare degree.

When Lachmann moved to Palestine as a Jewish refugee from Nazi Germany in 1935, he set about recording and studying all the music he could find. He loosely shared some of the hopes of Europeans who saw Palestine as a site of biblical relics, thinking regional musical practices might be traces of the ancient past, whether the courts of the Abbasid Caliphate or the Temple of Jerusalem, for example. However, he used this framework for asking questions rather than answering them, something that led him into difficulty at the Hebrew University where he acquired some work.[33] This institution had been from the start a Zionist initiative whose main role was to encourage a unified Jewish nationalism in Palestine, and Lachmann's scholarly, comparative approach did not serve that purpose.[34] It explored the diversity of Palestine's music and musicians, and drew on Wasif as a primary representative.

> At my request, the singer and player, a well-known amateur of Jerusalem, Wasif Gauharija [*sic*], started a series of instrumental preludes and vocal introductions representing the different melody-types (*maqamat*) of Arab classical music, and promised to complete it on the next occasion. These records will be particularly useful for anybody who wishes to obtain a precise idea of the traditional Arab systems of melodies and scales.[35]

While Wasif was willing at several venues to disseminate music "as a demonstration of the theories" about which Dr. Lachmann was writing,[36] his memoirs also document his protest about the way that Lachmann presented him. A scene on one particular occasion provides us with an iconic example of how a very broad conflict about culture played out in the Palestinian context. At stake was the extent to which Arabic music should draw on Western technologies in order to develop, and at a much-discussed musicological conference held in Cairo (mentioned by Wasif), the Egyptian vision had clashed with a European one. Whereas Egyptians were keen to transform their work by connecting up with Western trends, European ethnomusicologists such as Béla Bartók and Lachmann argued that the riches of the East should be preserved as they were.[37]

Wasif recollects his own angry response to Lachmann about such desires for preservation made on stage at a venue in Jerusalem. While he appreciated Lachmann's view that Arabic music could not be entirely reduced to Western notation, he went on to point out that if regional music education relied on the privileges that he himself had enjoyed, then Arabic music would die out. He knew from the rest of the Arab world that this need not happen, however, and that adaptations of Western notation could enable more effective dissemination. When Lachmann did not accept this point, Wasif responded by making the political significance of his discussion crystal clear. He accused Lachmann of aiming to "prevent Arabs from spreading their music, and from ever evolving beyond what they have already achieved," and referred to this as "a Zionist, anti-Arab point of view."

Lachmann's reaction, according to Wasif, was to celebrate Wasif's exceptional quality, and insist that this was to be valued more highly than mass dissemination. Setting aside the points that were of concern to Wasif, Lachmann also said that it "has nothing to do with politics." It is intriguing to compare Lachmann's reaction with comments he had made with regard to the radio in November 1935, when his position was less preservationist, more concerned to see opportunities for Arabs to *develop* their musical activities. Attempting to shape policy for broadcasting, he proposed that the radio should be an engine for stimulating creativity in Arab music in the region. He stated explicitly that there were "excellent and inspired performers" among "the singers and players, urban, rural and Bedouin, of this country," and that it would be a "gratifying task for the Jerusalem Station to support the original music existing in this country, and thereby to promote its development."[38] His hope would be borne out by the Arabic Section.

While Lachmann's comments about the radio are insightful, it is the wealth of Wasif's reminiscences that truly reveal the complexity of the Palestinian situation. The universal question of development versus preservation was, after all, particularly fraught in Palestine, because Jewish settlers seemed to have it all ways. Supported by the British, they had institutionalized a European-style music culture that enabled them to continue their then-established musical activities. Meanwhile, they increasingly claimed "Oriental" repertories, religious music, and even folk song and Arabic regional dance not only as their own but also as a part of a Jewish "national" identity that belonged on the land of Palestine. Wasif, on the other hand, the long-standing resident once proud to be in a position to learn from all musicians encountered (we recall all the musicians he encountered as a child), was increasingly faced with the bounded categories brought by outsiders that set limits on his community's musical expression.

With the best intentions, such limitations placed colonized musicians in a no-man's land, one that was a neat correlate of the "timeless" and "immovable

East" often invoked by Western visitors.[39] Here we gain a unique perspective on (the causes of) the region's presumed immobility. Even so, after Lachmann later passed away Wasif would note in his diary, "I was very saddened by his death, may God bless his soul. I will not forget the time I spent with this great artist."[40]

* * *

Shortly after the lecture-demonstration exchanges with Lachmann, the partition of Jerusalem led Wasif to flee his home and abandon his possessions, including his entire collection of instruments. At the close of the memoirs we find him living as a refugee in Beirut, apparently having survived for a number of years without playing music at all. He is finally able with some difficulty to scrape together enough money to rent an oud, the instrument that had in Palestine provided the means to such an effervescent existence.[41]

INTRODUCTIONS

I. WASIF JAWHARIYYEH'S JERUSALEM

by Salim Tamari

Wasif Jawhariyyeh's memoirs span sixty years of Jerusalem's turbulent modern history, from 1904 to 1968, a period covering four regimes and five wars. More significantly, this period marks the transition of Palestinian society into modernity and the breakout of its Arab population beyond the ghettoized confines of the walled city.[1]

Wasif's father, Jiryis Jawhariyyeh, was the *mukhtar* (communal leader) of the Eastern Orthodox community in the Old City and a member of Jerusalem's municipal council serving under the mayoralty of Salim al-Husseini and Faidy al-Alami. Trained as a lawyer, he was well versed in Muslim sharia law and fluent in several languages, including Greek, Turkish, and Arabic. He worked briefly as a government tax assessor but later turned to private business, becoming a successful silk farmer in Ezariyyeh and proprietor of a public café over the Jraisheh River. He was also a skilled icon maker and amateur musician who encouraged Wasif to learn the oud early in his youth.

Wasif's mother, Hilaneh Barakat, descended from a leading Orthodox family from what later became known as the Christian Quarter. Wasif's father, having lived in the Barakat family compound as a youth before he moved to Haret al-Saidiyyeh, became friends with Hilaneh's father. When the latter died at an early age, Jiryis took responsibility for the care of his two children. Later Jiryis would marry Hilaneh.

Where do we place the Jawhariyyehs in the social networks of Jerusalem at the turn of the nineteenth century? On the one hand, the father and grandfather seem to have occupied important public positions in both the Ottoman civil service and in the city's institutions. Jiryis was also a prominent member of the Orthodox Christian community and a delegate to the city council. But the rest of the family seems to have worked at a number of more modest occupations. At one point Wasif refers to his grandfather as a shoemaker or tanner. His elder brother Khalil apprenticed as a carpenter before he was conscripted into the Ottoman army. Wasif himself worked at a number of odd jobs including, briefly, as a barber's assistant before becoming an itinerant oud player and singer for wedding parties. His main income came from employment in the Ottoman and British civil service. It is not clear whether he was paid for his early employment.

Certainly the family was not happy with his career as a musician and wanted him to settle into a more respectable job. Later on, the family's fortunes improved significantly, with the father becoming a prominent lawyer and bailiff. Khalil owned a successful café near Jaffa Gate, and Wasif joined government service. We can say with some certainty that the family members skirted that precarious space between skilled labor and the middle ranks of the civil service. From the detailed description of the ceremony accompanying Jiryis's funeral, it becomes evident that the family had achieved social prominence in the Old City just before World War I. In any case, they were solid urbanites and held a remote, though benevolent, attitude toward the peasantry of the neighboring villages, with whom both father and son had substantial dealings.

It is impossible to understand the Jawhariyyehs' place in pre-mandate Palestine without considering their critical bonds as protégés of the Husseini family in Jerusalem, feudal landlords and patricians of the city's inner circle of *ayan* (notables). Jiryis spent part of his early career looking after the Husseini estates in Jerusalem's western villages, particularly in Khirbet Amr. After his father's death, Wasif was "adopted" by Hussein Effendi, later the mayor of Jerusalem. Hussein Effendi set Wasif up in a number of jobs in the city and ensured that he was treated well in the Ottoman army. The family was on such intimate terms with their patrons that Wasif was entrusted with the welfare of Hussein Effendi's mistress, Persephone, when she became ill.

Wasif's vivid rendering of daily life in Mahallet al-Saadiyyeh, an area situated between Bab es-Sahira and Via Dolorosa, during the first decade of the twentieth century marks one of the most valuable records of Palestinian urban life that exists anywhere. His memoirs combine anecdote, social history, and ethnography into a unique account, one in which shifts in domestic living arrangements are periodized and described in detail.

Jawhariyyeh's cognitive map of Jerusalem's neighborhoods, and his recollection of communal boundaries prevalent in his youth, reinforce the view that the division of the city into four confessional quarters was a later development. The British demarcated new boundaries between the city's populations to preserve equilibrium and create a modern sectarian balance among the four ancient communities. This balance preserved the status quo in the administration of the holy sites, an arrangement carefully negotiated during the late Ottoman period, and elaborated and codified in the early mandate rule over the city.

The diaries implicitly challenge this notion of quarters, based on the regulation of relations between Jerusalemites in terms of their religious and ethnic habitat. In Wasif's version of daily life in the alleys of the Old City, we are struck by the weakness of this notion in two respects. One suggests that there was no clear delineation between neighborhood and religion; we see a substantial intermixing of religious groups in each quarter. Furthermore, the boundaries of habitat were the *mahallet*, the neighborhood network of social demarcations, within which a substantial amount of communal solidarity is expressed. Such cohesiveness was manifested in periodic social visits and sharing of ceremonial occasions, including weddings and funerals, and by active participation in religious festivities. These solidarities undermined the fixity of a confessional system derived from a premodern—perhaps even primordial—network of affinities.

But confessional boundaries also were being undermined by the rise of the nationalist movement in Palestine. Initially this occurred within the context of the constitutional Ottoman movement at the turn of the century, especially after the 1908 coup which received a great deal of support among intellectual circles in

Jerusalem; and later, in the anti-Turkish trends within greater Syrian nationalism. These shifts can be gleaned in these memoirs in a haphazard and selective manner. Jawhariyyeh—who was not involved in any political party but was an Ottoman patriot, and later a Palestinian nationalist—clearly believed that the move towards modernity (and presumably post-Ottoman nationalism) was linked to the move outside the city by the rising middle classes.[2] By the mid-nineteenth century, members of the notable clans already had established base in Sheikh Jarrah to the north and in Wa'riyyeh to the south.[3] Within the Jewish population a similar move had taken place with the construction of the new neighborhoods of Mia Shiarim and Yemin Moshe, signalling a separation of ways between modern Palestinian Arab nationalism and Jewish communal consciousness—even before the entrenchment of Zionism among the city's Jewish population.[4]

Jawhariyyeh's relationship with the Jewish community of Jerusalem is more complex. His narrative is no doubt colored by retroactive memories of the clashes of the twenties and of 1936 with the Zionist movement, and with a vision mediated by the events of the 1948 war. But he is also aware of a different era, when as a teenager he used to participate in the events of Purim (which he describes in great detail, including the costumes he used to wear with his brother Khalil), and in family picnics in the spring at the shrine of Shimon as-Siddiq in Wadi al-Joz. He also mentions a number of Sephardic families with whom his family was on intimate terms, including Elishar, Hazzan, Anteibi, Mani (those from Hebron), and Navon. Wasif himself performed or became aquatinted with a number of Jewish musicians—including Shihadeh, Badi'a Masabni's oud player.[5] He also mentions the prominent role played by groups of Aleppo Jews, known as Dallatiyyeh, who resided in Jerusalem. Those were Sephardic choral musicians who performed Andalusian music in weddings of Jerusalem Arabs.[6] Before the onset of the Mandate he used to play in a number of Jewish communities surrounding Jerusalem.[7]

The Growth of the Modern City

The Jawhariyyeh diaries add to our understanding of Jerusalem's social history a contemporary record of the growth of the city outside the city walls. Although Sheikh Jarrah, Yemin Moshe, and Wa'riyyeh were established before his time, Wasif narrates the growth of Musrara and the Mascobiyyeh neighborhood along Jaffa Road in his boyhood, followed by Talbieh, and Katamon in the 1930s. He witnesses the inauguration of the new road linking the Old City to Musrara under the patronage of Mayor Faidy al-Alami in 1906. This expansion—and a similar one which preceded it in Baqa—saw the move by hundreds of families (many of them individually named here) to modern, tiled buildings and to ones made of mortar fortified by iron railings. All of these new dwellings continued to be constructed with rain-fed water reservoirs in their courtyards to sustain them through Jerusalem's long, dry summers. In these neighborhoods the implements of modernity first appeared: electricity, in the Notre Dame compound just opposite the New Gate; the automobile on Jaffa Road; the cinematograph, the early motion-picture projector; and, above all, the phonograph, which introduced Jawhariyyeh to the worlds of Salameh Hijazi and Sayyid Darwish.

The memoirs devote extended entries to Jerusalem's musical and artistic life during the Ottoman period. He includes a long list of oud makers and performers, dancers and singers. Many of them performed as family teams in local weddings, and later—during the mandate—in café-cabarets outside the walled city. In combination with his special compendium on the typology of musical traditions that prevailed in Palestine at the turn of the century, Jawhariyyeh's observations provide us with an original and unique source on the modernization of Arabic music in Bilad ash-Sham and the influence of such great innovators such as Sheikh Yusif al-Minyalawi and Sayyid Darwish on provincial capitals like Jerusalem.[8]

A self-taught chronicler and musician, Wasif had a photographic memory which enabled him to recall not only the dramatic (the entry of Jamal Pasha, and later Lord Allenby, into Jerusalem's) but also the quotidienne thrill of the seemingly mundane. Accompanying his father—a trained solicitor who served as an administrator for Salim Affendi al-Hussaini's rural estates (in Khirbet Deir Amr and its environments)—he was able to observe, firsthand, the links that tied Jerusalem's feudal aristocracy to the surrounding villages and their peasant populations. As he grew up in the shadow of his father, Wasif was able to forge for himself a local reputation as a foremost oud player and composer-musician. Playing in the mansions of Jerusalem's urban notables, he recorded, with great wit and satire, the musings and tribulations of the city's patricians and paupers.

What comes out of this is an intimate portrait of Jerusalem's Ottoman modernity at the very moment when Zionism was about to clash with an emerging Palestinian nationalism. He recounts the introduction of the phonograph and movie projector to the city's cafés in 1910, and the wonderment he experienced as he saw motion-picture images for the first time, in the Russian compound. In 1912 he first saw a horseless car ("a Ford") driven by Mr. Vester of the American Colony at the Municipal Park by Jaffa Street. In the summer of 1914 he rode a donkey with his father to Baq'aa in Jerusalem southern suburbs to watch the landing of an Ottoman military airplane. Unfortunately the plane crashed in Samakh (Tiberius), and its two Turkish pilots, officers Nuri and Isma'il, were killed. Wasif composed a special eulogy in their honor. In the autumn of that year he did manage to see for the first time the landing of an airplane, in Upper Baq'aa, manned by German and Turkish officers.

Deeply involved in the affairs of the Arab Orthodox community, the writer nevertheless exhibits a unique affinity to the Muslim culture of his city. His narrative compels us to rethink the received wisdom about Jerusalem's communal and confessional structure in Ottoman times. Endless stories—often scandalous and satirical—draw a picture of profound triadic co-existence of Christian and Jewish families in the heart of what came to be known as the Muslim Quarter. This was not the tolerant cohabitation of protected *dhimmi* minorities, but positive engagement in the affairs of neighbors whose religion was coincidental to their wider urban heritage. There is no doubt, however, that the Jawhariyyeh family, though deeply conscious of its Orthodox heritage, was also immersed in Muslim culture. Jiryis, the father, made his sons read and memorize the Qu'ran at an early age. When he died in September of 1914 he was eulogized by Khalil Sakakini, followed by his close companion, Sheikh Ali Rimawi "... I cannot believe that Jawhariyyeh's soul will remain in Zion [cemetery]...for tonight surely it will move to Mamillah," referring to the Muslim cemetery. Such an attitude clearly went beyond the current normative rules of coexistence at the time.

The Vagabond Years

As was customary among the population of the Old City, Wasif in his boyhood was sent to be apprenticed in a number of jobs. These assignments supplemented his formal schooling and often involved his evolving musical career. Wasif also learned creative truancy during this period. He would escape his master's shop to listen to the oud being played by Hussein Nashashibi at another barbershop, that of a certain Abu Manawail, whose shop was owned by the Nashashibi family. It was during this time that Wasif's obsession with oud performance began, and he counted the days until he would play one himself.

His musical career occupies a substantial portion of the diaries. We are fortunate to have his Musical Notebook, which he began to record just prior to World War I and later salvaged from its hiding place in the family's Botta Street house in West Jerusalem after the 1967 war. The book reflects the progression of Wasif's interests in Arabic music, from classical *Andalusiyyat* and Aleppo muwashahat, to choral music which he used to perform in weddings and family celebrations, to love songs, to melodies based on classical poetry, and finally to *taqatiq* and erotic songs. Not being trained formally in reading musical notation, Wasif devised his own system. He also wrote a chapter on the adaptation of Western musical notation for the oud.[9]

The Jawhariyyeh house was the perfect setting for his budding musical talents. All the family members, with the exception of Tawfiq who was tone deaf, either played instruments, sang, or enjoyed good music. His father was one of the few Jerusalemites who owned a Master's Voice phonograph, and they had a number of early recordings by leading Egyptian singers, such as Sheikh Minyalawi and Salameh Hijazi. Jiryis would encourage his children to lip-sync in accompaniment with these records. He was particularly severe with Wasif when he made mistakes. Jiryis was also keen at hosting prominent singers and musicians while visiting Jerusalem. One of those, the Egyptian oudist Qaftanji, spent a week with the Jawhariyyehs, and from him Wasif learned a number of melodies which he used to sing during summer nights on the roof, and more often in the *beit al-khala* (outhouse).[10]

Contrary to the impression that he gives about his truancy and rebelliousness, Wasif had a substantial degree of formal schooling. This is reflected in his polished language and rich poetic imagination. His elegant handwriting was phenomenal, and he kept up this standard until his old age.

References abound in his diaries to diverse sources from classical poetry, as well from contemporary literary figures including Sakakini, Ahmad Shawqi, and Khalil Gibran. His favorite quotation came from Gibran, whom he quoted on the occasion of his expulsion from his primary school: "They say to me, 'Be a slave to him who teaches you the alphabet'... thus I decided to remain free and ignorant."[11]

When Khalil Sakakini established his progressive Dusturiyyeh National School in Musrara, his father intervened with the mayor to have him admitted as an external student. Sakakini had acquired a reputation for using radical methods of pedagogy in his school, strictly banning physical punishment and written exams, and introducing two disciplines which were unique to his school at the time—physical education and Qu'ranic studies for Christians. Sakakini himself was a music lover and had a special fondness for the oud and violin. Some of the Dusturiyyeh students had seen Wasif performing in local weddings and taunted him for being an *ajeer* (paid street singer). Sakakini defended him and brought the students to enjoy Wasif's music. Eventually, and despite his love for the Dusturiyyeh and its liberal environment, Wasif was compelled to leave it at the insistence of his patron, Hussein al-Hussaini, and enroll in al-Mutran School (Saint George's) in Sheikh Jarrah "… in order to gain knowledge of the English language and build a solid base for my future."[12] He remained there for two years (1912–1914) until the school was closed with the beginning of the war. Wasif had finished the fourth secondary class (his tenth year of studies) and with it the end

إني لست بذلك الأديب الفاضل أو الكاتب الماهر أو المؤرخ الشهير
أو الرحّال القدير الذي يحسن نشر علمه وأدبه وإرشاده على العالمين، فكل ما هنالك
أنني موظف بسيط أغلقت أبواب المدارس في وجهي في الحرب العظمى الأولى عندما كنت على وشك
إنجاز دراستي الثانوية ولم يساعدني الحظ على ترك بلادي فلسطين طيلة حياتي، ولكنها
طرأت على ظروف ومفاجآت وحوادث مختلفة منها الطريفة وذلك في العهدين العثماني
والبريطاني جعلتني أفكر في تدوين البعض منها معتمدًا على سببين أظن أنهما الساعدين على حدوث
مثل هذه المفاجآت والظروف التي سأدونها في كتابي هذا:-

١- العلاقة الأخوية المتينة بين المرحوم والدي والأسرة الحسينية بالقدس التي ربطتني بأحد وجهاء
هذه الأسرة الكريمة ألا وهو المغفور له حسين هاشم الحسيني ابن المغفور له الحاج سليم الحسيني، تلك
الشخصية الفذة فكنت فخورًا برفقته في رحلاته وجلساته منذ نشأتي فوقفت على عادات أهالي القرى
وموسيقاها في قضاء القدس ومن ثم في أريحا والبحر الميت والكرك وذلك قبل وإبان الحرب العظمى.
وكذلك ميولي الفطرية للفنون وأهمها الموسيقى العربية ذلك الفن الرفيع الذي احتل القسط
الأكبر من حياتي فقد تمتعت بحضور مجالس أنس وليالي سمر مع شخصيات عالية ولها فيها أشكال متعارفين
وقواد وحكام وأدباء وفنانين من مواطنين وغرباء في العهدين العثماني والبريطاني يتعذر لغيري
الوصول إلى مثل هذه المجالس وقد أتيح لي معاشرة كثيرة لأشخاص من الأسر الراقية والعائلات
من مختلف الطبقات والأجناس والأديان اكتشفت بواسطتها على كثير من حوادث خفية يصعب
لغيري الحصول عليها والوصول إليها.

٢- عملي بوظيفتي في حكومة الانتداب البريطاني كمدير مال في القدس للضرائب ورئيس لجنة تخمين أملاك
المدينة ذلك العمل الذي يقضي أن أدخل بيوت العائلات للسكن والمتاجر والمعاهد والأديرة
وغيرها من الأملاك وأحتك بأهلها وأصحابها وسكانها مما ولا شك قد زاد في معلوماتي العامة
في الحياة فشجعني على جمع واقتناء التحف الشرقية النادرة على اختلاف أنواعها فكانت هوايتي هذه
بالنسبة إلى حبي الفنون أساسًا وموفقية كبرى لوجود المجموعة الجوهرية التي سيجيء البحث عنها مطولًا
في صفحات هذا الكتاب.

نعم هذه الأسباب التي ساعدتني بأن أقدم على تدوين أفضل ما حدث لي مشاهدة وسمعًا
وقد شجعني على ذلك أخي وصديقي الأستاذ محي الدين مكي فوافقته على تسميته "الذكريات الجوهرية"
وجعلته تقدمة مني إلى ولدي :-

Page one of Wasif's diary

of his formal schooling without receiving the secondary certificate. At Saint George's Wasif excelled in acting in school plays where he was able to develop his musical talents. Among his classmates were Saliba al-Jozi, the well-known playwright and brother of Bandali, the Marxist historian who emigrated to the Soviet Union, and Shukri al-Harami, the noted educator and founder of al-Umma College.

With the termination of his formal schooling, Wasif was able to continue his musical education in the company of Jerusalem's foremost oud players and composers. Those included Muhammad al-Sibasi, Hamadeh al-Afifi, who taught him the art of muwashahat in the Turkish tradition, and Abdul-Hamid Quttaineh, who was his first tutor. But he did not reach his maturity until he met the great master oud player Omar al-Batsh. In the spring of 1915, after his father's death, Wasif was attending a party in the company of Hussein Effendi and several Turkish officers in the house of Hajj Khalil Nashishibi. A section of the army military band known as the Izmir Group was performing Andalusian muwashahat. Wasif was mesmerized by the playing of a young oud player wearing military uniform who was introduced to him as Omar al-Batsh.[13] For the duration of the war period, Omar became his constant companion. Wasif prevailed on Hussein Effendi, who was now his official patron, to hire Omar's services to give him four oud lessons a week at the headquarters of the army orchestra in Mascobiyyeh.

Throughout his Ottoman years, and beyond in his adult career, Wasif saw himself as a musician and oud player above all else. When he sought employment in various government and municipal authorities, it was only to survive and release himself to his passionate obsession— the oud—and the company of men and women who shared his vision.

His first paid "job" was that of a clerk in the Jerusalem Municipality in charge of recording and classifying contributions in-kind for the Ottoman war efforts. The job was created for him by Hussein Effendi al-Husseini after the death of Wasif's father as an effort to alleviate the material conditions of his protégé. At the end of the war and beginning of British military occupation, Wasif resumed his career in the municipality after his short bout of service in the Ottoman navy, and was now promoted to a court clerk in the Ministry of Justice, serving under the judgeship of Ali Bey Jarallah in Mascobiyyeh. Government employees were still paid in inflationary (and virtually worthless) Turkish paper pounds, but that was soon replaced with Egyptian pounds minted in stone, which was much preferable. Both Wasif and Khalil used to deposit their salaries to their mother.[14] With the death of Hussein Bey ("my second father"), Wasif resigned from his job at the central court and went on to help Hussein's widow (Umm Salim) in the administration of the Husseini estates in Deir Amr.

Hussein Effendi was succeeded in the mayoralty by Ragheb Bey Nashashibi (after a brief stint by Ismail Husseini). Ragheb was an amateur oud player and socialite. He hired Wasif to give him, and his mistress Umm Mansour, oud and singing lessons. To reward him Ragheb interceded so that Wasif would be on the payroll of the tax bureau with a monthly salary of twenty Egyptian pounds. At the end of each month Wasif would go to the Regie Department and collect his salary, with no further duties incumbent on him. Thus began a series of jobs based on patronage. His relationship with the Husseini family, and later with the

Nashashibis—who with British rule were now on the ascendancy—was established and helped Wasif to continue his career as a musician while maintaining a steady income from public coffers.

The Ottoman era was coming to a close. Wasif was entering his adulthood, but not quite an age of reason. These were the years of bachelorhood, before he got married and settled down. He had been overwhelmed by what he called a "period of total anarchy" in his life, ushered in by the death of his patron, the mayor of Jerusalem, Hussein Effendi al-Husseini. Living like a vagabond, sleeping all day and partying all night had left him bereft, in a condition he describes as "vagabondage." When his mother complained about him coming home late at night, if at all, he retorted with the famous line, "*Man talaba al-3ula sahar al-layali*" ("He who seeks glory, must toil the nights").[15]

Postwar Jerusalem

Wasif's episodes of abandon, which lasted most of 1918 when he was twenty-one, and part of the next year, also reflect a mood which had engulfed the city as a whole. His memoir introduces us to a rich social milieu of postwar Jerusalem in the early 1920s that could be described as hedonistic. Wasif records numerous occasions of public celebration in the streets of the Old City, marked by musical processions and open consumption of alcohol, as people savored a "short-lived... breath of freedom." Nightly episodes of drinking, dance, and occasional hashish smoking recur during this period and throughout the manuscript, as well.

These outbursts of street festivity soon found an outlet during the years of military government through the mushrooming of local cafes and café-bars. These were places where Jerusalemites could meet at leisure, listen to gramophone music, drink *araq* and cognac, and smoke an *arghileh*. One outstanding café from this period was Maqha al-Arab in Ain Karim, owned by Abu Abd al-Arab, which stayed open all night. Wasif's family made a significant contribution to this milieu with the opening of the Jawhariyyeh Café, which opened in 1918 near the Russian compound at the southern entrance of Jaffa Road and which featured live entertainment by visiting musicians from Cairo, Alexandria, and Beirut.

Wasif's brother Khalil brought to this café the skills he had acquired in Beirut while in the Turkish army. Those included serving a special mezze menu with araq orders and iced water, which was a new innovation for Jerusalem, made possible with the introduction of electric power. Within months after its opening, the café became a major attraction for pleasure seekers from all over the city and became renowned for bringing in the best singers in the country, including Sheikh Ahmad Tarifi, Muhammad al-Asheq, Zaki Afandi Murad, and not least the Lebanese dancer and singer Badi'a Masabni.

Later on, Wasif would meet privately with Badi'a at intimate parties either in the mansions of Jerusalem notables such as Fakhri Nashishibi and Mustafa al-Jabsheh, or in the Hotel Saint John which belonged to his father-in-law. Heavy drinking and cannabis enhanced the atmosphere of these evenings, and we are told that cocaine was also used habitually by both Masabni and Rihani. On one occasion, Wasif himself accompanied Badi'a on his oud at an all-night party which started at the Jawhariyyeh Café and continued at his father's house—a night which he fondly kept a photographic record of.

Wasif was blessed with an exquisite voice which, even as a teenager, placed him in high demand for performances in weddings. But his eternal love was the oud, which by 1918 he had mastered enough to make him a sought-after player in Palestine. He played the oud mainly for members of the city's élites, usually in special homes kept by and for their mistresses. Several members of Jerusalem's patrician families—including the Husseinis and the Nashashibis—kept in suburban areas of the New City special apartments for their mistresses, many of whom were Greeks, Armenians, and Jews. The most famous of these was Persephone, a Greek-Albanian seamstress who in 1895 became the mistress of Hussein Effendi al-Husseini (and possibly before him, his brother Musa Kazem Pasha).[16] She lived in a special apartment on Jaffa Road and used her clout with Hussein Effendi to trade in cattle in Beit Suseen and Deir Amr—both Husseini estates. Wasif became her musical companion and helped her in marketing *za'atar* (thyme) oil, which she successfully processed and sold as a medicinal. When Hussein Effendi became mayor of Jerusalem in 1909, he distanced himself from her and gave her permission to marry Khawaja Yenni, a Greek confectioner. During the war Persiphone became sick and, deserted by her husband, was brought to the Jawhariyyeh household where Wasif took care of her until her death. The diaries relate numerous episodes of festive events spent in the company of members of the social élites and their concubines. Muslim, Christian, and Jewish entertainers catered to these events.

Another feature of cultural life in Ottoman Jerusalem recounted here is the *oda,* a bachelor's apartment equivalent to the French *garconierre.* It was customary for middle-class single men from the Old City to rent a furnished one-room apartment where they would spend their evenings playing cards, smoking and drinking, and, during the long winter nights, having oud sessions. The apartments were also used to conduct love affairs, or to meet with prostitutes. The oda did not necessarily have a negative reputation, although it is clear from Wasif's narrative that elder family members—certainly the female ones—were not privy to what went on. Jawhariyyeh lists a number of well-known odas in the Old City and in Sheikh Jarrah where he used to perform his music. For several years he himself had the key to Hussein Hashem's oda behind Mamilla Cemetery, where he used to entertain "Russian and Greek ladies" in the company of Ragheb Bey Nashashibi (later the mayor of Jerusalem) and Ismail al-Husseini.

These episodes compel us to rethink the image of turn-of-the-century Jerusalem, which is often falsely characterized as a grim, conservative, and joyless city—as described by visitors and natives alike. "The only thing he ever said about it [Jerusalem] was that it reminded him of death," Edward Said relates his father recalling of his early life in the city.[17] How do we account for this incongruity? We have to remember that Jerusalem was a city of religion, but not an excessively religious one. Its religious status generated a large number of industries and services that catered to a visiting population of pilgrims, but its native inhabitants were not necessarily more religious than people in other urban centers in the hill country. Nablus, Hebron, and Nazareth, for example, had decidedly more religious reputations than did Jerusalem.

The explanation for this tolerance of what seems to be a libertine atmosphere lies elsewhere. Wasif's narrative comes from an earlier era of the city's history when class boundaries and seigneurial privilege created an atmosphere in which the upper crust felt relatively insulated in their behavioral patterns from the moral encroachments of the public eye. In many cases they even flaunted this behavior, as was the case with public drinking and the keeping of concubines, without fear of retribution. Another source of protection for these latitudes was that Jerusalem was still a reasonably closed city, with limited influx from the surrounding villages or from Mount Hebron of peasant migrants who later exercised the more conservative influence on the city's norms for which it became renowned.

The complexity of Jerusalem's Ottoman identity is revealed in the formation of the Red Crescent Society in 1915, ostensibly to garner local support in Palestine for the Ottoman armed forces against the allies.[18] Despite his several references to the brutality of Jamal Pasha and the Triumvirate, Wasif himself was an active supporter of the society and acted as a secretary to one of its leading members, Hamadeh al-Afifi.[19] The society, prominently based in the Russian compound, was headed by Hussein Effendi, who by now was forced to leave his position as mayor, and also included several prominent Christian and Jewish citizens among its founders: Ibrahim (Abraham) Entaibi, Izhaq Elishar, Salim Khoury, and Wadie Kittaneh, as well as two leading Ottoman army officers. Through its public musical events and through direct solicitations, the Red Crescent was able to raise substantial funds for the war effort against the British and French enemy. But Wasif sees the society also as aiming to create a bridge between the interests of the Jewish community in Palestine and the Ottoman government before the appearance of Zionism as an active force. Both Ibrahim Entaibi, the director of the Alliance Israelite school system in Jerusalem, and a Miss Landau—described as "the liaison between the Jewish community in Jerusalem and the Ottoman military leadership"—were pivotal in cementing those ties. With this objective, they mobilized a large number of young Jerusalem women who wore ceremonial Ottoman military uniforms with Red Crescent insignia, and solicited contributions in-kind and money for the army.

The first volume of Wasif's diaries ends with the chaotic retreat of the Ottoman army from Jerusalem and its environs. Turkish and German saboteurs were blowing up the Jerusalem rail lines, while British planes bombarded military installations. Wasif himself was preparing to go to Jericho for his naval assignment after reading a public pronouncement threatening court-martial and execution for AWOLs. Then, on December 8, 1919, the entire southern front collapsed. Young men were out in the street from hiding and burning their Ottoman uniforms. The Turkish governor of Jerusalem, Izzat Bey, signed an order transferring civil authority of the city to deposed Mayor Hussein Effendi and a council of the city's notables. Ten days later, General Allenby officially entered the city through Jaffa Gate.

British Rule

The memoirs for the years following World War I, covering the mandate period, convey the spirit of emancipatory anticipation that engulfed Jerusalem—and Palestine—during the critical three years of military rule. Wasif himself was maturing as a musical performer and had reached a point when he was able to reflect on the future of Palestine and Jerusalem from the momentous events that he witnessed. He also occupied a strategic vantage point in these events: as an entertainer to members of the city's notable élite, as well as civil servant in the nascent British mandatory government in the capital of the country.

It is often forgotten that the British mandate over Palestine occupied barely three decades of the country's modern history. In scholarly literature and in Palestinian popular imagination the mandate has acquired a colossal, if not mythical, impact on the molding of modern Palestinian society and its destiny. A quick list of its often cited achievements—and disasters—would include: the creation of modern institutions of government, with a new civil service and police force, and the centralization of the national bureaucracy in Jerusalem; the modernization of the land code and the taxation system; the creation of a legal corpus to replace, and supplement, the Ottoman code; the conduct of a national census (1922 and 1931), and the creation of the population registry; the creation of the rudimentary features of citizenship and icons of unfulfilled sovereignty (currency, stamps, passports); a modern secular educational system; and an infrastructure of roads and communication, including a broadcasting authority—Palestine Radio, in 1931. A major consequence of these administrative changes was the separation of Palestine from Greater Syria. All this happened in three short decades, less if we deduct the years of initial military rule. But the mandate is also especially remembered—retrospectively—for one major accomplishment: the laying of the groundwork for partition and the creation of the state of Israel.[20]

Wasif Jawhariyyeh's memoirs from the mandate period help us to reread these changes not only because they offer lived experience by a contemporary observer but because they challenge the idea of a clean rupture between Turkish and English rule. They undermine the notion that the Ottoman and British regimes were opposites, one representing oriental despotism, and the other, modernity.

Here, by contrast, the presumed creation of these institutions of colonial modernity is seen not as an innovation over a decrepit Ottoman system but as an elaboration on foundations which were already introduced by Ottoman reforms—secular education, the civil service, constitutional reform, urban planning. In certain areas, British political plans constituted a regression from the Ottoman system. This was the case, for example, with the confessionalization of quarters in the Old City, and the enhancement of religion as a marker of national identity.[21] Wasif reminds us that many celebrated reforms of the mandate administration were already in place during and before the First World War. But the tragedies of the war, and the disastrous consequences of conscription (*safarbarlik*) in poisoning the relationship between Turkish rulers and the subject Arab population in Syria and Palestine, erased these features of Ottoman modernity from Palestinian collective memory.

Naturally the British administration is recalled as the conscious instrument—through the Balfour Declaration—which laid the foundation for the displacement of the Palestinians in 1948. Much of Wasif's narrative, since he was writing in a later period, is permeated with this foreknowledge. It explains to a large extent his ambiguity about the liberation of Jerusalem from the Ottoman yoke, even as Jerusalemites were dancing in the streets and as he and his brother Khalil were burning their Turkish military uniforms.[22]

The years that preceded the fall of Jerusalem were particularly harsh. The devastation of war was accompanied by major social dislocations and ruthless suppression of the urban population in the major cities of the region. The last three years of Ottoman rule were also years of famine in Syria and Palestine. Hunger was not induced by draught or any other natural cause, but through the confiscation and forced diversion of wheat supplies to the Fourth Army, under the command of Jamal Pasha.[23] To compound these disasters Palestine in 1915 was subjected to a severe attack of locust swarms that compelled a massive relocation of coastal populations inland.[24] Lebanon was first hit by famine in the spring of 1916, and the famine soon spread to other the urban centers in Syria and Palestine.

The Jawhariyyeh memoirs shed a revealing light on the critical postwar years during which much political ambiguity about the future direction of Palestine prevailed. These were the years in Palestine when the Ottoman system had collapsed militarily but the colonial system was not yet ushered in. "We lived in a state of ignorance," Colonel Storrs, military governor of Jerusalem, later confessed, "and my word was the law."[25] Under the administration of General Moonie, all civil laws were suspended in favor of the military administration. Suddenly in Palestine, according to mandate historian Bayan al-Hut, there were no lawyers, no judges, no courts, and no newspapers.[26] In 1918 the northern part of Palestine was still under Turkish control, and the British were mobilizing resistance in the name of Sherif Hussein against the fledgling Ottoman army. But even after the defeat and final consolidation of British rule over the country, the borders between Transjordan, Lebanon, and Syria with Palestine remained "Ottoman," with fluid boundaries and a common cultural outlook.

While the legal vacuum was filled in the countryside by a reversion to common law (*al-Qanun al-Surfi*) and tribal law, the situation in the big cities allowed appointed judges and senior administrators, both British and Palestinian, substantial leeway to exercise their discretion in applying the law at the local level.

Early Rebellion and Ottoman Nostalgia

The honeymoon with the colonial authority did not last long. One of the first government acts was to conduct the General Census (1921) in which Palestinians were divided into three confessional categories—Muslims, Christians, and Jews. The Jerusalem leadership of the Jewish national movement saw the census not as part of the planning instrument, as it was heralded, but as a prelude to the realization of the national Jewish home project. A call to boycott ensued but was not entirely successful.[27]

As soon as the Bolshevik government exposed the terms of the secret Sykes-Picot accords, Palestinian Arabs began to link the terms of the British and French mandates with the implementation of the Balfour Declaration. The national movement began to focus on the twin issues of Jewish emigration—now encouraged by the new authority—and the transfer of land for Zionist settlement.

Unlike the situation in the Ottoman period, public ceremonials acted as the linchpin of confrontation with the British authorities. The main focus of clashes between demonstrators and the military government was the Nabi Musa procession. These clashes began in the spring of 1919 and intensified over the next two years. Colonel Storrs, in his capacity as the new military governor of Jerusalem, began to regulate the Nabi Musa processions under government supervision—partly as a measure to control the crowds, but also as a plan to regulate religious ritual within the new civil administration of Palestine. In this effort he was acting in collusion with Hajj Amin al-Husseini, the recently appointed mufti of Jerusalem and rising star of the nationalist movement who also saw himself as a successor of Salah ed-Din in this regard. Both the nationalist movement and the British saw in the control of religious ceremonials a mechanism for realizing their different objectives.

Another striking turn within the nationalist discourse related to the manner in which British "perfidy" had made people, initially exhilarated by the end of Turkish rule, nostalgic for the Ottoman era and even towards the "Turanic" regime of Mustafa Kamal Ataturk, despite his openly anti-Arab credentials. Wasif narrates a performance in 1921 by Egyptian-Jewish composer Zaki Murad (the father of singer Laila Murad) in which he sang a tribute, "Ode to Ataturk," which became widely popular in Jerusalem.

> The heart beckons to you in adoration
> and the eyes are cast towards your beauty
> Royalty seeks your concord
> the soul is enlivened by your presence
> Nobody is your equal
> Nobody radiates in your brilliance

Although the song was ostensibly composed for King Fuad the First by Ibrahim Qabbani, it was nevertheless seen in Syria and Palestine as a tribute to Ataturk's victory over the allied troops. The record of this song was in constant demand for some time after the war, especially when Palestinians began to feel "the pernicious objectives of British rule." Abu Shanab music store, the main importer of Egyptian records, could hardly keep up with popular demand.[28]

Public Space and Voice

On the eve of the British Mandate in Palestine, war and upheaval had drastically altered urban life. Famine, disease, and exile had torn apart the social fabric of entire communities. In Jerusalem new public spaces and social patterns began to emerge. A growing state sector created a new civil servant class. Investments in the national economy invigorated the rising merchant class along the coastal regions. Residential communities extended outside the Old City walls. Secular education, cafés, social clubs, and recreational centers responded to the growth of middle-class tastes and sensibilities. The personal writings of the period reflected a changing sense of individualism.

The Jawhariyyeh memoirs, in common with most Arab autobiographies of the period, are infused with this new spirit. They are especially valuable because they record, expose, ridicule, and celebrate the conventional, the hidden, and the unmentionable—the insular goings-on of Jerusalem's upper classes, the foibles of Ottoman and British military and political leadership, and the hilarious heroics and scandals of ordinary people. These writings help us to perceive people and events of the times in new ways.

For the greater part of his narrative, the events Wasif describes are more anecdotal and expository of human faults, weaknesses, and limitations than they are intimate. This scarcity of self-disclosure is particularly poignant given the substantial amount of "scandalous" disclosure about the private lives of Jerusalem's notables: their bachelor apartments, defiance of public morality, mistresses, indulgence in alcohol and other implements of keif, and the self-revelations (often self-depreciating) on his youthful indiscretions. These disclosures are recorded in detailed, anecdotal fashion as social observations of changing ways of life in Ottoman and mandate Jerusalem. And, these events happen to other people, and are ones in which he often appears as spectator and witness, as much as subject. His own family is significantly absent from these observations. Except for a brief passage on the lineage of his mother and father, the profile of his siblings (particularly his sisters), his wife, and his immediate circle remains opaque.

But a shift occurs with the memoir entries Wasif devotes to his betrothal and marriage to Victoria, to their forced flight from Jerusalem to seek refuge in Beirut, and finally to Victoria's death in 1958 and his ensuing exile. These revelations are of special value not only because they stand out as intimate recollections of courtship, marriage, loss, and exile but also because they talk to the reader in a more direct way about what has gone unsaid. Wasif is candid with the listener, as if questioning himself about his own self-doubts. He drops his satirical defenses and expresses himself as a fragile, hesitant, but dignified husband and father.

With his memoirs Wasif Jawhariyyeh repatriates to collective memory, and to historical record, nearly a half century of Jerusalem's complex mix of local, and foreign, voices. Through his immersion in the life of the city, these voices come to include his own.

II. FROM OTTOMANS TO ARABS
by Issam Nassar

Memoirs offer an important source for understanding Ottoman Palestine. This is so because no official Palestinian archive exists from this period. Also, memoirs shed light on fragments of history from daily life that we can never find elsewhere. In the case of Palestine, the story of the late Ottoman period is heavily dominated by Zionist narratives and reference points, and by a limiting focus on the Palestinian-Israeli conflict itself. Even if alternative histories of Palestine or a national archive existed, memoirs provide a rich record of social and cultural life. They give us a more close-up look at life coming from the margins as well as the mainstreams, as in the case of the Jawhariyyeh memoirs.

The memoirs that we have at hand document personal, communal, political, and collective events that were witnessed by the author himself. They cover events in Wasif's life that were familial, social, cultural, and political. In most cases, the author placed himself inside the picture and managed to tell the story from a personal perspective and to place himself inside the event—both as a participant and as an observer.

What Jawhariyyeh left us is essentially a memoir written—and rewritten—after the fact. Even so, we encounter places in the memoir where he appears to be speaking *from* the period, not a future vantage point. This suggests that when Wasif decided to write down his memoirs, he must have used notes or diaries that he had written earlier. Since he sometimes makes reference to what a particular place or location is "today," it is safe to assume that the original notes were written before he collected his memoirs together in a series of notebooks. For his references to what a location is today appear to belong to the British Mandate period in Palestine, and not to the late 1960s and early 1970s when the manuscript we found appears to have been written.

Although the memoirs of Wasif Jawhariyyeh encompass half a century, those sections he devoted to the last decade of Ottoman rule are of special importance. While narrating his life and that of his city during the period, they highlight the effects of the Great War on Jerusalem's society. Most historical studies on Palestine during this period deal with the later periods of British rule and post-1948. The handful of books on the late Ottoman period in Palestine are most often either written by Zionist historians who insist that Palestine was an underpopulated, underdeveloped land or focus on the administration of this Ottoman district. The few serious studies that do not fall under either of those two categories tend to highlight aspects of life of the elites in Palestine and bring to the forefront either the normality of Palestinian life before Zionism or the development of Jewish life since.

Therefore, the memoirs of Wasif Jawhariyyeh provide a primary source for narratives that seek to reconsider the effects of modernity and the Great War on life in Palestine in the last Ottoman decade. In this sense, they are a primary subaltern source for any understanding of the period that takes into account native voices and their historical agency. This translation into English of selections from the memoirs is intended to encourage readers of history to take more seriously voices from the margins in their searches for Palestine's modern history.

A neglected theme in the history of the Great War is the relations between the Arabs and the Turks before and during the war period. Although this topic has received some attention with the appearance of publications specifically treating the subject of Arabs and Young Turks, it is still largely understudied—especially in the case of Palestine.[1] The fact that Ottoman rule over Palestine ceased to exist, coupled with an obsession with the roots of the Palestinian-Israeli conflict, has contributed to a general disinterest in relations between the Ottoman rulers and their subjects. The emergence of various nationalist discourses in the states that emerged in the region after the fall of the Ottomans, or in the few decades that followed, had the effect of transforming the Ottoman period in the collective historical imagination of the peoples of the region and to shrink it to their experience of the Great War years. The Ottoman centuries thus, were transformed and reduced in collective memory to military conscription, hangings of nationalists in public squares in Beirut and Damascus, and famine.[2] As Salim Tamari has pointed out, an erasure of the Ottoman past in Palestine and the region took place in which the memory of four centuries of Ottoman rule was replaced by the memory of the last four years of that rule.[3]

Palestine and Ottoman Rule

In the second decade of the sixteenth century, Palestine, and the rest of *Bilad al-Sham*— today's Syria, Lebanon, Palestine, and Israel—fell under the control of the Ottomans. During the Ottoman centuries, a political and administrative tradition gradually took hold in the region, which in many cases intersected and represented a continuation of the regime of the *Mamluks* who had ruled Bilad al-Sham from the mid-thirteenth century until 1517–1518. From the inception of the empire, the Ottoman administrative system rested largely on the power and prestige of the empire's armies. Some of the most powerful rulers of the sultanate arose from their ranks. As historian Naim Turfan points out, this was partly due to the fact that the state itself was built up by *ghazis* and fighters who later on assumed positions of power within the empire.[4] This fact might account for why the Arab lands of the empire were well-integrated into the Ottoman imperial system, but not their Arab residents, who were absent from high government positions for the entire four centuries of Ottoman rule. Out of the two hundred and fifteen grand viziers in the history of the sultanate, not one of them was Arab—although three were possibly of Arab origin.[5] This is a significant point, especially in light of the fact that only seventy-eight of them were Turks whereas many others came from the ranks of other ethnic or national communities in the empire.[6] This might also help to explain Arab animosity towards the Turks, particularly in the last two decades of the empire.

Still, this does not adequately explain why Muslim Arabs from Bilad al-Sham did not occupy high offices in the ranks of the state, or why those offices they did hold tended most often to be in the ranks of the judicial *sharia* institutions. The answer to this question relates to the existence of a class of *ashraf*, or members of families that claim descendence from the family of the prophet. Members of such families traditionally specialized in Islamic jurisprudence and served in positions of power in the Sunni religious establishment. This placed them in the most suitable position to serve in the various ranks of the Islamic religious establishment in the Ottoman sultanate. The positions they acquired became hereditary, passing from father to son. Jews and Christian Arabs were part of the *millet* system where they had rights and duties, and were under the control of their religious hierarchy. This fact in itself might account for some of the special ties they had with their respective communities of faith abroad. In this regard, Ottomans of the Arab lands, whether they were Muslims or members of the millets, lived in a region considered periphery by the authorities in Istanbul. Therefore, they were not trustworthy enough to be appointed administrators or viziers in the capital. Still, Arabs of all religions served in the administrations of their cities, towns, villages, and communities.

Perhaps the *Tanzimat,* or reorganization, reforms of the nineteenth century diminished the status of Arab officials in the empire. The *Islahat Fermani,* or reform edict, known as *Hatt-i Humayoun* issued in February 1856, decreed "the equality of all religions in the Empire" and granted "Ottoman citizens equal access to educational institutions and equal treatment before the law."[7] The millet system was annulled and replaced by the authority of the government. Arabs who had played a significant role in the life of the empire were now marginalized because of the declining position of the religious establishments. It is worth recalling that the Young Turk Revolution in 1908 was motivated partly by the reinstatement of the Ottoman Constitution (itself a product of the Tanzimat period) which confirmed the reforms discussed here.[8]

Furthermore, the 1908 revolution itself, although it resulted in a general liberalization or relaxation of repressive policies and promised major reforms, did not represent an attempt to seriously challenge the existing Ottoman system. The Committee of Union and Progress (CUP), or *İttihat ve Terakki Cemiyeti*, was not essentially a progressive movement despite its overthrow of the Hamidian regime and its slogans such as "liberty, equality, fraternity, and justice."[9] Even though the new leaders proclaimed "equality of all Ottoman subjects without distinction of religion or race," the fact remains that most of these promises were never implemented or seemingly carried out.[10] The period of freedom of the press and assembly, and the right to form political parties came to an abrupt end even before the Ottoman sultanate officially entered the Great War.

Local Challenges to Ottomanism

In an entry written on September 15, 1914, about a month and a half before the Ottomans officially entered the War, the Jerusalem based educator Khalil al-Sakakini commented on the ban of newspapers in Palestine. He complained that "people do not read these days, other than the telegrams they get, as most local newspapers have been stopped and the Egyptian ones are banned by the government."[11] Aside from the implication regarding censorship of papers, Sakakini's comment might also reflect disappointment over the interruption of the flow of ideas between the Arabic speaking regions of the empire and Egypt. At the time, issues of Arab national rights within the Ottoman Empire were at the forefront of the debates in the newspaper media. While Arab nationalism might have been at its embryonic stage, ideas about local Arab interests apart from those of their largely Turkish rulers in Istanbul were starting to take hold in Palestine. Louis Fishman discussed a specific instance in Jerusalem when the local leaders confronted the imperial ones regarding an issue considered pivotal to the people of Jerusalem suggesting that it may represent one of the first signs of an emerging Arab mobilization in Palestine and the desire to challenge the central authorities in Istanbul.

In 1911, the *waqf,* or religious endowment, authorities in Jerusalem discovered that an English archeological team was carrying out excavations in the *haram* area (al-Aqsa Mosque and the Dome of the Rock). Jerusalem's Muslim elites were quick to mobilize a campaign to stop the excavations. It is worth pointing out that the wrath of the *ayan*, or notables, was directed, not against the intruding archeologists but against the central authorities in Istanbul, as well as the local Ottoman rulers of the city, especially when it became clear that the excavating team had the approval of the authorities in Istanbul. It did not take long for the protest to be joined by the Muslim elites in other cities in Palestine. Nablus notables from the families of Tuqan, Tamimi, Nabulsi, Hammad, and Abdu sent letters to the Ottoman parliament and the Muslim Higher Court in Istanbul protesting work in the haram. The governor sent a report to the authorities in Beirut protesting the excavations.[12]

The protest by the notables is significant particularly in light of the fact that it came only three years after the Arab regions enthusiastically welcomed the arrival of the Young Turks to power, a celebration depicted by Wasif in his memoir. He describes in detail and favorable tone how the Damascus Gate of the Old City of Jerusalem was ornamented and how the authorities erected four victory arches in the area between the gate and Notre Dame de France to the west. We also find a description of what he considered the impact of the coup on the economic situation in the city.

> Because of the Ottoman coup and the granting of freedoms to the masses so they could improve their social and political rights, in particular the Arab regions [...] the standard of living rose and the will to learn increased.[13]

In fact, this viewpoint appears to dominate the passages in Jawhariyyeh's memoirs that deal with the pre-War period. It does not appear that the changes in government and the struggle between the political orientations within the CUP had any effect on his view; he does not even mention them. A few years later, by 1914, Jawhariyyeh's apparent excitement seems to have faded. Recalling the dire economic situation in Jerusalem, he complains about the "injustice and despotism" of the authorities and the taxes demanded by the government as its troops entered the Great War.[14]

Such injustice could, perhaps, explain the peculiar behavior of Jawhariyyeh's neighbor Mikhail who hung pictures of Sultans, Abdülhamid and Muhammad Rashad, in his toilet. Mikhail would often go to the toilet to hit the pictures with his shoe, declaring, "You are wearing us out with your taxes!" Having the pictures of Abdülhamid who was removed by the Young Turks, and Rashad who was appointed by them, is rather significant and is confirmed by Jawhariyyeh's description of the period as "the time of despotism." Coming from someone who praised the coup as putting an end to Hamdian despotism, Jawhariyyeh's lumping together of both eras appears to be an indicator of a new development in ways in which he, and the perhaps the people of Jerusalem, looked at their Turkish rulers.

Such a complaint about the economic situation is also found in the diary of Ihasam Turjman, a local conscript in the Ottoman army stationed in Jerusalem during the war years. In an entry in his journal dated July10, 1916, Turjman wrote:

> Jerusalem has not seen worse days. Bread and flour supplies have almost totally dried up [...]. Every day I pass the bakeries on my way to work and I see a large number of women going home empty-handed. For several days the municipality has distributed some kind of black bread to the poor, the likes of which I have never seen. People used to fight over the limited supplies, sometimes waiting until midnight. Now, even that bread is no longer available.[15]

Turkish–Arab Relations within the Empire

Despite such expressions of disapproval, the relations between the Turks and Arabs did not reach a dead-end before at least a year into the war. There is little evidence that Arabs entertained the idea of separation from the empire, despite their substantial grievances against its government. A situation of cooperation and negotiation between the CUP and the emerging Arab nationalist movement appears to have existed before the war began. In fact, on a few occasions, the CUP chose to support representatives of the emerging Arabism movement at the expense of their own party's interests. One example is the 1914 parliamentary election when they supported Arab candidates who ran against their own party candidates. In Acre, for example, the authorities arrested supporters of Sheikh Asa'ad al-Shuqayri, the Unionist candidate, to enable his Arab nationalist competitor Abdel Fattah al-Sadi to win. In Nablus, the Unionist Hayder Touqan was made to lose the elections in favor of the opposing candidates. Still, these were perhaps select attempts by individual leaders to safeguard the empire, rather than a principled endeavor to see the Arabs as equals. It did not take long for essentially a small group of leaders to hijack the CUP, even if the organization's membership continued to surge (by 1908 it had 83 branches throughout the empire with a total membership of 850,000).[16] The triumvirate of Enver, Talaat, and Jamal pashas unseated the government of Kamil Pasha on January 23, 1913 following the empire's humiliating defeat by Italy in Tripoli (today's Libya).

The surge in membership of the CUP though did not always reflect their popularity or a commitment to the party's line. While many must have joined the party out of conviction, a large number joined for various other reasons including pressure, personal or economic interests, or simply curiosity. Khalil al-Sakakini, for example, was visited by a sheikh in his home on September 25, 1908, who asked him to join the committee. Al-Sakakini asked him questions and for a few days to think it over. Several days later, he pledged in a secret ceremony to uphold the constitution and the orders of the CUP.[17] Nothing in the rest of al-Sakakini's diary indicates that he was ever active in the Committee. In fact, he clearly became an advocate of Arab and Syrian nationalisms immediately after the ceremony.

Despite promises of equality in the empire by the Unionists, and the conciliatory tune of the Arab nationalists, it is clear that the leaders of the CUP did not trust anyone but Turks. Four years before the beginning of the war, Talaat Bey, who would become a prominent member of the triumvirate after the coup, told a meeting of the local branch of the CUP in Salonika in 1910, that "there can be no question of equality, until we succeeded in our task of Ottomanizing the Empire."[18] Although Talaat was referring at the time to the failure to incorporate non-Muslims in the Balkans and Greece (or what he called *ghiaur*), his statement applied to all non-Turks in the empire since his premise was that of Ottomanizing. At a time when all the people of the empire were already Ottoman citizens, especially after the reinstatement of the constitution, Ottomanizing could only mean Turkifying of non-Turks in the empire, including Arabs, Armenians, and others.

The leaders of the triumvirate embraced the ideology of Pan-Turanism, particularly after the defeats in Tripoli and the Balkans.[19] As Zeine Zeine has argued, "the shock of [the] disaster of war losses between 1911 and 1913 resulted in a wider spread of a genuine desire for national regeneration among all educated Turks."[20] The ideas of the Ottoman reformer Namik Kemal, with his emphasis on Turkishness (*Türkçülük*) were gaining popularity among the rank and file of the army. A recollection by Selahttin Bey, a veteran of the Great War and Turkey's War of independence, illustrates that the idea of being a Turk was strongly associated with service in the high ranks of the army. Recalling a meeting with one of his friends at a café in Istanbul following his acceptance at the Ottoman Military Academy (*Herbiye Mektebi*) in the city, Selahttin reported the following conversation.

> What are you?
> A student at the military school
> What else?
> I don't know.
> Think about it.
> I am an Ottoman.
> What else?
> I am a Muslim.
> *No. Before everything else, you are a Turk!*[21]

Salehttin's recollection demonstrates how his allegiance had changed during his time at the academy, a point he stresses in his story, notes Ryan Gingeras.[22]

The claim could be made that an anti-Arab sentiment, as part of a more general sentiment toward non-Turks in general, was already visible among the Turks on the eve of World War I. Such anti-*ghiaur* sentiment, coupled with what Ussama Makdisi called "Ottoman Orientalism," are significant signs of a Turkish view of Arabs as second-degree Ottomans.[23] Still, the rise of a separatist movement in the Arab regions was not as apparent. Rather, Arab leaders and parties were calling for a decentralized Ottoman state composed of two nations—one Arab and one Turkish.

At the same time, within the ranks of the CUP, talk of an "Arab Question" started to become public, not to mention the broad references to it among British officials after the Ottomans entered the war. Only ten days after the sultanate entered the conflict, Enver Pasha, the minister of war, told Jamal Pasha—who is noted often in Wasif's memoirs—that "the news from Syria points to a general disturbance in the country and great activity on the part of the revolutionary Arabs."[24] This is why Enver instructed Jamal to take command of the Fourth Army, which led the latter to arrive shortly afterwards in Syria where he soon implemented ruthless policies against his Arab subjects. Jamal's insistence on carrying through with the executions of Arab leaders in Beirut in August 1915, and in Damascus in 1916, sent a clear message that he was not going to tolerate any Arab nationalist sentiment. Similar executions took place in various other cities in Syria, Lebanon, and Palestine, including in Jerusalem on several occasions. Wasif kept a photo of a hanging of a man in front of the Jaffa Gate of the Old City of Jerusalem in one of his photo albums that he kept with the memoirs.

Based on the impression one gets from Jamal Pasha's memoirs it is clear that, although publically advocating Turkish-Arab cooperation and partnership, he harbored anti-Arab feelings. This is especially obvious in his treatment of those sentenced to death and his Arab subjects, as well as his attitude toward Emir Faisal and his father, the Sharif Husain of Mecca. Arabs in his book are often referred to as treacherous and as traitors, and he discusses the literary hypocrisy of the Arabs in general.[25]

Similarly, advocates of Arabism were also changing their tone and policies, and inching gradually more towards separation from the Turks. The mood among Arabs was changing, and the ruthless policies of Jamal Pasha must have played a pivotal role in the change of heart among inhabitants of Palestine in particular. Nevertheless, it cannot be said that they had given up completely on the empire until more than a couple of years into the war. What is clear is that the people of Palestine were organically connected to the peoples of Syria and Lebanon, and their positions followed suit with those of the intellectuals and leaders in those places.

Changing Allegiance in Jerusalem

On the eve of the Great War, Jawhariyyeh writes:

> The soldiers of the Ottoman army were ravaging this tranquil country in such a way that some of the locals began to worry. At the time, Germany and France were at war and rumors were spreading whereby the Ottoman state was soon going to have to join this war.[26]

Indeed, the state did enter the war shortly after, and Wasif describes the announcement made in Jerusalem, adding that it was "a black day, for our country" that "the Ottoman state could have spared [us], had it pondered the consequences."[27] It did not take long for the state to start conscripting young men from Jerusalem, and elsewhere, into the army. In 1917, Wasif himself would become one of them, serving in the navy at the Dead Sea. This, along with other consequences of the war, became a source of resentment against the state. On September 10, 1915, Ihsan al-Turjman asks in diary:

> What does this barbaric state want from us? [Do they want] to liberate Egypt on our backs? They promised us and other fellow Arabs

> that we would be partners in this government, and that they are seeking to advance the interests and conditions of the Arab nation. However, what have we actually seen from these promises? Had they treated us as equals, I would not have hesitated to give my blood and my life—but as things stand, I hold a drop of my blood to be more precious than the entire Turkish state.[28]

This sentiment clearly reflects how the general mood in Jerusalem—and in Palestine and Syria—had turned anti-Turkish as the war entered its second year. While it states just one person's view, considering Turjman's social circles, this view was probably more representative than not. He was close to the mayor of Jerusalem Hussein al-Husseini, and a regular visitor to the house of Khalil al-Sakakini and his friends. A similar expression of local sentiment toward the war and the authorities in Istanbul is also found in the diary of the Spanish consul in Jerusalem, Antonio de la Cierva y Lewita. In an entry dated February 16, 1915, de la Cierva notes that "the Arabs are angered at the Turks as they have sent them to die."[29] The entry then turns to what de la Cierva thought was a weak national consciousness among the Arabs at the time, stating that they are not "able to resist the oppressors" and lamenting that the Arabs "have no awareness of the spirit of nationalism." However, his claim would be proven wrong in light of events that would unfold over the next few months.

One example that could serve to challenge the Spanish consul's claim relates to the establishment of the Ottoman Red Crescent society in Jerusalem in 1915. Following the authorities' quick dismissal of Hussein al-Husseini from his position as mayor, along with the other members of the city council, al-Husseini

Military Labor Corps road building and laying pipe between Kuseimeh and Ibn (1915). John Whiting Collection. © Library of Congress.

moved to establish the Jerusalem branch of the society. It is very possible that such a move was designed to strengthen his power in relation to the new council and mayor that replaced him. But it is worth keeping in mind that in contrast to the newly appointed council members, most of whom were Turks and all of whom were Muslims, the board of the society's chapter was native and inter-communal. Along with al-Husseini who became its head, its members came from the ranks of Jerusalem's prominent families and included Jews and Christians and did not include any Turks. In fact, it is perhaps more important to highlight "prominence" over religious affiliation. The board of the society consisted of five other members, two prominent native Jews, two prominent Christians, and one Muslim. In a sense, the society was more about local representation and communal solidarity than about doing what the Ottomans required. As Abigail Jacobson suggests, the composition of the board was a sign for a sort of post-Ottoman alternative that al-Husseini was starting to advocate.[30] His alternative, unfortunately, did not have a continued impact. Jacobson points out that this was possibly the last national or communal committee or organization on which Jews served voluntarily along with Muslims and Christians in support of a national government.

Far from being a pioneer in interrelations among the different religious groups in the city, al-Husseini maintained the state of coexistence that was already prevalent in Jerusalem at the time. The best evidence for the religious mix in the fabric of Jerusalem comes, once again, from the Jawhariyyeh memoirs. Throughout the memoirs from the period before and after the Young Turk Revolution, Wasif describes to his reader how rich and multireligious life was in Jerusalem. From his depiction of the ritual practices of every religious group and the role that members of other religions played in such rituals, he paints a picture of a mosaic in which intercommunal solidarity was a prime feature.

As a Greek Orthodox Christian, he appears to have attended every celebration in the city—be it Muslim, Christian, or Jewish. During Ramadan night festivities in Jerusalem in his childhood, Wasif and his brothers would take part in the chanting of the *Zikr* celebrations at the shrine of *Sheikh Rihan*,[31] and then sing and perform music with neighbors.[32] Similarly, he describes the annual Jewish picnic (*shat-ha*) in which "Christian and Muslim Jerusalemite Arabs used to participate" with the mostly "Eastern (Mizrahi) Jews who kept their traditions, in particular... Palestinain Jews." The picnic, which featured "musical string groups and choirs" and singing of "*muwashahat* of Andalusia," constituted a visitation to what Jews believe to be the tomb of Simon the Just.[33]

The fluidity that existed between the communities was reflected in new local educational practices in the city such as the *Dusturiyeh*, or constitutional school, that was set up by al-Sakakini along with 'Ali Jarallah, Aftim Moushabeck, and Jamil al-Khalidi in the aftermath of the revolution. The policy of the school was to reject the physical punishment typical of missionary schools in the city at the time. In an entry recorded on Sunday, January 1, 1911, al-Sakakini notes:

> The Dusturieyeh School stands out in a number of ways:
>
> (1) It brings together students from different religious and denominational backgrounds [...].

> (2) The school functions on the principle that the pupils are honorable and not subservient, and need assistance to grow in pride, not the opposite, and in need of emotional growth and freedom to be creative.[34]

Jawhariyyeh and his brother Tawfiq attended the Dusturiyyeh School after their father took them out of the German Lutheran School (*al-Dabagha*), following a violent assault on Wasif by one of the teachers. Wasif describes the education he received in his new school, listing the topics they studied, including "grammar, literature, mathematics, English, French, Turkish, physical education and Qur'anic studies for Christians"—the Qu'ran for non-Muslims.[35]

Such a secular and multicultural spirit is exemplified by the life of Jawhariyyeh himself. He grew up in a religiously mixed neighborhood in the Old City, learned to love and appreciate the *adhan*, or Muslim call for prayer, and became a musician playing in a group composed of musicians from all religious orientations. His own name was given to him to honor a leading Arab figure, Wasif Bey al-Azem, from Damascus. At the same time, after his conscription into the Ottoman navy, he also befriended many Turkish officers and was fond of telling about his adventures with them. In a sense, Wasif embodied the various identities prevalent, or emerging, at the time—Ottoman, Arab, Palestinian, Jerusalemite, and Christian-Arab. Yet, the concept of "Ottoman identity" appears to have gradually diminished as the war progressed, a feeling expressed clearly in an entry in his memoirs about the war and the Ottoman involvement in it.

> The Arab people of the empire were under the threat of annihilation at the hands of Ahmed Jamal [Jamal Pasha] the blood-shedder who rules our lands now and who is killing its devoted children.[36]

While Wasif's statement conveys a strong sense of Arab identity as well as opposition to Jamal Pasha's policies, it also suggests that a new sentiment was emerging since the term "Arab people" could also have meant the natives of Palestine. It is comparable to the attitude that appears to have been behind the structure that former mayor al-Husseini had in mind when forming the board of the Red Crescent Society. Jacobson described this attitude as that of a *local patriot,* one who "combined a dedication to the city of Jerusalem as an urban locale and for its residents, of all religious beliefs."[37]

The idea of a "local patriot" is evident in the writings of Khalil al-Sakakini, even if it is presented in more indirect terms, most likely to avoid showing opposition to the state. In a notebook entry dated December 3, 1917, written shortly before his arrest by the Ottomans and imprisonment in Damascus, and just a few days before the British forces entered Jerusalem, he affirms:

> I am, I am simply a human being, nothing else. I do not belong to political parties or religious factions. I consider myself a patriot wherever I am, and strive to improve my surroundings whether they are American, British, Ottoman or African, whether they are Christian, Muslim or pagan. I only work to serve knowledge, and knowledge has no homeland.[38]

The Ottoman rulers reinstated al-Husseini to his position as mayor before the British forces took over Jerusalem, and he delivered the message of surrender to them. Why did the Turkish officials choose not to deliver the letter themselves and negotiate an honorable withdrawal of their forces? The fact that the surrender resulted from a meeting to which the army's leaders in the region called local notables from the various religions in the city might be significant, as it implies that the Turks recognized that the local patriots were in charge of the city. This is a unique event in Jerusalem's history. The entry of General Allenby into the city on December 11, 1917 appears to have amounted to a national celebration. It was not because of the British and what they had in mind for Palestine, but rather that the population of the city was happy to see an end to Ottoman rule and to conscription. Describing his family's preparations for Christmas that year, Wasif observes:

> Truthfully, it was a joyous holiday for all our family because the British had come and the Arab people were rid of the nightmare of the tyrant Turks. We all had great hope for a better future, especially after what we had suffered... Thank God for saving our youth from the damned army service.[39]

Little did he then know of what was to come to Palestine in the decades that would follow. The people of Jerusalem, as well as the rest of the Bilad al-Sham, had had their fill with the war. The oppressive war-time rule of Jamal Pasha, coupled with famine due to the Franco-British blockade of the eastern Mediterranean and conscription, left them little choice but to rejoice at the end of Ottoman rule. They moved on from being relatively loyal Ottoman subjects to Arab, Syrian, or Palestinian nationalists in the years to come. The Jawhariyyeh memoirs from the late Ottoman period clearly illustrate this. It did not happen overnight but gradually over time during which the local identity was greatly fostered before it eventually embraced a larger collective Arab identity in the process of being born.

PROLOGUE

I am no skilled writer, famous historian, or experienced traveler. I am simply a civil servant who was forced out of school by the First Great War. But I feel compelled to document situations, surprises, and incidents which emerged in my life during the Ottoman and the British periods in my country of Palestine, some of which are amusing.

Two aspects of my life led to these situations and surprises. The fraternal ties which connected my late father and the Husseini family of Jerusalem also connected me and one of the notables of this honorable family, the late Hussein Hashem al-Husseini, who was the son of the late Hajj Salim al-Husseini. I was proud to accompany this man of great personality on his trips and socials from when I was a child. In this way I came to know the customs and music of the villages of the Jerusalem district, and later those of Jericho, the Dead Sea, and al-Karak.[1] This was before and during the Great War. Given my love for art and for Arabic music in particular—the fine art that occupied the greater part of my life—I had the opportunity to attend parties and evening socials which would have been inaccessible to others. Thus, I met great personalities of name including high commissioners, leaders, governors, literary figures, and artists of both the Ottoman and the British eras. I made acquaintances with upper-class families and people of various social classes and faiths. I was able to know the details of many mysterious events which others would have found it difficult to uncover.

While I was a civil servant in the British Mandate government, I worked as a fiscal manager in Jerusalem and head of the committee for the evaluation of the city's properties. My work required me to enter homes, shops, institutes, monasteries, and the like, and to be in touch with their owners and residents. This enriched my general knowledge of life and encouraged me to collect rare oriental antiques of all kinds. My job was both the starting point of my love for art and a great contributor to the growth of the Jawhariyyeh Collection. These reasons prompted me to write down what I had come to witness or hear about.

I am grateful to a dear friend, Mr. Muhyiddine Makki, for his support.

I dedicate this book to my son, Jiryis, who is without doubt my only hope. It will be for him a master key. If used correctly, it will enable him to open all doors and have an insider's look at the life of his father and his family and friends. It will be a reminder of his ancestors' deeds, anecdotes, and customs, particularly in Jerusalem, the city of the honorable Jawhariyyeh family.[2]

I.
THE OTTOMAN ERA: 1904–1914

MY BOYHOOD

I was born on January 14, 1897, which on the Julian calendar was the Orthodox Christian New Year's Day. My father was preparing a tray of *knafeh*, a tradition which the Greek Orthodox follow to this day.[3] My father named me Wasif after his dear friend Wasif Bey al-Azem from Damascus, who was sitting judge of the Criminal Court of Jerusalem at the time. I still have a nice photograph of him, which he gave to my father as a present.

From the family record, which my father wrote himself, I learned that he married my mother Hilaneh in 1884. Together they had three girls, Afifeh, Shafiqa, and Julia, and four boys, Khalil, Tawfiq, (Wasif), and finally Fakhri.[4]

My sister Afifeh married Costandi Abdel-Nour Al-Baghl, and together they had Widad, Nuhail, Fayez, and Nabiha. Shafiqa married George Costandi Adranli and had with him Aline, Costandi, Nada, Elia, Issa, Hikmat, and Naim. Julia married Tanas Yanko al-Sununu and emigrated with him to America. They married before the Great War and together they had Hanna, William, Janet, Madeleine, Ruth, and Margaret.

At my christening, the British consul, William Assad al-Khayyat[5] from Jaffa, acted as my godfather, while my godmother was Miss Nastas Sam'aan Abdu. Both were also godparents to all my siblings, God bless their souls.

My father told me that all he was ever able to find out about his grandfather, Suleiman, was his name. He was an only son and lived in the Damascus Gate home, on the eastern side of the Valley Road, below al-Qantara and in front of the stairs of the Jewish religious endowment's building and Mount Zion's Greek Orthodox cemetery. His father, Khalil Jawhariyyeh, was an only son, too, and lived in the house situated near the Mawlawiyah[6] complex, in which my father, Jiryis, was born. He, too, was buried at the Mount Zion Cemetery. When he died, my father Jiryis was still a minor. He said that he was playing marbles with the children when his father's funeral cortege passed by. His sisters were already married at the time.

DAR AL-JAWHARIYYEH IN SAADIYEH

Dar al-Jawhariyyeh—the House of Jawhariyyeh—in which I and all my siblings were born, was located in the Saadiyeh Quarter in Jerusalem, near the shrine of Sheikh Rihan, on a high hill overlooking the city. When approaching it from Damascus Gate, one had to ascend via the Mameluk arch, and when approaching it from the al-Wad Quarter, one had to ascend the steps of al-Asila archway. If coming from al-Rawda, one had to ascend the steps of the archway of the School of the Sisters of Zion of the order of France, going past Sheikh Rihan.

The house consisted of four floors, the top two of which belonged to my father. The third floor contained a separate room, and my father had arranged it in such a way that it seemed like a modern building. Forty-five steps led to the south-facing main entrance, where a wood-and-glass chest was placed to block the wind, which was particularly heavy in winter. Then one entered a spacious and elegantly decorated hall whose walls were lined with wooden cupboards where clothes, copper utensils, glass, books, *argilehs*[7] (kept in a dedicated cupboard), and coffee utensils were stored. The dinner table, at which we ate only in summer, was placed in the middle.

The hall had three doors. One opened to a well-proportioned room lined with seashell-covered pots made by my father and containing all kinds of homegrown flowers. Under the arch of this room was a jasmine tree and a snail vine. The room faced south, so when my father sat on the wooden sofa, smoking his argileh, he could enjoy the view of Old Jerusalem, which was particularly dazzling at night. The room also had an extremely beautiful and elegant window overlooking the main hall.

The second door led to the marvelous reception room, which had large stone benches in the main area and smaller ones by the double bay window overlooking the southern side, too. At the front of the reception room, a small door led to my father's bedroom, a beautiful room set over a very high arch and overlooking the main street through its northside window. The bed had an elegant mosquito net, and in the corner a bookcase stood next to a built-in wardrobe that had a special compartment in the middle for sweets and for the tray of marmalade offered to visitors, as was the custom at the time. There was also a white iron built-in safe whose keys were always kept by my father.

The third door opened to a large room which was a bedroom for my mother and all the children, male and female, including me. After spending some time together in the evening, we would take the mattresses from the corner where we kept them stacked, lay them one next to the other, and sleep, after drawing the large mosquito net which was hung by four rings in the corners of the room, to keep off mosquitoes and flies. I never stopped recalling with bitter nostalgia those beautiful nights and the sweet, natural sleep. Whenever my father needed something, he would ring a small bell that was always placed by his bed, and my mother or one of my siblings would attend to him. Every morning, particularly on winter days, my mother would bring him coffee in his bedroom and drink it with him, and we would bring him the argileh and the brazier, while he remained in bed to keep warm. In summer, he usually would smoke his argileh morning and evening in the flower room, which he used to call "the balcony," and enjoy the views of sacred Jerusalem from this veranda, or from the bay window.

From the main hall, the kitchen and facilities could be reached directly. Then one could climb eleven steps to a room with a mud-and-brick ceiling where provisions were kept, such as the box of flour, urns of chickpeas, beans, lentils, bulgur wheat, rice, couscous, vermicelli and *freekeh* (grilled green wheat), oils, olives, pickles, and cheese. In the corner of this room there was a wooden worktop, and on it a cabinet where father kept the carpentry tools which he used to fix things around the house. We always assisted him by bringing him the tools, handing him the nails, and then returning everything to its place. A harsh punishment awaited those of us who failed to return a tool, piece of furniture, argileh, jug, or pair of scissors to its dedicated place. He used to tell us, God bless his soul, "If I come for the tweezers at midnight, with no light, I want to find it hung on this nail in the argileh cupboard," pointing angrily to the nail.

In this room, there was also a big pigeon cage that had a window on the eastern side to let the sun in. We had more than forty pairs of pigeons that used to fly over Saadiyeh and return home in time for their regular feeding time. From this room, a flight of eight steps led to a wooden door that opened to the rooftop, where one truly felt like they were in a minaret or on an airplane, for each side of the rooftop of Dar al-Jawhariyyeh had its special feature. If you looked west, you could see Damascus Gate, the city wall, the New City, al-Musrara Quarter, the Italian hospital, and the Maskobiyyeh (Russian compound) building. Before them lay the houses of the Christian Quarter, stacked up inside the wall all the way to the Franciscan Monastery, the clock tower, David's castle, and Jabal al-Mukabbir.[8] To the east lay the beautiful view of the al-Aqsa Mosque, the Dome of the Rock, and the court of the mosque, with Jabal al-Tor and the Russian Church beyond. You could simply count all of Jerusalem's minarets and high belltowers from this rooftop. The rooftop area was surrounded by a beautiful wooden fence, through which we would often wave to my father when he was at the government offices, opposite our house on the southern side. My father was in charge of the municipal park of Jerusalem (al-Manshiyyeh), that had a room in which the municipality's decorations were stored. On many occasions we would take Ottoman flags, decorative lamps, and fireworks, put up the exquisite decorations, and set off the fireworks over Qabasiyyeh, especially at night. The people of Jerusalem were dazzled by the show, particularly because our house was located on an elevated spot and visible from most of the city's homes and locations.

A NOTE ON MY PARENTS' LIFE

I learned that my paternal grandmother belonged to the al-Sawabini family, one of the well-known Arab Greek Orthodox families of Jerusalem. She was the daughter of the late al-Sawabini. My father had on a number of occasions shown me the grave of his maternal grandfather, which was located in the middle of the Zion Cemetery and was made of faience. The glazed ceramic grave had the color of dark brown china and remains to this day the only such grave in Jerusalem, being of an old Russian make. I remember well the

The al-Saadiyeh neighborhood of Jerusalem. The arrow in the photo, drawn by Wasif, points to the location of the Jawhariyyeh home. Jawhariyyeh Collection. © Institute for Palestine Studies, Beirut.

residence of Banayot al-Sawabini in the alley that runs north of the Maskobiyyeh wall, near what is now the building of the Queen of Abyssinia. Vicars Farhoud and Qurban later used the building as a base for the Association of Arab Protestants. Banayot al-Sawabini was a venerable man and was head of the al-Sawabini family. He was over one hundred years of age, and I clearly remember visiting him with my father. I keep a photograph of Bayanot al-Sawabini, George Deeb, Yaacoub Ansara, my father Jiryis Jawhariyyeh, Theodore Yanko Theodori, Yaacoub al-Sununu, and a Russian prince. The photograph was taken on the occasion on which they dressed in Western clothing for the first time, with the exception of Bayanot al-Sawabini who was wearing the *shirwal*.[9]

My father told me that he had acted as godfather in the christening of al-Sawabini's children. They lived in Jaffa. I recall visiting them once as a child with my father and seeing in the room a clock that was enshrined in a large cornice-like frame and decorated with waterfalls, trees, houses, and puppets, which I believe was a representation of a farm. When the clock struck the hour, they would all move in an exquisite way.

MY MOTHER

My mother Hilaneh was the daughter of Andony Barakat, who belonged to one of Jerusalem's Arab Greek Orthodox families. Her mother came from the al-Baramky family, which was well-known in Jerusalem. I found out that her brother, Nakhla Barakat, died at our home in Saadiyeh after he lost his wife Anastas, the daughter of Hanna al-Ajrab. My uncle died childless. Thus his death sadly meant the end of this Jerusalemite Arab Greek Orthodox family.

My father, Jiryis Jawhariyyeh, had been living in the same residence as the late Andoni Barakat in the al-Saha compound in the Christian Quarter. After my mother's birth, her father passed away and my father stepped in to provide for the family, raising both my mother and her brother, Nakhla. When she reached adulthood, it so happened that my father married her when he was about forty years of age. My Uncle Nakhla Barakat was of a strong build and extremely opinionated, so my father had no choice but to make him join the cavalry where he became a skilled cavalryman in the Ottoman era. He died of asthma in Jerusalem. Margot, the daughter of al-Baramky and the widow of Ibrahim al-Lengy (the al-Lengy family also died out) often visited our home. Margot was my mother's aunt.

MY FATHER

My father taught himself Arabic, Turkish, and then Greek, before studying law and becoming a well-known lawyer at the civil courts that were established in Jerusalem after Wasif Bey al-Azem, the judge of the criminal court, arrived from Damascus. During that period, my father traveled twice to Istanbul. His second visit was a special mission for Patriarch Damianos, accompanied by the late Yaacoub Said and his sister, Umm George Adranli, while his first visit had been for trade business.

My father had learned the Qu'ran by heart and could recite it very well. When I was a student at the Dusturiyyeh School, he used to correct me as I practiced my Qu'ran lessons at home. Whenever I misread a sura, he would tell me from the reception room, and I would correct my error.

My Father's Professions

My father was appointed *mukhtar* (head) of the Greek Orthodox community in Jerusalem in 1884. I still keep the mayor's stamp with his name on it. With the help of Hajj Salim al-Husseini, my father became a member of the Administrative Council of Jerusalem and received from Istanbul an honorary costume and a sword which I still keep in the Jawhariyyeh collection. (Matia Sarophim represented the Latin community.) He was also a member of the municipal council at the time of Hajj Salim al-Husseini's headship of the municipal council, and later at the time of Said Effendi al-Husseini and that of Fayd Effendi al-Alami.

Studio portrait of Wasif's father, Jiryis Jawhariyyeh, in official attire. Jawhariyyeh Collection. © Institute for Palestine Studies, Beirut.

He was appointed an inspector for the animal census in the Jerusalem district the first time that the government organized this census. He was also appointed many times as property surveyor at the committee for the evaluation of the werko[10] and the tithe taxes on behalf of the locals. The government also assigned the tithes of the villages of the district to him and to his partner, Jiryis Kutn, a number of times.

His Work and Interests

My father was passionate about agriculture. For this reason, the municipality put him in charge of the *al-Manshiyyeh*, or municipal park, for at least twenty years, and he became the founder of this park which he managed entirely by himself, with no supervision.

He planted mulberry trees to breed silkworms, since silkworms feed on mulberry leaves. He did this work at home, so we would watch the silkworm eggs turn into worms, then into caterpillars, before turning into cocoons. This last stage took place in the orange grove of George al-Homs in the village of al-Aizariyah. This was carried on for nine years, becoming a profitable business. I also remember that he planted bird-feeding seeds, which we sold profitably via Hajj Idriss al-Mughrabi in Damascus Gate. In his younger years, he ran a nice riverside café in a private orange grove for six years.

He was an art-loving person who liked to listen to fine music and was particularly appreciative of it. I never saw him play the oud, but Nakhla Kattan told me that he had once seen him play in his father's tent during the picnic of our Lady Mary.[11] My father knew the rules of singing and encouraged me to learn to play an instrument and to sing correctly.

He liked to paint and was good at it. He used to draw at our home in Saadiyeh, with egg yolk and then with oil, following the common technique. Four icons that he painted himself are on display in Saint John's Church in the Christian Quarter. He presented the government offices with the coat of arms of Sultan Abdul-Hamid, which was displayed above the entrance, inside the fence, between the two police offices. He also presented Said Effendi al-Husseini with a smaller replica of this icon when the latter was head of Jerusalem's municipality.

When the late William Khayyat, who was the consul of the British government in Jerusalem and godfather to the children of our family, sent us a British-made wooden horse, my father painted a zebra pattern on it and gave it to Fayd Effendi al-Alami, the head of the municipality of Jerusalem, as a present for his son, Moussa. I still keep a large-sized photograph of me with my father standing next to the horse. My father also liked to hunt. He told us that he once shot an eagle with his number twelve rifle, and when he was convinced that the eagle was dead, he went and moved his head with the rifle, only for the eagle to catch the rifle's pipe and squash it with his beak!

While he was a fine horse rider in his youth, in our time, when he was over sixty, he rode a donkey. The donkey was white—the color my

Studio portrait of Wasif Jawhariyyeh at age three, with his father Jiryis, some time in early 1900. Jawhariyyeh Collection. © Institute for Palestine Studies, Beirut.

father preferred—and was famous for the way that my father kept it looking elegant. He knew a great deal of poetry and wise sayings by heart. Many times, at our home, we watched his poetry competitions with the late Sheikh Ali al-Rimawi, as well as with the late Sheikh Taher Abu al-Saud. He could also communicate with his fingers, which he did with the late Hassan al-Azhari, moving them in a way that dazzled the audience. I learned this beautiful art from him and I will provide details of the symbols on a page of this book, lest they might be lost forever.

Father liked to acquire rare objects, such as antiques and the like. We had at home two African Boa snakeskins, one of which still had the head on it with two rows of teeth in the upper jaw. I still keep it in the Jawhariyyeh Collection, and all those who see it are stunned by it. He had a very small china collection (candy pots), as well as some rare manuscripts and a valuable collection of rare ancient stamps. The furniture he owned was rather modest, but rare in comparison with the furniture that his friends owned at the time. His collection also included my mother's trousseau chest, which was made of Turkish walnut wood. It was adorned with copper engravings and had an unusual padlock with a bell. He also had a brazier from Istanbul made of yellow copper, and a Russian samovar. I have kept these items as souvenirs.

OUR HOME LIFE

My father liked order and tidiness. He was a great socializer who taught and encouraged us to be righteous. For instance, when my sisters Afifeh, Shafiqa, and Julia were married, he ordered my brothers Khalil, Tawfiq, Fakhri, and me to help mother in all the housework, tidying away, cleaning, sweeping, and mopping the floor, laying out mattresses and bedding, and storing them away, whitening copper, and transporting water from the ground floor to the first floor, climbing forty-five steps. We even helped with meal preparation, to the great surprise of the neighbors who envied us for our housekeeping skills.

In the summer, we used to sit at the table to eat. We would take our seats and each would eat off their own tin plate,[12] as is the custom nowadays. We had given up the widely used wooden spoons that were imported from Anatolia and Greece in favor of copper spoons that were bleached from time to time. We also gave up the habit of drinking from a common metal bowl that was tied to the water jar, since each of us had acquired his own glass. In order to refine our lifestyle further, my father also bought for each of us an iron bed. So from 1906 on we no longer had to sleep on the floor, thank God, and were able to make the beds in no time, as we no longer had to store away the mattresses.

There were two stables for the white donkey my father used to ride—one that was outside the house and had a street door, and another one inside, in the corridor entrance, in the corner of which we used to keep charcoal and wood for winter days. My brothers and I looked after the donkey daily, making sure he was fed, given water, and kept clean. We loosened the saddle when Father wanted to ride it, sifted the barley and mixed it with hay, and did all the chores according to Father's instructions. Indeed, the stable looked as though it was meant to house a genuine Arabian horse, for everything was tidy and well kept because Father was angered by the slightest negligence and sometimes would even beat us. In winter, he liked to sit on his oriental mat in one of the corners of our sleeping area, wrapped in his *abaya*[13] or sheepskin coat, smoking a water pipe and drinking coffee. In the evening he enjoyed sipping arak with delicious mezze dishes laid around him. For his comfort and pleasure, we prepared the "feast" by placing a round table that was about thirty centimeters high in front of him, and laying on it the spoons, plates, and food my mother handed us in the kitchen. We would then all sit around it to have lunch or dinner, and after dessert, we would happily put everything back in its place, all four of us, under Father's watchful eye and Mother's supervision.

My father, God bless his soul, had a great sense of humor. He never missed a chance to joke with us, but within the rules of politeness, and none of us dared to use vulgar language. He complimented those of us who made a good joke and tried to correct mistakes and to teach us the true meaning of humor. That is how we spent our leisure time, after which we would go to work or to school. My mother, God bless her soul, was not literate, and my father used to joke with her wittingly, as though she was one of the kids. On *a'yad* (special occasions), she was the first one to congratulate him by kissing his hands. Then we would follow suit and kiss his hands and hers.

Whenever any of us had been disobedient to Mother or had behaved badly— whether towards brothers, neighbors, or friends—all Mother had to say was, "I'll have your father deal with this." These words were enough to discipline us and make us obey her, fearing that she might indeed complain to Father who was ruthless and could punish us harshly, but fairly and justly. Often his chastisement was accomplanied by a relevant story, the moral of which would deter the culprit in the future and preclude the need for physical punishment.

For instance, my brother Tawfiq was good at witty replies. He was very intelligent and skilled at manual work, able to repair all sorts of clocks and machines. But, as the saying goes, he was a jack-of-all-trades and master of none. He did not succeed at a single job, and his skills, frankly, did not yield any fruit throughout his entire life. Once he made a cardboard model of a building which Jews had built outside Jaffa Gate to sell goods made at the Alliance Girls School, and put it on display in the hall. Just as he had finished it, my father happened to be coming back home from Government House. He looked at the model thoughtfully and asked, "Who made this?" "I did, Father," answered Tawfiq. So my father said, "What am I to do with you, son? The only mistake I made in my life was to have named you 'Tawfiq'" (success). "What should you have named me instead?" asked Tawfiq. My father answered, "Talfiq" (contrivance). He carried on, saying, "Tawfiq, tell me, what benefit does this model bring you? I agree that it is beautiful, but it has no use. I sent you to school, but you did not do well. Then you managed to join an evening school in Jaffa but ran away back to Jerusalem. Then you tried to work in carpentry at your brother-in-law's workshop and left him, then you tried to become a mechanic and also gave it up. Then you went to train as a painter with that famous Armenian master, Aram, but he sacked you because of your disobedience!" Tawfiq was embarrassed by these words but carried on, nonetheless, as before.

OUR STRONG FRIENDSHIPS WITH THE NEIGHBORS

Dar al-Jawhariyyeh was entered via a long paved corridor, which was dark even during the day, as the main entrance was its only opening. After climbing a flight of twenty-five steps to the first floor, to your right was a large room where Andoni al-Muna lived with his mother and his siblings. They used this room both as a living room and bedroom, but also had a large dark room on the ground floor which they used as a kitchen and dining room, and which contained a communal well for use by all the occupants. Next to Andoni's room was another large room used as a reception room and bedroom by Salim Fasha's large family. They had a large dark room on the ground floor to use as a kitchen and dining room. Next to Salim Fasha's room on the first floor was a large room that was used by the "senior" Mitri al-Muna and his family, both as a living room and bedroom. They, too, had a room on the ground floor, used as a kitchen and dining room, which also contained a communal well. Next door, a small room was built for

Mitri's unmarried sister, Nour, when Mitri married. The family of Abu Shehada Muluk lived in the same arrangement and had access to a communal well on the ground floor. There were also the families of Costandi Fasha and Yaacoub Fasha, and finally a small room occupied by their elderly mother, Umm Salim.

All these rooms opened to an outdoor space used to hang the laundry to dry. There was also a well in the house's laundry room. The main entrance had a large well for drinking water. The facilities for these families were of the rough, older style. They consisted of two pit toilets near the entrance to this corridor, which made the corridor smell foul more often than not, given that these two WCs were intended for use by all the families living on the ground and first floors. Imagine what life for them must have been like. For the second floor, my father had installed modern facilities.

When Salim Fasha moved out, Costandi Ata Kuttab moved in, since he was married to Jamila, the sister of Andoni al-Muna. Costandi was a first-class alcoholic who liked to carouse at night, disturbing his neighbors. He was the subject of many incidents and was not always in a conscious state. He even tried to kill his wife with a knife, prompting us to interfere to protect his family.

Dar al-Jawhariyyeh was more like a monastery than a house,[14] for it had spacious outdoor courtyards on both floors. If you entered the house on a Sunday, you would find families and relatives of both sexes with their children, some playing cards or backgammon, others singing or playing music with their friends, some smoking argileh, or telling stories and anecdotes, while the young ladies played in the middle of the ground floor on a swing they tied to the iron bars of the courtyard of the upper floor. On walking into our house for the first time, a stranger with no knowledge of our lifestyle would have thought that he had walked into a club or some institute or a fair. My brothers and I were always the first to take part in our neighbors' celebrations, for it was a time of true friendship and loyalty, and we were all like one family.

Life with neighbors was fun-filled and relaxed. We treated each other like brothers. For instance, whenever one of us had been baking *lahem bi ajeen* or *mraddad*[15] or spinach pasties or sweets, one sent some to the neighbors to taste. At engagements and weddings, all would gather like one family to cook, eat, and get drunk together. Salim Fasha was famous for a game called "the tray." Festive occasions were celebrated. The first was Saint Jacob's Day (Yaacoub Fasha being the saint's namesake), celebrated on the twenty-third of October. All the families would gather to sweep the entire corridor, the steps leading to the courtyards, and the ground floor, as well as those leading to my father's place on the second floor. The house was cleaned again on the third of November for Saint George's Day, since my father Jiryis Jawhariyyeh was the namesake of Saint George. The same was done on the eighth of November for Mikhail Fasha, and then again on Saint Dimitri's Day for Mitri Abdullah al-Muna. The latter was blessed with a large extended family, so on his saint's day the house was gripped with celebratory fever, as we were joined by the families of Ansara, Allouchia, Jawzi, Theodosi, Mansour, Fattalah, Khanouf, Shebr, Zakharia, Qort, and Harami. Since Mitri was an only son, they would make him *simat,*[16] *labaniyeh,*[17] or lentil-filled pastry, and all the families would eat lunch together. It was a beautiful sight. My brothers and I and some of the other children would then take plates of simat to the prison in Habs el-Dam and offer them to the inmates, as was the custom at the time. Then the men sang until midnight. The relatives and friends of our neighbor Mitri al-Muna, who were amateur musicians, had formed a band. It included Mitri Costandi al-Muna and his friend Costandi al-Sous, who had beautiful, high-pitched, and voluptuous voices, Mitri al-Zaer who played the flute, and Issa al-Sous who played the *darbuka* and the *naqqara*.[18] It was indeed a good band, and it was from them that I learned the basics of singing. The ladies ululated and the celebration was worthy of a wedding. This house witnessed all kinds of fun and play, but always within the boundaries of Arab traditions, abiding by the values of honor and decency, despite the intermingling of men, women, and children which my brothers, sisters, and I were also a part of.

Our Muslim neighbors, both men and women, used to join us at times of joy or sorrow alike. Even on carnival nights, the first nights of Lent, we would all dress up—men and women—and hide our faces. Then we would make an entrance and dance. We would also dance the dabkeh, and each one of us would act out the role of the character we were dressed to impersonate. For instance, the bride would be my brother Khalil, and the bridegroom would be a girl from the al-Daoudi family or from the al-Samman or al-Salihani families. Honor and fraternity were our motto, for which I thank the Lord. As for the neighbors of Dar al-Jawhariyyeh, they were the families of Abdul-Qawwas al-Daoudi, Mustafa al-Salihani, al-Samman, Mustafa al-Jabsha, and al-Ansari. A little further away lived the families of Abd-Rabbu, Omar Darwish, Al-Sheikh Muhammad Salih, Atef Darwish, and others.

THE BATHS IN JERUSALEM

Apart from those belonging to illustrious families, Jerusalem's homes had no bathroom facilities or bathtubs. Instead, they had small rooms with a small receptacle and a drain in the ground. People thus had their baths at the city's public bathhouses. These included the al-'Ain bath in Mahallat al-Wad,[19] which remains famous to this day and at which masseur Nuuman Ghannam used to work. He was tall, dark, and of a strong build, and he was sought after in cases of bone fracture problems, giving doctors fierce competition. There are many anecdotes about him in this regard.

There was also the Hammam al-Batrak—Patriarch's Bathhouse—which was located in the Christian Quarter and was owned by Jerusalem's Islamic mortmain. Water was channeled to the bathhouse from the nearby reservoir known as the "pool of Hammam al-Batrak." The pool is surrounded by many buildings, such as Abu Abdallah's café, Khan al-Aqbat, and others, all the way to Amdursky Hotel near Suwaiqat Allun.[20] I have learned that the Ma'man Allah pond, located near the Ma'man Allah—also known as Mamilla—Cemetery outside Jaffa Gate, was connected to the al-Batrak pond through an old channel that pumped water into it when the first pond filled with rain. As for the masseur of the al-Batrak bathhouse, he was Hajj Salim al-Bitar, a Muslim Jerusalemite. The bathhouse was demolished and a store was built in its place. Salim al-Bitar was the father of our friends Omran, Mahmoud, and Arafat.

The Greek Orthodox Patriarchate had a modern bathhouse that was built right next to the monastery and the Church of Saint Joachim and Saint Anne, near Saint Stephen's Gate inside the wall. The bathhouse, named the Baths of Our Lady Mary, was the best of all the Jerusalem bathhouses in terms of organization, cleanliness, and space. It is traditional in Jerusalem for the bathhouse to be reserved for the use of men in the evening and through the night, then again in the morning and until noon. Men often spent the night in the bathhouse and slept there. In the afternoon of each day, the bath was open to women only. When the ladies went to the bath to wash themselves, they took along all sorts of food, sweets, fruit, vegetables, and nuts, as though they were going to a park or on a picnic.

At the Bathhouse with My Mother

Once when I was little, I went with my mother to Hammam al-'Ain, or Hammam al-Wad, as they used to call it. When I entered the bathhouse, the matron of the bath gave me a kiss after my mother paid two matliks for my admission.[21] But there was a revolution among the ladies who were nearly naked and thought I was too old to be allowed to bathe among them. Some protested, "Come on, he's not young!" while others mocked, "God bless, he is quite old." As for me, I stood there embarrassed but unable to run away because my mother was holding me tightly by the hand. In the end, I passed the exam and was allowed to stay. When it was my turn to wash, I wished I had not passed. Water in Jerusalem's wells was scarce, so at the bath women poured water over us with merciless generosity. My mother began to scrub my body meticulously. I will never forget how much hot water she poured over my head. I kept my eyes closed and struggled to breathe, until I was about to faint, wishing I had remained filthy, cursing the bath and its abundant water that let my mother save on her rationed use of well water at home. The ladies attended to themselves, using the towels, soap, and the like, which they had brought from home, not to mention the food, drinks, and nuts.

THE SCHNELLER SCHOOL[22]

My brother Tawfiq and I received our primary education at the German Schneller School, known as the Dabbagha School, which was located near the German church, inside the city wall. The school was mainly attended by Arab Greek Orthodox pupils and had two schoolmasters and two schoolmistresses: Jiryis Mansur Tishto, an old man from Birzeit; Beshara Costandi from the village of Taiba; Miss Tharwat who taught the older pupils (the students had noticed the romance between Mr. Beshara and Miss Tharwat, and it was later revealed that they got married and left Jerusalem for Jaffa); and finally Miss Julia Abu Raqaba, a Greek Orthodox who taught the younger schoolchildren and was in charge of cleanliness and hygiene in the school. We learned Arabic and some German, but the most important lesson was to learn and memorize the verses of the Holy Bible. We started with "The Lord our God, the Lord is One" and went on to learn hundreds more verses. We also had to learn the well-known hymns of the Protestant Church. The teacher would play a small organ, or sometimes the violin, while we sang, "A voice was heard from Heaven, what could the news be," "We spread, in the morning, the good words," and "O happy day." I was the best student and the teacher's favorite pupil in this domain. At the time, only teachers wore trousers, while we still wore the *qombaz*[23] and those Syrian-made red shoes that we used to buy at the spice market for seven piasters. I remained in this school until 1909 (age twelve).

MY DESIRE TO SING AS A CHILD

Singing had been my hobby ever since I was a youth. I used to sing whatever music I heard at home or from the neighbors. This I owe to my father, God bless his soul, for he was an art lover. Whenever a musician was visiting Jerusalem from any Arab country, my father would make his acquaintance and spend some nights in his company. My father also was the first Jerusalemite ever to own an oud at his home, and the famous oud player known as the Egyptian al-Koftanji stayed at his home as a guest for a time. I used to sing songs like "Rozana" and "al hani" while on the rooftop, and often in the bathroom or with the neighbors' children: "al hani al hani al hani" ("I beg you to have pity on me").

Our neighbors and acquaintances liked my performance of this song. They acknowledged that I had a soft, sensuous voice, and they listened to me passionately whenever I sang at an evening gathering. I remember a celebration of Saint George's, my father's saint's day, on the third of November. I was about six years old at the time, and the Sons of Abu al-Sibaa band, which was famous then in Jerusalem, came to our place bringing along the popular oud player Abu Khalil. He used to live opposite Dar al-Jawhariyyeh, and my siblings and I would listen to him play through the window. Abu Khalil's playing was accompanied on the *qanun*[24] by Abdullah Abu al-Sibaa. The percussionist was Omar al-Sibaa (who wore over his qombaz a redingote which he had probably been given as a present by a Jerusalem notable). That night I longed to play an instrument, and as it happened, my father had made a cover for the cupboard where we kept the charcoal and shaped it like a qanun so it would fit in the staircase that led to the storage room. I fetched the cover immediately and placed it on my knees, drawing the attention of the band members. After they had a few words with Father, he asked me to sing, so I sang "Rozana" while the band musicians accompanied me on their instruments. They complimented me on my voice and handed me the qanun. I plucked its strings a little, unable to contain my joy. I was now longing to sing even more and wondered when I was going to be able to play an instrument like those people.

My father acquired a His Master's Voice phonograph at the time when the phonograph was still a new invention. A tall wooden neck held up the trumpet, which had complicated hinges, and the discs were only playable on one side. Monk Hanania gave the phonograph as a present to my brother Khalil. We used to play the disc recordings of Sheikh Salama Hijazi (*Romeo and Juliet*).[25] I learned the songs on this recording by heart and became able to sing them to perfection.

Whenever I sang the wrong note, my father would twist my ear and play the song again and again until I had totally mastered the phrase. His love of music and singing were such that he forbade me to learn cheap songs. He tried to bring songs of poems such as the one by Sheikh al-Manyalawi, *Dayya'ta 'ahda fatan li 'ahdika hafizun* (You forsook a young man who would never forsake you), and similar recordings by fine, established musicians. He also kept an eye on the language and content of what I sang.

I recall once singing *Jaddidi ya nafsu hazzaki* (Renew yourself, my soul), which I had once heard Costandi al-Muna sing. The song contained the following verse which I sang exactly as I had heard it: "He who blames me for being lovesick knows not what love is. Oh God, what makes me lovesick is this gazelle." My father had been in the reception room with Sheikh Salim Mamluk, writing government documents. When he heard me sing those verses, he stopped and came out to the parlor shouting, "I do not want you to sing such vulgar things and will never allow you to. You are an educated schoolboy, not a handyman." When I asked what had angered him, he responded, "What is that you were singing about gazelles and rabbits? You are supposed to end the verse with the word 'blaming' (not gazelle) to make the two verses rhyme." I never forgot that advice and did my best, from then on, to avoid incorrect language, even when singing *taqtouqas*.[26]

MY FIRST MUSICAL INSTRUMENT

I had learned a considerable number of songs, but I always longed to be able to play some musical instrument in order to accompany myself while singing. As it happened, my father had bought a can of Easter egg dye powder. Once the powder had been used, I took the rectangular can and inserted a wooden stick through its square opening and out another which I had made on the opposite side of the can. I then hammered three nails into each end of the stick and tied to them some strings which were, of course, untuned, and which I plucked with a pigeon feather, imitating oud players. I played alone, or with the neighbors' children. Since I could not play the music I was singing on my instrument, I would sing first, without playing, and after I had finished singing, I would strike the untuned strings in a self-congratulatory manner. I was between six and eight years old at the time, if I remember well.

I loved music so much that I used to deprive myself of candy, sugared almonds, and chocolate, and save the piasters Father gave me as pocket money to buy a string from a Jewish shopkeeper in Bab al-Bazar, near the Dabbagha School. Whenever the teacher was away, I would tie the string to a student desk and pluck it, producing a beautiful sound that greatly entertained my classmates. Back at home, I would tie it to a nail which I would hammer into the corner of the dinner table in the parlor, making my mother angry. And so, music and singing occupied most of my time.

MY FATHER'S FRIENDSHIP WITH THE VENERABLE HUSSEINI FAMILY

My father was a dear friend of the late Hajj Salim Effendi al-Husseini (the father of Musa Kazem Pasha[27] and Hussein Hashem al-Husseini). Hajj Salim al-Husseini rose to a high status in the country, and the Ottoman government had to bear him in mind, given his patriotic stances and the love that people—particularly the farmers—had for him. He was, God bless his soul, a member of the Administrative Council of Jerusalem and head of Jerusalem's municipality for twenty-two years and truly served the city. It was he who had the public sewage system built within the wall. He is also responsible for paving the streets of Old Jerusalem, which he both conceived and saw through, thus transforming the city into a model for cleanliness, beauty, and marvel, particularly for foreigners who used to come to visit its holy sites. He was well known for his diplomacy, generosity, honesty, justice, and humility, which earned him the love of the people. He set a "divan," a special reception at his home in Sheikh Jarrah, where farmers who had been subjected to injustice went to see him to seek help, preferring to resort to his judgment rather than to the courts of the state. Since my father was a lawyer with a profound knowledge of the law, Hajj Salim came to rely on him in his divan work and during his trips to the villages and lands of the Jerusalem district, which included Beit Susin, Beit Jeez, and Deir el-Hawaa, among other places.[28] In return, the Hajj lent Father his support and appointed him a member of the Administrative Council of Jerusalem representing the Greek Orthodox community. He also managed to have the Sublime Porte in Istanbul award him an "honorary costume" in appreciation of his knowledge and trustworthiness, by seeking the mediation of Shukri Bey al-Husseini with the Grand Vizier. I still keep this official costume, and its sword, as well as a photograph of my father wearing it.[29]

My father was also a member of the municipal council and kept Hajj Salim company throughout his time as president of the council. When Greek Orthodox Patriarch Kyrios Damianos the First was consecrated, he appointed my father as a member of the ecclesiastical court at the patriarchate, for which he received a monthly salary.[30] This appointment shows the extent of the trust which Hajj Salim and Patriarch Damianos had in my father, and which saw him become the mediator between the patriarchate and the Jerusalem government at the time. On festive occasions, he would join the archbishop and the patriarch's head translator, and together they would visit the notables of Jerusalem on behalf of the patriarch, and hand each high official their allocated share of gold, packed in a small bag of pure white silk, as a gift from the patriarch. These allocations were given in view of the patriarch's status and power in the country, and in this way, the Greek Orthodox Patriarchate in Jerusalem had the sympathy of the entire government. In all honesty, the patriarchate itself was a government within a government and enjoyed total freedom of action, which only made it more powerful. It thus increased its purchases of property from city residents and farmers alike, and began to build properties and markets in Jerusalem and Jaffa, earning the Greek Orthodox Monastery large revenues that continue to this day.

I keep a gold-incrusted faience set of coffee cups and matching plates that my father used at our home to serve coffee to visitors, particularly to the late Patriarch Damianos. When he visited my father, the patriarch used to go to the rooftop of Dar al-Jawhariyyeh to enjoy the beautiful and exquisite view of Jerusalem.

One of the good deeds of the late Hajj Salim al-Husseini's towards my father, and a proof of how he trusted Father and his good taste in all matters was that he put him in charge of al-Manshiyyeh when the municipal park and the building in its center were built. He dedicated an upper room to His Excellency the *mutasarrif* (governor) of Jerusalem, and a special room next to it for the use of my father who supervised the entire park. There was a large store where decorations were kept, including flags, lamps, and the like. The park and its trees, plants, ponds, and fountains were all designed by my father and extended, in the beginning, as far as the road leading to the Sisters of Compassion. A base was placed over a well and covered with an engraved wood and tin rooftop, and wooden chairs were fixed around it for the members of the state's military music band. The band played on Friday, Saturday, and Sunday afternoon of each week to entertain the people, the army, and the government, while His Excellency and my father watched these celebrations from the courtyard of the governor's room on the upper floor. My father turned the lower floor into an Arab café that served coffee and argilehs to the customers who sat under the trees. Abu Hassan was in charge of the café. Adjacent to the café was a bar that was run by a Greek called Aristidi who was the father of Miss Nina, the current mistress of Archbishop Epiphanius. My father did not have to pay any dues in return for running the café, thanks to his good taste and management, and to the power of Hajj Salim al-Husseini, God bless his soul.

Salim Effendi al-Husseini was almost like a family member. Once, Easter was upon us and my father's finances had deteriorated, so much that he was unable to meet the basic needs of home. When Holy Week began, my mother, who was unaware of my father's financial situation and how precarious it had become, was asking for food and clothing for the children to be on a par with children of our acquaintances and neighbors during Easter celebrations. Our family comprised eleven members, including my father, my mother, my aunt, the seven children, and my mother's helper at the time, Sultana al-Lengy. My father used to visit Hajj Salim Effendi at his home in the morning, when the divan was held, but had started missing these visits. When he finally managed to visit the Hajj during Holy Week on Wednesday afternoon, the Hajj noticed that my father was going through some financial trouble. He received him extremely well and insisted that he stay the night at his home because he was bored. So my father stayed and they spent the evening chatting and playing backgammon. In the morning, the Hajj told him, "Abu Khalil, let us stay here away from people. By God, do not refuse to stay with me for another night, and tomorrow, Friday, you will travel with me by carriage to Damascus Gate. Then you can return home, and I will go to pray in Temple Mount." So it was, but my father could not brush off his worries. How could he, when Easter was approaching and he still had not bought anything my mother had asked him to buy for the celebration?

He spent Maundy Holy Thursday and the morning of Good Friday with the Hajj, and then accompanied him to Damascus Gate. When they parted ways, my father went to the Christian Quarter, instead of going home, and remained with his friends until nine o'clock. As he entered the house, my mother met him with a smiling face. "This is too much, Abu Khalil! What did you buy all this for?" she said, pointing to the provisions placed in one of the hall's corners: a large hamper of rice, a canister of ghee, a canister of oil, a small hamper of green coffee, a bag of flour, a canister of castor oil, fifteen kilos of soap, fifteen kilos of sugar, nine kilos of semolina for making *maamoul*, as well as dates and walnuts for the fillings. My father smiled, having understood that the sender was the magnanimous Hajj Salim Effendi. When he entered his bedroom, he found that a new black broadcloth suit lay on his bed, with three gold Ottoman liras in the pocket of the waistcoat.

This is but a small picture of the strong ties between my father and the venerable Husseini family of Jerusalem and of how friendship used to be, *effendim*![31]

A Brief Note on the Ways of Hajj Salim al-Husseini

My father told me that he often accompanied the late Hajj Salim al-Husseini around the villages of the Jerusalem district and that he was always amazed by the Hajj's extreme humility. When he sat to eat a *mansaf* in any village, he made sure that all that the villagers—the men, the poor, and the children—also sat down and ate their fill. He often grabbed the meat himself and handed it to the poor, until everyone was fed.

Once as he was eating he saw a snake, so he squashed it with his foot and placed his knee on the mat so that no one was aware he was sitting on a dead snake. After he had made sure that all the villagers, from the oldest to the youngest, had eaten, the snake was removed. He had not wanted any of the guests to be disturbed by it while eating.

These good deeds earned him the unreserved love and respect of the farmers who, even after his death, would only swear to the life of the country's master, Hajj Salim Effendi, may God bless his soul and bless him with paradise.

The Ties of Friendship Remain Between My Father and the Late Hajj Salim al-Husseini's Children

The ties of friendship and mutual trust between my father and Hajj Salim also extended to his sons, Musa Kazem Pasha, Hussein Hashem, and Hajj Sherif. In private matters, whether with regard to their affairs in the city or their properties in the villages, they acted only on Father's advice, Hussein Hashem in particular. My siblings and I often spent summers at the village of Deir Amr which Hussein Effendi had come to own with my father's help.[32] We enjoyed such freedom of action in all matters related to Deir Amr that we believed that it belonged to my father.

To give you an idea about the true bonds of fraternity between my father and Hussein Effendi, my father had been a lawyer in his younger years and stood out as a Christian lawyer at Jerusalem's Muslim sharia law courts. As such, he had witnessed many amusing incidents at a time when Jerusalem had no civil courts yet. Sheikh Asa'ad al-Shuqayri, of Akka, was a colleague of his, but was keen to be in constant competition with him. As it happened, Sheikh Asa'ad al-Shuqayri visited Istanbul and obtained a post as a judge at the sharia court in Jerusalem. So he sent my father a telegraph saying, "Jiryis Effendi al-Jawhariyyeh—Jerusalem, I have been appointed Judge for Jerusalem. Thanks be to God."

Father had to leave Jerusalem at a time when he was affluent, so he went to the village of Deir Amr which was in ruins. He built two rooms on the higher part of the mountain and planted trees around them. He also cleaned wells in the rocks, which might have been Roman, so they were functional again. Then he discovered a muddy puddle in the bottom of the valley, on the southern side of the house. So he went there with some Greek Orthodox construction workers, Yaacoub, Salim, and Costandi (Constantine) Fasheh, and together they succeeded in discovering a sufficient amount of water dripping from the ceiling of a grotto. He built an open canal inside the grotto to collect the water, which was a beautiful sight. The water was then channeled through a pipe outside the grotto and into a red stone pool that measured five meters square. When necessary, the bottom of the pool could be accessed via a flight of stone steps. We used to sit happily around this pool, amid the high mountains. The water of this pool was also channeled through four sluices down a slope to water the gardens and orchards on the eastern side. My father built a special room for the guardian of these orchards, Khalil al-Yasini of Deir Yasin, who worked there with his brothers. This water was known as "the new fountain" and could be reached in two ways: the first was nearer the house but was rough and bumpy; the other was easy and long, and went past Kherbet al-Sufayr which was on the eastern side of Deir Amr. He then planted a vineyard on the top of the mountain to the west of the house, with various types of grapes, and built a terrace in the backyard where he used to sit on early summer mornings with Hussein Effendi and smoke the argileh. As for the divan (court) where Hussein Effendi looked into judicial matters when he came from Jerusalem, it was set near the shrine of a saint called al-Saii Amr, near an old huge carob tree. My father was his judicial assistant in all matters relating to the problems of the farmers who preferred to come to him with their problems, for they had the utmost confidence in Hussein Hashem Effendi al-Husseini.

My father did all this with his own money and without obtaining the permission of the owner, Hussein Effendi, who was away in Paris at the time. Upon his return from France, my father surprised him and wanted to take him to Deir Amr without telling him about the improvements he had made. Hussein Effendi hesitated at first saying, "Abu Khalil, we've got no business to do in Deir Amr now! Why would we go to a remote ruined place, especially since we would have to take along our own drinking water from Suba?"[33] My father answered, "Don't worry, I've sent some water over there. So by God, don't turn down my request." Finally, they headed for Deir Amr, and when they reached Suba, Hussein Effendi could see in the distance the house on the top of the mountain. When they arrived in Deir Amr, Hussein Effendi was surprised to see what my father had done and was amazed by his courage and serious work, and thanked him. Thus, my father remained in Deir Amr until, with the help of the powerful Hajj Salim al-Husseini and his honorable children, he managed to have Sheikh Assa'ad al-Shuqayri removed from his post as a judge in Jerusalem's sharia courts, and he returned to Jerusalem with his head held high among his acquaintances at the court.

As for the lands of Deir Amr, they consisted of a group of villages which surrounded it, namely Kherbet al-Amour, Beit Naquba, Suba, Kherbet el-Loz, Mataf, Kherbet al-Mays, and perhaps Kasla. The majority of the inhabitants of these villages worked in the fields of Deir Amr and continued to do so after these fields were acquired by Hussein Effendi. In return, they paid him the tithe tax[34] which my father collected on his behalf. We spent the evenings sitting in the moonlight near the house looking out over the fields of this village, and beyond them the fields of Kherbet al-Sufayr, which turned out to be Roman.

As for the area of the village, it was four thousand square kilometers. The village was situated on a very high spot. Mr. Stubbs, the director of the Department of Land Registration of Palestine under the British

Old house belonging to Husseini Salim al-Husseini in the village of Deir Amr. Jawhariyyeh Collection. © Institute for Palestine Studies, Beirut.

Mandate, once said, "If I had to choose a place to buy in Palestine, I would choose Deir Amr at any price." This is a valuable testimony to its strategic location, beauty, and charm.

When leaving Deir Amr, we would ride donkeys, all of us, male and female. Sometimes, we would ride a camel. I remember once riding a camel with my sister Afifeh—who was very skilled at riding camels by herself—and passing Bab al-Bouweib. The mountain of Kherbet al-Akrad was part of the lands of Deir Amr and had been planted with oak trees, which made it impossible to enter it, even in the middle of the day, as one feared being attacked by wild animals. If you made your way via the top of this mountain, on the southern side, you could enjoy the beautiful sight of the Jaffa-Jerusalem train in the Wadi Ismail Valley. You could also see a cave on a high spot that had a narrow opening overlooking the rail tracks. It was a historical cave called "the cave of Samson the great." On leaving Bab al-Bouweib, one entered Kherbet al-Mais, which belonged to a member of the magnanimous al-Hamdan family that was a neighbor to Deir Amr. Then one went down a valley called Wadi Ayn al-Arab, which was indeed isolated and frightening, and had a feel of awe to it. There was a water fountain in the middle of the valley, so we had some drink and also gave some to the donkeys, camels, and horses. Then we all rested—my mother, father, brothers, and sisters. We were quite young, particularly the boys. Then we climbed a road which not even a bird could have managed to take, until we reached the top of the mountain, going past the villages of Kasla,[35] Mirah al-Basal, and Kasleen beyond it. Then we passed the village of Saraa and finally entered Beit Susin, which belonged to the late Hajj Salim. The villagers of Beit Mihsir and Sarees paid the tithe to the Husseini family via an employee called Ghantous, of Jaffa, who had been appointed by Hajj Salim.[36]

My father's strong ties with the Husseini family afforded me and my siblings the opportunity to go to these villages and enjoy spending the whole summer there every year. We used the buildings and ate from the trees, vineyards, orchards, and orange groves, and even the wheat flour produced in these places, so much so that we were under the impression that we were the owners and masters of these villages, for all the servants and farmers showed us respect. When I was no more than ten years old, the mayor of the village of Sarees, who was an elderly man with a long beard, used to kiss my hand and call me "Master Effendi."

I remember these beautiful times, particularly the moonlit nights we spent on the threshing areas of Beit Susin, where the crops of wheat, barley, corn, and the like would be piled up like mountains. On hot days, we would lay mattresses over the straw and hay, and sleep on them.

ACQUIRING MY FIRST DECENT MUSICAL INSTRUMENT—THE *TANBOOR*

Since I was extremely fond of music and singing, I invented an instrument out of a can of dye powder and took it along to the village of Beit Susin where I used to pluck its untuned strings, having no technical knowledge of how to play.

Hajj Salim el-Husseini had appointed a Moroccan man named Hajj Mohammad Mu'een as keeper of the grain produce of the village, and of Hajj Salim's share in particular, so that the farmers had no chance to cheat. Hajj Mohammad always slept by the wall of the house known as the residence of Hajj Salim Effendi, where we were staying.

When Hajj Mohammad saw my "tin instrument," he said to me enthusiastically, "This one is no good, Wasif." I was about nine years old at the time. "Go to the orange grove and ask Abu Salem to give you a dry pumpkin, and I will make you a beautiful tanboor like those we make in Morocco." I was overjoyed, so I thanked him and rushed to the orange grove where I fetched a dry rectangular pumpkin. Using the knife he carried by his waist, Hajj Mohammad halved the pumpkin, cleaned one of the halves, and wiped it thoroughly. He then carved a piece of hard wood and split off a stick that was curved on its higher end to look artistic as it held the peg heads, and flat on the lower end which was attached to the pumpkin. Next, he inserted the peg heads. I was asked to fetch a piece of goatskin or sheepskin. A sheep had been slaughtered on that day. Hajj Mohammad cut out a piece of the skin, scraped the wool away, covered the hollow side of the pumpkin with it and started stitching it around the edges, completely covering that side of the pumpkin and turning it into a decent soundboard. He then made the bridge of the tanboor out of a solid piece of wood and, when the skin was dry, tied one end of a pair of strings to the peg heads he had carved with his knife, stretched the other end over the bridge, and tied it onto a piece of wood. The process must have lasted over a week, while I watched impatiently, waiting for this extraordinary instrument to be ready. The first time Hajj Mohammad played it I was overwhelmed with joy. He was a capable musician who played exceptionally well, although the Moroccan airs of his musical pieces were foreign to me.

He handed me the instrument and started explaining to me how to place my fingers on the strings. If I placed my second finger on a string, the tone would go up by one degree. He also taught me how to pluck the strings and made me grow the nail of my index and play with my nails, rather than with a feather or anything else.

I treasured this instrument proudly. Hajj Mohammad had taught me to play it, and more importantly, he had taught me how to tune the first and second strings. I started playing the Jerusalemite music that I already knew, "Rozana," "Akh Mash'aal," and other songs, and was soon able to play these taqtouqas with a remarkable skill that impressed Hajj Mohammad al-Mughrabi. In return for his favor, I used to bring him whatever food, fruit, and sweets I was able to obtain, and I remained generous to him, thanks to my late father who always encouraged me to.

As the summer went by, I returned with my tanboor to Jerusalem, where I showed it to the neighbors' children, having abandoned my first tin musical instrument in Beit Susin. I would walk around the parlor, corridor, and open air spaces of Dar al-Jawhariyyeh playing and singing, while they followed me singing the chorus. In the evening, I would give a repeat performance for the neighbors and guests who visited us. My mother and sisters often took me along on their Ramadan evening visits to Muslim neighbors of ours like the al-Daoudi, al-Salihani, Quttaineh, and other families. I thanked God that my dream had come true. At last I owned an instrument that was an excellent one for a young boy, and I had also acquired a good understanding of music. When, the following summer, we went back to Beit Susin, I presented Hajj Mohammad with a tobacco case that I had bought for him from some Indians in order to show my appreciation.

LEARNING *UHZUJAS,* DABKEH, AND PEASANT FOLK SONGS

Being ambitious, I was never satisfied with the amount of musical knowledge I had acquired, or happy to stop at the point I had reached. As it happened, my family and I had the opportunity to enjoy the beauty of nature among the villagers in both coastal and mountain areas. I often had the chance to listen to their *uhzujas* (folk songs), attend their celebrations, and hear the shepherds sing behind their sheep flocks and cattle herds while they played the *nay*, *arghool*, and *mijwiz*,[37] and danced the *dabkeh*.[38] I began to learn those popular airs of theirs that had piqued my interest and entranced me. From al-Abd, Hussein Effendi's shepherd in Deir Amr, and his friend who was known as the son of Yamina al-Sarisiya, as well as from a famous person called Deeb bin Ahmed Muslih who was from the village of Kasla or Sarees, I learned the taqtouqa.

In addition to those people, in Deir Amr I met a man who was famous for his dancing of the dabkeh. His name was Salih Sha'arawi, and he was tall and plump, with sharp eyes and a handsome face. He was a good horse rider and famous for being skilled at dabkeh, which I had seen him perform at celebrations. From when I was a kid until I became a young man, I used to dance it in Jerusalem for family and friends. This attracted the attention of anyone who happened to hear it or see it. I remember that when the band of Abu al-Sibaa once came to our home for one of my father's celebrations, my father allowed me to dance and sing the taqtouqa, while the band played its tune on the violin, the oud, the qanun, and the *riqq*.[39] The guests were pleased, particularly the band members themselves who complimented me generously. After learning this song, I learned to sing other songs and to dance their dabkeh, too.

PERSIFON, THE MISTRESS OF HUSSEIN HASHEM AL-HUSSEINI

For a long time, the custom in the country, particularly in Jerusalem, was for the notables of Jerusalem's well-known families, al-Husseini, al-Khalidi, an-Nashashibi, and others, to have a mistress, provide a home for her, and spend their leisure time with her. Ragheb Bey al-Nashashibi had a Jewish mistress, and Hussein Effendi had a Greek mistress from Albania who was of great beauty and tenderness. Her name was Persifon, and she was well-known in Jerusalemite society, particularly for her ravishing figure, stunning beauty, and elegant style. When she went to visit the Church of the Holy Sepulchre, people would say that the patriarch visited. Hussein Effendi had brought her over from Istanbul, and she remained with him for over seventeen years. She learned Arabic and he granted her total freedom to go out and spend summers in Beit Susin, and particularly in Deir Amr.

In these two villages she worked at distilling wild thyme using a machine and special scales, and sold thyme oil at high prices to Russians who came to Jerusalem in large numbers each year to visit the holy sites. She also worked in grain agriculture in partnership with Hussein Effendi, Khalil Bey al-Daoudi, Fouad Bey (the son of Musa Kazem Pasha), and others. She also had a flock of black-and-white sheep, cattle, hens, pigeons, and the like, and thus lived like a queen, thanks to the power which Hussein Effendi had over the villagers of Beit Susin and Deir Amr who obeyed Persifon's orders and carried them out to the letter. Indeed, Hussein Effendi delayed his search for a legal wife because of Persifon's presence in his life. But in the end, my father lost his patience and put his mind to persuading him to wed, insisting that he marry the honorable Fatima, daughter of Muhammad Taher al-Khalidi. Hussein Effendi got married when he was mayor of Jerusalem. On the invitation of the German state, he spent his honeymoon in the German building known as the Augusta Victoria, which was situated on Um al-Talaa' on the Mount of Olives. Fatima gave him four children.

I had the privilege of accompanying Persifon in Jerusalem, Beit Sueen, and Deir Amr, for she was very fond of me and was a friend of my father and my family. She was the godmother of my brother Fakhri,[40] and thanks to her help I was able to learn more songs and dabkeh from the people who obeyed her orders. I used to play songs for her on my tanboor while she toured Beit Susin and Deir Amr.

LEARNING TO PLAY THE REBECK

A peasant who was from Ain Karem, I believe, happened to be working in the fields of Deir Amr, and I noticed that he played the rebeck rather well. He was widely known at the time by his nickname, Abu Sanduqa. So, I went to Persifon and suggested to her that he should teach me to play the rebeck. Indeed, Persifon at once met with the man, who agreed to give me private lessons. She also bought me a rebeck made by Abu Sanduqa himself for eighteen Ottoman piasters. Abu Sanduqa taught me how to play the rebeck, and I worked hard until I had learned to play it well. Whenever Hussein Effendi came by and heard me play he was impressed. I remember that he used to bring Abu Sanduqa food or watermelon in person, so that he would take good care of me. Thus, within three months, I was able to play all the peasant folk songs which I knew, such as *Dakdookah, Isma'u ya nas* (Listen, folks, to what the wise man has said), *Abu jdailah, Akh mash'al, Mijanah*, and *Dal'unah*.

When, in 1906, I went back to Jerusalem, bringing with me my tanboor and rebeck, I began to play frequently at evening gatherings of our neighbors, in particular at the evening parties thrown by the famous Mitri Abdullah al-Muna's family. I would sing and play the tanboor, then the rebeck, then I would dance the dabkeh for acquaintances, friends, and family. I must have been eight or nine years old at the time. My father offered me a lot of encouragement. He bought me a fake beard which was skillfully made of black hair and which I could easily wear by slipping a string behind my ears. I would then play the rebeck, dressed in Arab costume. The incidents behind a lot of wonderful anecdotes involving this fake beard happened to me at homes, school theaters, and other places.

By luck, my father, God bless his soul, was able to buy me an Indian rebeck. He bought it from a Kurd who used to play it in the streets in return for change. The instrument was made with unmatched precision using a coconut, a piece of leather, and two beautiful hair strings. My father paid a mere six piasters for it.

When I needed some hair for the strings, my brother Tawfiq and I would stroll by the Jerusalem-Bethlehem horse carriages, known at the time as "the bus carriages," which used to wait at Jaffa Gate for those heading to Bethlehem. We would then tiptoe unnoticed past the driver, and once behind the horse's back, we would quickly grab its tail and pull it for whatever we could get.

HAJJ SALIM EFFENDI AL-HUSSEINI PASSES AWAY, BUT TIES OF LOVE AND FRIENDSHIP CONTINUE WITH HIS SON

I was in Deir Amr when Hajj Salim Effendi al-Husseini passed away and was buried in his last abode in 1322 Hijra (1903) in the cemetery of Beer al-Kalb in Sheikh Jarrah, near the American Colony.[41] I saw my father's sorrow, and the pain and agony of Hussein Effendi, following this devastating event. I remember that shortly after the period of condolences, my father met with Hussein and they exchanged warm words.

DAMASCUS GATE IN OTTOMAN TIMES

Damascus Gate, where my siblings and I wandered around on the way to our home in Saadiyeh, was indeed an example of love, fraternity, and friendliness. The butcher's, baker's, and grocer's where my father always shopped were there.

On entering Damascus Gate, you found a police station to your left, near the shrine of Sheikh Lulu which was attended to by the Wahbah family. Abu Amer Mahmoud al-Shaweesh was a simple man known to everybody in the quarter. The café belonged to Ali Zuhaiman Abu Zuhdi, and the mill to Muhammad al-Sibasi. It was located underground, beyond the soap works that later became the café of Khalil Najm who performed the first part of *Karakoz*[42] there. The café was later converted to a shop run by Ibrahim al-Khatib Assi. Before reaching the soap works was the small café of Aref Zaatara (Abu Tawfiq), and finally a tobacco and roasted nuts shop kept by the grocer who lived near Maghibo's café at the time. This small shop was later run by Faez al-Alami. On leaving the alley leading to Saadiyeh, one passed Mustafa Abd's (al-Jabsha) grocery shop, then the café of Ahmed al-Samman (Abu Jumaa) which later changed hands and was run by Abu Kamel Qlibo.

Also, on entering Damascus Gate, you found to your right the barley shop of the well-known al-Nabulsi (Abu al-Deeb al-Nabulsi) and the entrance to the mill of Muhammad (al-Sibasi). There also was Aref Faydi al-Alami, the barley merchant, Asaad Hijazi's hummus restaurant, al-Mughrabi, the butter and yogurt seller, and before it the mute chap who was from the family of Abu al-Sibaa. After the turn leading to Taqsh's bakery in the Christian Quarter, there were more shops on the right, starting with al-Qabbani's shop that sold yogurt, cheese, milk, and white wall rocket (salad green), then Abdul-Muuti's shop for roasted nuts and tobacco, then al-Ikrimawi's shop for the same. Then, there was Hassan al-Awi, who was from the al-Khuja family, Rushdi Qursh's kebab restaurant, the grand grocery of Muhammad al-Jabsha and Ragheb Qutayn (the father of Muhyiddine Qutayn), the grocery of Muhammad Maatouq, the shop of Rushdi Rasas, and next to it the shop of Moussa Kamal (Hankro) who sold yogurt and white wall rocket, the grocery of Abu Shehadeh Muluk, our neighbor, the shop of Abu Ghazala—who was both a barber and a doctor; then, after passing Al-Haru Alley, the residence of Saudi Ismail Aziz who sold various types of halawa, particularly white halawa. Then came Ali Bayda Alley, and next to it al-Sununu's olive press which was owned by Omar al-Dijani, the father of Hassan Sidqi al-Dijani. Then there was the barbershop of Abu Daoud, a Latin Christian who was living in Dar al-Mameluk (the residence of al-Mameluk) in Saadiyeh, Abdeen al-Arnaout, the construction worker, Hassan Khamis' bakery for ready-made bread, Hajj Mustafa Abdul-Latif's flour shop which was run by the late Futa Zakharia, the father of Saba and Yaacoub Zakharia, and finally al-Battikh Archway. Retracing your steps, you would pass on your right the late Hanna al-Halabi shop for washtubs and other East Jordan imports. He was the father of Andoni and Ishaq al-Halabi, and used to wear his Moroccan fez. The shop was used later by Mustafa Abd al-Jabsha for wholesale of foodstuffs in Jerusalem. There, you also found the alley leading to Mahallat al-Wad and Wabur Salah, which was known as al-Nota Archway. Then came the shop of Ali Khamis, the father of Saleh Khamis, who sold charcoal and flour, then Qutayna's soap works which was run by Rasheed Qutayna, then the shop of Suleiman Wafa, then that of Hassan Qlibo, and then Qutayna's olive press.

Then there was Hajj al-Mughrabi who was officially responsible for distributing permits to peasants from other regions, then Khayruddin Najm who sold groceries and coffee, Abu Umar Ghusha's grocery, Muhammad Rasas's grocery, Ashur's grocery, the grocery of Sheikh Abu Hassan al-Mushaashaa Abu Halaqa, the fruit and vegetable shop of Ali Qirsh Abu Mustafa and Abu Abdul-Muuti Qirsh (who was later followed by his lame son Mustafa), Muhammad Khalil Abdul-Latif who sold butter and yogurt, Hajj Khalil al-Hidmi, and then the grocery of Abd and later his brother Muhammad al-Maddah.

And finally, the mosque.

SINGER MUHAMMAD AL-ASHIQ

I remember the nights of singer and oud player Muhammad al-Ashiq with emotion and joy. He used to come to Jerusalem in the summer and make arrangements with the owners of the Hospice Café, which was located opposite the Austrian Hospice.[43] He would sit on a wooden platform at the corner of the main road crossing opposite the hospice and sing with his affectionate voice and play the oud. People sat around him and on every street pavement in that quarter, silent and mesmerized, drinking beverages and coffee, smoking argilehs, and cheering, particularly during the Ramadan nights when he sang exceptionally well, until the cannon was fired. His voice, especially at that time of the night when all went silent and there were no cars in Jerusalem, could be heard from our house, pure and natural, despite the considerable distance. The majority of people of that neighborhood would be at their windows or on their balconies or rooftops, listening to his beautiful singing.

I used to go with my brothers down the steps of the archway of the Sisters of Zion and sit near the café. We often took along a small padded mat to rest on, taking turns. I still remember a favorite which he used to sing, a taqtouqa on the maqam Bayyati: *Joz el-hamam, meen yishtirih*, (A pair of pigeons, who will buy them from me?). I was fascinated by the way he went back gradually to the keynote when repeating the word *joz* (pair). This taqtouqa became a hit with Jerusalmite music lovers, both men and women. I listened to this singer passionately and begged my brothers to stay longer until my brother Khalil lost his temper. I wished and prayed I would meet this singer one day, and indeed, my dream came true when I grew older. I met him, we sang together, and I played the oud for him.

WORKING AS A BARBER'S ASSISTANT

Matthia, a Jerusalemite Latin Christian, was a famous barber in Jerusalem, and sort of a "doctor" too. Those who wanted to have a suction cup treatment, or any other traditional treatment, would go to Matthia Abu Abdallah's barbershop that was located in the Latin Patriarchate's *khaniqah*, opposite the alley leading to the Christian Quarter where Jerusalem's Latin Christians lived.[44] His partner, Ziyadah, was also a Latin Christian. My brother Khalil, who was a friend of Abu Abdallah, arranged for me to work at his shop as a barber's assistant for two months during the summer of 1907 (age 10). I would hold the customer's neck, while Abu Abdallah washed his head from the back so that water did not drip on his back. The customer would rest his head on a copper basin that curved around the neck. Then water was poured out of a copper bucket with a tap near the base. I was extremely delighted about this occupation of mine. In the evening, two of the bravest young men of Damascus Gate, namely my brother Khalil and Muhammad al-Maddah who had taught him bravery, would take me to the bachelor's apartment[45] in Damascus Gate where I would play the tanboor and sing for them.

During the day, I used to leave the shop and go to listen to Mr. Hussein al-Nashashibi play the oud at Abu Manaweel's barbershop, which was located near his father Sheikh Khalil al-Nashashibi's olive press. His *taqasim*[46] were indeed breathtaking; he had learned them piece by piece from the finest oud master of that time, an Egyptian. As I listened, intoxicated, to his fascinating playing, I wondered when I would be able to play the oud myself.

After school I would take a detour to listen to Muhammad al-Sibasi and Abdul-Hamid Quttaineh whenever they happened to be playing the oud at the shop of oud maker Farah al-Qaraa. The shop was situated right by the eastern gate to the roof of the Holy Sepulcher, which leads to Khan el-Zeit. I felt overjoyed and wished I could hold this instrument and talk to the players. Then I would leave the shop and go home, all my thoughts filled with the oud.

JOINING THE MUSICAL PROFESSION

Saint Mitri's was the saint's day of our neighbor Mitri Abdullah al-Muna. It was a happy day, and many families from the confession gathered together. Around sunset, Mitri Costandi al-Muna, who had a beautiful voice, arrived with Mitri al-Zaair, the superb *nay* player. Such celebrations used to take place at Dar al-Jawhariyyeh, and therefore, we took part in them, particularly myself, having learned to dance dabkeh and play the rebeck, and the Hajj's tanboor.

That night Muhammad al-Mughrabi, my brother Tawfiq, and I sang and listened to al-Muna and al-Zaair, and carried on for quite a while. Later, Costandi al-Sous and his brother Issa arrived. Costandi al-Sous, a Greek Orthodox, was famous for his singing voice and oud playing. He was particularly good at the songs of Sheikh Salama Hijazi. His brother Issa, played the darbuka beautifully. It was the first time that I listened to them. Later, I was asked to sing, so I did. Then I danced the dabkeh and played the rebeck, and in the end, I sang Sheikh Salama Hijazi's poem, "Romeo and Juliet," while Costandi al-Sous accompanied me on the oud. He liked my performance, my voice, and the way I sang the song on a high pitch despite being just nine years old. I was entranced by the voice of Costandi al-Sous, so he handed me the oud, and I was over the moon. I began to pick it, tried to place my fingers on the first fret, and managed to play the song of *Zena, zena, zena*. Mitri Abdullah's good friend, Nakhla al-Hashsha was also present.

Everybody was happy on that unforgettable night. The music and singing went on until midnight, as women ululated and men cheered whenever the singing or playing stopped. Costandi al-Sous told me, "Come to my home tomorrow, and I will give you a beautiful oud neck which you can attach to a small oud. It would be better and bigger than this tanboor." But Nakhla al-Hashsha said, "No, I have a big old dry pumpkin which you can attach the neck to. That would be better."

Having been given this promise, I could not sleep a wink that night. In the morning I went to al-Sous, and he gave me a beautiful oud neck. I thanked him and danced the dakdookah dabkeh for him and his family, and they were pleased. On the following day, I went to Nakhla al-Hashsha's. He and his brothers worked as carpenters in the archway of the Greek Orthodox Monastery. He took me to his warehouse that was situated next to the old house of Reverend Yaacoub al-Baramki, under the arch and near Saint Nicholas Monastery (before the demolition of al-Baramki's house). I entered the dark warehouse with him, and with great difficulty we managed to find the pumpkin between the piles of wood. I took it and thanked him. Since my brother Khalil worked as a carpenter at Mitri Abu Shanab's, he was able to fix the oud neck to the pumpkin, and he made its body with reverse veneer that is used on the back of carriages. A three-string tanboor was almost ready but was missing a very important part—the sound hole. My father grabbed the tanboor, and using his knife, he carved a sound hole with a beautiful pattern in its middle. Father carved as he sat by the bay window of the reception room, while the snow fell heavily on Jerusalem. That was the year of the seven snows, which may have been 1907. And so, my tanboor was ready, earning me a higher status in the field of music. But since the neck was too short, I played it with my fingers close to one another, as one would do playing the mandolin.

A GLANCE OVER MODERN WESTERN INVENTIONS THAT REACHED JERUSALEM DURING MY BOYHOOD

Luckily, while I was growing up, lamps (kerosene lanterns) were already in use at our home. They included versions number two, three, or four, and later we got number forty, indicating the size of the wick. After lighting the wick, we would put back the lamp's glass cover, which was cleaned daily. This was the light we relied on in our daily life and in our evenings. But I used to see Andony al-Muna's family, who lived on the ground floor of Dar al-Jawhariyyeh, having dinner by a lamp lit by olive oil, as the custom had been prior to the invention of gas lamps. When we used to take the dough to Al-Zawraq's bakery and stay until after sunset, we saw that the bakery was lit with a kind of large conic-shaped tin container filled with kerosene, in which a thin wick was placed and lit with a match. No glass cover was placed on it, so it was quite dirty and it spewed smoke on all that was around it.

The Primus Stove

When the primus stove arrived in Jerusalem, we were amazed by this invention that made it possible to cook without the hassle of wood and charcoal. Enthused at this invention, and thinking he would be making my mother happy, my father paid four Ottoman *majidis* (eighty piasters) to acquire one, knowing that the monthly salary of His Excellency the Governor of Jerusalem did not exceed five liras, so you can imagine what four majidis were worth at that time. But this handy invention did not meet with the approval of my mother who complained day and night, saying that it was too noisy and that she was not used to it. For example, someone would knock twice on the door of the main entrance, but my mother would not hear it because she would be near the stove. Then, surprised to see the guest walking in, she would start cursing the stove and its inventor. I remember my father once coming home while my mother was fuming about it. She met him angrily and told him, "I swear to God, Abu Khalil, this stove will make me run away! I swear it will make me renounce my religion and go straight to Temple Mount and become a Muslim. Damn it and damn the day you bought it. We were alright without it. What's wrong with charcoal?" My father laughed and then comforted her. But as he arrived home one time, he was greeted by my mother: "How are you, Abu Khalil? I got rid of the stove. Look what I swapped it for!" She showed him a water jug and six glasses made of cheap crystal and decorated with gold patterns.

The Gas Lux (Lantern)

My sister Afifeh was living in Bethlehem, where her husband worked, and Tawfiq and I once visited her, staying for twelve days. As it happened, the municipality of Bethlehem had hung a big gas lux lamp on the rooftop of the Church of the Nativity for the Christmas visitors. The whole city was amazed by this new invention the first time they saw it. Some people, including the mayor, Saleh al-Qanawati, who was a friend of my father, gathered some mattresses and laid them over a straw mat under the lantern and lay down on them. Tawfiq and I were with them until our brother-in-law, Fayez, came for us at nine o'clock, and so went home raving about the gas lantern and its joyous light. Within a short while, the use of the gas lantern spread across cafés and streets, and Jerusalem became engulfed by light. When the clock tower was constructed on the wall of Jaffa Gate, the municipality had a gas lantern lamp hung on each of the clock tower's four sides. They were lit at night and could be seen from the villages, as well as from a long distance, transforming the clock tower into a lighthouse. Thus, we thanked the Lord for allowing us to see this invention in our city.

Electricity

Electricity came to Jerusalem for the first time when a power engine was brought to Notre Dame de France in order to illuminate this great institute. When passing the building, we used to see the electric lights through its main entrance and windows. Luckily, my father took me and Tawfiq along for the first time to an evening with Hussein Effendi near the municipality park. When it was time to leave, we brought him his white donkey which he rode while we walked along on both sides. When we reached the entrance of Notre Dame, he stopped and asked the gatekeeper (who had lost a hand) to show us how electric lighting worked. We went in with him to the hall and stood by the entrance. He pushed a button on the wall, turning off the lights in the entrance and part of the hall, and plunging the place into darkness. Then, in the blink of an eye, he placed his finger on a button, switched it on, and the whole place was lit instantly. We were extremely puzzled by this process and exclaimed that it was indeed greater than the lantern. For a long time afterwards, we related what we had seen to our friends, mother, and siblings, who were also surprised by what they heard. We thanked the Lord that we had seen electricity for the first time. Needless to say, this invention spread gradually to many other grand buildings.

The First Edison Phonograph

When the first Edison phonograph came to Jerusalem, we had heard about this unique invention and how it could record sounds, just like a camera transmits and copies a man's image on paper. But some time passed before we got lucky, and *nay* player Mitri al-Zaair, who was a friend of our neighbor Mitri al-Muna and a member of his music band, became the first to acquire the machine. All the neighbors—adults and children alike—gathered to see it, and my brothers and I were in the lead. We saw the phonograph and were surprised to hear the sound come out of the disc's spiral groove, clear and audible. There were also earphones with rubber wires, which one could place over one's ears for a clearer sound.

Mitri began to make some recordings. For example, he recorded the neighbor girls singing religious hymns such as *Ranna Sawtun fi al-a'ali* (A voice was heard in the heavens), some ululations by Noor al-Muna, Zumurruda, Hilana al-Muna, as well as some songs that were in vogue at the time. My brother Tawfiq and I also recorded some songs. I remember recording *Al-ghusnu idha ra'aka muqbil sajada* (The tree branch prostrates when you appear) and also the Druze song *Fihukm al-sab' salatin* (During the rule of the seven sultans). We recorded all these songs using a special recording needle, which Mitri later replaced with another one so that we could listen to the sounds we had recorded, and each one of us listened to their own voice for the first time. We were amazed and said to ourselves, "He taught man what he knew not. God speaks the truth."

P.S. The disc is wiped with kerosene and can then be recorded on again.

THE SECOND, OR "ORDINARY," PHONOGRAPH ("IT'S LIKE EATING WITH ARTIFICIAL TEETH.")

There was no tangible demand for Edison's first phonograph in Jerusalem, and I believe that was due to two reasons. It was beyond the means of people at the time. The late Yaacoub Said bought one for twenty-five French liras. I believe that no more than ten machines were sold in total, and they were bought by some of the rich Jerusalemites. The other reason is that the sound was not sufficiently clear. In any case, it was not long before various brands of the phonograph still in use nowadays arrived in Jerusalem. These included His Master's Voice, Polyphone, and Gramophone, among others. So the phonograph became widely spread in Jerusalem, and we started listening to famous singers and musicians, particularly those from Egypt.

Then disc recordings arrived. These were recordings of *dawrs* (songs in dialect) and *muwashahat* (sung poems) by the late Sheikh Yousuf al-Manyalawi, Muhammad Uthman, Sheikh Salama Hijazi, Muhammad Salem al-Ajuz, Abdul-Hayy Hilmi, Daoud Husni, Zaki Murad, and others, and above all, by al-Safati. Starting in cafés, music spread throughout the city. I remember that I used to take a coin from my father in order to go to the late Ibrahim al-Beiruti, a blind man who owned a large phonograph with four spiral springs and a twisted yellow copper trumpet with a big sound-magnifying opening. In order to protect the phonograph against the evil eye, he used to cover it with a red prayer costume and attach to it a big blue bead with some alum (a stonelike chemical substance) and a garlic clove. Then he would surround the trumpet with pictures of beautiful ladies and lady artists. This phonograph was placed on the pavement in front of the café of Ali Izhiman (Uncle Abu Zuhdi) in Damascus Gate, and next to it were placed two boxes full of disc recordings by the most famous music masters of that time. These were looked after by Mahmood al-Arnaaout. In front of Uncle Ibrahim, there was a yellow copper tray where the café customers could put some coins to listen to these recordings. I would throw a coin in the tray and say, "Please, Uncle, I would like to listen to Sheikh Salama Hijazi." In the blink of an eye, he would reach for the requested disc although he was totally blind, to everyone's astonishment! Then, we would stand there listening to the song until the end. On this note, the famous musician Kamel al-Khalii in his book on the subject of the phonograph said that listening to it was like eating with artificial teeth. But my opinion is that this invention made it possible for the various types of music to spread all over the world and for music to become accessible to all the peoples of the world who became able to sample it and appreciate it, as well as to tell good music from bad. What a great invention this is! I pray that the Lord bless the soul of the man to whom we owe it, and I thank Him for making it happen in our lifetime.

OUTSIDE THE CITY WALL—AL-MUSRARA AND AL-BAQ'A

Al-Musrara Quarter: Since the Schneller Orphanage[47] was founded in 1860, people felt encouraged to allow Jerusalem to expand and to begin gradually to live outside the wall. Thus, the Mea Shearim and surrounding communes were built for the Ashkenazi and Yemenite Jews, then the commune of Najarlia, and some of these communes became connected to Jaffa Road on the west side of Jerusalem.[48] Then the grand Russian complex was erected, and thus, by the beginning of the twentieth century, there was a vacant space between these buildings and the Damascus Gate part of the city wall. So the Georgian Jews started to build a commune near Damascus Gate, on the right side of the entrance to al-Musrara Quarter, later expanding to the left side. Then, the families of al-Dizdar, Youssef Agha, and Daoud Agha established their properties there and were followed by the families of al-Khalidi, Muhammad al-Taher, Sheikh Moussa Shafiq, al-Ikrimawi, al-Mutawalli, and finally, still within the same area, Hassan Bey al-Turjuman, all the way to Mea Shearim Road. Many families built homes in the area, including Daoud Yaacoub, Yaacoub Said, al-Khayyat family, and the Swedish School was built there, as well. As for the area stretching from Damascus Gate to the alley of Notre Dame de France, there were some buildings near the land of Issa Nakhla Qurt. After the road linking that alley to al-Musrara Quarter was inaugurated by the late Fayd al-Alami when he was the head of Jerusalem's municipality in 1906, Doctor Kanaan[49] built his well-known house and was followed by teacher Issa Moussa Isbitan, of al-Tor, then by Hajj Ismail al-Najjar, then by the al-Ansari family, and finally by Fayd al-Alami. Indeed, the alley remains known as Fayd Alley to this day. Then the building of the Ashkenazi Mortmain was erected near the Silesian School (for carpentry), before Shakib al-Nashashibi built a property, followed by Aref al-Alami, then Tomayan and Abu Hermas, and Tleel (his building had previously housed a school), then Costandi and Saliba al-Daadoush, then Yaacoub al-Mahshi, then Reverend Khalil Ibrahim Farah, then teacher Issa Moussa al-Tawri, the al-Ansari family, Nqula al-Shimali, Dahbour, George al-Harami, al-Shaghuriya, Hajj Bakr al-Nashashibi, George Baddour, Muhammad al-Khalili's family, then al-Sheber, al-Mahshi, Mustafa al-Jabsha, al-Yafawi, al-Aref, Abu Shanab, al-Daruti, Qamar, al-Muwaqqat, and Said.

Thus, many families left their homes inside the wall and moved to live in al-Musrara Quarter. The quarter's archway was erected using iron bars, and its roof was covered with Schneller bricks. Just as the custom remains to this day inside the wall, the majority of these buildings had really useful wells in which rain water was collected. As for the way of living, most families lived just as they had done inside the wall. For example, the families of Salim al-Skafi, Afteem Akra, Isbir al-Khayyat, and Costandi Abdul-Nur lived as follows on the first floor of one of the buildings in al-Musrara Quarter.

Salim al-Skafi and his family occupied two rooms, using one as a reception room and the other as a bedroom. The kitchen and dining space were located on the ground floor.

Afteem Akra and his family occupied two rooms, using one as a reception room and the other as a bedroom. A small room on another floor served as a kitchen and dining space.

Isbir al-Khayyat and his family lived in two rooms.

Costandi Abdul-Nour occupied two rooms. The kitchen was a wooden room with a tin rooftop (measuring one by one and a half meters), built over one of the balconies of this floor. As for the main hall, it was for communal use. The four families shared one toilet which was built of tin sheets and had a hole in the ground. The toilet had no flush and was situated outside the building, near the entrance. The houses had no bathrooms, so people used to wash using copper washtubs, either in the kitchen or in the bedroom. From time to time, perhaps once or twice a year, they used to go to those big bathhouses known as Arab *hammams*.

Al-Baq'a Fawqa Quarter: In my opinion, the spread of urban development south of Jaffa Gate was due to the railway and the location of the Jerusalem station near the Bethlehem-Jerusalem Road. Another reason for it was the German Colony being located on the western side of the railway station, and finally the erection of the khaniqah building while Hajj Salim al-Husseini was head of the municipality of Jerusalem, which was during 1879 and 1897. The vacant space between these historical buildings came to be known as Baq'a al-Fawqa (upper Baq'a).

Thus, some of Jerusalem's Muslim Arabs (no Jews were living in this area) gradually began to build there. Among them were Daoud Abu Jadam, Tanas Faraj, Jiryis Semaan, George Zakharia and his brothers, George al-Khouri who is known as George Bayda, the Mikel family, Andony Asaousa, Ibrahim Asaousa, Semaan al-Zaghloul, Hanna Theodosi, Tanas al-Halabi, Yousif Jahshan, Abd Akra, Semaan Sahar, and other Christians. As for Muslims, they had already started building there, and among them were the large al-Waari family and the families of Nassar, Arnaout, and al-Dijani. It was the al-Waari family who set the foundations of this development, having lived for a long time in their properties that were connected to those of al-Namamreh.[50] And so the area was called al-Waaria, or Mahallat al-Waaria. As for the building style, most people went for crossed arches and did use bricks because they had begun construction before the building of al-Musrara Quarter had begun, knowing that the owners retained the tradition of having a well to collect rain water in winter. Nakhla Effendi Katan's house stood out, for it was a special house which he built near the properties of Fayd al-Alami on Mount Sharafat, and it was the most distant building in Jerusalem at the time.[51]

RELIGIOUS FESTIVALS CELEBRATED BY THE PEOPLE OF JERUSALEM

It is fortunate that since the olden days, religious festivals have been celebrated in and around Jerusalem, providing the people with some recreation. Without these religion-based celebrations, people would have succumbed to gloom, particularly in the days when they lived inside the wall and the gate was closed at sunset in order to prevent potential attacks by Bedouins. The geographical location of Jerusalem was optimal for this purpose, as there was no waterfront, fountain, river, sea, or forest in this purely religious site, but only monasteries, churches, *zawiyyas*, and synagogues. It is without doubt a city of great historical value, given that it is home to the world's greatest religious sites. But credit should be given to those who devised these celebrations, for they have provided entertainment of a religious nature to people from all sects and denominations.

The Festival of Our Lady Mary

It was traditional for Greek Orthodox families to begin the fast of Our Lady Mary by spending fifteen days, from the thirty-first of July until the fifteenth of August of the Julian calendar,[52] in the valley, under the olive trees surrounding the shrine of Our Lady Mary, located on the eastern side of Jerusalem. During this fortnight, many families spent their days and nights under the trees, hanging their blankets or sheets (or loincloths) from the branches of olive trees down to the ground to protect their children and themselves from the dew and the heat of the sun. The wealthier ones set up tents and enjoyed their time inside.

Everyone observed the fast, and fruits and vegetables were consumed profusely during that season of the year. In the late afternoon, they would start drinking, while some of them sang to the rhythm of the darbuka or the *riqq* (tambourine), and others sat around someone playing the oud or violin, and joined in the chorus. Thus, people sat in circles huddled together, either in the moonlight or by the light of gas lamps and, more recently, gas lantern lamps. Friends and relatives who came to visit the families staying in these shelters and tents or under the olive trees were invariably met with due hospitality. Whenever someone came over and greeted them, he was presented with a glass of arak or wine, while the other hand stretched out offering *mezze*.[53]

Being at this festival was like being at a wedding party, for you could hear the men cheering and the women ululating, as well as the singing and playing of all those who happened to be taking part in this gathering. The custom was that when the men stopped cheering, the young men would take their guns and rifles and fire into the air. We were moved to hear the shots resounding in the silence of the night and echoing in the valley in that marvelous, entrancing way. In the morning, people went to work and returned in the afternoon. And so they carried on, until the feast day.

The Eve of the Feast, "the Paramony," was an occasion well-known to all, particularly at that time (between 1900 and 1914). The government contributed to its success in every way it could, in appreciation of Patriarch Damianos and his compassion and generosity towards the people. Thus, the army musical band played music from the morning of that day until midnight under a special tent set up for the occasion, accompanied by an army parade, while His Excellency the Governor and the notables of the state gathered in another tent and the whole nation feasted all day on stuffed lamb, courtesy of the Greek Orthodox Patriarchate.

As for spectators from outside the Greek Orthodox community, they would gather on this day from Saint Stephen's Gate all the way over cemeteries, hills, and streets up to the vicinity of Ras al-Amud. Some, particularly the children, played on swings, while some bought small darbukas and horns for the kids, while others sat in the municipal café or along the streets and around the shrine of Our Lady Virgin Mary. One could walk through these crowds only with great difficulty, as everyone was gripped by celebratory fever, Christians and Muslims alike. I have great memories of these festivals, during which I spent wonderful times enjoying music day and night with many fellow Jerusalemites.

The day after Paramony was the glorious feast day of our Lady Virgin Mary, and church was visited throughout the following nine days.

Those who had made a pledge to the Virgin Mary would visit the church early in the morning, perhaps at four o'clock, proceeding barefoot from the city to the shrine, each one bringing the amount they had pledged to donate, and they would light small candles, lining the steps of the church. On entering the main entrance to the church, particularly when approaching it from the tomb of the Virgin on the lower level, the church seemed like a ball of light.

After the ninth day, as the custom remains to this day, the clergy of the Greek Orthodox Patriarchate performed a symbolic funeral of Our Lady Mary. Lying on a bed, the head of the church would hold in his hands an icon of Virgin Mary, intricately made with white pearl and precious stones, while the bishops, priests, and monks walked at the front, chanting hymns. A huge congregation of people joined in this grand procession that went from the tomb of Lady Mary on the street leading to Saint Stephen's Gate, on to Via Dolorosa, then to Aqabat al-Mufti (al-Mufti Archway), up the steps of the khaniqah past the bars and on to the Christian Quarter, before finally descending the steps leading to the Church of the Holy Sepulchre and depositing this precious icon in the House of Our Lady Mary, which was located opposite the main entrance of the Church of the Holy Sepulchre, near the Mosque of Omar.

During this festival of Our Lady Virgin Mary, the Paramony, the feast day, and the nine days that followed it, the people of Jerusalem basked in joy, happiness, and love, in the absence of beaches, rivers, cafés, cabarets, and forms of entertainment available in other countries. I will never forget the thousands of Russians who visited the Holy Land, staying at the Russian institutes all over Palestine. They joined with the clergymen on every religious occasion, particularly at Easter, chanting hymns with their melodious voices.

Celebration of Easter Week by Jerusalem's Christian, Muslim, and Jewish Communities between 1900 and 1914

Having lived under both the Ottoman rule and the British Mandate, I decided to describe the religious feasts as celebrated by all three religions during Easter Week, in order to provide a clear depiction of the Ottoman rule and way of government. I do not deny that the Turks, too, were considered colonialists. But what is important is that the individuals—whether governors, directors, and police—were among the city's most honorable citizens, and so problems were solved amicably, quickly, and fairly. Only a few Turks were sent to our country, and with the exception of the governor, they mattered little. It is amazing to see how the huge festivals and wide national celebrations of each religion and every confession followed one another in this small region, in peace and security.

On Passover, Jewish shops and workshops in Jerusalem were closed for seven days. The custom was for Jews of all the communes around Jerusalem and in the nearby villages to march to Jaffa Gate and on to Swaiqat Alloun[54] until they reached the Wailing Wall. After the Friday prayer (the week before Christian Holy Friday), the procession of Prophet Moses proceeded from the al-Aqsa Mosque in a majestic religious ceremonial attended by the governor, the sharia judge, government high officials, notables, and Muslim clergymen. The procession exited via the court of the mosque with the flags held as follows.

Two members of the al-Qutb family held two flags, one of the rights that continues to be observed.[55]

Two members of the al-Dijani al-Daoudi family held two flags considered to be the flags of Prophet Daoud.

Two members of Youssef al-Husseini's family held two flags considered to be the flags of Prophet Moses, since the family is in charge of the shrine of Prophet Moses.

One person from the Qlibo family held one flag for Prophet Moses, and this flag was usually that of the Mufti of Jerusalem.

The flag holders proceeded on horseback, resting the flag stick on a special piece placed over the knee. The tradition was for these flags to be preserved in the well-known *Bayraq* (Flag) House which was located on al-Mufti Archway and belonged to the al-Ragheb al-Husseini family. The grand procession descended via Saint Stephen's Gate, preceded by the army music band and then by the young men of Mahallat Bab Hatta. The "flag of the youth" was held by someone from the Zaed family or the al-Qarjouli family, who were among the notables of Mahallat Bab Hutta. The procession was accompanied by a special group called the *sayyara*[56] who carried large and small drums, tambourines, and copper cups that were used to play percussion. This group was formed of members of the al-Deesy family and led by Sheikh Atef, who was in charge of the mosque of Sheikh Jarrah. Another band was led by Sheikh Abu Abd al-Qazzaz, who sang muwashahat and recited Qu'ranic verses in a high, strong, far-reaching voice and who was marvelous at playing percussion with the drums or copper cups. Farmers also joined in with many more flags, having come from the villages of the Jerusalem district, particularly Salwan, al-Aayzariyyeh, Abu Dees, and others. Every village had its own sayyara band and brought along its own uhzujas, dabkeh, and dances, while laudations for the Prophet and patriotic cheering were heard from the brave men of Jerusalem. These included "Open the gate for us, triumphant Abdul-Hamid; we brought the wall down with your sword," "Line the chairs; we are coming to you," and other soul-stirring songs. You could see the horses dancing to the music and to the rhythm of the drums and copper cups, and watch a full parade of the power of the Jerusalem city-state, including the gendarmerie, the police, and the crossbred camels which they rode dressed in their official attire.

I clearly remember those people, including Mustafa Effendi al-Salihani, Mahmud Effendi Jarallah, Abdul-Qader al-Alami, Hajj Khalil Rasas, and others, walking in an amazingly well-organized way, followed by the special carriage carrying the judge and the governor. On reaching Ras el-Amud, the head of the municipality gave them an official reception in a huge tent where they were served refreshments and coffee. Then they would make their way to the shrine of Prophet Moses, some in horse carriages, some on horseback.

The main streets running from the gate of the al-Aqsa Mosque to Ras al-Amud, over the city wall and the hills and cemeteries on both sides of the main street, and on to the end of Ras al-Amud, were so crowded that one could not see the ground, only people, most of whom were Muslim ladies who had dedicated the day to watching the celebrations with their children. They would come at dawn to secure a place to sit, even if on top of the wall. Most people left their homes on that day and had their meals in the streets, buying them from ambulant sellers who sold all kinds of food, drink, nuts, sweets, fruits, and vegetables, but also children's toys, sticks, cigarettes, hoses, water pipes, and other hard-to-find items. I recall an ambulant seller, whom I believe to have been Egyptian, once coming to sell reed sticks. When he wandered among the ladies, he would shout at the top of his voice, "Discipline your husband, for one piaster." Once he was among the men, he amended his phrase, shouting, "Discipline your wife, for one piaster." The procession remained at the shrine of Prophet Moses in the Jordan Valley for a week, during which Palm Sunday was also celebrated.

Palm Sunday

Muslim traditions: On Saturday afternoon, the people of the city of Hebron began their procession. Holding their flags, drums, and cups, they were led by the clergy, the mufti, and the notables of the city. The tradition at the time was for people to dine together, hosted by the late Suleiman Jacir who was reputed for his generosity. His was one of Bethlehem's most honorable families, and he was also one of the city's most respectable wealthy figures. The dinner was hosted at his palace, which was located near Rachel's Tomb, on Bethlehem Road.

On the morning of Palm Sunday, the procession would enter Jerusalem in a majestic celebration and be given an official reception at Jaffa Gate by the government as well as by the people of Jerusalem—the notables of the Muslim community and the young men, who welcomed them with uhzujas and patriotic anthems.

This procession advanced so slowly that it took four hours to pass the station road which ran from Birkat al-Sultan (the pool of Ottoman Sultan Suleiman) to Jaffa Gate. The roadsides were crowded with women and children who had come to watch, particularly on Mount Zion. They would arrive at dawn to reserve a space where they could sit and watch this national festival. Men sat at the cafés of Jaffa Gate—al-Maarif Café, al-Ballur (the crystal) Café located in the zawiyya belonging to the mortmain of al-Aanabusi, the "Hanging" Café which was known as the Bank Café. The procession arrived at its destination around midday, entering the city through the gap in the city wall which was originally opened when Kaiser Wilhelm II of Germany visited Jerusalem in 1898. It then visited Jerusalem to pray. After prayer, it proceeded on to the shrine of Prophet Moses, where the procession joined the crowds that had assembled there since Friday afternoon.

Christian traditions: On this day, the rites of the Christians' religious celebration began at the Church of the Holy Sepulchre, particularly in years when Palm Sunday fell on the same day for all denominations, including the Latin, Roman Catholic, Syriac Orthodox, Syriac Catholic, Coptic, Abyssinian, Maronite, Protestant, and other Christian denominations. From the start, the rituals were well-organized thanks to the supervision of the government with its police force and the army, according to the Status Quo arrangement.[57] Each denomination had its own characteristic rites, which were performed at a particular time and place, as well as its own circumambulation ceremony inside the Church of the Holy Sepulchre. Perhaps since the conquest of Jerusalem by Caliph Omar bin al-Khattab, the Judeh family, one of Jerusalem's illustrious families, has kept the key of the Church of the Holy Sepulchre. Omar also ordered that the Nussienbah family also be given the right to open and close the door of the church, as well as that of the Garden Tomb, and the two families have retained these rights.

So imagine the visitors to the Church of Holy Sepulchre on this great day, wandering around it and on its rooftop, including clergymen from all the various denominations, ordinary people, European pilgrims including Greeks, Cypriots, Bulgarians, French, Germans, and, most of all, no less than thirty thousand Russian pilgrims, men, and women. Imagine the task of the government, security forces, and civil authorities on such occasions, and how forces had to be carefully deployed during this week in order to protect Jews and their beliefs, protect the celebrating Christians, and deal with emerging problems that could turn badly if it were not for the government's intervention, despite the small number of its forces at that time. This success was largely due to the fact that only the most honorable citizens were chosen to fill offices. These individuals were never intimidated by the large number of visitors and ensured that security measures were in place for the celebrations to happen without incident.

Easter Monday

Muslim traditions: The people of Nablus began a grand procession starting in Jabal al-Nar. They entered Jerusalem at Sheikh Jarrah before proceeding to Damascus Gate in exactly the same way as the Hebron procession the day before. After visiting Jerusalem, they would make their way to the Shrine of Prophet Moses, where they would join the people of Jerusalem and Hebron already present there. All these people remained for a week at the shrine, which provided them with full boarding. The Yunis family, which was in charge of the shrine, also had the right to oversee how the funds allocated to the shrine by the religious endowments were spent over the year. On this occasion, their task was to cook the rice and meat, and feed everybody, rich, poor, and strangers alike. I had the good fortune to visit the Shrine of Prophet Moses with Hussein Effendi al-Husseini when he was head of the municipality of Jerusalem.

Holy Thursday

Christian traditions: On this glorious day, Jesus's washing of his disciples' feet is reenacted. All denominations would perform their rites at their dedicated places and times inside the Church of the Holy Sepulchre. The Greek Orthodox, particularly during the time of Patriarch Kyrios Kyrios Demianos, developed the tradition of holding Holy Thursday service on the church rooftop, rather than inside. This service was one of the most beautiful Christian celebrations in Jerusalem. The patriarchate would set up a large wood-and-iron platform and affix thirteen chairs to it, symbolizing Christ and his disciples. The Arab Greek Orthodox priests would take their places first, then the Greek priests would join them to complete the number. They would ascend to their dedicated seats via a special ladder. After the patriarch had delivered mass inside the church, he would make his way up to the platform. As special prayers were offered and hymns sung, the priests would remove one shoe and sock while, suddenly, the patriarch would be changed into all white attire. As the clergy sang melodious prayers, he would wash the foot of the priests in a silver bowl, each of whom represented a disciple of Christ, while the deacon poured the water out of a silver jug. He would then dry the priest's foot. Every balcony, window, and rooftop around the Church of the Holy Sepulchre was crowded with spectators. On a sign from the patriarch, some of the Arab Greek Orthodox young men standing on the rooftops of the entrance to Saint Jacob's Church began to clap, cheer, and play the darbuka, while the prayers continued.

Standing on a temporary platform, a priest would read the story of Jesus washing his disciples' feet, in many languages and from all twelve gospels. The platform was set up near the entrance to Our Father Ibrahim Monastery, and a green olive branch was hung above it on the adjacent wall. Special scaffolds were built for this occasion using wooden boards tied with rope to the walls surrounding the church rooftop. The seats were rented out at high prices to pilgrims visiting Jerusalem. Long wide flights of steps were also built on the rooftop of the House of Mary Monastery, on a section of the monastery's orchard, as well as on the rooftop of the Greek Orthodox Monastery, by the bell tower of the church. All these seats were often rented out to Russians who came in large numbers and were so fond of Jerusalem's historical sites that they spared no expense during their stay. Once back in their country, they sent monies to the patriarch and the monks, and particularly to Ephtimios, the head of the Church of the Holy Sepulchre. The Greek Orthodox Monastery enjoyed such wealth, power, and support that it could indeed be considered as a state within a state. This religious celebration ended at nine-thirty on Thursday morning, allowing the government and leadership to turn their attention immediately to the flag ceremony of Prophet Moses.

Muslim traditions: All visitors, pilgrims, officials, and guests would leave the Shrine of Prophet Moses and gather in Ras al-Amud, where the head of the municipality received them in a reception tent set up for the occasion. After drinks were served, this huge procession would descend the road leading to the Shrine of Our Lady Mary, and then the road leading to Saint Stephen's Gate, before entering the city in a more nationalistic spirit than the week before. For the number of visitors to the Shrine of Prophet Moses had been increasing throughout the one-week visiting period with the daily arrival of people from Hebron and Nablus and their mountains, and farmers from Ramallah and the villages of the Jerusalem district. Thus, numerous flags and instruments were in the procession now that it had been joined by the holders of the flag of Nablus, the flag of the youth of Nablus, the flag of Hebron, the flag of the youth of Hebron, and the flag of the youth of Jerusalem. The latter had the right to be in the lead, making sure the flags of Jerusalem—and in particular the flag of Prophet Moses—were at the forefront. For the privilege of leading the procession had always been reserved for the people of Jerusalem.

So imagine what Jerusalem was like on this Holy Thursday, as Christians from the various denominations held an unequaled celebration in which they were joined by foreign tourists and pilgrims visiting the Holy City. Then imagine the gathering of Muslims who were either from the city itself or from neighboring villages, in addition to the people of Hebron, the Hebron mountains, Nablus, and the Nablus mountains.

Good Friday

Muslim traditions On this great day, Muslims who had returned from the Shrine of Prophet Moses on the previous day would gather on the Temple Mount at the Aqsa Mosque, the Dome of the Rock, and esplanade. The Temple Mount overflowed with people, making it impossible to move around its vast spaces without difficulty. You could see flags everywhere held aloft by the people of Jerusalem, Hebron, Nablus, the villages of the Jerusalem district, and Ramallah, while large and small drums and finger cymbals played, and people gathered in groups, hovering around the flags and singing religious and national anthems on this day referred to as the flag celebration day of Muslims. All this would take place after the Friday prayer. On leaving the mosque, they would begin celebrating within the courtyards of the Temple Mount and continue until late afternoon. Then they would bid Jerusalem farewell and start to leave in groups, returning to their towns and villages. However, a number of visitors, namely the Christian tourists and pilgrims that season, remained in the city until all the celebrations were over.

Christian traditions On Good Friday, Christians held prayers and services inside the Church of the Holy Sepulchre, each denomination at its own time and according to its own traditions. Throughout the day, church bells of the various denominations resounded all over Jerusalem. They rang slowly on this sad day, the day of the funeral of Jesus Christ, particularly throughout the evening, and until midnight.

Tradition states that the Greek Orthodox denomination has the right to join the Greek clergy in the circumambulation of the church courtyard, which is known as "the rooftop." The procession, made up of clergy holding candles and Arab Greek Orthodox priests, would complete three circumambulations while singing the hymns of Good Friday in Greek and Arabic, while consuls, officials, and notables of the Arab Greek Orthodox community followed behind. It was indeed a beautiful sight, particularly in good weather. Shops in the Christian Quarter selling crosses, candles and shroud, olivewood, and shells to visitors, particularly to Russians, seemed to be on fire. They all made massive profits in these much awaited blessed hours and days, which were the only time of the season for them to earn their family's expenditures for the whole year. Funeral ceremonies could also be held by the patriarch at midnight at the Church of the Holy Sepulchre. These were attended by large crowds from the various denominations.

Holy Light Saturday in Jerusalem

On this great day, in years when Easter would fall on the same day for all Christian denominations, Eastern-rite churches—Greek Orthodox, Armenian Orthodox, Syriac Orthodox, Coptic, and Abyssinian—would hold their celebrations together inside the Church of the Holy Sepulchre. All these denominations unanimously agreed to receive the Holy Fire and blessing from the Greek Orthodox Patriarch, after which they would bring them to their own churches and denominations. The Latin denomination kept their own Holy Light ceremony which their patriarch held before the ceremonies of the other denominations, striking the fire himself.

The ceremony would start at nine o'clock on Saturday morning. The patriarch entered, then exited the Holy Sepulchre. Standing in front of it, he began the service, later serving the Holy Eucharist to the clergy, monks, nuns, schoolchildren, and believers of the Latin denomination. Once mass had ended, government officials and members of the Nusseibeh and Judah families would rise and enter the Holy Sepulchre and inspect it meticulously for any combustibles, such as matches, wicks, lighters, or electric wires. Then they would all leave it, closing the main entrance behind them. This task of closing the Holy Sepulchre has been entrusted to a member of the Judah family who would then hand the key back to the Nusseibeh family. The door remained sealed with red wax until the arrival of the patriarch at precisely twelve o'clock.

At this point, people began to enter. Greek Orthodox clergy took their seats in the katholikon, then Coptic clergy, believers, and pilgrims who had come from Egypt for the occasion took their seats by the special windows on the ground and first floors, followed by clergy, believers, and foreign visitors of the Syriac denomination who took their dedicated seats by the Holy Sepulchre. Then, led by the Armenian patriarch, the Armenian clergy, community, and their foreign visitors took their seats on the left side of the Holy Sepulchre as well as on the first floor, where windows overlooked the sepulchre. Finally, the Abyssinians made their entrance. One must not forget that at the same time, thousands of Russians—both men and women—were huddled together inside the church around the sepulchre, in and behind the katholikon, in the vestibules and corners, and on the steps leading to Golgotha, on Golgotha, and finally in the rotunda. All these places were crowded with people, including rich foreigners, Russians, Greeks, and others, who payed the clergy of their denomination huge amounts of money in return for a small seat anywhere around the sepulchre, on one of the balconies overlooking it, or in the katholikon. Special tickets were issued for these excellent seats, often by the patriarchate. The balconies facing the Holy Sepulchre were reserved courtesy of the patriarch for His Excellency the Governor and his family, the police commander in chief and his family, and other senior officials. Arab Christian visitors, too, were in the church, having come from Syria—especially Aleppo and Damascus—Lebanon, East Jordan, and above all Greece and the Greek islands, Bulgaria, Montenegro, the Balkans, Cyprus, and Crete among others. Not an inch of space was vacant inside the church, as visitors from all over the world gathered inside, some of them staying for four or five days together with their families and children, sleeping on the floor in its many vestibules.

On the second floor, under the Dome of the Holy Sepulchre, a door opened to the rooftop of the Greek Orthodox Monastery. The patriarchate's head translator issued tickets allowing entry to the church through this door. On this upper floor, whose windows overlooked the interior of the church and the Holy Sepulchre itself, some Greek Orthodox Arabs attended the celebrations of Holy Saturday, as did some tourists who would have come from faraway countries and gained entrance with special tickets. The Franciscan Monastery's seven windows which overlooked the Holy Sepulchre remained vacant. The monastery allowed only Latin Christians to watch through these windows, but I remember that not a single person could be seen in any of them since the Catholic ceremony would have already taken place. On many occasions, government officials were also denied access to these windows during the Holy Fire Ceremony of the Eastern Orthodox churches.

After visitors had taken their places, the rest of the people crowded together inside the church before the young men of the Greek Orthodox community would be allowed in. Dressed in traditional costume, they entered holding their flag—the flag of youth—accompanied by the sword-and-shield dancers and darbuka players. Arabs visiting from neighboring countries such as Syria and Lebanon also entered the church, as did Christian visitors who had come from the villages of the Jerusalem district such as Ramallah, Birzeit, Bethlehem, Beit Jala, Jifna, and al-Taybeh. On many occasions, visitors from Nablus entered cheering and singing uhzujas with their high voices that reached to the sky, chanting an old Holy Saturday hymn that is well-known to the people of Jerusalem.

Wearing simple black clothes symbolizing his grief, the patriarch then left the patriarchate and marched down the street, accompanied by some of the clergy. When he made his entrance into the Church of the Holy Sepulchre, the Judah and Nusseibeh families formally closed the door behind him, transforming the Church into the semblance of a prison. Prior to the patriarch's entrance, the young men had been cheering for about an hour. Around noon, the patriarch reached and entered the Holy Sepulchre, which earlier had been sealed with red wax under the supervision of government officials. The sepulchre was opened and the red wax removed by the Nusseibeh family, in the presence of the Judah family and government officials. The patriarch then donned his special white robe, as the audience and the government representatives looked on, and then entered the sepulchre alone.

When the young Arabs entered the church, the thirteen flag holders were handed the flags by the mayor (previously, this was done by the family of Hanania Mikhail al-Taweel, the father of Hanna Hanania). And then, holding the flags, they would march three times around the Holy Sepulchre, after which the cheering and singing stopped. The flags would later be handed back to the church employee in charge and stored at the church. Thus, people in the church—on the ground floor, on the balconies overlooking the Holy Sepulchre, around the rotunda, under the large dome, and in the katholikon—all awaited the Holy Fire ceremony, holding candles which they would then light to have the blessing.

At around one o'clock, the light poured forth, announced by the ringing of the bells of the dome of the Orthodox Church which was located above the entrance, then the Armenians' gongs and bells began to resound, and the rejoicing people of all denominations began to cheer and sing. To pass on the Holy Fire, the patriarch handed a special torch lamp to the priest of the Greek Orthodox community, another to the Slehit family who received it on behalf of the denomination and Arab visitors, and another to the delegated Armenian clergyman who passed it on to the Syriacs and Copts. Another torch was then tied to a long rope and pulled upwards from the top of the windows of the dome above the All-Holy Sepulchre—the dome with the door opening to the rooftop of the Greek Orthodox Monastery. Thus, in the blink of an eye, the whole church was illuminated with the Holy Light. It was a marvelous sight, despite the fear that all those handheld candles could cause a fire. At this awe-inspiring hour, the church resounded with the ululations of the ladies—Coptic ladies from Egypt, in particular—and cheers went up from every direction, while the crowds gradually hurried to leave through the door which was opened immediately as the light poured forth.

The convoy of young Greek Orthodox Jerusalemite men left the church, followed by the convoys of young men of Ramallah, Bethlehem, and villages surrounding Jerusalem, as well as by visitors who were mostly from Aleppo and Lebanon. Following tradition, these processions would start at the Church of the Holy Sepulchre and ascend the steps inside Saint James Chapel which led directly to the spacious rooftops of the Greek Orthodox Monastery, where young Greek Orthodox men such as George and Saba al-Harami, Mitri al-Muna, Khalil al-Hakim, Issa al-Ghouri, and Elias al-Kharouf excelled at performing sword-and-shield dances. The famous master of this art was the late Nakhla al-Hasha, who performed the dance dressed in its special authentic Arabic costume. However, it was Orthodox visitors from Aleppo who gave the most beautiful performances, with remarkable swiftness and agility. I remember that most of them wore red shoes and sang their own special hymns. Often the man with the sword stood on another strong man's shoulders and chanted soul-stirring verses such as "Holy Saturday," "Our Feast," "Saint George Ali Khidr," "We Christians are holding the candles," and "Oh Virgin, peace be upon you." Depending on the political situation, he might cheer for the Sultan, chanting, for example "Abdul-Hamid, may you remain glorious" or "Abdul-Hamid, may you remain victorious, with your sword, we brought the wall down," as well as other religious, national, and folk hymns, while everyone joined in the chorus.

Long hours were spent performing the sword-and-shield dance on the rooftop of the Greek Orthodox Monastery, while people looked on from nearby rooftops and from further away, even from the minaret of the Caliph Omar bin al-Khattab Mosque that faces the Church of the Holy Sepulchre. I recall that at the moment of the Holy Light's pouring out, about four or five young Jerusalemites of the Greek Orthodox and Arab Armenian communities, all dressed in white *shirwals*,[58] would run on the heads and shoulders of the audience as though they were walking on the floor. Thousands of people were crowded inside the church at the moment of the Pouring of the Light.

"The Carnival"—Jewish Purim

On Easter eve, the last day of Lent, it was traditional for the people of Jerusalem and for the Arab Greek Orthodox community in particular to hold the well-known nightlong parties, known as *huruma*, at their homes. Most families, men and women together, made the necessary arrangements for these parties, and they would dress in traditional Arabic costume and hide their faces so that it was difficult to recognize them. For instance, when a wedding was acted out, the bride wore an elegant dress with special attention given to her hairstyle, makeup, and the jewelry on her chest, ears, and neck, although the bride was a man, not a woman, and vice versa. Thus, they would make surprise visits to homes, dressed in various costumes. For example, one would dress like a priest and act out the mass service, while the sword-and-shield dancers sang and danced, giving one the impression that one was watching a masquerade wedding celebration.

Some also dressed as Jews or Ashkenazi Jews by wearing fake sideburns, others like a farmer and his wife, the latter wearing the traditional Ramallah dress with its luxurious embroidery or the Bethlehem traditional dress, while someone else donned the Cossack costume, complete with trousers, karakul hat, belt, and breast cartridges. One would dress like an Albanian, wearing a red Moroccan fez with the navy tassel hanging over his shoulder and all the way down to his chest, while another dressed like a consul in official costume, wearing a top hat. And so, accompanied by music bands playing the oud, riqq, and various wind instruments, they visited their neighbors and other people in their quarter.

One of these unique costumes was mine. I used to wear a ladies' skirt, which I would tie to my waist over a pair of white trousers, and place a sifter over my head. Then someone would lift the skirt up and tie it together over the sifter so that my upper body and head were inside it. While inside, I kept my arms up in order to hold the skirt's split open and see through it. Dressed like that, we would enter the room where spectators would be waiting, and I would dance to the music and the rhythm of the darbuka, to the astonishment of the audience who could hardly believe that they were watching a human being! Then another person would come, my brother Tawfiq, for example, and stand on two hand-held stilts, after putting on the scary mask and a tall conical hat. A long dress known as the Berlin was placed over his shoulders so that it covered his entire body, transforming him into a giant who could not enter homes through the door. And so this giant walked next to the dwarf I was, making everyone laugh, even the unhappy.

The patriarch used to give some money to one of the community groups, which made this group take special care of their show. The group was led by Jalil Qamar who would dress in caricaturesque clothes and carry a broom. Together they would march on the afternoon of Paramony from the monastery in Wadi al-Rababah, south of Jerusalem's Sultan Pool, donning their elaborate costumes and walking to the sound of the darbuka, while their leader rang a big bell that he held, until they reached the Jaffa Gate and later on, the Greek Orthodox Monastery. This was a famous day for the people of Jerusalem—Christians, Muslims, and Jews alike. Starting at dawn on that day, families and children kept their seats and places on Mount Zion, overlooking the road to Jaffa Gate. They would sit at the many cafés of the quarter, while others stood around on their feet all day, awaiting the arrival of the carnival, known as "the welcoming of the monk," at Jaffa Gate.

The carnival tradition was also acted out by the Jewish community of Jerusalem at their homes and in their communes that surrounded the city. They called it Purim, and we spent long evenings among them in the communes marveling at what we saw, particularly at the time of the Ottomans.

Ramadan Nights

Ramadan nights in Jerusalem were nights of warmth and cosiness, particularly when this holy month fell in the summer. Since my brothers and I lived in the Saadiyeh and Damascus Gate locality, and given my father's strong friendship with our Muslim neighbors, we used to attend parties and get-togethers that allowed us to have an insight into Muslim traditions which other Christians would not have had the chance to experience. My brothers and I often took part in the *Zikr* rituals held at the Shrine of Sheikh Rihan, in the vicinity of Dar al-Jawhariyyeh, and we sang religious hymns with the professional and amateur singers. In the evening, we would visit our neighbors, Sheikh

Muhammad al-Saleh, the great master Sheikh Adeeb Judah, Sheikh Salim Mamluk, Mustafa al-Zawraq, Abdul-Daoudi, Mustafa al-Salihani, Mustafa al-Jabsha, and others, and enjoy a musical evening at their homes, particularly when I took my tanboor along. I played and sang together with my brother Tawfiq, as we enjoyed the various beverages, *barazek*,[59] and sweets.

The tradition was for the children of Saadiyeh and Damascus Gate to get together, bringing along a baker's bowl and go around to homes after the cannon was fired. Together they were called the praisers, since they went around reciting verses of praise. When they visited our home, they would stand in the dark corridor and recite at the top of their voices: "If it were not for Khalil (my brother), we would not have come. So, open your bag and hand us some halawa and two plates of baklawa." Then their leader would shout on the top of his voice, "May God keep his mother" (that is, Khalil's), and everyone would say, "Amen." "May God keep his father." "Amen." "May God keep his sister." "Amen." On they went until my father came down to the corridor and generously handed each one of them a coin. Someone named Hassan, who worked at al-Zawraq Bakery, used to play a trick on us. Once he had received his coin from my father, he would change his voice and say, "Uncle Abu Khalil, I did not get anything." Unable to see in the dark corridor, my father would hand him another coin, thinking this person was someone else, until he finally realized he was being fooled and told the boy off, knowing that he loved him for his good humor.

Those who are familiar with Damascus Gate Square during that period, particularly when the cannon was about to be fired, would certainly approve of the good taste in which it was organized. Every seller had his own dedicated space where he could set up his stand. These stands resembled those set up on the rooftop of the Church of the Holy Sepulchre to sell religious souvenirs in the time leading up to Easter. On one of those small café stools, opposite the café of Khalil Najm where the first part of *Karakoz* was played after sunset, a tray of Aleppo *karabeej* was on display with its magnificent topping of *natef*[60] sprinkled with ground cinnamon, the speciality of George Daoud Yasmina, the famous master of this speciality. In front of the water fountain located opposite the corner of the street leading to Mahallat al-Wad, there was a man called Flous. He was bald and had a sense of humor. Flous also sold this sweet speciality, but since his was dirty, he sold it cheaper than Yasmina's. He also shielded the natef from flies with a cake bell glass cover which he took care to decorate. However, the flies refused to part ways with him and instead lingered in their thousands over his face and clothes. Next to bald Flous was a blue wooden cupboard containing old white glasses filled with carob syrup. This cupboard was like a "branch" of the famous Hajj Khalil's shop that specialized in the sale of this delicious drink and which was located opposite Zalatimo's in Suq Khan al-Zeit.[61] The carob syrup seller would shout at the top of his voice, "God is the healer, carob!" In the middle of this square which was located at a crossroad, sellers of Ramadan barazek sesame cookies, bread, *kaak*, licorice juice, lemonade, and ground *qudama*—roast chickpeas (which was consumed in large quantities by fasters when experiencing dizziness) were everywhere, and it was difficult to walk between them, as each one of them shouted at the top of his voice, advertising his merchandise and praising its quality. And on they went until the cannon was fired. At that moment, everything went silent in the square, and every merchant proceeded to break his fast in his own shop, knowing that the most popular food in this month was barazek.

Speaking of the cannon of Ramadan, traditionally, the cannon was placed on the rooftop of David Castle in Jaffa Gate. When it was fired, particularly at night, it shook the entire city, and the sound could be heard anywhere because of the cannon's elevated location. My brother Tawfiq and I used to sit at the top of the stairs in Dar al-Jawhariyyeh, which was located on a high spot, and watch the cannon being fired from the rooftop of the castle as though it was happening right in front of us. We would have food and drink ready, then each one of us would hold one mouthful in his hand and wait with his mouth open, having made a bet over which one could down the mouthful first after the cannon is fired.

In the evening, the square was decorated and illuminated all the way to Damascus Gate. People sat on the street pavement, under the light of lux lamps, smoking water pipes and listening to the phonograph of Ibrahim al-Bayruti, or to one of the famous singers visiting Jerusalem, such as Sheikh al-Safati or Muhammad al-Ashiq who often visited during Ramadan and sang at the Hospice Café which was located on that street.

PICNICS

The Yahudia Picnic

There are two caves in the quarter of Sheikh Jarrah in Jerusalem, near the lands of Abu Jubna's mortmain which Jews believe to be the graves of Shimon. I think Jews visited these graves twice a year, spending the day under the olives trees. Most of them were Eastern Jews who observed the Eastern traditions, the country's Arab traditions in particular. They had string bands. I remember Haim, the oud player from Aleppo who had a voluptuous high voice and sang Andalusian muwashah mostly.[62] And so, everyone spent the entire day singing songs and uhzujas. The Christian and Muslim Arabs of Jerusalem celebrated with Jews, and families went along to take part in what is known to the Arabs as the Judea Festival. That part of the mountain was therefore crowded all the way down to the valley with locals and ambulant sellers. My brothers and I never wasted an opportunity to be among them.

Daily Summer Picnics at Saad-wa-Said

The festivals held in the Saad-wa-Said Quarter of Jerusalem were merely intended to provide locals, both Christian and Muslim, with an opportunity to go out, and had no religious basis like the other festivals.

The Saad-wa-Said Quarter could be found between the Mosque of Saad-wa-Said, opposite the Dominican Monastery[63] on Nablus Road, and the road running behind al-Mutran English School (Saint George School), near the entrance of Sanhedria.[64] To its south lie the recently built houses of al-Musrara Quarter, starting with the properties of the al-Dizdar family and stretching all the way to those of Hassan Bey al-Turjman.[65] Olive trees abound in this area, and since it is close to the Old City, to Damascus Gate and Bab al-Sahira (Herod's Gate) in particular, the people of Jerusalem have long taken to the habit of going there at sunset when the gates of the city are closed. Thus, in summer, families with children left the city every afternoon and went there for a promenade.

Each family, sometimes joined by another one or two, sat under an olive tree. When the sun was too hot, they shielded themselves with white sheets and blankets, which they tied to the tree branches and let hang down to the ground. And so, they remained there until sunset, smoking water pipes, eating with their children, drinking arak or wine (those of them who were Christian), buying sweets, nuts, grilled green chickpeas, cookies, and the like from ambulant sellers. Saad-wa-Said was indeed the only public promenade for Jerusalemites at the time.[66]

My brothers and I used to accompany my mother to these picnics and enjoy some of the unusual food sold there, despite it being unhygienic, because we found it delicious. I have wonderful memories of the picnics of Saad-wa-Said which, alas, have now ceased due to the decreasing number of olive trees, as well as to the amelioration of living standards.

The Bir Ayyoub Picnic

There is no doubt that it used to rain heavily in Jerusalem, which meant that the sky was gloomy most of the time and we only saw the sun for about three weeks, as ceaseless rain was followed by snow and cold. On the eastern side of the village of Silwan near Jerusalem, there is a well that is known as Bir Ayyoub[67] that has a poor water flow. With the heavy rains, however, the well would fill up and the water would gush out of a hole in it and down into the eastern side of the valley, from where it flowed on until it drained into the Dead Sea. This flooding period lasted about a month, providing the various communities of Jerusalem with an opportunity to bask in the warm rays of the sun after having had to remain indoors, inside the city walls, for a long period of time. Men, women, and children would head there in groups, strolling on both sides of this spring, which was like a river for Jerusalemites. Some took along baskets of food, while others put whatever provisions they were able to buy in a saddlebag and headed for the spring on their donkeys' backs.

The location of Bir Ayyoub was unfortunate, for it happened to be right next to the city sewers. Although waste was channeled out of the city in underground pipes, these turned into open sewers on reaching Bir Ayyoub. So imagine us picnicking and washing our feet in the pure water of Bir Ayyoub, while before us, alas, flowed a large river of foul-smelling waste. I believe that all Jerusalemites have enjoyed this landscape since their early childhood and grew up by the foul smell of the waste.

KARAKOZ (BLACK EYES) AND HAJJ MAHMOUD

The word *karakoz* has a Turkish etymology, *kara* meaning "black" and *göz* meaning "eyes." Karakoz were flat shadow puppets made of animal leather that was thinner than horse leather. Every piece of the shadow's clothing was then colored to match real-life clothing. So to us children, this perfectly made picture seemed to be of real men, women, and animals, and the small objects represented also seemed real in a way that caused both puzzlement and admiration, for this was like a miniature version of today's cinema.

The most important part of this unique art was that of the puppeteer manipulating and animating these small shadows. This was done by just one person who was able to control all the shadows with his hands by himself, by holding a wooden rod for each character. Sometimes he had to hold additional rods in order to move the arms or legs of the characters, depending on the events of the relevant part of that beautiful play. As if that was not enough, the puppeteer also did the voices, keeping his voice in tune with the character he was presenting, so that when he was uttering a certain verse, it was possible to tell if the character speaking was Karakoz, Iwaz, or a lady or boy. Thus, the spectator was under the impression that he was watching real people acting on stage, as those human dwarves moved around, danced, and spoke in a truly dazzling way.

We watched many professionals of this art, who were known as *karakozati*. But we were fortunate to be able to see the most famous one of them all, Hajj Mahmoud, from Tripoli in Lebanon. The late Hajj Mahmoud used to visit Jerusalem for the entire duration of the holy month of Ramadan. Throughout his life, he preferred to visit Jerusalem rather than any other place, moved by the love and popularity he had earned there.

Hajj Mahmoud would begin his show every Thursday at one o'clock Arab time, one hour after Iftar, performing the first act at the café of Khalil Najm. This one-hour act was intended to entertain children before bedtime and told the stories of Arab knights such as Antara bin Shaddad, Abu Zaid al-Hilali, and others. The children watched these tales of Arab bravery and knighthood, and took sides during battles, some siding with Antara, others with Abu Zaid, and so on.

As for the second act, it was also aimed at children and was performed in Bab Hatta. The third act took place at the Austrian Hospice Café in Mahallat el-Wad, and the fourth at a café in Khan el-Zeit or Mahallat al-Nasara, until it was finally time for the fifth and final act, which was the most important one. This act combined literary prose, poetry, unique morals, and poignant criticism, thus attracting the cream of society, including writers, professors, and intellectuals. The audience sat in silence, hearkening and following attentively the movement of the dwarf shadows projected by the lamp that was placed between the shadows and Hajj Mahmoud, and so as not to miss a word or a joke that the great raconteur could utter in one of his moments of genius and creativity. He was talented and intelligent, without a doubt, and I have been told that he knew by heart over ten thousand verses of various genres of poetry. He was, God bless his soul, known for his spontaneous wit, friendly smile, sense of humor, bright mind, and humility, and these fine qualities of his earned him the love of the people.

The ensemble of these shadows was known as *khaymat* Karakoz (Karakoz's tent or "the clown's tent") and comprised a large group of characters. Each act of the play had its own characters, and each one had its own funny name: Karakoz, Iwaz, Shakk Qrina (the wife of Hajj Karakoz), Maouza, Mudallal, Fatfout, Hajj Daqamiqo, Hajj Qraitem,

Khumkhum Bared, the Agha, al-Bakri Mustafa, Ashao Agha, Taraman, and Abu Ouu'. I obtained a number of puppets representing these characters, which I kept in the Jawhariyyeh Collection.

As for the clown's tent, it consisted of a white screen tied on both ends to two opposite corners facing the audience. Hajj Mahmoud sat behind the screen with the lamp placed on a wooden shelf in front him, and in this way the audience could see the shadows in their natural colors. Next to Hajj Mahmud sat a man called Abdul-Salam al-Aqraa who played the riqq and sang part of a muwashah at the start of the act. For example, he would start singing *Ya Hilalan*, (Oh crescent moon), and Karakoz would appear and attempt to dance to the rhythm. All the while, Hajj Mahmoud remained glued to his water pipe, despite being busy with all the hard work. At the end of the act, which lasted about an hour, he would put the light out and, despite his old age, make a quick jump to the café's main entrance where he would stand and take a coin from each of the spectators as they left the café, making sure none of them got away without paying his due and seeing them off jokingly as he addressed each one in their own dialect.

The fifth and final act was performed in the big spacious café of Ali Izheiman and Uncle Abu Zuhdi. In summer, the performance moved to the café's rooftop, which was laid with straw mats. The play later moved to the al-Nabulsi Café which was located opposite Damascus Gate, outside the city wall, and was owned by Hindiya. The act started at midnight and ended just before the cannon was fired.[68]

I honestly remember the majority of Jerusalem's intellectuals being present for this act, such as Sheikh Muhammad Saleh, Nakhla Zureiq, Hajj Sheikh Ali al-Rimawi, Khalil al-Sakakini, Isaaf al-Nashashibi, and others. On Sunday, the play also attracted some Christians who were indeed among the élite of the Christian communities.

The plays were truly superb. Each one—known as an "act"—had its own significance and moral that reflected aspects of our own lives and society. Many of Hajj Mahmoud's words of wisdom remain imprinted on our minds, and to this day we Jerusalemites repeat them proverbially on many occasions. In between the acts, comedy sketches, known as *gharza* in the karakoz slang, were performed. These sketches made spectators laugh so hard that they had to physically struggle to contain themselves. Indeed, my friends and I often fell off the small café stools but did not mind being seen in that state, as everyone else was in the same situation.

Advertisements

Hajj Mahmoud used to incorporate advertisements for the city's merchants within the play. Once Karakoz and Iwaz were discussing a party that the latter was intending to host, and suddenly, Karakoz began making recommendations to Iwaz. "Iwaz, my friend, I have seen the nicest pine nuts today at Hajj Khalil al-Daoudi's spice shop—pure as gold! They just arrived today from Syria. You must buy some for the kunafa. But make sure not to be late because it will all be gone by tomorrow." Then he mentioned a bag of *Ajami* (Persian) tobacco had just arrived at some grocery, pomegranate seeds in Suwayqat Allun, and other merchandise, just like in cinemas today.

Since Hajj Mahmoud was one of the finest water pipe smokers, Uncle Abu Zuhdi, the café owner, had to keep a watchful eye on his water pipe, continuously changing the charcoal. Otherwise, a merciless complaint would be immediately introduced into the dialogue between Karakoz and Iwaz, for he was unable to be creative with his comedy when he was not smoking the water pipe.

We Jerusalemites of the twentieth century remember with deep emotion a man called Fahim Abu Nuuman, from the Nusseibeh family. He was a passionate comedy lover and a great fan of Hajj Mahmoud, and did not miss a single karakoz show throughout the holy month of Ramadan. His seat was in the first row, right next to Abdul-Salam al-Aqraa's, and his laugh was recognizable to all the people of Jerusalem. When he was particularly amused by a joke, he would burst out laughing at the top of his voice.

The customers went on smoking water pipes and drinking beverages, especially soda, until the cannon was fired.

THE *ODA*, OR BACHELORS APARTMENT

At the time, it was customary for Muslim friends or neighbors in any of Jerusalem's neighborhoods to rent a private apartment in one of the buildings of Old Jerusalem, consisting of one or two rooms, with facilities, and hold long evening parties in them, particularly during winter. This kind of bachelor's apartment was known as the *oda* (room). Whenever a musician or singer was visiting, they would take him to the oda and have a special party with their friends. Sometimes they would play cards, dama, dominoes, backgammon, and adrali together, or listen to the good reader among them read out stories of *One Thousand and One Nights*, or Antara, or Abu Zaid. Some people rented such apartments as a place to have love affairs with prostitutes. But many apartments were rented by honorable people, such as the one in

Sheikh Jarrah that was frequented by the finest citizens and intellectuals of Jerusalem.

THE OUD AND I

I continued to play tanboor number one, the rebeck, tanboor number two, and the Indian rebeck for about three years, until I was able to play them all with virtuosity. I played what I had learned from my amateur teachers and succeeded in playing well-known taqtouqas, that I had been singing at the time, with remarkable precision and skill. But given my deep passion for the art of music, I became more ambitious as I realized that I was capable of achieving broader knowledge in this field. So I longed to play the oud, the instrument which, in my belief, has a special status in Arabic music, and in oriental music as a whole.

ABDUL-HAMID QUTTAINEH

My father took it upon himself to do all he could to help me learn this art, and so he had to find me a private teacher. Abdul-Hamid, the son of Asaad Quttaineh, who belonged to one of the oldest families of Jerusalem, was one of the finest amateur oud players around. He was also a friend of my father, who had been a friend of his father, Asaad. It was agreed that Abdul-Hamid would give me oud lessons twice a week at our home. This is how I began to learn to play artistically for the first time. My father would bring him wine and exquisite mezze dishes in person, which made Abdul-Hamid take extra care of my learning. In the beginning, he taught me a dolab, then *Ya sah al-sabr*, and then a piece from the *Basheraf Tanios*,[69] in which I took thirteen lessons. That was all I ever learned from a teacher in terms of playing the oud.

As for tuning the oud, in the beginning I had difficulty with it. Whenever the evening had ended and Abdul-Hamid had left us, I would discover in the morning that the tunes of the strings were different from the night before, as the change in weather conditions had affected the wood. It was difficult at my age to know whether each one of the five double strings was tuned properly, so I came up with a solution. When my teacher left me after the second lesson with my oud perfectly tuned, I took a ruler and placed it crosswise on the strings of the oud between the sound hole and the neck, and traced a line perpendicular to both the body of the oud and the strings. And so, whenever I saw that a string had moved in relation to that straight line, I would pull it back to its initial position using its respective key. I stuck by my invented method until I was able to understand the tuning process both artistically and technically. All visitors to our home who could play the oud were amazed to see this technique.

HAMADA AL-AFIFI

Uncle Abu Fuaad (Hamada al-Afifi) came from one of Jerusalem's well-established Muslim families. He was a senior official in the judiciary and a friend of my father. He was considered one of the finest music amateurs who played the oud and had a good voice. So if he sang a muwashah or a poem, you thought you were actually looking at one of Cairo's most famous musicians. His playing, and the way he picked the string with the feather, could not be emulated by any of the Jerusalemite amateurs. Luckily, after the oud made it to Dar al-Jawhariyyeh, Uncle Abu Fuaad made his visits to my father more frequent. He sang extremely beautifully, entrancing himself, which is, in my opinion, what art is about. For as philosopher Gibran said, "A singer cannot enchant others unless he is enchanted himself." I picked up some unique pieces from him, and our friendship continued after my father passed away. I still sing one of his favorite muwashahat, and I admit that most of what I have achieved in the art of Arabic music, I owe to Abu Fuaad.

As for the teaching method at the time, through which I learned to play, it consisted of the teacher showing the student where to place his fingers while playing short phrases from longer songs or musical pieces, and then handing him the oud so that he would attempt in his turn to play the phrase as he had heard it from the teacher, and which he should be able to remember by heart. Such was the learning method before the shift to Western music notation, and that is the reason why few people excelled in music. For only the truly gifted and passionate were happy and willing to apply themselves and learn through the difficult old method.

AL-SALFITI AND THE OTTOMAN PORTRAITS

Once, on a family visit to the al-Salfiti family who lived right next to Nqula Abdu's home in the Christian Quarter, and while a large number of people chatted in the courtyard and my father smoked the water pipe, we heard a loud noise. Malaka, al-Salfiti's sister, was standing at the top of a flight of steps that led to a toilet at the ground floor. She was angry and distressed, and shouting at the top of her voice, "May God punish you, Mikhail! Enough! Have some pity."

My father left the water pipe and went to check out the matter with the others. We found that Malaka had been talking to her brother who was in the toilet. She told us, "For God's sake, come and see how heartless he is." Suspecting an emergency, we all rushed downstairs, only to find Mikhail in a state of rage, holding an old shoe in his hand and with it beating some portraits that were hanging on the wall in the toilet. These large color portraits were of Sultan Abdul-Hameed, Muhammad Rashad, and other great figures of the Ottoman dynasty. He was in a state of unimaginable agitation and beating the head in the portrait saying, "Enough is enough, you devil. You are wearing us out with your taxes!"

AL-SALFITI AND THE FLEET

For a long period of time, the Turkish government in Jerusalem would urge the people to help buy supplies for the army, the Red Crescent charities, or military aids. The financial situation was dire, and while all these requests and taxes put unbearable strain on the people, no one dared not to comply at that time of injustice and despotism.

It so happened that a police force, headed by Saleh Effendi al-Alami, was going around the city as a special committee to collect donations from the citizens, and stopped by the shop of Salim al-Salfiti who worked as a money changer under the arch of the Christian Quarter. "The despots' vehicle," as people used to call it, stopped and asked for "donations" for the Ottoman fleet. Uncle Mikhail was thrilled by the request and said to them, "You couldn't have come at a better time!" He then went inside, reemerging a moment later with a piece of an old black chain which he presented to the chief, Saleh Effendi, saying, "Take this. You could use it for the fleet's anchor. I can't wait to get rid of it." Saleh Effendi and his company laughed and left the shop, never to come back.

THE TURKS AND THE KURDISH SERGEANT

My father related to me a true incident that occurred at the time of the Ottomans. The Bani Zeid villages of the Ramallah district[70] were refusing to pay any taxes, and payments due for previous years were piling up. The government sent a unit of gendarmerie to escort some of the civil servants of the Finance Department, including my late father, on their mission to forcibly collect the monies due, to protect the image of the state and its tyrannic ruler, Sultan Abdul-Hamid. One of the gendarmes, a sergeant of Kurdish origin, only spoke Turkish and had convinced his companions that he ought to be in charge of collecting the taxes, which he would do in his own way, and very efficiently. All they had to do was to grant him freedom of action. They agreed.

This force, which people referred to as "the tyrants' machine," arrived in the first rebelling Bani Zeid village and went as usual to the village *madafa* (guesthouse). The farmers came at once, and the clerk began his job and read out the name of the first taxpayer, whom I shall call Muhammad Hassan. When Muhammad Hassan, a venerable villager with a long beard, stood up, the Kurdish sergeant sprung with exceptional swiftness, straddled his shoulders and started whipping him, saying, "You pimp, the money." When the man was told the amount, he went off with the Kurd still on his shoulders, until he reached his home where his wife and children saw him in this shameful situation. He asked his wife to get the purse hidden under the clay urn, opened it up, took the money, and handed it to the Kurdish sergeant. The sergeant got off, showering him with strong Turkish swearwords and returned to the madafa.

The clerk then called on another, whom I shall call Hassan Musa and who owed forty-eight piasters. As soon as his name was called, the sergeant had the gendarmes drag him out, tied a fine rope to his testicles, and dragged him in the alleys of the village while the villagers looked on, until he reached his home in that terrifying and shameful state. After the clerk received the full amount from him in the presence of his family, he undid the rope, also obliging him with some strong language and returned immediately to the madafa to get creative with his tax collection mission.

After this ghastly show, the villagers immediately dispatched a messenger to the neighboring villages, warning them of the horrific deeds of this Kurdish sergeant and advising them to have the required amounts ready immediately. And so it was. When the clerk called on a certain taxpayer in the madafa, the latter was standing there vigilantly, holding a considerable sum of money which he would then hand immediately to the sergeant inside the madafa, lest he might get straddled or tied to a rope. In a short time, the government collected all the overdue taxes from all the Bani Zeid villages and returned to Jerusalem jubilantly victorious.

The injustice and tyranny of the Ottoman state ruled the country with fire and iron for more than four centuries, until it finally met its end. "A tyrant's home is doomed to ruin, even if only after much delay."

THE COUP D'ÉTAT CELEBRATIONS

When the Ottoman coup d'état took place in Istanbul in July 1908, there was much jubilation among government officials, and more so amongst Arab people who labeled it the "Coup of Freedom" that would bring them "freedom, justice, and equality." Jews in Jerusalem secretly mocked the coup, which they described as scorching, saying that it would lead to disaster. This coup was led by the army officers who together formed the Committee of Union and Progress under the leadership of Niazi, Anwar (Enver), Jamal, and others, and who succeeded in deposing Sultan Abdul-Hameed, the tyrant who ruled over thirty-three years of brutality, injustice, and despotism, plunging the country into a state of unequaled poverty and ignorance. If he ever heard of someone rebelling in his country, or any Arab country, he would diplomatically but cunningly send after them and bring them over to Istanbul where he would end their life, until people were gripped by fear and terror, and all potential rebels were eradicated.

Following the coup and the accession of the sultan's brother, Muhammad Rashad, to the throne, decorations were put up and

Portrait by Khalil Raad of Jamal Pasha and his staff.
© Institute for Palestine Studies, Beirut.

celebrations held all over the country. I clearly remember those days and nights. At the time, my brother Tawfiq and I were attending the primary school known as the German Dabbaghah School (the Schneller School). The city of Jerusalem was glowing with lights, as every house, building, institute, shop, and street was lit with candles (there was no electricity at the time) placed inside small lamps. For weeks, the city was decorated with flags, flowers, and tree branches, and the people celebrated with great joy and jubilation. Since my father was in charge of the municipal park, al-Manshia, my brothers and I were able to enjoy watching many of the official celebrations that were held there on a nightly basis. The military band marched in the city streets every day, entertaining the citizens, and in the afternoon it played in the park until after sunset. Every citizen owned a gun, for at the time, possession of all kinds of weapons was allowed. As people were carried away by the trance of victory, shots were fired into the air, in the streets or at home, giving the impression of a battlefield.

Damascus Gate stood out for its decorations which exceeded all others. The people of Damascus Gate, Saadiyeh, and al-Wad neighborhoods had come together and spent profusely to build four arches of triumph above the roads leading to Notre Dame de France, al-Musrara, Nablus Road, and finally Jericho Road. The gate itself was adorned with the best decorations and lights, and the spacious square between these arches was packed with people, as the singing, dancing, cheering, national anthems, and soul-stirring hymns went on until dawn. The people of Bab Hutta and other neighborhoods were also invited to join in the celebrations and partying, so they did. I remember that outside Damascus Gate, there were barrels full of fresh rosewater-flavored lemonade for people to help themselves to. These unique celebrations were the first of their kind to be held in the country to mark the end of the age of force and despotism of Sultan Abdul-Hameed the tyrant, and I will not forget them as long as I live.

HUSSEIN EFFENDI IS APPOINTED HEAD OF THE MUNICIPALITY OF JERUSALEM

Following the Ottoman coup, elections were held in Jerusalem to elect a head for the municipality, as well as the two representatives.[71] Hussein Effendi won the head of the municipality of Jerusalem and immediately took over from his predecessor, Faydi Effendi al-Alami, while Ragheb Bey al-Nashashibi and Said Bey al-Husseini became the representatives of the Jerusalem district.

I recall that following his new appointment, Hussein Effendi renovated the building located outside Jaffa Gate which belonged to the municipality and was at the time a hotel (Al-Jamal Hotel). He had a special flight of steps built outside, and the building thus became the headquarters of the municipality of Jerusalem, based outside the wall for the first time. Previously, it had been based inside the wall, near the offices of government which were part of the mortmain and which were later turned into an Islamic orphanage run by Jamil Wahbah.

SHEIKH SALAMA HIJAZI IN JERUSALEM, SUMMER 1908

"O Lord of the chosen one, grant us what we seek, and be pleased with us, O Most Generous."[72]

From the minaret of a mosque of the seaside city of Alexandria, a voice reached the ear of theater artist and entrepreneur, Iskandar Farah.[73] Later on, during his trip from Cairo to Alexandria, Farrah conceived of the idea to bring to the stage the muezzin who was not known at the time. By doing so, he marked the beginning of a new era for Egypt after the age of al-Naqqash and Abu Khalil al-Qabbani,[74] that of the muezzin Sheikh Salama Hijazi. The famous musician and great actor Hijazi was born in Alexandria in 1278 Hijra.[75] In his first appearance, he performed the role of Curiace in "May and Horace." His teacher Suleiman Haddad played Horace,[76] and he remained in Iskandar Farah's troupe for about fifteen years.

The late Hussein Hashem al-Husseini became mayor of Jerusalem at a time when the Ottoman coup was proving to be a historical revolution, thanks to which the people were now basking in justice, equality, and freedom. Great celebrations were organized to entertain the people. One of Hussein Effendi's good deeds was that he brought Sheikh Salama Hijazi from Cairo to Jerusalem. He came with his large troupe that included George Abyad,[77] and Hussein Effendi rented a tent for them that was set up adjacent to the city wall. The tent, which Hussein Effendi rented from the Franciscan Monastery in Jerusalem, was one of the largest in the country.

Sheikh Salama and his unique troupe gave performances of a number of immortal plays and stories, including the story of Saladdin, in which he sang with his affectionate voice *In kuntu fi al-jayshi* (If I were in the army, I'd be the flag holder). He also gave a performance of the story of the love martyrs Romeo and Juliet, and we listened to the famous poem (which I had always sung since I was a child) starting with *salamun 'ala Husni yadi-l-mawt* (Peace be upon the beauty of the hand of death). His performance of this song was more than excellent. Sheikh Salama was suffering from partial paralysis, and as all his roles involved singing melancholic music, the audience cried out loud as they listened to him sing, unable to walk, and dragging his bad leg along while he placed his other hand over his head. He only went on with his singing and acting career out of love and dedication for this fine art, which was his raison d'être. There were some Greek spectators who did not understand Arabic, and yet they cried as though they were at a funeral, moved by his unique, affectionate voice and by the way he sang and acted.

A ticket to see Sheikh Salama cost half a French franc, a high price at the time considering the living standards, as this great musician was highly regarded and extremely popular. Thanks to Hussein Effendi, I had the fortune to be able to attend all his evening performances in Jerusalem. The cherry on top was that I was able to kiss his hands in the reception room of the municipality. I was eleven at the time. I went in and kissed the hands of Hussein Effendi and begged him to give me the opportunity to kiss those of our Sheikh. My wish was fulfilled immediately, and then I went to see my father who had been in the office of Elias Effendi Habib, the department's chief clerk. I was over the moon.

WHY WE LEFT THE SCHNELLER SCHOOL

In 1909, the time when my brother Tawfiq and I were attending the Schneller School, my brother Khalil was working as a carriage carpenter at the workshop of Mitri Abu Shanab and his brothers, which was located on Jaffa Street, outside the wall. My father was managing the municipal park. Every night the events of our school day were the only topics of conversation my brother Tawfiq and I could think of while chatting with our parents. Like all the other schoolchildren, we hated Mr. Beshara who was harsh and despotic, and used to beat the children for no good reason. So my brother Khalil, who was known among his friends for his boldness, had a good idea. Once when Mr. Beshara was walking down Jaffa Street, he passed Mitri Abu Shanab's workshop while Tawfiq and I were playing there. Since we were keen for Khalil to see what Mr. Beshara looked like, we said to him, "Khalil, this is Mr. Beshara! Look, look!" Khalil left work and went after Mr. Beshara, clapping his hands and shouting as loudly as he could, "Mr. Beshara, Mr. Beshara!" Mr. Beshara turned around and recognized only Wasif and Tawfiq. After all, he did not know Khalil. When we realized that

Mr. Beshara had noticed us, we said, "We're dead. God knows what he will do to us tomorrow. What do you think you are doing, Khalil?"

We left Khalil and headed for al-Manshiah Park where my father was smoking a water pipe with his friends. Since he was a lawyer, we brought our complaint to him. His reply: "Don't be afraid. When he asks you about it, tell him it was your brother calling *Uncle* Beshara, not *Mr.* Beshara!"[78] We said "But Father, he'd never give us a chance to explain what happened. You don't know what this teacher is like." "Don't worry," he insisted. So the next day we went to school against our will.

At three o'clock Mr. Beshara entered the classroom for his one-hour mathematics class, but knocked on the door so hard and with so much anger that I thought, "God help us." He stood there with evil glowing in his eyes, pointed at me with his right index finger, and shouted, "The young Jawhariyyeh." I went to him, and he slapped me so hard I fell over, hitting the organ, then the first row of benches, and finally landed on the floor. I wet myself and held my head in my hands, screaming as loud as I could. So he left me and turned his attention to my brother, Tawfiq. The teacher chased him from one bench to another, beating him with his cane stick, first between the benches, then between the students, as Tawfiq quickly gave in to him, until Mr. Jiryis and the schoolmistress arrived at the end of the session. I kept looking at the door, thinking could I manage to open the latch and run away?

We went back home and told Father what had happened. My father intervened and wanted to take the case to court, so teacher Beshara came to our place and offered his apologies in the presence of teacher Jiryis and some others. We continued to go to school for a few days and then transferred, with the help of Mr. Hussein Hashem al-Husseini, to the school of Khalil al-Sakakini. Such was the despotism in education at the time. God bless the soul of Gibran who said, "They told me one was the slave of him who taught one a letter, and so I remained ignorant but free."

JOINING THE NATIONAL SCHOOL

In the wake of the Ottoman coup, citizens were granted freedom to rise in their social and political lives. People finally breathed relief, particularly across the Arab nations which still constituted one body at the time. Indeed, the country begun to see improvement in the standard of living, as well as a rise in ambition, particularly for education. The great teacher and educator Khalil al-Sakakini embraced this opportunity to set up the Dusturiyyeh National School in one of the properties of Hajj Ismail al-Najjar, in Musrara. He was joined in his enterprise by

Mr. Ali Jarullah, Aftim al-Moushabeck, and Jamil al-Khalidi, and the school soon became extremely attractive to the various communities of the city. The school also included a boarding section, in which Arabic, Turkish, and French were taught. After Tawfiq and I left the German Dabbaghah School, my father made my brother join the Greek Orthodox boarding school in Jaffa. Unfortunately he ran away and returned to Jerusalem, forcing my father to take him out of education and make him learn a vocation instead.

As for me, after a long period during which I accompanied my father on his business journeys, particularly around Deir Amr, the late Hussein Effendi al-Husseini intervened for me, after he was appointed mayor of Jerusalem, and I joined Dusturiyyeh as a day student, to my great fortune. For there I acquired enough education to secure my future.

Mr. al-Sakakini taught us Arabic in a way that was very popular with the students. He used a method which, to my knowledge, few teachers in the East liked to use. He did not make students memorize rules of grammar like most teachers used to do, but instead would give them a short sentence in which he had combined all the relevant rules of grammar and conjugation, without resorting to course books. His lessons included anecdotes which the students of this great educator received with eagerness and excitement. For with him they were able to understand what it took them long hours to grasp with other teachers. He instilled in them patriotism and manliness. He valued honesty, virtue, and integrity, and his humanity knew no boundaries. He always told us to look after our bodies, reminding us of the saying "a sound mind in a sound body," and urged us to keep exercising regularly. He also advised us to nourish ourselves by eating plenty of meat, particularly chicken, although he himself passed away for a reason that I still do not know.

Having chosen to name his school the "Dusturiyyeh," or National, School, al-Sakakini was the first to ban corporal punishment in education, and this wise stance spread to other schools. Whenever he noticed the slightest inappropriate conduct on the part of a student, particularly on the moral level, not withstanding his fatherly love for the pupil in question, he went berserk and pulled on an angry face, frightening the student who had the utmost respect and esteem for him and who would then amend his behavior immediately. There is no doubt that he instilled high values in his students and was an exemplary teacher and educator.

Professors Aftim Moushabeck and Jamil al-Khalidi taught us beginner's English and French, while Hajj Sharif al-Husseini taught us Turkish. I benefited greatly from the English lessons I took for the first time with Teacher Labiba. I think she was from Lebanon or Syria, and thanks to her I did well and succeeded in being admitted to an upper level. As for Adib Abdu, the brother of Mrs. Sultana, the wife of Professor al-Sakakini, he taught us arithmetic. He later left the country for America and remained there, alas. I also remember Hanna Zakharia, who also taught us after joining the Turkish army in the wake of the Ottoman coup. He was the brother of Mrs. Farida, the sister of Andony Atallah. Mr. Jadaoun was from Lebanon and taught us sports the impeccable French military way.

More importantly, Professor al-Sakakini decided to give Christian pupils the opportunity to read the Qu'ran, if they chose to. Encouraged by my late father, I seized this opportunity with both hands. Her ladyship the late Umm Musa Kazem Pasha al-Husseini presented me with an elegant copy of the Holy Qu'ran that was printed in Istanbul and taught me how to respect the Qu'ran and observe hygiene when touching it. So I learned the Qu'ran from the subject teacher, Sheikh Amin al-Ansari, who was an illustrious figure in Jerusalem. Professor al-Sakakini was of the opinion that the essence of the Arabic language, particularly elocution, consisted in the ability to perform classical readings of the Qu'ran. I took these classes along with my brothers and many of my Muslim Jerusalemite classmates. I began with *Surat al-Baqarah* (The Cow).[79] I am most grateful to this opportunity for the

Teachers and students of al-Dusturiyyeh School in Jerusalem. Khalil Sakakini, the school's founder, is seated second from the left. From the private Collection of the Theodorie family in Bethlehem.

impact it had on my life, particularly with regard to singing and Arabic music, for I felt proud of my pronunciation when I sang muwashahat, and more so when singing poems, in the presence of masters of the Arabic language.

THE CINEMATOGRAPH

I recall one time when my brothers and I, as well as my mother and our neighbors, particularly the family of Mitri Abdullah al-Muna, decided together to see the cinematograph[80] for the first time, in 1910 (at age thirteen) when I was still a student at the National School.

When the shows started at the cinema, we were able to see them at the theater hall located in Feingold House on Jaffa Road, opposite the Russian Compound (the intelligence section in the mandate era). A ticket cost one Turkish *bishlik*.[81] We were amazed to see the silent footage, particularly that the characters were moving as in real life, which we had never seen before, and so we thanked the Lord for his blessings.

As for the building itself, it was a monumental bloc of stores and apartmentss. It was sold later on to the mayor of Beit Jala, Mr. Makhlouf, while the eastern part of it, which was owned by Mrs. Catlinek, was the residence of Ibrahim Antebi, the head of the Jewish Alliance School in Jerusalem. The building was sold during the British Mandate period.

THE MAGIC LANTERN

A magic lantern projects a magnified picture onto a wall or screen. The picture is in color, but motionless. We got to see it at a show by a German troupe that had been invited by the Schneller School to perform at the Dabbaghah Building where the school was based. It was a good thing for society, and for students in particular, for it enabled them to see places which it would have been hard for them to see in real life, particularly the historical sites in Arab countries such as Petra (Wadi Musa) in East Jordan, Jerash, Wadi al-Mujib, the Dead Sea's Lisan Peninsula and Mount Sodom, Amman Philadelphia,[82] Baalbeck, and other places. Educator Elias Haddad from the Schneller School provided detailed information and description to go with each scene.

SANDOUK AL-AJAB, OR THE WONDER BOX

The Wonder Box (Magic Box) looked much like a cupboard. It was semicircular and had six thick wooden compartments. Each of these compartments had a circular glass hole through which one could look inside the box and see magnified pictures in natural colors. The pictures slid around a wooden pole which the box's operator rotated with his hand, making them move in a succession. There was, of course, another wooden pole opposite the first on the other end of the box.

The box had five or six peep holes. We used to sit on a wooden bench and look through them at the pictures, while the box's owner loudly explained, "This is Egypt! This will blow you away! Have a look!" and other catchphrases designed to attract children like us. The Wonder Box was often ambulant, moving around the streets, particularly during festivals and yearly occasions in the city. In order to protect it from the evil eye, the box was decorated with a blue bead and garlic clove. We used to await its visit to Jerusalem with overexcitement.

THE STORYTELLER

It was traditional for the cafés of Jerusalem which were located inside the city wall to bring storytellers to tempt customers into the café and entertain them with something appealing, particularly in winter. The storyteller used to sit on a high platform at the most central spot in the café so that he could be seen and heard by everyone. Then, he would loudly read to them the stories of Antara and Abla, Abu Zaid al-Hilali,[83]

Photo of the Wonder Box by Khalil Raad.
© Institute for Palestine Studies.

and Prince Umara, for these were folktales with morals on heroism, chivalry, virtue, and knighthood. Hajj Jawdat bin Moussa al-Halabi, who was one of the well-known Muslim figures of Jerusalem in his younger years, was particularly fond of reading these tales, which he did at the café of Abdul-Latif in Bab Hatta, drawing large crowds of people who came all the way from al-Baq'aa al-Fawqa in cold and rainy weather, and stayed until midnight. Such was the appeal of Hajj Jawdat's full, rotund voice and great personality. His reading, elocution, and pronunciation were impeccable, and the way in which he articulated words made him seem indeed like the hero of that story. He usually read out the story of Antara and Prince Umara, and the audience attended every evening until the story ended.[84] In this way, young men of the time learned and understood the true meaning of patriotism, virtue, revenge on an aggressor, and knighthood.

JERUSALEM'S RUSSIAN COMPOUND IN OTTOMAN TIMES

Al Maskobiyyeh, the Russian compound, was built on Jaffa Road on a piece of land that was known as Umm al-Summaq and belonged to the village of Lifta. It was sold to the Russians by the families of Nasr, Salama, and Khalaf, who were all from the village of Lifta.[85] This majestic compound consisted of a number of buildings, each one comprising two floors dedicated for a particular purpose. It was built according to Arabic architectural design, with masterfully erected cross-arches. The walls of these buildings were no less than one-and-a-half meters thick, and the windows were made with two sets of glass shutters, with space between them to block the cold. These buildings had heavy wooden flooring which, following the Russian way, was painted with a dense layer of oil paint once a year until it turned into one large warm tile that insulated the room against humidity and cold. The buildings had large wood-burning stoves which were especially brought over from Russia. No buildings of other countries in Jerusalem had a similar one.

These buildings had their own green spaces, with orchards, cypress, pine, and olive trees, and were surrounded by a massive stone wall with the municipal park to the east; the Russian Compound Street, the Mea She'arim Road to the north; and Jaffa Road to the south. So imagine what the plaza of this building looked like! At the center of these buildings was the famous Russian church. Everyone in Jerusalem recognized the sound of the bells of this beautiful church, particularly when they resounded at four o'clock, every day of the year. The walls of the buildings had four main gates, one on each side. The most important one was the eastern gate that led to Jerusalem. When we were children, citizens were allowed to enter the bloc through the eastern gate and wander under the trees in the orchards until prayer time at four o'clock. The gates were guarded by strong, black gatekeepers. We also used to see some unique dogs, almost the size of donkeys and with pitch-black frizzy hair, which had also been brought from Russia. During Easter the children of the city were allowed to enter the compound and climb the church bell tower to ring the bells. We awaited this opportunity impatiently, and we rang the different-sounding bells with joy and pleasure.

The Russian pilgrims went around the Holy Land on foot, for example walking from Jerusalem to Jericho to the River Jordan and back, although some of them were over eighty or ninety years of age. Wherever they happened to arrive, they would sit to drink tea on the side of the main roads. Many families in our country depended on these pilgrims for their living, selling them tea, sugar, bread, cheese, and meat, earning large sums of money which sufficed them for the whole year. There were also the donkey riders, carriages, horses, and mules that ferried the food and provisions needed to maintain these thousands of people. They used to pray on the slightest occasions. We used to see the ladies among them walking around the streets. When they needed to relieve themselves, they would spread their legs while standing, sign the cross three times from the forehead to the chest, and then relieve themselves. You could hear the gurgle of the water as it flowed on the ground in the street. Finally the lady would sign the cross again and resume walking.

The Street Leading from the Russian Compound to the City

Since my father was in charge of the municipal park, which was located opposite the eastern gate of the Russian Compound, my brothers and I headed for the park every day after school and stayed there with my father until evening. I have the warmest memories of the street that runs along the northern fence of the park. This street remains imprinted on my mind, and I will never, ever forget it. I recall it as though looking at it for real and remember how it was crowded with Russians, particularly during the two-month period before Easter. This street became deserted after the Russian revolution.

All the stores located on the ground floor of Lord Bayouk Building, which was built on the left side of the street leading to the city through the eastern gate of the compound, sold foodstuffs that were popular with Russians, including bread, cheese, pumpkins, raisins, and all kinds of alcoholic beverages, knowing that business in these shops did not cease day or night.

Likewise, all the stores located on the ground floors of the adjacent buildings, including those of Kukia and Salim Meo, sold all the requirements of the Russians. Opposite Lord's building, on the right side, inside the iron fence of the park, sellers set up stalls offering all kinds of goods and defended their allocated space to the last centimeter. Russian bread was baked in bakeries inside the compound. We enjoyed eating a particular variety of it, called *khleb*, which was sour and salty. This loaf was made to perfection and so dry on the inside that we were puzzled by how they were able to bake it like that.

Heaps of red-dyed Easter eggs were also piled up on the pavement, next to the samovars. These were sold to Russians day and night. It seemed as though a herd of black sheep was grazing up and down the street, one shopping, one drinking, another praying and signing the cross. It was a beautiful sight, and the locals made a lot of money from those sheep.

The children of al-Zaghloul used to sell walking canes which they made out of cypress seed balls. They made handles from olive wood, carving them in the shape of a camel and decorating them with crosses. All pilgrims—men and women—used these sticks to lean on while walking. As for the block located to the east of the municipal park, on the spot where the municipality of Jerusalem now stands, and where Barclays Bank was built at the time of Ragheb Bey al-Nashashibi,[86] it comprised a number of wooden stores which were let to people from the Arab Greek Orthodox community. The first of these shops belonged to the late Youssef al-Harami, the father of Hanna, Shukri, James, Farah, and Elias, and sold rosaries, crosses, olive wood crafts, and particularly thyme oil, which he sold in small white bottles at relatively extortionate prices (he used to buy thyme oil canisters from Persifon, the mistress of Hussein Effendi al-Husseini). He also sold icons of the various saints. There was also the shop of Nicola Mitri al-Brinkh, who sold various kinds of alcoholic beverages such as arak, wine, and cognac to the Russians, and particularly to the women who were addicted to alcohol. We used to see them downing white alcohol as though they were drinking pure water. There was also Gibran al-Ajrab's excellent grocery, then the shop of Mitri Khashram and his brother who specialized in selling pictures of the country's historical holy sites, as well as magnifying glasses.

Peasant women used to come from the villages of the Jerusalem district— most of them from Ain Karem—and line the two sides of the street, from the gate of the Russian Compound all the way to the gate of the Greek Orthodox Monastery via New Gate. Russians filled these long streets day and night. Most of these peasant women spoke Russian and sold flowers of the Holy Land, as well as sage, rosemary, thorns, and wood. I remember the varieties of dried meat sold on these streets to Russian pilgrims, including fesikh, baccala, smoked fish, octopus, sardines, palamida,[87] as well as snails, vegetables, leek, potatoes, spring onions, and other products.

As for the New Gate neighborhood, all the shops in it were rented to Arab members of our community[88] such as Gregory Anastas and Costandi Anastas, and the families of al-Sahhar, al-Habash, Qurt, Atallah, and others who used to lathe olive and cypress wood and make wooden camels, walking sticks, boxes, cigarette boxes, and crosses, as well as the wood used in icon making. Russian pilgrims bought these items in daytime as well as at night, particularly the various camel models which were made from the holy olive wood, as well as from cypress wood.

THE JERICHO FESTIVAL

On the Greek Orthodox Epiphany in 1911, my sister Afifeh, who was married to Qustandi Abdul-Nour, made arrangements to attend this holy festival in the River Jordan with about seventeen families of their friends and acquaintances. Since I had succeeded in learning to play the oud, my father allowed me to go with Afifeh and her family, and so all of us—men, women, and children—rode on donkeys and mules, leaving through Saint Stephen's Gate.[89] I would never forget this trip, for many times a lady would fall off the donkey's back, then the donkey of another lady would trip while she was riding on it, and another lady would break the saddle's strap. In the meantime, everyone cheered and sang throughout the journey, and the hunting rifles and guns that most of the men had brought along were fired into the air.

We had a first rest at Amarat al-Hawdh where we had some of the food we had brought, and after the animals were fed and given to drink, we traveled on until we reached Khan al-Ahmar,[90] before arriving in al-Marazi where we also had a brief rest. Our convoy finally descended via Aqabat Jaber, as it was closer to the Nabi Musa Road.[91] It was afternoon, and unfortunately the weather changed and there was a thunderstorm followed by heavy rains that poured misery on us, particularly on the women and children. As for me, my only worry was to protect the oud I was carrying and which I covered with a raincoat.

We reached our destination at sunset, after the weather had improved, and we agreed to stay at Al-Jalajal Hotel which was run by Abu

Nimr al-Shemali and Iriqat, the hotel's owner at the time. This hotel is currently located opposite the Latin Monastery on the eastern side. It was sold by the Iriqat family to the Greek Orthodox Monastery and then annexed to the lands of the monastery and the adjoining church. Since the hotel's few rooms were already full, we had to sleep on the mattresses that had been laid out on the floor in the hotel's spacious hall. There were about sixty of us, so imagine, my friend, what that night was like with all these people lying one next to the other all over the floor in the hall.

The party kicked off, we began drinking, and I sat next to Mitri al-Muna (Abu Costa). Our darbouka player Issa al-Sous and Mitri al-Zaair sat next to me, and together we formed an ensemble and started to sing. Abu Costa sang on a high pitch, particularly when he was singing folk songs and *mawwals*.[92] Everyone was singing the chorus of the beautiful taqtouqas that were popular at the time, and we were all in a state of enchantment and joy. I remember it was at this party that I had my first drink, as Uncle Elias al-Qazzaz forced me to drink two glasses of arak. I recall that the late Rashid Ereqat called on us early in the evening. He was a venerable man who wore his sword strapped to his side, and was accompanied by Uncle Abu Nimr al-Shemali and Abu Jamila al-Shemali. Then, the women started laying mattresses on the floor, which was a pleasant sight. After everyone went to their own spot, in their nightclothes, and all gas lamps except a small one were turned off, I sat on my mattress, reached for the oud that had been lying above my head on the wooden floor, and started playing. Since most of the men were drunk, we started again and kept going until daybreak. Because the rain was terribly heavy, we could not resume our trip to River Jordan, particularly since the roads were rather bad at the time, and we stayed at the hotel for three days and kept partying.

When the weather improved a bit, Uncle Abu Nimr, who was swept away when he heard me sing and play the oud, presented me with a large orange branch from his own orange grove to bring to my father who was his good friend, and we returned home the way we had come to Jericho.

KHALIL JOINS THE GENDARMERIE

Since his youth, my brother Khalil had been finding himself embroiled in troublesome incidents. This became a source of worry for my father who was concerned about them, soon ran out of patience, and thought of a solution that would both benefit Khalil and relieve him of having to deal with his aberrant behavior. When Khalil neared army enlistment age, my father submitted an official application to the government and expressed his wish to present his much loved and cherished son, Khalil, who was born to him after four girls, to serve in the gendarmerie in Beirut, starting immediately, before he was called to duty by the government. Indeed, Khalil was accepted and traveled to Beirut where he remained for the entire duration of the Great War, during which my father sadly passed away without seeing Khalil.

Had my father wanted to, he could have withdrawn Khalil from the service and made him marry a foreign girl, as Christians used to do at the time,[93] or made him learn a vocation so that he did not have to go through the ordeal of carrying a weapon and serving in the Turkish army while he was still a youth. But his love and loyalty for his country, as well as Khalil being the ideal young man to carry arms, made my father gladly accept the idea of Khalil serving in the army.

Wasif's brother Khalil in military uniform during his service in the gendarmerie in Beirut. Jawhariyyeh Collection © Institute for Palestine Studies, Beirut.

JOINING THE ENGLISH SAINT GEORGE'S SCHOOL IN JERUSALEM

Hussein Effendi, who was like a second father to me, wanted me to leave the Dusturiyyeh National School. He had me enrolled at the English Saint George's School in order for me to improve my command of the English language and my prospects for the future. I joined the school in the beginning of 1912 (at age fifteen) and continued to attend it until Turkey joined the First World War, which saw the school being closed down in the beginning of 1914. I was in the fourth year of secondary school at the time, and the closure of this school regrettably marked the end of my education, as I was not able to resume my studies or even obtain a certificate from this school.

A TRIP WITH HUSSEIN EFFENDI AND MY FATHER

I was lucky to enjoy the privileged treatment of my father who took me along on a trip with Mr. Hussein Effendi al-Husseini when the latter was the mayor of Jerusalem. It was summer, and after spending three days in Deir Amr, we grabbed tanboor number two and headed for Beit Suseen where we spent five days, during which Hussein Effendi worked really hard, seeing the farmers of Saris[94] and Beit Mahsir. The tribunal was set up in the orange grove, and from morning until afternoon he dealt with the farmers' complex disputes which could not be solved in court. After these disputes were resolved, we had to go to Beit Mahsir.[95]

The Village of Beit Mahsir

We headed for this village of the Jerusalem district with Hussein Effendi riding a gray-blue bicycle, while my father traveled on his donkey, and I on the donkey of one of the farmers of Beit Susin, which gave me a hard time during this journey.

On arriving, we were warmly received by the locals who insisted that we spend some time in their village. But, after a brief rest we resumed our journey to the top of the village's mountain and were amazed to be able to see all the neighboring villages, including the more remote ones, considering the elevation of the spot which was strategic and one of the unique village locations of the Jerusalem district.

This mountaintop was populated with old pine trees, which added to the beauty of our surroundings, particularly as it was summertime. This was in 1912 (at age fifteen), if I remember well. The tombs of the village were interspersed in the shade of these trees. What impressed us was the large size of these tombs, as well as their height, which made them seem like small houses and meant that visitors did not recognize them as tombs. One felt at ease and wasn't terrified or frightened to be there. We spent four days and nights in that place. They laid mattresses over the tombs for us, and what a sweet sleep it was. Around us, the good villagers partied and danced to the music of the reed in the moonlight. It was one of the moonlit nights of the twelfth to sixteenth of the lunar month, and I will not forget this trip as long as I live.

The sheikh of this village, God bless his soul, was famous for his generosity. Sheikh Ali Saleh was an elderly man of about eighty who loved Hussein Effendi and had been one of the men of his father, Hajj Salim Effendi. In the morning and evening we ate a delicious *mansaf*,[96] which was always a rather majestic one, given the wealth and luxury that this village enjoyed compared to the rest of the villages of the Jerusalem district. I did not have the opportunity to sing while playing the tanboor when I was there, because the villagers themselves were singing continuously, but I joined them to dance the dabkeh to the song "Listen, folks, to what the wise man said." My father had brought along his famous bag; they were inseparable on such trips. In it, he kept some orange blossom water, rose water, onions, garlic cloves, some *qershalleh*,[97] a piece of pastrami, some thread, a packing needle, some needles and pins, a pair of pliers, a pair of pincers, candied chickpeas, sugared mints, liquorice extract, Epsom salts, cotton, antiseptic liquid, some mercurochrome, a box containing the coffeepot, coffee, cardamom, a small water pipe inside the box as well as a small alcohol stove, some charcoal, and most importantly a large bottle of arak and an arak flask. And so, every day, before dinner, and often in the afternoon as well, my father enjoyed a drink, secretly, passing a glass over to Hussein Effendi, which he often did through me. I will never forget this village, particularly the great Sheikh Ahmed Saleh, may God bless his soul and rest him in heaven, for he was one of the most respectable farmers of the entire district. Four days later, and after I exchanged my donkey for a better one that had a modest Jerusalem-made saddle, we headed for al-Sanabira and Umm al-Burj.

PROFESSIONAL MUSICIANS IN JERUSALEM DURING THE OTTOMAN ERA

As a Jerusalemite music lover, I believe that there was a shortage of musicians during the Ottoman period, particularly male musicians, in this peaceful city. Instead, Jerusalem was visited by well-known singers and chanters from Egypt or Syria.

Between 1900 and 1914, I listened to the ensemble of the Sons of Abu al-Sibaa'. This excellent band played for the people of Jerusalem, entertaining them in cafés and at celebrations. The ensemble members were qanun player Abdullah, percussionist Omar who was from the same family, and Ibrahim Abu Khalil who was from Haifa and was, I think, Jerusalem's first oud player. There was also their son Arif Abu al-Sibaa who was talented. He had a good voice and consistently tried to emulate the singing of Egyptian singers, particularly in *dawrs* and mawwals.[98] As for oud player Uncle Abu Khalil, he was a neighbor of ours, since he lived opposite Dar al-Jawhariyyeh in Saadiyeh. I used to listen to him through the window play exercises on the oud, and I learned from him how to pick the strings with the feather and how to do it with vehemence, when needed.

Abdul-Salam al-Aqraa' used to sing some muwashahat while playing percussion and accompanying Hajj Mahmoud, the Karakoz and Iwaz animator, on Ramadan nights. As for professional Arab janaki who performed at celebration parties, I remember. Asmaa al-Qaraa', the wife of Fayyad, who was famous for singing on a high pitch. She lived with her husband opposite our house in Saadiyeh. There was also Khayzaran, the qanun player who performed beautifully at parties. She had a daughter who tried to become a musician but did not do well. I have heard both of them play, so I am able to give this testimony. Then came Amina al-Ammawiya who was from the Jerusalemite al-Ammawi family. She danced with agility and grace, and was very popular, particularly with men, because she lisped, pronouncing the *s* as *sh* which made the extremely inebriated men very excited.

After Amina, there was Thuraya Qaddoura and her father who was a sergeant at the prison. She was an exceptional singer and had a strong, entrancing voice. Jerusalem had musical bands which were known as "instrumentalist ensembles," and which were made up of Eastern Jewish musicians from Aleppo. These musicians were passionate about Arabic music and made sure the muwashahat were immaculately preserved, but they used to change the language and the content of the songs. We often went to see and listen to them in the Jewish Halabia Quarter,[99] as well as in Habsa Street and al-Basal and Montefiori. Arabs used to invite them to their wedding celebrations where they gave excellent performances. Among these musicians were Haim, who played the violin and also the oud for which he was famous, and Zaki al-Halabi the percussionist and tireless singer who had a voluptuous, although not sufficiently affectionate, voice. As for the Jewish janakis, there was Sulika, who was well-known to the people of Jerusalem. She was the leader of the band and was accompanied by dancer Fariha and others. There is not a single Arab Muslim or Christian house in Jerusalem whose celebrations had not been led by Sulika, who converted to Islam. Singer Khayzaran Abdu married a man from the Jerusalemite al-Assaly family.

Finally came the time of Frusu Zahran, an excellent singer and oud player who famously provided entertainment at unforgettable evening parties in Jerusalem, particularly wedding celebrations of the rich peasants of the district of Jerusalem, like Abudis, al-Ayzariyah, and al-Tour, as well as in Bethlehem. She played an important role with the Turkish army, playing music and singing, and her singing was broadcast by Jerusalem radio station under the name of "Rajaa al-Filastiniyah" (Palestinian Rajaa). Her singing was truly beautiful. She married Hussein al-Fitiani who was a lancer in the army and a thug. She was accompanied on the violin by Elias as-Salfiti, who was nicknamed "al-Karsha" ("intestines" or "guts").

The city of Jerusalem relied for its entertainment and pleasure on the amateurs of this art, who were some of the finest people of Jerusalem.

MY FATHER AND THE MUEZZIN

The window of the hall (the sitting room) of Dar al-Jawhariyyeh in Saadiyeh overlooked the red minaret, so we used to listen passionately to the muezzins who had good voices. When Sheikh Muhammad al-Silwani came from Egypt, he had graduated from al-Azhar. He was a master of the *adhan* (call to prayer) and his vocal stretching skills were on a par with those of the greatest musicians. God had blessed him with a beautiful voice, and my father used to wake me up to listen to his morning call to prayer. As it happened, though, Sheikh Muhammad al-Silwani was transferred to one of the minarets of Temple Mount and replaced by Sheikh Umar Wahbah who had a most horrid voice that disturbed our peace. My father could not bear to listen to him, particularly having become used to Sheikh Muhammad's angelic voice.

Encouraged by his status as one the most respectable residents of Saadiyeh, my father went to the Awqaf Administration (Islamic religious endowment) and submitted a request to have the new sheikh removed, expressing his dismay at his voice and asking for the return of Sheikh Muhammad al-Silwani. The staff members were surprised since my father was a Christian, and the director of the Awqaf recited the following verses, referring to Sheikh Wahba.

"I heard a muezzin whose voice hurt the ears of the listener, when the call to prayer is heard. So with pain in my ears I said to him, do you mean to call to prayer, or do you mean to hurt?"

The employees were pleased and said to him, "Abu Khalil, the father of this Sheikh was killed by a gang of bandits in an attack on the post carriage on the Jaffa-Jerusalem Road and we must help him for the sake of his children." My father replied that he did not want him to lose his source of income but that it was possible to appoint him at the minaret of Mahallat Saad-wa-Said where there are no houses, but just some gypsy tents and the Dominican Monastery. They laughed, and my father succeeded in having Sheikh Muhammad transferred back to the red minaret, which was a happy day for us.

THE SARAYA IN OTTOMAN TIMES

During Ottoman times, the government offices were housed in a building[100] that belonged to the Islamic religious endowments of Jerusalem, which later housed the Islamic Orphanage run by Jamil Wahba. The building was located on the road leading from the northern spice market to al-Wad, with an additional gate facing Aqabat al-Takiya.[101]

This building housed all of the government's administrations, bodies, and departments, and so on entering it, you would find the high commissioner, the Administrative Council, the Registry Department, the Tapu Department (land titles and deeds), the Werko Department, the Finance Department, the Justice Department, the Land Mortgage Bank, the Public Works Department, the cash register, the police force, the gendarmerie, the prison, a prayer area surrounded by a wooden fence, and finally a large and organized stable for the horses of the gendarmerie and the lancers.

THE PRISON

The prison consisted of a cage that was placed opposite the Justice and Werko Departments and the Registry on the ground floor. Next to it, under a mulberry tree, there was a public café where people who had come on business would sit on locally made stools and wait until their papers were ready. The cage was a temporary prison where people under arrest awaited the verdict.

THE HORSES

The horses of the lancers and the gendarmerie were tied up in the corridor-like stable of this building, which was located opposite the main entrance and had its own door that opened to another road known as Aqabat al-Takieh. The stable could house a large number of horses while their owners were on business out of town.

THE MUNICIPALITY

As for the Municipal Department, it was adjacent to this building and could be reached via a wooden flight of steps through a window that was turned into a door. It also had a door that opened to Aqabat al-Takieh. I often climbed these steps to see my father when he was a member of the municipality in 1907. The last person to head the municipality while it was still based in this building was the late Hussein Effendi al-Husseini who was appointed to this post in 1908. After that, he made the necessary repairs to Al-Jamal Hotel, which was owned by the municipality and was located outside Jaffa Gate, at the intersection of Jaffa Road and Ma'man Allah Street. The municipality moved outside the wall for the first time and remained based in that building until the end of the British Mandate.

INSTABILITY IN JERUSALEM

At the start of 1914 the soldiers of the Ottoman army were ravaging this tranquil country. Germany and France were at war. Rumors spread that the Ottoman state would soon have to join this war. We noticed Ottoman army officers renting homes even in the neighborhoods of the Old City. Thus, Muhammad al-Qoulaghsi and Abdul-Rahman Bey, who became the masters of Jerusalem after Turkey joined the war, moved to Saadiyeh where they rented a place in Mamluk Arch from the late Mustafa al-Zawraq. They often joked with us and held my father's donkey when we came across them on our way to Dar al-Jawhariyyeh. In this way we became friendly with each other.

When Mustafa al-Jabsha was the mukhtar of Damascus Gate and the Saadiyeh Quarter, he once invited them to an evening at his home in Saadiyeh, located opposite Hajj Abd Rabbu's bakery. My father was among the guests, and also with us were Mustafa al-Sirriya al-Mu'aqat, Ibrahim al-Alami, Hussein al-Arnaout, Muhammad al-Sibasi, and others. In this way we and al-Qoulaghsi and Abdul-Rahman Bey became well-acquainted with each other.

Uncle Muhammad al-Sibasi sang beautifully. I remember the dawr of *Fu'adi amruhu 'ajib* (My heart is strange in matters of love) which was of the maqam Karawan and was composed by Daoud Hosni and sung by Sheikh Yusuf al-Manyalawi[102] and Sheikh al-Safati. Al-Sibasi sang for more than one and a half hours, and when he sang *lamma mana't el-wad*, we cheered him so much that despite not having any knowledge of the Arabic language, the officers had to admit that Arab music was more enchanting and civilized than Turkish music, for it is so emotional it literally shakes the listener. I played the oud and sang for hours, which pleased al-Qoulaghasi. He thus became a great support for me throughout the Great War.

The rooftops, windows, and courtyards of the neighboring houses were packed with veiled women who stood listening to this celebration, which unfortunately was to be the last one of its kind for Jerusalemites. For the Great War meant the end of the Arab people, and the end of their lives, too.

TURKEY'S ENTRY INTO THE GREAT WAR IN JULY 1914

The situation deteriorated and the people of Jerusalem were gripped by panic. The commissioner of Jerusalem had distributed envelopes sealed with red wax to all the mayors of the country, with strict instructions not to open them before drums were beaten to announce these letters. This was in April 1914. People worried and feared the worst, particularly the Christian communities. They wondered what the content of the letters could be. Was the country going to descend into chaos? Were Christians and minorities going to be under threat? Adding to citizens' fears was that these decrees remained with the town and village mayors for over two months without anyone knowing what they were about. Finally, one Friday during noon prayers at the al-Aqsa Mosque, the drums were heard and orders were given to open the sealed decrees.

They turned out to be a light red sheet, about seventy centimeters long and fifty-five centimeters wide, with a green flag on one side and red flag on the other. Between the two was the picture of a cannon and written underneath it the sentence *Seferberlik birinci günü Temmuz 1914* (First day of mobilization July 1914).[103] I kept one of these decrees in the Jawhariyyeh collection, thanks to Uncle Mustafa al-Jabsha, the mayor of Damascus Gate, who had given it to my father at the time.

This decree said that the Ottoman state had indeed joined in the Great War alongside Germany. The country was thus in a state of war, although no alarming incidents happened on the day that war drums were beaten in the al-Aqsa Mosque. It was nonetheless a black day, for our country had become involved in a war whose ending nobody could predict and which the Ottoman state could have spared, had it pondered the consequences.

THE FIRST PUBLIC HANGING OUTSIDE DAMASCUS GATE

The country had joined the warring countries overnight and citizens, particularly in the Arab countries, lurked in expectation, for they had great hopes for liberation from the oppressing occupiers. In the wake of this, the famous Decentralization Society[104] was formed. Freedom-seeking Arab members of this society, some of whom were from Jerusalem, such as Baytar Ali al-Nashashibi, began to dress in Arabic dress and wear the *qumbaz*, the *abaya*, and the *kaffiyeh* with the head-rope. It was refreshing and hope-inspiring to see them wearing the *kaffiyeh*, having taken off Turkish and foreign costumes, including the fez. Some of these people had been breeding ideas, while others were preparing the ground to free Arab countries from Ottoman control and establish an Arab caliphate that would be based in Egypt and subject to British military control. Fearing the reaction of the Ottomans, they fled to other Arab countries. Their fear was shared by Arab people across the Arab countries under Ottoman rule. With the Ottoman state's entry into the war, people began to fear the worst, and rightly so, for it became clear that the state was going to take revenge.

A few days after war was declared, I was on my way from our home in Saadiyeh early in the morning. On exiting through Damascus Gate, I saw the first Arab to be executed, hanging on a high wooden gallows in a corner outside Damascus Gate. It was a terrifying sight. He was dressed in a white gown and had a long announcement hanging on his chest, perhaps stating his crime. He was from a village and had been imprisoned. So Jerusalem witnessed the first public hanging of an Arab, which sowed terror in the hearts of its citizens and was soon to be followed by many more executions.

THE SEIZING OF FOREIGN INSTITUTES AND ESTABLISHMENTS, INCLUDING THE SAINT GEORGE'S SCHOOL

The government began to replace the Civil Administration with a military one. Foreign establishments were closed down because they belonged to the enemies—the British, the French, the Russians—and the ambassadors of these countries were expelled. All banks were closed down and foreign establishments in the country seized, including the

Saint George's School. Alas, I lost the opportunity to complete my education when I was in my second year of high school and just about to finish my studies.

Military Costs

Food prices rose dramatically due to the army's tyranny and despotism. They confiscated the foodstuffs stored in the foreign establishments they had seized, as well as grains, oils, and even textiles from markets and from Jerusalem's well-known merchants, on an incredibly large scale. Since these goods were seized without payment, this confiscation was called "assistance for the military" (military costs).

The Map

Since my father did know a foreign language, and since he was following the news of the war in Europe and Asia, I drew for him a large map showing all the countries in Europe and Asia, and wrote the necessary details in Arabic script. My father would place the map in front of him as though he was the commander in chief and trace the advance of each state towards Germany as he had heard about it in the official daily news circulated to the people. He was very happy to have this Arabic map at his disposal.

THE CLOSING DOWN OF FOREIGN POST OFFICES IN JERUSALEM

In 1914 immediately after the Ottoman state joined the Great War, these post offices were closed:

The Austrian post office, located in the Armenian Quarter inside the wall. This was the first post office to be set up for foreigners in Jerusalem. Later, it moved to one of the buildings of Doctor Pascal al-Armani (Doctor Pascal the Armenian) which was located near David Castle, inside Jaffa Gate, next to Cook Travel Agency.

The German post office, based in one of the shops of the building of the Anbusi Mortmain outside Jaffa Gate, under the Ottoman bank.

The French post office, based in one of the shops of monk Hanania, which belonged to Jerusalem's Greek Orthodox Patriarchate, near the shop of Raad the photographer and Boulous Said's Palestine Bookshop.[105]

The German and French post offices were opened at the same time.

The Russian post office, based in the Armenian building opposite the municipal park on Jaffa Road.

The Italian post office, based in one of the shops of monk Hanania, which belonged to Jerusalem's Greek Orthodox Patriarchate and was located next to Boulous Said's Palestine Bookshop and opposite Fast Hotel on Jaffa Road.

I kept photographs of the locations of the post offices of these five countries in the Jawhariyyeh collection. The Ottoman post office continued to be based on the second floor of the building of the Greek Orthodox Patriarchate outside Jaffa Gate. This building was adjacent to the city wall from the outside. The office was located on the second floor of this building, above Credit Lyonnais and next to the public debt administration and the Regie Department,[106] and it remained based here until the end of the Ottoman occupation of Jerusalem.

When the administration announced that foreign privileges would be abolished in the Ottoman Empire, the *Palestine* newspaper wrote the following about the foreign post offices in its issue of October 14, 1914.

> Foreign post offices in the Ottoman Empire date back to when each one of the relevant countries obtained its privileges. The people of Napoli and the people of Venice were the first to set up post offices in Istanbul while they were still two separate kingdoms. In 1721, the Austrians and the Russians followed suit. It was agreed that France would set up post offices in the Ottoman Empire in 1812, England in 1831, Greece in 1834, Germany and Egypt in 1870, and Italy in 1908.
>
> The Sublime Porte had made repeated attempts to close down these post offices in 1874, 1880, 1888, 1901, 1908, and 1909 because they were a burden to the empire and were detrimental to its economy, but he only succeeded in closing down those of Greece and Egypt in 1881, and the Italian one in 1883. As for the remaining countries, they opposed the plan vehemently, while Austria conceded in 1909 the closure of five of its postal branches across Ottoman countries where there were no other foreign post offices that could threaten its sovereignty.

THE FIRST AIRPLANE LANDS IN JERUSALEM

In 1914, after the Ottoman state entered the war, the government issued an official statement announcing that a military airplane was going to land in Jerusalem for the first time. The landing would take place near the pharmacy and petrol station in al-Baq'aa Fawqa, on the Jerusalem-Bethlehem Road. It was decided that the landing would take place at noon on the day following the announcement. Government officials, the military, and ordinary citizens all hurriedly made their way early on the designated day, which was a hot day, if I remember well. Only a few people remained in the city. My father got on his donkey to see the plane, and we went along. Talpiot seemed festive, as the crowds gathered in the sweltering heat and the ambulant sellers sold all kinds of food and drink. I also remember that people had to buy their drinking water. Food was sold out, as people had become unpleasantly hungry and thirsty while waiting for the airplane which, unfortunately, never arrived. So we returned home with my father after the heat, hunger, and exhaustion got the better of us.

That afternoon, we learned that the plane had crashed over Samakh[107] near Tiberias and that the military pilots on board had been killed. I recall that one of them, Nouri, was among the best-educated young pilots and was new to the field. The following days were ones of grief and mourning for the state, the army, and the people. A special song was composed and sung all over the country to commemorate their deaths, which were seen as a bad omen. The name of the other pilot was Ismail.[108]

An Ottoman plane in Jerusalem, 1914. Cropped from a stereoscopic photograph. Courtesy of the Library of Congress.

II. THE MANDATE YEARS: 1917–1948

BRITAIN OCCUPIES JERUSALEM

When Sunday, 9 December 9, 1917, dawned on Jerusalem, the city had fallen overnight into the hands of the English and their allies. This fortunate moment saw the end of Ottoman rule and of the tyranny and despotism that had prevailed, particularly from 1914 to 1917. We began to breathe relief and praised the Almighty for this blessing. Little did we know at the time that this cursed occupation was in fact a curse for our dear country. We thought, "But perhaps you hate a thing and it is good for you."[109]

I remember that day as being one of the happiest for the people. They were dancing on the pavement and congratulating each other. Many young Muslim and Christian Arab men, most of whom had been conscripts in Jerusalem during the Turkish era, had changed their army uniforms into civilian clothes in a ridiculous fashion, fearing that the occupying British army might arrest them in their military uniforms and take them as war prisoners. One would be wearing his military trousers and a pair of wooden clogs, with one of those jackets normally worn over the qumbaz and an ancient fez on his head, while another wore a qumbaz and a *kalpak*,[110] as he did not have a fez.

Some people were cutting down the Turkish telephone wires in the streets and taking them home, while others looted mules, donkeys, or carts which the former government had left behind and impatiently drove them away in order to sell them.

The British army had rapidly deployed in the city's streets, and those in charge of public works began to take over Turkish departments, such as the post office. They started replacing the old telephone lines, using their vehicles, known as the "automobile boxcars," which we were seeing for the first time. They were fast and small-sized, and we were surprised by these sights which had been unknown to us only yesterday. As for me (age twenty), I was dancing in the streets with my friends and raising toasts to Britain and the occupation. I then began to shiver and came down with a fever that forced me to stay in bed for three days, for the joy and ecstasy of victory that we felt had been extreme, and we had drunk excessively as we celebrated.

Early in the morning on that day, I went with my brother Khalil and some friends to Sheikh Badr[111] and headed for the very site where the mayor of Jerusalem had surrendered the city. There, in Romema,[112] we noticed how Jews in those quarters were keeping close company with the British soldiers who had made their way to the city, surrounded on both sides of the road by Jewish young ladies who accompanied them, chatting to them in English with smiles on their faces and giving them an excessively warm welcome, until they went their separate ways.

After Balfour's declaration and sinister promise, we would remember back to this warm welcome of theirs. We did not realize that, thanks to this occupation, Zionist dreams would come true. The Arabs had fallen victims to a shameful trick which put an end to our being and to the future of our children and grandchildren, and we lost what was dearest to us.

On this day, my brother Khalil, my mother, my brother Fakhri, and I were at my sister Afifeh's home on the western side of Saint Julian Street. I recall that on that day all Christian denominations rang their church bells to celebrate this happy occasion and held services in their churches. After Hussein Bey al-Husseini officially surrendered the city, the American Colony in Jerusalem published a photograph of historic value, which I have kept in the Jawhariyyeh Collection. The photograph includes Hussein Bey al-Husseini, mayor of Jerusalem; Tawfiq Muhammad Saleh al-Husseini; Ahmed Sharaf, police commissioner; Hajj Abdul-Qader al-Alami, police commissioner—lancers; Shamseddine, policeman; Amin Tahboub, policeman; Jawwad Bey bin Ismail Bey al-Husseini, who was wearing short trousers; Burhan, son of the late Taher Bey al-Husseini; and behind Hussein Bey, the white flag of surrender, held by Jamal Pasha's driver, a Lebanese called Salim who was married to the sister of Hanna al-Lahham. The latter was standing by his side. Only two individuals were present from the other party (the British army). I myself delivered the white flag of surrender to the person holding it.

A VALUABLE REMARK (AND MY COMMENT ON IT)

This photograph of the surrender of Jerusalem to the British army is genuine. However, the British Empire refused to acknowledge it, since their habit has always been to lie, deceive, and spread propaganda for the benefit of the empire. So I was told that Prime Minister Winston Churchill, in his book, proposed the following: The two British soldiers who appear in this photograph were in fact looking to buy eggs from the farmers of the village of Lifta and happened to come across Hussein Effendi al-Husseini and his company, so this photograph was taken. And that is all there is to it.

Behold, dear reader, the hypocrisy! First you should know that the weather was rainy and biting cold, particularly that year. This was the

photograph of the surrender of Jerusalem to the British army, courtesy of Library of Congress

end of December, so if Churchill's story was true, what makes a delicate person like Hussein Effendi stand in Sheikh Badr at such an early hour and in such cold and rainy weather? And would British soldiers drop their responsibilities in the middle of a heated battle over the city of Jerusalem, to go looking for eggs? Is it possible that a British soldier would suffer from hunger? Perish the thought.

The location of the surrender of Jerusalem was in the neighborhood of Sheikh Badr. Following the British occupation, it became a purely Jewish neighborhood known as Romema and one of the most famous Jewish communes. The British Empire intended to place a cross of no less than three to four meters in height in the very spot where the photograph of the surrendering of Jerusalem was taken. But Zionists refused to allow this cross to be set up in the Jewish area of Romema, and in the end the British acquiesced. Thus, this great tall cross, which was made with impeccable skill and precision, remained lying on the ground, and Britain had to set up an enormous iron-chain fence around it.

If Churchill did not acknowledge the genuineness of this surrender, then why did his government have this gigantic cross made in order to

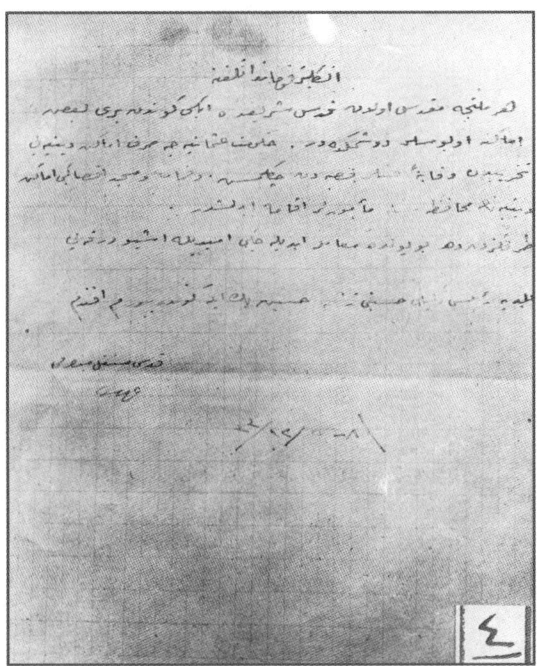

The surrender note handed to the British by the mayor of Jerusalem on December 9, 1917. Jawhariyyeh Collection. © Institute for Palestine Studies.

place it as a memorial at the very site known to us as Romema, where the late mayor and his companions were standing and where the surrender of the city took place? And why was the mayor carrying the official authorization signed by the governor Ezzat Bey during the meeting held at the home of the English bishop? Why was the mayor in Lifta—or what is Romema today—at that scary and dangerous moment?

RETURN TO DAR AL-JAWHARIYYEH

Now that we were rid of the Turks, with God's help, we were free from the yoke of military service, and my brothers Khalil and Fakhri, my mother, and I returned to my father's home, Dar al-Jawhariyyeh in Saadiyeh, inside the wall. During the war, my brother Fakhri and my mother had settled at my sister Afifeh's home at the building of Reverend Youssef. The building belonged to the Greek Orthodox Patriarchate and stood on Saint Julian Street, near the building that currently houses the YMCA.[113] A number of Jerusalem's Arab Greek Orthodox also lived in this building. The neighbors were Youssef Qurt and his family, Menia Btouli and his family, Umm Hanna Zakharia, the wife of the late Issa Zakharia and her daughter Farida, the Meqhar family, and others. I recall also that the al-Khouri family, of Jaffa, were living with us in this house. Their men had deserted the army and were on the run at the time.

We tidied up and cleaned the house in preparation for Christmas 1917. It was a merry one for everybody, thanks to the British occupation that freed the Arab people from the despotic Turks. We were all nurturing great hopes for a better future, particularly after what we had been through—the miseries of war, famine, diseases, epidemics, and typhus that spread throughout the country, and we thanked the Lord who saved all our young men from the damned military service.

Given the strategic location of Dar al-Jawhariyyeh, we would go to the rooftop and watch the bloody battles between the British army and the Germans and Turks, which were still taking place on the Mount of Olives and Ard al-Samar, which lies flat on the eastern side of our house.[114] We often feared that these battles would bring the Turks back, God forbid, until their total defeat put our minds at rest and we said, "May your departure be for good."

GENERAL ALLENBY'S ENTRY INTO JERUSALEM

General Allenby entered Jerusalem in a grand military celebration marking victory and the official conquest of Jerusalem. The celebration took place on Sunday, December 18, 1917, eight days after the surrender of Jerusalem in Sheikh Badr. I still remember this great day and how he entered the city through Jaffa Gate. The celebration was followed by another one when he visited the city at Christmas and was received with due ceremony in Bab al-Qala inside the wall. After General Allenby gave his famous speech in which he made the unfortunate remark that "only now have the crusades ended," Muslim leaders protested. Some of them withdrew from the celebration.

MY APPOINTMENT AS A CLERK AT THE JUSTICE DEPARTMENT

Since the occupation, I had always kept company to Hussein Effendi al-Husseini. As mayor, he was responsible for all matters related to Jerusalem. Through Haddad Pasha, he served as the link between the local population and the occupying British forces, which gave him considerable influence among the latter.[115] Hussein Effendi gave me a recommendation and sent me to see him, and I went into Haddad Pasha's office with Ali Bey Jarallah. After asking me a few questions, and with the help of Ali Bey Jarallah, he agreed to appoint me.

This was the first court of its type to be established in Jerusalem following the occupation, and Ali Bey Jarallah was its president. It was based in a room on the upper floor of the second building that you passed on entering the Russian Compound through its main gate on the eastern side. Under the mandate, it became the central court.

The court employees were Ali Hasna, Fakhri Bey, who was the son of Assem Bey, Muhammad al-Zawraq, Salim al-Naja, Muhyiddine Qami', and office boy Abdullah Deeb. We had good times working there. The court was the only one in Jerusalem where the people could seek settlements to their problems, and these were many, since the country was under occupation. The late Ali Bey Jarallah solved these problems without ever parting with his smile or his sense of humor.

Thus, with God's grace, I became a civil servant earning a reasonable salary, and with the help of Ibrahim Bey al-Duzdar, my brother Khalil was appointed as a lancer in the Jerusalem gendarmerie by Haddad Pasha. I should mention that we preferred to receive our monthly pay in Egyptian coins which we would happily put on some plates inside our father's cupboard and then spend what was necessary to cover the daily expenses, while recalling with bitterness the worthless notes of the Turkish currency which had devaluated to sixteen piasters per Ottoman lira.

HADDAD PASHA

Gabriel Haddad Pasha was in fact one of the men of the British intelligence in the Orient and a guardian to the interests of the British Empire. He was attached directly to the Arab Office, which was established in Egypt by the English and counted among its men McMahon, Gilbert Clayton, Lawrence, Storrs, and others. When the British army advanced under Allenby, Gabriel Haddad Pasha joined the leadership and became one of the most senior assistants. He had been selected for this post because, on the one hand, he had been working for the intelligence service, and on the other hand he was fluent in Arabic, having previously worked with the government in Sudan. In brief, Gabriel Haddad Pasha was a prominent member in the Occupied Enemy Territories Administration,[116] and his official mission ended with the end of the military administration in Palestine. He also oversaw the administration of Jerusalem for a period of time as an attaché of the Higher Military Command. Thus, from the first day of the British occupation, Haddad Pasha was running the administration of the country, particularly in Jerusalem, and had total freedom in this respect.

Mr. Ronald Storrs was appointed military governor of Jerusalem, and his headquarters were in the Schmidt Building[117] outside Damascus Gate. Haddad Pasha's rank was higher than Ronald Storrs's.

During the occupation, Haddad Pasha was based in the Armenian Building located opposite Jaffa Road in Jerusalem. When I went in to see him, seeking to be appointed at the Justice Department, I found a robust giant speaking Arabic in the Egyptian dialect with an imposing voice. Later on, I learned from my great brother and good friend, Judge Abdul-Wahab Bey al-Nashaba, that Gabriel Haddad was from Tripoli in Lebanon.

Haddad Pasha at the Table of Ismail Bey al-Husseini

Haddad Pasha visited Uncle Ismail Bey al-Husseini for dinner on a special invitation. It was a marvelous party attended by many of Jerusalem's prominent notables and chiefs. Thanks to Hussein Effendi, I was present at this party, and I did my job well, serving the coffee to Haddad Pasha and Ronald Storrs. The two had robust bodies and enormous heads that made them seem worthy of their high posts. The generosity of Uncle Ismail made this a lavish night, as one would expect from this house that was known as the House of the Nation and was a source of pride both for his family and for the people of Jerusalem.

MUHAMMAD BIN MUSA AL-ZARDAQ

And what should make thee know who al-Zardaq is.[118] Al-Zardaq was actually an intelligent, bright, good-humored, and generous man who spent much of his life making merriment. There are extraordinary anecdotes involving him which one could not possibly describe in writing. He had been a well-regarded civil servant at the Justice Department in Jerusalem at the time of the Ottoman rule, and fate decreed that I should become his colleague just after the British occupation at the court over which Ali Bey Jarallah presided. He had a broad knowledge of all matters related to the courts and particularly to the Office of Public Prosecutor, of which he became the head later during the British Mandate. He was fluent in Arabic and Turkish, and did extremely well at Hebrew during the occupation. Since Muhammad al-Zardaq was a small man and had blonde to ginger hair and blue eyes, when he spoke Hebrew one mistook him for one of Jerusalem's old Ashkenazi Jews. He once happened to be in Tel Aviv where he was summoned to testify at court. When he stood before the Jewish judge, the Torah was put forward for him to place his right hand on and take the oath according to custom. For the judge had thought al-Zardaq to be Jewish and was surprised like the rest of the audience to learn that his name was Muhammad and to watch him request a copy of the Qu'ran. He was fluent in Hebrew like a Jew. Muhammad al-Zardaq remained a close friend of mine throughout the mandate era. He was quick-witted and was well-known to the people of Jerusalem of various denominations. He was also hot-tempered and could not tolerate cold-tempered people. He even carried in his pocket a list on which he wrote the names of Jerusalemites he found to be insufferable.

"Musliman, Thanks be to Allah"

We Jerusalemites of the various denominations had always lived like a family during the Ottoman rule, and there was never any difference between a Muslim or a Christian. But when Britain occupied Jerusalem, it tried to sow trouble, particularly among Muslims and Christians. As though it had not been vicious enough in issuing the sinister Balfour Declaration after the occupation, causing the loss of our homeland, it banned Muslims from the Church of the Holy Sepulchre and Christians from al-Haram al-Sharif.

One Sunday morning in April, I was with some of my Jerusalemite Muslim friends—Daoud al-Fityani, Tahsin al-Khalidi, Mahmoud Aziz al-Khalidi, Saleh al-Danaf al-Ansari, Fakhri al-Nashashibi, Amin

Tahboub, Munir Darwish, Nu'man Aql, and finally Muhammad al-Zardaq, and others.[119]

We each had a glass of the Italian-made Vermouth Bianco and then went to the bar of Aristidi the Greek for a second one. Since it was a warm and sunny day, we bought some green almonds. Each one of us put his share in his pocket, and off we went, having decided to picnic in the courtyard of the Dome of the Rock.

We stood at one of the gates of al-Haram al-Sharif and noticed that a police force had been stationed at each one of the main gates. It was made up of bigoted Muslim members of the Indian army who asked everyone who wanted to go in, "Musliman?" If the person in question was Muslim, they were allowed in. If not, they were denied entry. So each one of us answered, "Musliman" to the question. When it was my turn, the Indian officer asked me, "Musliman?" I answered "Musliman, thanks be to Allah." Behind me was Uncle Abu Eid al-Dallal, who used to wear a turban. Since he was a loyal friend of my father's, he shouted at the top of his voice, "I swear to Allah that he is Musliman." Imagine, dear reader, Wasif, the son of Jiryis Jawhariyyeh, standing as a Muslim before God. So to my luck, after the Indian made a gesture at me and mumbled some words, I went through the door and got in.

When it was our friend al-Zardaq's turn, the Indian officer denied him entry without any discussion, threatening him with his bayonet rifle. Al-Zardaq went out of his mind and turned all red with anger while everyone laughed. He began shouting at me at the top of his voice, "My name is Muhammad and I was banned from al-Haram al-Sharif. But you Wasif, you're a graduate of al-Azhar and a devout Muslim!" We laughed so hard we almost passed out. But there was no way around it, and when al-Zardaq tried to enter through another door, the Indian officer blew his whistle and gestured to his colleagues not to let him in.

And so we all threw ourselves on the grass in the court of al-Haram al-Sharif, eating the green almonds, while al-Zardaq stayed outside, thundering and fuming.

EAST JORDAN REFUGEES IN JERUSALEM

In the winter of 1918, Jerusalem received a large number of refugees from the towns of East Jordan, towns such as al-Salt, al-Fheis, and others, when the Turks (or the Germans, in fact) launched a counter-attack which allowed them to regain possession of al-Salt and al-Fheis and begin their descent towards Jericho. This prompted the residents to flee during the night, before the arrival of the Germans and Turks. The German forces entered Jericho and threatened to advance towards Jerusalem, and people became terrified by the possibility of the Turks taking vengeance on them. I still remember the bad state in which the families of Jericho, including those of al-Qazzaz, Nazzal, Saliba, Saad, and al-Baida, arrived in Jerusalem, having fled in the night and having made a horrific journey on foot. The English soon bounced back and resumed their advance towards the east. Having said that, the Turks reentered Jericho just after the fall of Jerusalem because the British forces had failed to defend it, and also because Jericho was not a good base for defense, although it might have served as a good base for our friends Abu al-Qazzaz, Naser, al-Mustaklib, Nazzal, and Karakoz.

For memory's sake, the massive cannon used by the German forces remained for thirty years on the heights of Wadi Shuaib where it had been positioned, and continued to threaten Britain as though it was a great power, for it was one of the many cannons involved in Germany's famous cunning war tactics.

THE DEATH OF HUSSEIN EFFENDI AL-HUSSEINI

I was devastated, by the death of my second father, Hussein Effendi al-Husseini, in February 1918. He passed away after coming down with acute catarrhal pneumonia which ended the blessed man's life after confining him to bed for no more than five days. He fell ill one night while carrying out a night mission between Jerusalem and Ramallah on the orders of Gabriel Haddad Pasha, who relied on him and trusted him from the first day of the British army's occupation of Jerusalem.

Some malicious people said at the time that God had struck him for surrendering Jerusalem to nonbelievers. This unique and extraordinary Arab personality had fallen out of favor with Jamal Pasha, who had removed him from his post as mayor of Jerusalem and replaced him with four Turks, some of whom had plundered the funds of the municipality during the Great War. He was, God bless his soul, one of the most prominent patriotic figures and was well-versed in politics and fluent in English, French, Turkish, and Arabic, and also knew some Russian and Greek. This helped him to solve problems thanks to his frequent dealings with foreigners who lived in Jerusalem or visited the city, and all his actions were for the nation's benefit. I am certain beyond doubt that had Hussein Effendi's death been delayed by a few years, politics in Palestine would have taken another course.

My Personal Relation with the Late Hussein Effendi

Hussein Effendi was kind to me from when I was a boy. When he saw me in the street, God bless his soul, he would call me immediately. I would kiss his hand, and he would give me a bishlik. In the summer, I accompanied him on his trips to his lands, as though I was one of his children. It was thanks to him that I joined the National Dusturiyyeh School of the great educator Khalil al-Sakakini without my father having to pay the fees. Later, and also thanks to him, I transferred to al-Mutran School (Saint George's) where I continued to receive my education in the same way until the Great War caused the school to close down.

When my father passed away in September 1914, he gave me support and comfort. I would not be exaggerating to say that he often had the famous tailor Solomon make my suit of the same cloth as his so that I would not feel hurt. It was he who encouraged me to learn to sing and play musical instruments. During the war, he always made sure the needs of my mother and our home were promptly supplied. He also had me send money on his behalf to my brother Khalil who was in the gendarmerie in Beirut, and sometimes also to my brother Fakhri who was in the gendarmerie musical band in Damascus. From the time of the closing of the English al-Mutran School, I would accompany him on his trips while he was still mayor and later on his trips to Kerak across the Dead Sea. I carried his money for him and was the one in charge of buying the provisions his wife asked for. He never checked the expenditure but simply gave me money whenever I ran out; his trust in me had no boundaries. I was truly loyal to him and never coveted anything because he always made sure I had everything I needed in this life throughout my time with him, thank God.

I truly felt I had become an orphan (at age twenty-two) after he passed away, a feeling I did not experience at my father's death, for Hussein Effendi had taken care of me during that time. The news of his death struck me down like lightning, and the shock left me unconscious of what was going on around me. His death left me with no support but God's, and I frankly admit that I owe him everything that I achieved in my life on every level. It is thanks to him that I was able to enjoy a good life and recognition in society. But what can one do? Such is the will of God. To God we belong and to Him we return.

Hussein Effendi left behind him his sons Salim, Omar, Ali, and Hashem whom he had with his honorable wife, Mrs. Fatima, the daughter of Muhammad Taher al-Khalidi of Jerusalem.

THE APPOINTMENT OF MUSA KAZEM PASHA AL-HUSSEINI AS MAYOR OF JERUSALEM

After the death of Hussein Effendi, the military governor appointed his brother Musa Kazem Pasha al-Husseini as mayor. Since Musa Kazem Pasha hardly knew any English, he used the services of a secretary, Mr. Tawfiq Farah, a Greek Orthodox Arab who had a good command of the English language and who kept this job after the dismissal of Mussa Kazem Pasha.

MY RESIGNATION FROM THE JUSTICE DEPARTMENT

Umm Salim, the widow of the late Hussein Effendi, sent for me and complained to me about what had happened with the lands of her late husband. Some farmers, particularly in Deir al-Hawa and Beit Jeez, had broken faith with the deceased and grabbed some of the lands, trespassing the borders in a shocking way when they had been extremely loyal to him in the past. She had appointed her brother Taher al-Khalidi to represent her in her business, and he based himself in Deir Amr. But since he did not know the ins and outs of these properties, she asked me to become his companion. I was the only person who knew what the situation was like during the life of the deceased, having accompanied him on all his tours and become aware of all the problems, particularly the dispute between the deceased and the so-called Omar Mahmoud al-Saleh of Beit Jeez, a village near Beit Suseen. I gladly handed in my resignation to the Justice Department and traveled to Deir Amr. On this same trip, I discovered that the oak bush that the deceased had been growing and looking after, known as Kherbet al-Akrad, was gradually disappearing because Taher had cut the trees down in order to provide for the needs of the house in charcoal.

AL-JAWHARIYYEH CAFÉ

In 1918 my brother Khalil resigned from his job as a gendarme lancer, during which he served under Ibrahim Bey in Jerusalem. He entered into a partnership with our friend George, a Greek Orthodox who was the son of Ibrahim al-Halabi and was renowned for his bravery during the Orthodox upswing led by George Zakharia. They were joined in this partnership by Habib el-Mondo (Abu Sami), and together they opened a café and bar in the Russian Compound by the southern main entrance located on Jaffa Road. This café and bar consisted of four spacious stores with six doors on the ground floor. The first and second floors were used by the British Intelligence Department and some other departments of the mandate government.

The café became extremely popular with the locals of all denominations and religions. You could see the customers sitting on chairs all the way from the first corner of the café's building to the road turn leading to the properties of 'Amma'il, the Travel and Immigration Department, or the Kantura Road. Al-Jawhariyyeh Café shot to fame in no time thanks to my brother Khalil's fine taste in presenting and preparing mezze and accompanying beverages. He introduced us to the appetizing presentation styles he had learned in Beirut while serving as a gendarme during the Ottoman rule. Arak glasses were arranged on a special tray among delicious mezze dishes presented in a variety of small matching plates and were stylishly served to the customers by the waiter with a glass of ice-cold water. This was unseen in Jerusalem at the time. Many friends of my brothers Khalil and Fakhri, and particularly the friends I myself had made as a music lover, were quick to begin frequenting the café, becoming regulars at it. We thus happily spent days and even nights at the café, of which we have good memories.

I remember hosting an evening with singer Badi'a Masabni at the café. We shut the doors and spent an exquisite evening at which many of Jerusalem's well-known figures of the time were present, such as Tahsin al-Khalidi, Daoud al-Fitiani, Rashid al-Muhtadi, Sheikh Nazzal Abu al-Saoud, Judge Muhammad Yousuf Al-Khalidi, Fawzi Darwish, and others. Reverend Sutiri Hanania was also present, and I still have in my collection a photograph of the group, showing an intoxicated Reverend Hanania who has taken off his cap and placed it beside him on the table.

We had some extraordinary times and wonderful evenings with the famous singer Sheikh Ahmed al-Tarifi, the well-known singer Muhammad al-Ashiq, the brilliant qanun player Abu Hussein al-Sousi, the famous singer Zaki Effendi Murad, and others. One could not possibly describe those days and nights, for as soon as the Turkish nightmare was over, everyone felt free like a newborn and started eating, drinking, and spending and squandering their money, the economy having improved immediately with the start of the British occupation.

My job every afternoon was to verify the records of the snooker table. There were three snooker tables in one of the café's backrooms. Those who were skilled at this royal game, such as the late Nasri Aroum, Issam Murcos, Mariusi Bicari, Francis al-Awi, and others never left the café. My brother Khalil and his partners thus earned a lot of money, but they did not save any because of the way they used to spend and squander.

RAGHEB BEY AND THE OUD

I had known Ragheb Bey al-Nashashibi since I was a youth. I met him on various occasions during the Ottoman times while he was Jerusalem representative, and our acquaintance became stronger during the British occupation.[120] Known for his generosity and lavish lifestyle, as well as for his love for music and merry times, Ragheb Bey used to spend his time at the home of his Jewish mistress, who later became his wife and the mother of Mansur and his brothers. She was a French Jew, and Ragheb Bey provided a home for her in the second building on the alley located on the left-hand side off Kantura Street, which became known as the Department of Travel and Immigration Street after the occupation. The building was owned by a Greek tinsmith. Ragheb Bey did not have an occupation, and he had a small carriage—the type known as a tok—drawn by an English horse, which Ragheb Bey drove himself with grandeur and pomposity.

He liked to listen to the oud and was fascinated by my singing of Arabic music, Andalusian muwashah in particular. He often sang some old poems with his loud voice at our gatherings, and his favorites were recordings by the late Sheikh Yousuf al-Manyalawi. I recall that Ragheb Bey used to add to the poem two verses that were not on the recorded version, and which I picked up myself in order to sing the poem to his liking.

Ragheb Bey asked me to teach him to play the oud, and so I did. We used to meet at Umm Mansur's, and I am not exaggerating when I say that no one ever entered that house. Thus we were able to spend long hours there. We would drink arak, have lunch, and take a nap. Then we would resume the playing and singing lessons. I would sing what he requested, then he would sing it in his turn, and then we would take a carriage, often to go to Kalounia and Ain Karem, and so on. If one day I did not go to him, I was doomed. He would come to the Jawhariyyeh Café in his private carriage and ask about me, "Where is Wasif? Where did the wretch go?" He would remain standing there until I was found. Then he would take me with him to his house of cheer.[121] We carried on like this until he was appointed mayor of Jerusalem following the resignation of Musa Kazem Pasha al-Husseini.

My Job at the Regie Department

A first-class socialite, Ragheb Bey styled himself as a highly respected figure in all social milieus. He had earned the love and respect of both civil servants and ordinary people during the Ottoman time and had become a powerful figure at all levels, particularly after becoming

Jerusalem representative in Istanbul. At the time when I was teaching him to play the oud, he once took me along to the Regie Department, which was located near the properties of Hassan Bey al-Turjman, on the road leading to Sheikh Jarrah and the Mea Shearim Road, opposite the Italian Hospital. We entered the Regie Department and were received by the director, Farid Bey Sawaya (Najib), a Lebanese if I remember well, who was a friend of Ragheb Bey. "Do you know this young man?" he asked pointing at me. The director answered, "No. Who is he?" Ragheb Bey answered, "He is the son of our late friend Jawhariyyeh." The director smiled, and I concluded from his facial expression that he knew my late father. Ragheb Bey then talked about me, my character, my penchant for music, and finally said, "I wish you to appoint him at your department, Najib." The director replied, "Of course, as you wish, sir" and immediately wrote down my name, noting a monthly salary of twenty Egyptian pounds. Ragheb Bey then said, "But be aware that while Wasif will be an employee of yours, he will work for me." Najib Bey smiled and laughed and said, "Again, as you wish." Thus, for nine months, I went to the Regie Department at the beginning of each month just to receive my salary, until I was appointed at the Governorate.[122] The unique deeds of Ragheb Bey, God bless his soul, were many.

SIX NIGHTS AT MESHKINOT[123]

My friend and oud teacher, Hamada al-Afifi, was the first one to teach me to play the oud. My father was still alive at the time. Since I was very young, I always made sure I was present at all the social getherings that Hamada al-Afifi (Uncle Abu Fuad)[124] went to. I learned a lot about the fine art of music from him. He really liked my company, God bless his soul, particularly when I was a young man, and he would take me along and introduce me to his dearest friends. I used to go with him to evening parties at the home of the Karriouz family on Saint Julian Street.

At one of those parties one day, Uncle Abu Fuad came to me and told me, "Prepare your oud, Wasif. We are off for a long evening, and could even spend the whole night in the Meshkinot Jewish Quarter, at our friend Rena's place." I knew Rena well. I remember that it was a Saturday night. I took my oud and bid farewell to my mother who had given me a nightgown and some other nightclothes, assuming that we would be spending a couple of days in Deir Amr. I kissed her hand and went off with Mustafa Ali al-Nashashibi, taking my oud along. When we arrived at dear Rena's home, we found it packed with guests, most of whom were Jewish and other young ladies who lived in the neighborhood.

We tuned the ouds, played whatever we felt like playing, and then raised a toast to Rena and another one to Sultana, a Moroccan Jewish lady who was good at singing simple folk songs and who also danced sometimes. The evening gradually became more and more spirited, and everyone was swaying with enchantment until daybreak when the guests left, while we remained in that house, the House of the Nation.[125]

Mustafa al-Nashashibi assisted Rena with domestic tasks. He would buy food and beverages, then he would help her with the cooking and presentation of the mezze and the drinks. We carried on like this, sleeping day or night, whenever we had the chance to rest. Then we would resume playing music, singing, and drinking. Many neighbors came along and joined the party, so we ended up spending a whole week in that house.

We had started off on Saturday evening and only left Rena and Sultana on Friday morning, after which I went with Uncle Abu Fuad to visit the honorable Umm Michel Karriouz. We spent all of Friday at hers, so I returned home on Friday evening at around eleven o'clock, when my late mother welcomed me saying, "It's been a long time, Wasif! Damn Deir Amr and and its people. You said you'd be gone for two days, but it's been a week now." When she noticed my shirt, which Rena had ironed that day, she said to me, "This is not Deir Amr's fashion." I answered her, inebriated, "Do you think Deir Amr is still like in the old days? Deir Amr has become a classy place since the arrival of the English." My mother replied, "Of course, and I suppose your ironed shirt is the servant's work? Ah, God bless you."

THE MONTEFIORE SOIRÉE AND "NOGHIM BNOGHIM"

The Jewish Mr. Solomon had been one of the most prominent tailors in Jerusalem since Ottoman times. City notables, particulatly Hussein Effendi, the mayor, were customers of Mr. Solomon who used to charge sixty francs (three French pounds) for a suit. My teacher Hamada al-Afifi was a friend of his and his family, since he was the chief clerk at the municipality. Once Mr. Solomon invited the employees of the municipality to his home, and my brother Tawfiq and I were among the guests. Led by Uncle Abu Fuaad, we sang and played until daybreak, which was only appropriate on that glorious night on which Mr. Solomon unleashed his generosity. All kinds of sardines and eggs, all kosher, were served on the drinking table. Some of the most beautiful Jewish ladies of that Jewish Quarter were with us at this delightful evening party, and some of them appreciated and savored Arabic singing while they disliked Western singing.

As it happened, one of Mr. Solomon's acquaintances, a young Ashkenazi Jew, decided with some of the young ladies to ask us to listen to them sing an Arabic song. Their request was met with unanimous approval, since we were all drunk and feeling cheerful. We were a truly exceptional group that included Ragheb al-Afifi, Fakhry al-Nashashibi, Abdullatif al-Nashashibi, Tawfiq Murad, Shakib al-Nashashibi, Fakhri Bey Assim, Tahsin al-Khalidi, Fawzi Darweesh, and other Jerusalemites.

The young Mordechai sat at the table and started setting the rhythm by tapping on an empty bottle with mezze forks, while the Ashkenazi young ladies sat around him. Together they started singing horridly in Arabic, may God preserve us.

Noghim bnoghim	(solo, in Mordechai's rough voice)
Ghaghikhon	(the chorus, sung by the group)
Waghaqu bnoghim	(Mordechai)
Ghaghikhon	(chorus)
Sheghshu bnoghim	(Mordechai)
Ghaghikhon	(chorus)

Unfortunately, none of us understood a word of this delightful song. We thought it may have been an Ashkenazi muwashah. I accompanied their singing on the oud as well as I could, and suddenly Uncle Abu Fuaad shouted at me, "Do you still not understand this song, Wasif? It's foreign, no? I bet my ass nobody does! They are singing, *Na'im na'im, Hal rihan, Waraqu na'im Shirshu na'im Hal rihan.*

It is so soft, this basil,
its leaves are so soft, this basil,
its stalks are so soft, this basil.

Everyone burst out laughing, and this song became the prelude to all our evenings. I would sing it exactly like the famous singer of Montefiore had done. That evening party was indeed one of our best. It took place prior to the fateful Balfour Declaration, thank God.

MY FRIEND FAHIM NUSSEIBEH

Abu Nu'man had the most cheerful character in Jerusalem, with a lifestyle that boiled down to having fun and celebrating. He was small, with blonde hair and blue eyes that he could not open in the sun, which earned him the nickname of Fahim the Fox. He was, God bless his soul, famous for his extraordinary and funny laugh, which he let out in such a playful way that it sounded musical and became known as "Fahim's laugh." If you heard him laugh as I just described, you could not but laugh along very hard. He was quick-witted and his jokes were many. We Jerusalemites of the early twentieth century recall the funny situations Fahim got himself into, particularly when he seated himself near the tent of Hajj Mahmoud the karakozati, in the first seat of the front row. He would sit there from the very first evening of Ramadan until the last, staring at Sheikh Mahmoud's movements throughout the *Karakoz and Iwaz* show. At evening parties, where everybody drank various kinds of alcohol, Abu Nu'man would sit among us without ever tasting a single drop of alcohol. Instead, he would bring a red bottle of soda pop and pour out a little in a glass of arak which he would then drink as though it was wine and act drunk just to humor the present company and make them laugh.

One night, we were extremely drunk when Abu Nu'man start getting undressed, keeping just his underwear on. He had had so much *gazeuz* (soda water) to drink that his belly was hanging out like a pregnant woman's. Each one of us had been asking him to drink more and more, so he ended up drinking more than seventeen bottles and seemed as though he was drunk for real.

At the time, the Turkish army was about to leave Jerusalem. It had set up its tents around the city, mostly opposite the mosque of Sheikh Jarrah. Fahim happened to trip over the phone wires connecting the officers' tents. So he cut off the telephone wires that army intelligence had been using during that critical period, rolled up as much of them as possible around his hand, and took them home to be used as laundry rope by his unmarried sister with whom he was living in that same neighborhood. It so happened that the army found out about it, and he was arrested by the soldiers, handcuffed, and taken around from one tent to another. Every time the guards took him into a tent, they would explain the incident in Turkish to the chief of the tent, saying, "This is the one who cut down the telephone lines." The officer would go into a rage and start beating him mercilessly, and so on, until he had made the tour of all the tents, when one officer rewarded him with a kick and the other with a slap on the face, until he finally passed out and was taken to prison.

PLAYING THE VIOLIN

After I left the Justice Department, I worked with Taher Effendi overseeing the business of the late Hussein Effendi in Deir Amr and did my work very well.[126] I spent the whole of summer 1918 there and took advantage of this opportunity by bringing along a violin so I could practice playing it on my own. Playing the oud I had memorized a lot of songs, dolabs, preludes, musical pieces, and most of all Andalusian muwashahat, all of which I practiced playing on the violin until I was able to play them well. When I returned to Jerusalem, I often played the violin at evening parties and celebrations, in addition to the oud, the rebeck, and the tanboor.

A PERIOD OF CHAOS IN MY LIFE

After the death of Hussein Effendi, who had been a second father to me, I no longer had anyone to give me guidance in life. Given that I had dedicated the greater part of my life to music and that I had fulfilled my duty in Deir Amr, honoring my promise to the wife of Hussein Effendi, Umm Salim, I found myself in a state of loss and chaos. Most of my time, day and night, I was unconscious because I was constantly drunk. I would party unil morning, sleep during the day, then go to an evening party followed by a picnic in one of the villages of the Jerusalem district, not caring for anybody or any responsibilities, only going to my mother's home to get changed. I slept at the homes of friends until all the partying and drinking got the better of me. I would go to an evening party in Bab Hatta, and in the morning I would go to a picnic with the finest families and notables of Jerusalem, and then to a private gathering in one of Jerusalem's secluded homes with street gangs. I did not even go to the Jawhariyyeh Café, except on rare occasions. I will never forget this period of my life. I only spent money on clothes, using the salary I was receiving from the Regie Department, thanks to Ragheb Bey al-Nashashibi.

ASSISTANT INSPECTOR AT CITY HALL

Musa Kazem Pasha al-Husseini, who was the mayor at the time, noticed that I had been out of sight and sent for me through the late Aref al-Nimri, one of the sergeants of the municipality. I met him at the city hall which was located in Jaffa Gate. He reproached me for not keeping in touch since the death of Hussein Effendi and asked me how

I was and how my family was doing, especially my mother. Then, he appointed me as an assistant inspector for a salary of twenty-four Egyptian pounds. I was appointed on a temporary basis until the decree institutionalizing the post was issued, as was the practice at the time.

I kissed his hands and thanked him. I assumed my new post under the late Abdul-Qader Effendi al-Afifi, who explained the job to me and handed me the receipt book. My job consisted of inspecting animals sold in Jerusalem by one individual to another, particularly on Friday morning of each week at the famous Friday animal market, which was located near the Sultan's Pool. I was entrusted to the care of the late Mustafa al-Kurd (Abu Darwish) who was an expert on this fine art.

Uncle Abu Darwish said to me, "Don't worry about doing anything yourself. Just sit at the café smoking the water pipe. I will do what is necessary and hand you the money, along with the receipts, on a daily basis." We agreed on this arrangement, and I carried out my job which consisted of a seat at the al-Maaref Café, where I smoked the water pipe with friends until ten or eleven in the morning. Then, once Uncle Abu Darwish had sat on his chair and taken the first three puffs, he would reach for the money in his Persian belt and hand me five Egyptian pounds, saying, "Here you are, Wasif Effendi...here is some spending money for you." Then he would pay me a separate sum against receipt, which I would hand in to the municipality.

I worked for about two-and-a-half months with Uncle Abu Darwish, whose charming and humorous conversation conquered everyone. Cheers to those wonderful days. I used to take Uncle Abu Darwish along to some of the evening parties I went to, especially those of the Montefiore commune[127] which were attended by many Jerusalemites such as Youssef Darwish, Hassan Fahmi, Rashid al-Daqqaq, Kamel Uwaida, Muhyiddine Zumurrud, and others.

JERUSALEM WITNESSES THE FIRST DEMONSTRATION SINCE THE OCCUPATION

When Britain made the sinister Balfour Declaration in 1918, it was forced to announce it publicly after the Russian revolutionists had divulged its contents. In 1922 a massive protest started inside the wall, as I remember, at the headquarters of the Muslim-Christian Association (the old Serail) led by the late Aref Pasha al-Daoudi.[128] The demonstration proceeded via Suq Aftimos, then through Jaffa Gate, and on to the Italian Consulate, which was located near the Hadassah Hospital in Jerusalem. I kept a historical photograph of this demonstration, in which

I myself took part. The late Musa Kazem Pasha al-Husseini actually led the many demonstrations, despite being the mayor at the time. These demonstrations sought to express Arabs' rejection of the Balfour Declaration and their commitment to Syrian unity.

THE LITERARY CLUB

The Literary Club was set up in 1918 on Maman Allah (Mamilla) Street, and Fakhri al-Nashashibi was one of its members.[129] The club was based in the house of Abu Swayy, near the house of Uwaida. My friend Saliba al-Jouzi was also one of its members. I remember well that Fakhri al-Nashashibi and Saliba once stood and gave a speech from the balcony that was above the Credit Lyonnais Bank. The building, which housed the Muslim-Christian Association at the time, belonged to the Greek Orthodox Patriarchate. They gave the speech in the course of the demonstration in order to voice both a unified protest against the Balfour Declaration and a demand for Syrian unity. It was an enthusing political speech in which they embraced each other, symbolizing that the cross was embracing the crescent. It was a wonderful event that clearly showed the British and Zionists the strong and true fraternity that joins Muslims and Christians of this country together despite its occupation by Christian Britain. The demonstration proceeded towards the Literary Club on Maman Allah Street.

THE RESIGNATION OF MUSA KAZEM PASHA

When the sinister Balfour Declaration was announced in Jerusalem, people were deeply stirred and upset to have been tricked; particularly that Article 22 of the mandate document stated clearly that "English, Arabic, and Hebrew shall be the official languages of Palestine." The late Kazem Pasha was deeply moved and submitted his resignation from his post as mayor of Jerusalem, categorically refusing to give his approval regarding the Hebrew language. He handed in his resignation in the autumn of 1920, after the first (anti-Zionist) uprising had taken place on April 4, 1920.

MY APPOINTMENT AS A CIVIL SERVANT IN THE MILITARY ADMINISTRATION

In 1919 I visited my teacher Costandi Labbat who was in charge of the Registry of the Military Governor of Jerusalem, which was based in the German Schmidt Building outside Damascus Gate. My colleague and friend Tannas Salmit was also working with him. After some discussion, Costandi Labbat decided to help me and sent me to see Mr. Reynolds, the head of the Saint George's School, who gave me a reference letter testifying to my good character, behavior, and competence. With this reference I was immediately appointed as a clerk at a monthly salary of five Egyptian pounds.

My appointment delighted employees at the Governorate, juniors and seniors alike. Most of them were friends of mine from Jerusalem. But why were they so happy? Because they had been joined by an amateur musician who was known not only in Jerusalem but in all of Palestine.

Since I took this job before the British Mandate began, all the heads of departments at the time, including the military governor, Mr. Ronald Storrs, were dressed in military uniform. Mr. Hanna Estefan,[130] who also dressed in military uniform, was transferred from the department of Haddad Pasha to the Governorate. The so-called Registry was based in a large room to the left of the entrance to the building. We, the male employees, worked in a separate section, and apart from us, behind a curtain, worked the ladies, and the young ladies—Farida Haddad, Julia Khadr, Mary Fattala, Emily Khod, and also Miss Lydia Tannous and Mary Hanania. The chief clerk was W. MacPherson.[131]

The Governorate was on the ground floor of the building. The first floor was used by the military administration officers, all of whom, such as Major Hedog Jones, Mr. Keith-Roach, Mr. Pollock, and Mr. Henderson, the head of the Public Health Department, wore military uniform. Sami Haddawi[132] was working in Mr. Henderson's office at the time as his personal servant. We often saw him polish Mr. Henderson's shoes. Later on, Sami was appointed as a clerk at the Governorate in Jerusalem. He used to wear shorts, and he worked with us and became our colleague. He could only write with a pencil, and his intelligence enabled him to come to Jerusalem and reach a high rank in the mandate government working in land estates.

The finance department was called the Tithe and the Werko Department, and was located in some of the ground-floor rooms. Its director was Mr. Harver, and among its employees were Hussein al-Arnaout, Ibrahim al-Alami, Abdul-Razzaq Qlibo, Muhammad Aref al-Costantini, Suleiman al-Waari, Sheikh Shehadah Abu Saoud, Said Mukhtar, Manuel Andrea, Tawfiq Manuel, Daoud al-Karimi, Abdullah Nasri Saghir, and others.

A small section of the basement level was turned into a café for employees and was run by Giryis Nassar, also known as Abu Mikhail al-Far, since he had been in charge of this building since before the Great War. The remaining rooms remained unoccupied and out of use. As for the department's collectors at the time, they were Shukri Ibrahim al-Nashashibi, Mustafa Awad, Bakr Awad, Uthman Abu al-Saoud, Shakib al-Daqqaq, Husam al-Sharfa, Khalil al-Qutb, Abdul-Rahman al-Danaf, Ibrahim Hassounah, and Yahuda Ibrahim.

We all worked together like a family. We were often allowed to have evening parties and play the oud and darbuka at the Governorate, so people who had business there were not allowed to come in until the following day. To tell the truth, the hall of the Registry was very convenient for throwing such parties. We have unforgettable memories of the good times we had there.

Mitri Costandi al-Muna, the maternal uncle of Andrea Qassis, our colleague at the translation section, ran a private café under the pine trees on the northern side of the building inside the building's fence. We used to have something to eat there in the morning at ten o'clock. All the employees, heads and subordinates alike, would meet and put their sense of humor and satirical storytelling skills to the test. My colleagues still bitterly miss those days and speak of how good they were. In winter, when the ground was covered with snow, they would all have snowball fights. One morning I went to work to find that many of my colleagues had been waiting for me. As soon as I arrived, they started throwing snowballs at me. I shouted, "Storrs, Storrs! Help me!" Storrs suddenly appeared and came to my rescue, frenetically pelting them with snowballs. Thanks to his strong build, we won the battle, and we all spent most of that day at the Governorate drinking whiskey and cognac. An atmosphere of friendship and understanding prevailed among all the civil servants; there was no room for hate or jealousy. Storrs liked this way of life, for having lived for a very long time in Egypt and Sudan, and having come to know the ways of the Orient and its passionate and cheerful nature, he decided to adopt them.

Unfortunately, this era came to an end when the British government established the Civil Administration in Palestine in the summer of 1920 and appointed Sir Herbert Samuel as high commissioner.[133] I recall that when we learned the news at the Registry, we were extremely disappointed to have been deceived. We had only been relieved from the tyrannical rule of the Ottomans to find ourselves under the rule of a Zionist high commissioner. We were gripped by fear and our hearts cringed.

This is how the Civil Administration was formed. The heads of the Education, Security, Finance, Customs, Legal, and Agriculture Departments were selected from among the British, while those for the Department of Travel and Immigration and the Land Commission were selected from Jewish ranks. The British Zionist Mr. Bentwich was also appointed as legal advisor, and we thought to ourselves that this was only a taste of what was yet to come.[134] It was the beginning of the implementation of the Balfour Declaration in Palestine.

OUR FESTIVE LIFE AT THE GOVERNORATE

At the Registry I worked every day from eight o'clock in the morning until one in the afternoon and from half past five until seven-thirty in the evening. As I used to drink regularly, especially towards the end of the day, I tended to be mildly inebriated when I returned to the Registry at five-thirty. My colleagues would welcome me with excitement and pleasure, and we would spend most of the two remaining business hours singing, joking, and telling anecdotes.

Now that they were liberated from the yoke of the Turks and from the Great War, and all the pain, displacement, and famine it had brought on them, people were enjoying a life of affluence with the occupation by the British army, the army that sowed money into the ground. We witnessed marvels at the Governorate. Often on official orders, the Registry room was turned into a celebration hall where singing, dancing, and acting went on during business hours in the presence of various local guests who attended on the invitation of Commander in Chief Mr. Ronald Storrs. I used to play the oud and dance the dabkeh among my colleagues of the first and second grades, and you could hear us playing the darbuka and singing at the top of our voices day or night in that stately building, the headquarters of the military governor of Jerusalem.

I was often amazed and wondered, What kind of government is this? What kind of governors are these? How is it possible to allow so much partying and drinking to take place in the very rooms where courts are set up and issues and problems of the people are resolved? How did we manage to live under the Ottomans? But I wish we had remained under their rule because we later realized that our country and homeland had been secretly sold. For those whose conquest made us breathe relief broke their promise and betrayed our trust after Arabs themselves helped them in occupying the country by rising against the Turks. But such was the will of the Almighty.

THE HEAD CLERK AND MACPHERSON

One evening, mildly inebriated as usual, I arrived at the Registry where my colleagues had been waiting for me. As I entered the room, I noticed in the corner a stack of those horrible cheap trousers made for

Turkish soldiers. They had been found in a cave in Jerusalem beneath the Damascus Gate wall and were confiscated and brought to the Governorate. I slipped on a pair that was so large that it reached up to my chest. In this ridiculous attire, I stood under the big lamp that hung from the middle of the ceiling and started dancing the dabkeh of *Dakdouka*, a well-known song I had picked up from the farmers. My lady colleagues stood around me clapping their hands and singing the chorus.

But as the proverb goes, calamities fall but on the calmest nights. Suddenly, the door opened and the head clerk, Mr. MacPherson, came in with a gloomy face, pointed at me with his finger, said, "Mr. Jawhariyyeh," and went back to his room. Everyone stood there, petrified, worried that I might be fired. I went behind the curtain that separated the employees from the lady typists, took off the trousers, tidied myself up, and went to see Mr. MacPherson, my heart pounding with fear at what the outcome of this embarrassing incident might be. He looked at me with a smile on his face and said, "Could you possibly take my sister home tonight after work?" I answered, "Of course, any time!" Then, I greeted him and his sister, a ravishing beauty. I said I was at her service and asked her to be ready at seven o'clock. She thanked me. Mr. MacPherson and his sister lived at the Austrian Hospice, near my father's home inside the wall.

At seven o'clock, all the employees looked on as I accompanied the young lady home. She knew me and knew about my musical interests. So she put her hand in mine, and we walked away while everyone laughed. Once I had brought her home safely, she refused to let me go before I had sat in her room and had a glass of whiskey. I then wished her a good night. The incident became a story for my colleagues to tell at their gatherings.

THE MILITARY GOVERNOR OF JERUSALEM, MR. RONALD STORRS[135]

My job at the Registry opening files, numbering them, and classifying them by subject in a special register was in the Big Hall of the German Building where all the employees, both male and female, were also based. As it happened, the governor of Jerusalem, Storrs, was giving a party in the same hall. The guests were Jerusalemites from all confessions—Muslim, Christian, and Jewish—and I was one of the employees in charge of receiving them. Costandi Labbat introduced me to Storrs and told him about my artistic inclinations and talents, particularly in the field of Arabic music, and how I could play the oud, the rebeck, and the tanboor, sing Andalusian muwashahat, Egyptian dawrs, folk songs and peasant uhzujas, and dance the dabkeh. Storrs was impressed and from that moment began to give me special treatment and invite me to his private parties, particularly those he gave at his home.

Sir Ronald Storrs. Photo by unknown American Colony photographer. © Library of Congress.

Mr. Storrs was one of the key men whose services to the British Empire in the Middle East were invaluable. He had joined the British occupation campaign, serving in Egypt for many long years. He knew Arabic, could read and write it fluently, including the Qu'ran, and he had taken marvelous and wonderful stances towards Arabs and Muslims on many occasions. Lawrence, who was well-known in the Middle East, was part of his entourage. He was fully in the know about the secrets of British politics in the East, and it was also through him that the McMahon Agreement had been negotiated with Sharif Hussein bin Ali of Mecca, his son Faisal, and Hussein Ruhi, who later remained in his job as civil servant at the British Mandate Education Department in Jerusalem. Storrs was knowledgeable about Arab countries, traditions, and instincts, and was appointed military governor of Jerusalem immediately after the occupation, through the influence of Gabriel Haddad Pasha. He helped in establishing the political administrative system in the wake of the occupation, and with his usual cunning, he conceived the idea of establishing political parties in the country. He set up the Supreme Muslim Council and appointed Hajj Hussein al-Husseini as its president after bringing him back home during the time of Sir Herbert Samuel. Against him, he set up Ragheb Bey al-Nashishibi who was as known for his links to the National Defense Party as for his support for the mandate government.

Storrs had a passion for acquiring various Oriental antiques. His home in Jerusalem was located in Mulk al-Alman, "the land of the Germans" (the slope leading to the Italian Hospital). It is said that on this site the German emperor's tents were set up when he visited Jerusalem in 1898. The home of Ronald Storrs was like a museum, housing the finest antique Persian carpets, a marvelous Persian copper collection, some antique weapons, rare braziers from Persia and Istanbul, manuscripts, and earthenware, among others. I used to acquire some of these antiques for him cheaply, so he became kinder and more sympathetic toward me. He appreciated these antiques and was a close friend of the late Nasri Ohan, the well-known antique seller in Jerusalem. I admit frankly that it was his collection of antiques that inspired and encouraged me to realize the dream I had always nourished and start acquiring memorabilia and antiques until my hopes turned into reality. My effort in building the Jawhariyyeh Collection has benefited from Mr. Storrs who broadened my knowledge and increased my fondness of this beautiful art.

Singing at the Home of Mr. Storrs

As my acquaintance with Mr. Storrs grew stronger, he never missed the chance to have me at his parties if it was convenient on the occasion. He once invited some of the notables and civil servants of Jerusalem for tea under the pine trees at his home. Among the guests were Sheikh Salim Qutainah, Sheikh Adib Jawda, Sheikh Yaacoub al-Azbaky, Sheikh Saoud al-Ouri, Sheikh Said al-Khatib, Sheikh Husameddine Jarallah, and others. He insisted that I play and sing for the guests in traditional Arab dress. It was an extraordinary evening in which Mr. Storrs gave a political speech in classical Arabic, impressing all those present. Storrs really liked listening to music. He played the piano and insisted on playing it for a long time every night, even if he was not back home until late, which was a nuisance to the residents of that quarter, particularly to the translator As'ad Khodr. Khodr used to keep some hens at his home, and Mr. Storrs was infuriated when the rooster crowed at night. He tried many times to put an end to it and even sentenced the rooster to death by hanging. But the late As'ad Khodr refused to allow the sentence to be carried out.

"And make ready for them whatever you can"

As soon as the Arab people of Palestine learned of Britain's malicious intentions, and the trick of the sinister Balfour Declaration was revealed to them, they launched a continuous series of protests and demonstrations led by the late Musa Kazem Pasha al-Husseini. I recall one occasion where people walked the city in a massive soul-stirring demonstration until they reached the governor's headquarters in Damascus Gate, voicing their anger in the strongest terms directed at Zionism, the Balfour Declaration, the partition of the country that was to follow the British occupation, and particularly the separation of Syria from Palestine.[136] The demonstration stopped for a while, and people demanded to see Storrs and hear what he had to say. After some hesitation, he came out of the Governorate and stood behind the fence that overlooks Nablus Road. Behind him stood a cannon that had been left behind by the army and placed there for memory's sake. When the crowds saw the governor, they fell silent. Storrs then spoke in his rotund voice and said, "And make ready for them whatever you can of force,"[137] and went back in immediately. It was an extremely funny act but these comedies did not fool the patriotic Arabs who knew Storrs well.

The emblem of General Ronald Storrs as military governor of Jerusalem.

WORKING AS A TRANSLATOR

I was appointed as an assistant at the Translation Section at the Governorate. The head of the section was the late Subhi Uwaida, and his assistant was the late Andrea Kassis. We had a great time together while I was working there, particularly as Andrea had a great sense of humor. Together we used to laugh and joke, and act at the various theaters of Jerusalem, particularly at the YMCA's, which at the time was housed in the wooden building located on the Armenian Monastery's land on Jaffa Road.

The late Andrea played the role of the village teacher, giving a hilarious reenactment of teaching in the old days. Another act was a representation of the village *madafa* (guesthouse), in which he and the audience listened to poet Elias and his rebeck. The poet Elias would enter limping and produce the rebeck from under his abaya. After greeting those present, he would sit down and begin to play the rebeck and sing songs. These plays drew a huge audience from all communities and from among locals and foreigners alike.

I had known Andrea since childhood. His grandmother, the mother of Mitri Costandi al-Muna, was our neighbor at Dar al-Jawhariyyeh. We had cheerful evenings with the whole al-Muna family. Andrea and my brother Tawfiq always led these parties, which were frequent and known to most among the Greek Orthodox community. Andrea was also my companion during my time at the Saint George's School. We were inseparable and would picnic together in the village of Deir Amr and also in Bethlehem at the time my sister Afifeh was living there in the house that belonged to his paternal grandfather, the late Reverend Assaf, and which was located near the fountain. I will never forget our picnics and evenings during the Festival of Our Lady Mary in Jerusalem, which lasted for two weeks each year.

MY FRIEND AND COLLEAGUE SAMI HADDAWI

I had known Sami Haddawi since I was appointed at the Governorate. I was an ordinary civil servant at the Registry, and he was the servant of Mr. Henderson who was head of the Health Department since the occupation and lived in a room on the upper floor of the governor's headquarters in the German Building in Damascus Gate. Our friendship grew stronger when he was appointed as a clerk in my section under the management of Hedog Jones. Sami and his brothers, Eddy, William, and James, were among the brightest young men. They were indeed self-made, and they all became some of the most prominent civil servants of the mandate government, particularly Sami.

I obtained the following information about his background from Uncle al-Abd Badran, who was the grandfather of Doctor Jaleel Badran.[138] Sami's maternal grandmother was a Muslim from Hebron. She was treated for an eye disorder at the English eye hospital in Jerusalem, which was known as the Ophthalmic Hospital, and converted to Christianity following her recovery.[139] She then married in Ramallah into the Shehadeh family and gave birth to Sami's mother. The latter married Sami's father, who was a member of the London Jews' Society and had converted to Christianity.[140] Together they had Sami and his brothers, and their only sister. I still remember the neighborhood-commune (mazal) where Sami's father lived. It was one of the many communes built especially for Jews in Mea Shearim in Jerusalem.[141] We threw many parties there after Sami joined the mandate civil service and became a colleague of ours. This ghetto was registered in the property tax records in 1929 in the name of the Haddawi family and remains so to this day.

SINGER SHEIKH AHMED AL-TARIFI

I was lucky to meet the late Sheikh Ahmed al-Tarifi at an evening party at the place of my dear friend, lawyer Fakhry Bey Assim. Many well-known Jerusalemites were present, such as Kamel Effendi al-Budeiri, Daoud al-Fitiani, Tahsin al-Khalidi, Ishak al-Budeiri, and others. Other friends of al-Tarifi had also joined us from Jaffa, such as late

Umar al-Bitar, Deeb al-Jaghlit, and others. Sheikh Ahmed sang wonderfully, and that made me play the oud in a particularly vibrant way. I was the only one to play the poems he recited on the oud, and he was impressed and began to treat me rather affectionately, all thanks to this fine art.

The voice of Sheikh al-Tarifi was one of the most voluptuous and powerful voices. He mainly sang poems which, although not very creative musically, were rather solid in that their meaning was powerfully conveyed despite the absence of elaborate singing. This induced the unsuspecting listener into a state of tarab and intoxication, thanks to a performance style which resembled Qu'ranic recitation, and to a powerful tenor voice.

Most of the sheikh's poems were of the Jiharka maqam. One of them was the poem beginning with *Tahayyartu fi amri* (I'm at a loss as to what to do). I truly enjoyed listening to him sing that famous poem of his, which was the most solid one in terms of musical composition, and perhaps his only poem of the maqam Sikah. It began with *Jarahata qalbi bi lahzika* (Your blink cut through my heart).

Sheikh al-Tarifi was an excellent reciter. He was keen on my friendship because he knew how much I loved music. That evening party was only the beginning of a strong and lasting friendship between the two of us. Thus, we dropped formalities with each other, and I gained a brother and a loyal friend. I recall that after that party, al-Tarifi went to Jaffa only to return to Jerusalem a week later. He stayed at our home in Saadiyeh for forty-two days and nights which turned out to be among our best ever. When he woke up in the morning, God bless his soul, he would respectfully and soberly go to my late mother and kiss her hand, and was happy to receive her blessing as though she was his own mother and there was no difference between us. Such was friendship at the time, thanks be to God.

I would not be exaggerating to say that Sheikh Ahmed al-Tarifi was one of the most handsome young men of his time. He was tall, upright, well-proportioned, and might have been taller than Doctor Yaacoub Nazha. He had a handsome, affable, smiling face, an extraordinary personality, and looked all the more handsome, marvelous, and elegant in his Arab dress which consisted of a *ghabani* or roza qumbaz (silk or satan coat)[142] and his "wool Sultan" Egyptian black abaya. Given his massive body, he was a big eater. In the morning, before breakfast, he would drink four warm eggs. When he sat down to drink, he would set out a large glass filled with arak, mixed with cold water, which we came to call "the milk jar."

In one party at Dar al-Jawhariyyeh, al-Tarifi sat in the middle of the lounge, as he used to, singing some of his poems. We learned later that the family of Umm Yusuf Abdu in the Christian Quarter had been sitting on the balcony listening to him and that they understood every word he said. This is how powerful his voice was.

With his death I lost a great support in music and became like an orphan in this art. May God bless his soul and accept him in his paradise.

THE LATE KAMEL BEY AL-BUDEIRI

I met the late Kamel Effendi al-Budeiri at one of the soirées organized by Hussein Effendi al-Husseini. Kamel used to call Hussein Effendi "Uncle"; the two of them might have been distantly related from the maternal side. Kamel, God bless his soul, was a great man and a true patriot who loved Arabs and embraced the idea of Arab nationalism. He was a civil servant during the Ottoman period, first as a district manager for al-Ramlah and later on for Jericho. He was one of the well-known figures of Jerusalem and the brother of Sheikh Musa al-Budeiri. He met a Greek Orthodox girl named Hannah Abu al-Sharr at the time that her father was working at the Al-Jamal Hotel, in the building located outside Jaffa Gate, and where Hussein Effendi moved the municipality building in 1908. Kamel became increasingly fond of her, and their story became a gossip topic for everyone in Jerusalem. Hannah ended up converting to Islam and marrying Kamel during the Ottoman period, which was indeed a rare and strange thing to happen at the time. This prompted some amateur to write and compose for the occasion a taqtouqa that was sung repeatedly at evening parties and weddings in Jerusalem. I played and sang this song in my younger years, too.

Oh, mother, adorn my hands with henna,
For I am about to lose my mind and renounce my faith.
Driver, start the carriage
And take me to al-Budeiri's.
(Chorus)
Hannah is standing on the balcony
Calling for Kamel on the telephone.
Eat your hearts out, Orthodox girls,
Mohammad's faith is now my own.

I have recorded this song as well as a number of old folk songs that used to be sung in Jerusalem at my daughter Yusra's.[143] The music was later transcribed by her husband Mr. Salvador Arnita when the couple were put in charge of compiling all folk songs in Beirut in 1959. The song is of the maqam Rast Nawa. My friendship with the late Kamel continued during the British occupation. He felt bitter, God bless his soul, about the situation following the occupation and how the British had tricked the Arabs and promised Jews through the sinister Balfour Declaration to set up a national home for them in Palestine. I remember a soirée at al-Budeiri's in Bab al-Sahira at which a great many Jerusalemites were present, and he was extremely drunk. He stood there lecturing enthusiastically with his poor language that was loaded with patriotism and dignity, while looking at Fakhri al-Nashishibi and giving him advice, or rather hurling rude insults at him and trying to awaken him after he had been appointed aide-de-camp to High Commissioner Sir Herbet Samuel. I still keep a historical photograph of him in the Jawhariyyeh Collection for memory's sake.

Kamel, God bless his soul, used to make his nephew Khalil, who was the son of Sheikh Musa el-Budeiri and a child at the time, stand on a chair and recite soul-stirring patriotic and folk poems to us. Proud and happy, Kamel would kiss his nephew lovingly and eagerly.

At one of the soirées in the Bab al-Sahira neighborhood, while some of Jerusalem's finest patriots were listening to me play the oud and sing—I believe it was New Year's eve—an extremely inebriated Kamel learned that some badly drunk British soldiers had been wandering around the city carousing and attacking bars. On learning the news, Kamel, who was very fond of his carriage that was drawn by two good horses, left the house and saw with his own eyes some of those soldiers trying to take his carriage away. Not knowing any English, he jumped forward heroically and with his strong arms threw two of the soldiers off the driver's seat and onto the ground. In the blink of an eye he saddled the horses and drove off, shouting to them, "I'll teach you, Johnny, I'll teach you, Johnny." He made his way to another neighborhood of Jerusalem and stayed there until morning. But a military force arrived and carried out an investigation and a search in Bab al-Sahira, when it turned out that the two soldiers who had been thrown to the ground had nearly lost their lives and had to be given first aid before being taken to the military hospital.

Kamel did not accept any posts during the British Mandate he detested, but rather remained in private business, launching *Al-Sabah* (*The Morning*) newspaper in Jerusalem in 1921. Unfortunately, Kamel was killed through betrayal in the Arabian desert, may God bless his soul and accept him in paradise, for he was indeed one of the martyrs of the Arab nation.

SOIRÉES WITH BADI'A MASABNI

Meeting Badi'a

Badi'a visited Jerusalem for the first time in 1920, accompanied by Jewish oud player, Shehada, and leading a modest musical ensemble and two female dancers dressed in national Egyptian dress. She stayed at a small hotel owned by her friend Mina Mikhail al-Halabi, located near Jaffa Gate right inside the wall. The building later housed the press of the *Mir'at al-Sharq* newspaper (*The Mirror of the East*) which was owned by the late Bulus Shehadeh of Ramallah. She performed at the theater of al-Maarif Café, a small theater that was nevertheless known to be the best in Jerusalem. She sang these songs while dancing along with her dancers and acting the story she was singing. For example, she would dress as a pistachio vendor and carry the pot used for the purpose when she sang the taqtouqa beginning with

Delicious, salted pistachio, Effendi,
Take an ounce or two.
Our country's pistachio is incomparable,
One nut is enough to give you a boost.

Likewise, Badi'a would hold some apples in her hands and wear a special costume when she sang in maqam Hijaz Kar the taqtouqa beginning with

Sweet apples,
Lovely apples,
Your vendor is fair, lovely,
And the best of all girls.

She would then move on to sing another taqtouqa, this in maqam Rast Nawa, dressed as a milkmaid.

Wake up, darling,
Start your day with some milk.
This creamy milk, I swear to my love for you,
Would cure the sick with just one sip.

She was indeed excellent at this kind of light singing. Her movement and dancing were just as impressive. Her perfect body, stunning beauty, gracious smile, her face and kindness, all made listeners and viewers feel like they were in paradise.

Badi'a often sang the songs and compositions of Sayyed Darwish. When she sang a song, particularly famous monologues, she uttered the words in a powerful, expressive way. I remember the monologue of the maqam Ajȧm *Ma 'ultilaksh inn el kutra* (Didn't I tell you that large numbers must one day defeat courage), particularly the verses mocking the rich who have no sense of patriotism.

It's all the fault of the rich.
There are loads of them, but they're no use to us.
They're just busy with Rosa and Maria
While disasters fall on their nation.
When will the Egyptian's penny
Stay at home and not go abroad?
You put in your money, and we our souls.
One hand alone doesn't clap.

When she sang the verse "It's all the fault of the rich" she would stare at some rich member of the audience who was known for his stinginess. The whole audience would look at the poor man and burst out laughing. If this rich man happened to be an idiot, too, she would repeat that part of the song with her fingers playing on her nose and look at him again, making him cringe with embarrassment.

Badi'a was a rare gem. She had a superior taste in this domain. To say that she excelled in her performances would be an understatement. No words could describe her justly. The oud player Shehada played very well. We had good times with him and Badi'a in Jerusalem.

Badi'a at al-Jawhariyyeh Café

Later on, Badi'a and I grew closer. As well as meeting at the theater, we began to meet at private musical gatherings, for Badi'a made a second visit to Jerusalem during which she stayed at the Saint John's Hotel that was located in the Christian Quarter, inside the wall, and that belonged to Uncle Saliba Saad. She thus became very close to us and our family. I remember once spending an evening at the al-Jawhariyyeh Café which my brother Khalil ran, along with George al-Halabi and Habib Mondo. Imagine an evening like that, in a café, after a day at work. It was an extraordinary party of drinking and music.

Many of our good friends were present including Fakhri Bey Assim, Tahsin al-Khalidi, Daoud al-Fitiani, Abdul-Qadir al-Alami, and Mustafa al-Sirriya. Reverend Sutiri Hanania was present in his uniform and had removed his cap, being in a state of inebriation and entrancement. I keep a photograph of this soirée.

I was playing the oud, and once everyone had been overcome with tarab, we moved to my father's place in Saadiyeh. Badi'a's musical band and the late Najib Bey Rihani were also with us. We stayed up until daybreak, and Badi'a was greatly impressed when the late Mitri Costandi whistled some taqsims, for he sounded like a violin. She rose from her seat, walked towards him, and gave him a kiss that was met with general applause. As for the late Najib Bey Rihani and the Egyptian artists who were in his company, they excelled at cracking jokes, particularly during a dialogue that took place between him and his wife Badi'a. We laughed until we almost passed out.

Badi'a at al-Jabsha's

A number of gatherings took place at which both Badi'a and myself were present. Some of these were held at the home of the late Fakhri al-Nashashibi with Ragheb Bey, Majed Bey, Ali Bey Jarallah, and others. The evening party which I never forgot, however, took place at Uncle Mustafa al-Jabsha's. Uncle Abu al-Abd was known for his passion for art and beauty. No musician ever came to Jerusalem and left without paying him a visit at his home. Uncle Abu al-Abd was a generous spender, and so he got lucky and invited Badi'a and her band to his house. It was indeed a bewildering evening. Badi'a was dressed in a see-through costume made for the purpose of dancing on stage only and was holding finger cymbals. As she danced among us, every part of her body shook while various musical instruments were played, particularly the qanun. Only Uncle Abu al-Abd, Ibrahim Shehada al-Alami, Mustafa al-Sirriya, Muhammad al-Sibasi, and I were present. We sat on a mattress on the floor, with all kinds of food and various alcoholic drinks laid before us. The house stood opposite Sabri Abd Rabbuh's bakery, and the room did not exceed three by four meters, but I can assure you that many of the women who knew Uncle Abu al-Abd were outside in the stable, listening to the music and watching this extraodinary scene through the door and windows of this small room. It was an unforgettable party. We were totally entranced until the morning, when we were surprised with a large tray of Zalatimo's famous *mutabaq*.[144] We had our fill of sweets, thanked Uncle Abu al-Abd, and left. I learned before leaving that he had paid Badi'a around thirty-five pounds. In return she gave an extraordinary evening of perfect artistry.

Badi'a was known for being a generous and kind soul with a sense of gratitude. Once, my daughter Yusra was visiting Cairo with some of her colleagues, and she wanted to see Badi'a on stage. When she arrived at the theater and sent her a message saying that Yusra, the daughter of Wasif Jawhariyyeh was there, Badi'a came to the entrance in person to welcome her and the other young ladies, and made her sit in the front row. Thus Yusra saw Badi'a on stage and was fascinated by her but without paying the entrance fee, and later returned home raving about this artist and touched by her kindness. May there be more people like Badi'a, and may God keep the unique gem she is for the East.

MY BROTHER AND FRIEND NAJIB AL-RIHANI

When speaking of Badi'a, one must mention her life companion Najib who later became her husband following the artistic cooperation between them. I met Najib in Jerusalem through Badi'a, and throughout his time in Jerusalem he did not let go of me a single day. I accompanied him to his private gatherings, particularly with Fakhri al-Nashashibi who was one of his most loyal friends. As for Najib's extraordinary personality, he was, God bless his soul, one of the greatest figures of the artistic scene in Egypt, and even in the whole East, as far as I know. It is entirely thanks to him that acting was able to mature the way it did.

He had performed on stage since he was a child. He once told me, "You see, Wasif, it is thanks to my late mother that I excelled at acting." I said, "Was she also an actress?" He told me, "As a child, I was an ambulant revolution, whatever I was playing or doing at home, and caused my mother a lot of nuisance. So when she cursed me, God bless her soul, she would say, 'May God strike you and make of you a sight for all people to mock.' God granted her wishes, and I ended up on stage where even sad people laugh at me."

I used to introduce him to many of my friends in Jerusalem, particularly to families, and we have good memories of our times with Fakhri al-Nashishibi at the homes of the most distinguished native Jewish families of Jerusalem. Najib truly felt at home at these gatherings and gave free reign to his humor—his raison d'être. I will never forget the exquisite gatherings with him when he was married to Badi'a Masabni. They were a dreamland of satire, wit, humor, and indulgence. Cheers to those days! Najib was a friend of our friend Agob Zeronian the photographer, who produced beautiful photographs of him while playing *Keshkesh Bey*. I kept some, signed by Najib, for the sake of memory and history.

THE FIRST ARAB UPRISING IN JERUSALEM DURING THE BRITISH MANDATE

In 1920 the Greek Orthodox communities of Jerusalem were celebrating Palm Sunday. Muslims were gathering to join the convoy of the flag of Prophet Moses. Saladdin had devised the majestic celebration as a national holiday upon defeating the Crusaders in order to keep the balance between the Muslim and Christian communities of Jerusalem.

I was standing in the pharmacy of my friend George Mashhour outside Jaffa Gate, waiting with everyone else to watch the convoy of Hebron pass. People grew fearful when they noticed that the convoy was proceeding too slowly, taking long hours, particularly from the moment it arrived at the Sultan's Pool until it reached the city at Jaffa Gate. The convoy was in a state of fury, chanting soul-stirring patriotic hymns against the Zionists, Jewish settlers, and the British in the wake of the Balfour Declaration as news spread throughout the country. When the convoy arrived in the outer square of Jaffa Gate, the whole city became like a battleground. The convoy's enthusiasm was inflamed when one free Arab standing on the balcony of the Literary Club raised the picture of Faisal I after they had listened to the patriotic speeches which the late Mahmoud Aziz al-Khalidi had given. This stirred their patriotic feelings, and they staged a massive uprising in which they took their revenge on native Jews,[145] killing and injuring many.

The government was furious at this audacious act, immediately imposed a curfew, and struck the Arab population, blaming the uprising on some of Jerusalem's figures, particularly Amin Effendi al-Husseini, the brother of the Grand Mufti of Jerusalem, Sheikh Kamel Effendi al-Husseini. In the evening, the forces of the British army shut the city gates, and I had to spend the night at my friend George Mashhour's place, which was located behind the Rex cinema, next to the Mamilla Cemetery.

Who Staged the First Uprising?

When I arrived at work at the Governorate in Damascus Gate on Monday morning, I learned that the government had arrested the following individuals overnight and that they were being held in a separate room on the second floor of the building, near what was the Finance Department—Sheikh Abdul-Qader al-Muzaffar, Abdul-Fattah Darwish and his cousin Said Darwish, Khalil Baydas who had given a soul-stirring speech, Muhammad Kamel al-Budeiri (I am not sure about this), and Musa Kazem Pasha, as far as I believe, and others. They were later transferred to Acre. I secretly helped to provide them with necessary items like cigarettes and other things. Later, we learned that following this uprising, Amin Effendi al-Husseini had fled Jerusalem on April 4, 1920 via the Dead Sea with the help of Muhyiddine al-Husseini, and moved between Jordan and Syria. After the collapse of King Faisal's rule, he returned to the East and remained there until the Civil Administration was announced and Sir Herbert Samuel took over.[146]

After the death of the mufti, Sheikh Kamel al-Husseini, Amin al-Husseini was elected by the citizens to be the Grand Mufti of Jerusalem. It was customary for the high commissioner to issue a decree to the effect, which he did, prompting people to believe that he was appointed when in fact he had been elected. When he fled Jerusalem, Amin Effendi al-Husseini was accompanied only by Aref Effendi al-Aref. After their return, Aref al-Aref accepted a post with the mandate government while Amin Effendi al-Husseini remained away from it, having been elected Grand Mufti of Jerusalem and the President of the Supreme Muslim Council.[147]

THE PRO JERUSALEM SOCIETY

The Pro Jerusalem Society was founded in the wake of Britain's occupation of the city by the military governor of Jerusalem Ronald Storrs, some state leaders such as Richmond, Ashbee,[148] and Luke, as well as the most respected notables of the various communities of the city. The society's aim was to secure the total preservation of the city's character, particularly in the historical Old City. Tough regulations were introduced, in addition to those of the Municipality and the Health Department, strictly forbidding the use of corrugated tin sheets, brick, cob, and concrete in any construction or repair works inside the wall, as this would disfigure the view of the old historical sites in Jerusalem. Mr. Richmond diligently supervised the state of affairs at the al-Aqsa Mosque and the Dome of the Rock on al-Haram al-Sharif, while the famous architect Mr. Ashbee, the then civic advisor as they used to call him, supervised preservation works on the wall. He made satisfactory repairs to the city wall and had iron railings put up along the inside edge of dedicated sections of the ramparts, creating a walkway where tourists could walk easily with the help of these railings and look at the city both inside and outside the wall.

The logo of the Pro Jerusalem Society, from the cover of Charles Ashbee's ***Jerusalem: 1918–1920*** (London: Council of the Pro Jerusalem Society). From the private collection of Issam Nassar.

I worked as a clerk at this society under Mr. Ashbee and had the opportunity to see much of the beauty and the historical monuments of the Holy City and al-Haram al-Sharif. The famous architect George al-Shebr, who became one of Jerusalem's rich personalities during the British Mandate, was working with Mr. Richmond as a technician, managing the repairs of al-Haram al-Sharif. I keep a historical photo-

Jaffa Gate, with the clock tower that was built in celebration of the jubilee of Sultan Abdul-Hamid. This photo was taken sometime between 1906 and the start of World War I. From the private collection of Issam Nassar.

graph of us with George al-Shebr after he had become a prominent civil servant of the government of Palestine. I could not bear to continue working under Mr. Ashbee because of the heavy workload. One winter evening, while I was fairly drunk, I went into the Registry where my colleagues met me with the usual cheers and laughter, and I started walking over the desks. Suddenly, Mr. Ashbee entered, staring at me, so I shouted at the top of my voice, "Hello, hello Mr. Ashbee." My colleagues burst out laughing, while he went back angrily to his office to write a damning report against me which turned out to be the final blow. In brief, I was transferred to the translation section and freed from his insufferable pestering. I thanked the Lord for this outcome.

To tell the truth, my work under Mr. Ashbee was extremely beneficial to me, as it allowed me to improve my knowledge of the unique monuments and historical buildings of Jerusalem which nurtured my passion for acquiring art objects.

THE CONSTRUCTION OF THE CLOCK TOWER IN JAFFA GATE

During the mayorship of Faidallah al-Alami,[149] the Jerusalem municipality built a unique clock tower in one of the corners of the rooftop of Jaffa Gate. I was told that the construction was financed with donations made by the people of the city in order to celebrate twenty-five years of the rule of Sultan Abdul-Hamid. This clock tower played an important role in Jerusalem and was of great use to the citizens. It was located on a high spot overlooking both the inside and the outside of the city walls, and could even be seen from as far away as Bethlehem.

However, the Pro Jerusalem Society would not allow it to continue to stand on the city ramparts and decided to demolish it. For despite its perfect construction, the quality of its stones, and its ornamentation, the architecture experts decided that it was not grand enough for the city wall considering its age and four-hundred-year history. This tower had been designed by the late engineer Pascal Effendi Sarufim, who also supervised its finalization. He was the municipality's architect and belonged to one of the most honorable families of the Latin community of Jerusalem. He adhered to the oriental architectural style, but his exuberant use of ornamentation, which was due to his being a graduate of French universities, resulted in a mix similar to the music of the great master Muhammad Abdul-Wahab, or the "Franco-Arab" style, as they call it.[150]

The Society thus had it demolished overnight. As for me, I agree to its demolition for the above reasons. But I feel that it is a real pity that it was not transferred to another site that would have been more compatible with its architecture, for example, on the rooftop of the Barclays Building or the lounge of the new municipality building. I am almost certain that these unique stones and ornamentations have gone with the wind or were perhaps grabbed by some to use in the building of private homes, at that time.

My total devotion for my city prompted me to make a wooden model of the clock tower and Jaffa Gate in the real-life colors of the old wall and the new clock tower built on it. Thus I have immortalized the entrance to the city as it was on the eve of the British occupation.[151]

OUR FRIEND HANNA BESHARAT'S PARTY

I promised to sing at a party at Hanna al-Besharat's[152] who lived at the time with his brothers Wasif and Raji in a property owned by the late Saleh Juqman in Musrara in Jerusalem, opposite the Toumayan Building. I did not know Hanna al-Besharat personally, but I had made a promise to Hanna Estefan who had occupied a senior post in the military administration since the beginning of the occupation and dressed in military uniform. The party was held on the occasion of the birth of twins Maurice and Victor outside Palestine, as far as I know. After picnicking in the village of Artas with my friends in my qumbaz and Arab dress, I made my way back to town extremely drunk and went to Musrara in the evening.

I had thought that this was a family party but was surprised to find that the iron fence surrounding the spacious orchard in front of the house had been covered with Persian rugs in order to deter the evil eye of onlookers. It was a joyful sight. The place was decorated with bright lux lamps, since there was no electricity at the time, and on both sides of the path leading to the building a large number of chairs had been arranged like in a theater and were filled with guests, while the rest of the guests stood around. Hanna and his brother Wasif, my namesake, welcomed me warmly at the entrance where I had remained standing for a while, unable to move; my embarrassment and cringing were such that I nearly fainted. I said, "Why all this, brothers? I am not a professional singer or musician. This great stage would be more suited for a professional master, not an amateur like myself!" I apologized, but after persistent pleading from my friends, and particularly from Hanna Estefan, I caved in and got on the stage which had been especially set up for me. Before I began to play and sing, a member of the Besharat family rose and read some words of praise, appreciation, thanks, and gratitude.

I played and sang some pieces which fit the occasion, after which there was much applause and whistling from the audience and from those who had been listening to the party from behind the fence. At the end, I sat with Hanna Besharat chatting and joking. I liked him as soon as I saw him, and a strong lifelong brotherly friendship was born between us.

Hanna Besharat had worked as a contractor in the British army since the beginning of the occupation and had conquered the hearts of most of the army leaders. I often had the chance to look at his correspondence with leaders such as Allenby and the generals who followed him, and saw that the letters were written to him in an informal style, as though Hanna was a brother of theirs. He was a debater and fluent in Arabic, French, English, and also knew some German and Turkish. His extreme generosity and hospitality made him the Hatem Tayy of our age.[153] During the Second World War, Hanna and his wife were staying in a private suite at Cairo's Continental Hotel. The generosity and hospitality he showed during his stay amazed all those who knew him. All those who visited the hotel's bar were offered drinks at his expense.

ISMAIL BEY AL-HUSSEINI AND MY BROTHER FAKHRI

A long time had passed without me getting the chance to see Uncle Ismail Bey al-Husseini. So he sent his servant to tell me that the Bey would like to visit me at my father's home in Haret al-Saadiyeh. I immediately made preparations to welcome him with due hospitality. When he came—my mother was still alive at the time—he rebuked me for not having been in touch, for he loved me like a father loved his son. I apologized to him, and on his request I played and sang some of his favorite songs. He was pleased and forgave me.

While we chatted, he asked how I and each of my brothers were doing in our work. When we discussed my brother Fakhri, I told him, "He has no luck, Bey. He has been working at the shop of our brother-in-law Costandi Abdul-Nur since the First World War. I wish we could help him to return to school now." He replied, "Wasif, we have the opportunity to do so. Send him to me tomorrow. I work as an inspector at the Education Department, so don't worry." My mother and I thanked him for his attention. My brother Fakhri went to him, and with the help of Uncle Abu Ibrahim he joined the Rashidiya School in Jerusalem. This was in 1921. Later on, the colonial policy in the country changed and the mandate government started working against the interests of the Husseini family, and thus appointed man of letters Is'af al-Nashashibi as education inspector. Thanks to his ambition and dedication to education, my brother Fakhri did well and successfully went on to join the Arab College at the time of our friend and brother, the educator Ahmed Sameh al-Khalidi who befriended him and placed his infinite trust in him.[154] Fakhri thus became like one of the al-Khalidis and succeeded in obtaining a teaching qualification, all thanks to the visit of Uncle Ismail Bey, God bless his soul.[155]

At the end of the evening Uncle Ismail took his leave, and I went down with him to see him off. When he stepped out of the house, he remembered that one of his many properties was located in the neighborhood. So with the gas lamp I was holding, we went down an alley and out again, going past one house after another until we finally found the house. It stood almost opposite our home, next to the house of the late Mustafa al-Salihani, and was occupied by the al-Sabbagh family. Uncle Abu Ibrahim was pleased and said, "Oh Wasif, I have not seen it since I was young."

THE APPOINTMENT OF RAGHEB BEY AL-NASHASHIBI AS MAYOR OF JERUSALEM

At the beginning of the Civil Administration in 1921, the mandate government appointed Ragheb Bey al-Nashashibi mayor of Jerusalem to replace the late Musa Kazem Pasha al-Husseini, who had resigned for political reasons.[156]

At the time, Ragheb Bey al-Nashashibi was in Aleppo and was recalled for this purpose. I had been close to Ragheb Bey and was always in touch with him thanks to the joyous gatherings he held. When he took his post, he proved himself to be truly worthy of this high position such that he made himself seem more like a king than a mayor. If you went to see him at the municipality, an attendant would take you through and leave you in the care of another, behind the screen, until you finally met this great personality.

Ragheb Bey was generous of spirit, and he gave away as he gained. His generosity and lavish lifestyle exceeded those of many Jerusalemites. He was a source of pride for the people of Jerusalem, particularly when he was receiving visitors to the city. This attitude of his earned him the liking of all those who knew him and whose requests he always granted. The story of one small incident will give an idea about his generosity.

Before his appointment as mayor, Ragheb Bey was living alone in his old home, the house of the mother of the late Sheikh Rashid al-Nashashibi. His Jewish wife was living in a private home on Jaffa Road. When he was appointed mayor of Jerusalem, he still owned his horse-drawn English carriage. He used to take me to the Bezelel store on Jaffa Road, in the very spot where Barclays and the municipality stand today.[157]

In his carriage he used to transport borrowed copper and silver showpieces, made by Yemeni Jews at the famous Bezelel workshop, such as vases, candelabra, cigarette boxes and holders, and more. As soon as we arrived at the home of his father, Sheikh Rashid, we would decorate the reception room with these showpieces so that they seemed like a part of the furniture. Immediately after his appointment, he began to host exquisite soirées at this house for the greatest figures of the British Mandate. These lively gatherings were attended by prominent figures of the occupation and their wives, as well as by heads of departments—English, Arab, and Jewish. Whenever a lady eyed one of the showpieces, he would throw a discreet look in my direction. I would immediately set it aside and find out the lady's name. On the following day, I would go in person to her home and present her with the showpiece as a modest souvenir from Ragheb Bey.

He carried on like this until his trip to Istanbul, from which he returned with his Christian wife, an Armenian who was an excellent host, in addition to being fluent in several languages. Ragheb Bey's popularity gained a boost, and his home became famous for its luxurious furniture and Persian carpets that conquered the leaders of the country.

THE FIRST CENSUS OF PALESTINE DURING THE BRITISH MANDATE

The mandate government of Palestine decided to set up a legislative council in Palestine that would include British, Arab, and Jewish parties and be proportionally representative of the population at the time (summer of 1921). Civil servants and teachers from the Education Department were appointed to carry out the census, and a census inspector was appointed for the neighborhoods of Bab al-Amud, al-Wad, and Saadiyeh, inside the city wall and all the way to the border with Mahallat Bab Hatta; along with Saadeddine Abdul-Latif (known as al-Khutt) and Fawzi Abbudeh al-Nashashibi, both of whom worked as teachers at the Education Department. But when we began distributing the forms for this purpose, strongman Subhi Hijazi, a well-known resident of Damascus Gate (nicknamed "al-Jaqman"), stood up to us with some colleagues and forced us to stop. Why?

Hajj Amin al-Husseini and the free men of his party had rejected this plan completely, just like the entire population, for many reasons. They feared it could be used for conscription. They did not want to cooperate with the current government, and they regarded it as a threat to the entire country. Since I was a resident of Saadiyeh Quarter, Subhi al-Jaqman came to my home at night and advised me not to go against his wish to stop the census. I supported whatever was for the good of the country and its people. But on this question, Hajj Amin differed with Fawzi al-Nashashibi[158] of the National Defense Party, of which Ragheb al-Nashashibi later became president.[159] He and his party, whom the people believed to be supporters of the mandate government, wanted to see a strategy of understanding adopted in the country rather than one of force. So the plan died in its infancy, and the forms remained just ink on paper on the shelves of the Governorate.[160] However, the mandate government did not rest after the Arabs voiced their rejection of a legislative council based on the results of the census. On June 22, 1922, the mandate government announced the formation of a legislative council, to which twenty-two members were appointed, including: ten English civil servants of the mandate government who would be appointed by the high commissioner; and eight Muslim citizens, two Christian citizens, and two Jewish citizens, by election.

The high commissioner would act as president of this council and have the power of veto, and the council would not have power to contravene the principle of mandate rule or that of the Jewish national home. Jews gave their preliminary consent to the formation of this council because its founder, Sir Herbert Samuel, had it examined and approved by the Zionist Commission. However, the Arab delegation that was in London at the time rejected the proposal on behalf of the Arab people.

Despite the Arab rejection of the proposal, the mandate government in Palestine called for legislative council elections to be held in February 1923, but Arabs immediately declared a boycott. Thus, the government was forced to abandon its measures and shelve its plan.

THE SECOND ARAB UPRISING IN PALESTINE

In March of 1921, the Third Palestinian National Congress was held in Haifa and rejected the British Mandate of Palestine. The influx of Jewish immigrants to the port of Jaffa intensified. It was the country's only port at that time, and its workers went on strike and boycotted the ships.

In early May 1921, on Labor day, the workers of Tel Aviv held a demonstration in which they shouted anti-Arab slogans. Escorted by government forces, they headed for Jaffa where they clashed with Arabs. The flames of the uprising spread all over Palestine and lasted for fifteen days during which 146 Jews and members of the armed forces and 147 Arabs were killed, and 700 people were injured, prompting senior clergymen and Arab leaders to intervene and end the uprising.

THE FIRST ARAB DELEGATION TO LONDON

On June 25, 1921, the Fourth Palestinian National Congress decided to send its first delegation to London. The delegation was made up of Musa Kazem Pasha al-Husseini as head, Shibli al-Jamal as secretary, Hajj Tawfiq Hammad, Amin al-Tamimi, Ibrahim al-Shammas, and Muin al-Madi. I kept a photograph of this delegation in the Jawhariyyeh Collection. The then Minister for the Colonies Winston Churchill issued the White Paper of June 1922.

IT'S OUT, IT'S TERRIBLE

Our rejoicing about the British occupation that had ended the despotic Ottoman rule soon turned into bitter disappointment as we sensed Britain's bad intentions for the country and its people when the fateful Balfour Declaration was announced to all so fearlessly and shamelessly. A first high commissioner for Palestine was appointed who not only was Jewish but was also a pillar of international Zionism.

I remember looking at *Al-Karmel*[161] newspaper, which had started to come out in Haifa after the arrival of the British, and reading the following verses:

It's out, the San Remo resolution
With its unbearable text.
Those who say it's not their business
May God strike them.

Being an artist, I was immediately inspired to compose a few more verses to add to the ones above, which are in fact a variation on the lyrics of the late Sayed Darwish's "The Beautiful Sun Has Risen."

(Chorus)
Didn't you, brother, read recently in the newspaper Al-Karmel
About the misfortune brought upon us by the appointment of

Mr. Samuel?
An auctioneer's voice is always heard by all
And those who do not like it can just pack and go.
Do not say "Christian" and "Muslim," now that they sold us all away.
How are we going to surrender to those who bought us?
They will force us to say "Shalom," brother,
And also "Ma shlomcha," may God end our ordeal.
Instead of Anwar and Jamal, our rulers will be
Shabtai, Sholem, and Haim, who hate us.
What a pity to lose you, dear homeland, and to lose our men,
And to see the gazelles around us turn into monkeys.

Shalom, ma shlomcha, shabtai, sholem, and *haim* are all Hebrew words that describe the state that Great Britain had got us into after the Ottoman rule of Jamal and Anwar, whom the people had ceased to hate as soon as they became aware of Britain's bad intentions, regretting instead the loss of the good days of their rule, despite how they had tyrannized the Arabs at that time.

I made this the opening song at many evening parties and gatherings I went to, and it gained popularity. At one evening party, Ronald Storrs, the military governor of Jerusalem in whose headquarters I had been working in, asked me to sing it. After he and the many guests present heard it, he burst out laughing, applauded passionately, then asked for a repeat, and I obliged.

But Storrs did not leave it there. Once I happened to be at an official party hosted by Sir Herbert Samuel at the German Augusta Victoria Building in Jerusalem. That party was worthy of royalty, and I was the only second-class citizen among a large group of notables who listened to me play the oud and sing muwashahat. At some point, Storrs came to me and asked me to sing this song. I was extremely embarrassed and thought I was doomed. But Storrs encouraged me to go on, saying, "Don't be afraid." Since I was a bit drunk, I sang it and gave a repeat. The hall was roaring with joy and laughter, particularly Storrs, who translated each word to His Excellency the High Commissioner.

In this way, the song marked the beginning of a strong relation between me and the high commissioner, who often sent the chief policeman, Ibrahim Bey Hbeish, to take me to his place in the commissioner's own car. We had nice evening parties at the Augusta Victoria Building, and I must say that, frankly, the commissioner and many of his foreign guests liked Arab singing and appreciated it greatly.

THE PUBLIC EDUCATION EXAMINATION FOR CIVIL SERVANTS

The mandate government of Palestine decreed that all civil servants were required to take an examination arranged by the Education Department. This outraged most civil servants, who were either the remaining employees of the Ottoman era or people who could speak English, even if just a little. The civil servants decided unanimously to refuse to sit the examination, especially since we were much like a newborn after what the country had been through under the Turks, during the Great War. After some negotiations, the government conceded, and a new decree was issued making the examination voluntary.

To celebrate the decree, Ronald Storrs invited all the employees of the governorate to dinner at Allenby Hotel (formerly the Fast Hotel), which was located outside Jaffa Gate on Jaffa Road. It was a long night in which Storrs and his entourage excelled as usual in humorous entertainment. After dinner, Governor Storrs rose and spoke about the government's examination.

> Although the government decided to make the exam optional, I would rather—and you are like my own children—each one of you took this examination because I am absolutely confident that it will be a useful foundation for the future of the civil servants of the mandate government. I promise that those who fail the examination have nothing to fear.

None of us felt able to refuse the governor's request. The Governorate was closed for three days, and the building became like a school. Every employee sat at a desk like a student and was monitored by a team of teachers and inspectors from the Education Department, with Hussein Ruhi at its head. Questions on all subjects were distributed, questions in declension, grammar, arithmetic, fractions, history, and geography. What kind of ordeal was this and what to do about it? Each of us did his best.

"God doth guide whom he will." Surprisingly, the only civil servant to pass the examination was Wasif Jawhariyyeh. My name was then published in the government's official gazette. The incident was regarded as a joke, particularly by all my colleagues.

Governor Storrs asked to see me, so I went to this office. He rose to greet me and congratulated me on my success, saying, "This must be thanks to the oud!" I thanked him, and he presented me with his autographed picture, which I kept in the Jawhariyyeh Collection.

THE GREAT ARAB LITERARY FIGURE, MR. MUHAMMAD IS'AF AL-NASHASHIBI[162]

I met Is'af al-Nashashibi at the time of the Turks through the late Hussein Hashem al-Husseini. He was in a state of misery and poverty, in dire need of a few piasters. I saw him more than once waiting inside a Jewish cobbler's shop in Souq al-Jadid, inside the city wall, for the soles of his shoes to be repaired, or replaced, as he had no spare shoes he could use in the meantime. The reason for his dire financial situation was that he had fallen out of grace with his father, the late Uthman al-Nashashibi, a well-known wealthy Jerusalemite who was police commissioner during the Ottoman period, along with his well-known colleagues such as Mahmud Jarallah, Badr Qutainah, Saleh al-Salihani, Khalil Darwish, and others, before attaining the high post of deputy for the Jerusalem district in Istanbul. Uthman was known for being extremely economical. I still remember once being at a picnic with Hussein Effendi and Ragheb Bey in the village of Abu Ghosh, when Uthman al-Nashashibi passed us in his carriage. Both the carriage and the horse were in an extremely lamentable state that matched Uthman's clothes. On seeing him in this state, alone, making his way back from his farm, al-Nu'manah, which earned him a substantial revenue, Ragheb Bey got so worked up that he plucked up the courage to lecture him on generosity before all those present.

In any case, Uthman remained at odds with his son Is'af, declaring him an apostate and an infidel at the sharia courts, denying him his money and his share of the inheritance. The story of Uthman and Is'af became the talk of Jerusalem's high society until Uthman married a second time and had a second son whom he named Dirar. But Is'af was a blessing compared to him. Dirar was cast out not just by his father but by the government and the people of Jerusalem of all three denominations. God has his ways. The great master remained at odds with his father Uthman until after the British occupation.

Some notables of Jerusalem, such as Ismail Bey, Ali Bey Jarallah, Ragheb Bey al-Nashahibi, and Hussein Bey al-Husseini, tried to mend relations between Is'af and his father. When they joined together in this cause, Haddad Pasha, whose first name was Gabriel, presided over the meeting. After they listened to Uthman's point of view, they asked Is'af to speak. He just stood up and said in an angry loud voice, "I swear to God that this business cannot be solved even by *Izraeel* (Satan), let alone by Gabriel!" and stormed out of the meeting while everyone roared with laughter.

After a short time, Uthman passed away. Is'af's rancor towards him was such that he went into the room where Uthman's body was laid, stood over his head, and said, "By God, I did not believe that Uthman could die," and left. But Is'af was able to persuade the courts and the judges that he was not an infidel like his father had claimed by showing them his massive and extraordinary writings on literature and religion, with their rich philosophical content, particularly in relation to Islam. This prompted the court to revoke the will of the deceased and allow him to inherit his share according to sharia law. This boosted the morale of Is'af who became one of the well-known wealthy figures of Jerusalem. His grand palace was in Sheikh Jarrah, where I spent many evenings in the company of the finest literary figures and notables of not just Jerusalem but also the various Arab countries.[163]

Is'af al-Nashashibi was appointed inspector at the Education Department in Jerusalem to replace the late Ismail Bey al-Husseini, and he became based in the very room in which I was working as a small employee, namely the Registry in the Governorate. At the time, there were only some fabric curtains (a screen) between us and the office of the inspector, Is'af al-Nashashibi. Is'af placed his trust in me and in my dedication, and put me in charge of translating into Arabic every letter sent to him by the government. Our friendship grew stronger. This was also helped by my brother being a student at the al-Rashidiya School, along with brother Mr. Sharif Hekmat al-Nashashibi.

I used to visit him informally at this palace and learned a lot from him, about language when singing. He talked to me about his life and how he had become a learned man through reading. He spent long nights reading one book after another until daybreak. He had received his primary education at the Jesuit School in Beirut. There is no doubt that Is'af became one of the leading Arab literary figures and that he was one of those who remained faithful to the foundations of the old language with its sophisticated vocabulary, for fear that it might perish. He used to visit me and enjoyed looking at the Jawhariyyeh Collection. His wedding present to me was one of the most valuable—an unusual silver tray for serving sweets, shaped like a seashell.

He often visited me at my department after it was moved to the Greek Orthodox Hospital Building, inside the wall, and then at the Governorate on Jaffa Road. He introduced me to the great musician Abdul-Wahab who complimented me on my music. Alas, this literary figure was removed from his post as an inspector in a shameful manner. His dismissal was announced in the official gazette, which came as a scandal for him at that late stage of his life.

A CIVIL SERVANT IN JERICHO

I was transferred to the Governorate of Jericho for two months to replace my colleague and friend Habib Mitri of Ramallah. Unfortunately, the job was for the months of July and August, may God help us. At the time, 1921, the Governorate was housed in the old building located at the main entrance of what had been the public park at the time of the Turks, on the eastern side of Jericho. The *qaim maqam* (subgovernor), Mr. Abdul-Raouf Jouda, was a well-known figure in Jerusalem. I made his acquaintance, and we liked each other and had good times together. I was staying in the upper room of the Jordan Hotel in the center of Jericho, which overlooked the terrace and was much like a lighthouse. We would have enjoyable evenings on this terrace, playing the oud and singing, while the people of Jericho listened to us as though we were on a minaret. The group was made up of Abdul-Raouf Jouda, Khalil Effendi Ereqat—the director of the Jericho police force, policeman Thoraya Effendi al-Ja'uni, Kamel Effendi al-Irani, Sidqi al-Hawwash, Musa al-Ragheb, Elias al-Kharouf, al-Qazzaz, Khamis al-Toubbeh, and others. Together we would drink cold beer until after midnight. I used to sing a song that was new back then and which begins, *Yalli enti naddik min naddi* (You who can challenge me) of the maqam Hijaz Kar Kurd. It was a delightful song, and both amateurs and professionals in Jerusalem picked it up from me. I had learned it from my brother and friend, the talented singer Muhammad Ali al-Osta from Damascus.

As for Abdul-Raouf Jouda, he was sympathetic to me, and on many occasions when the weather was too hot, he would send the Bedouins of al-Duyuk and al-Nuwaimeh[164] away and postpone their tithe and werko applications to another day out of concern for my welfare. Many times, the weather was so hot that I would go to the Governorate in my white sleeping gown, without the slightest objection from him.

As for my friend Kamel al-Irani, he was a dynamo whenever he was drunk. Whenever you brought up the subject of Britain, he would begin shouting the strongest swearwords, starting with King George and going all the way down the hierarchy. When he was drunk, he liked to walk around the homes of Jericho and whip whomever dared to contradict him, even if it was a woman. He would beat her in public and in front of all, particularly in Beit al-Khandaq. I found this painful to watch, but who would have dared to stop him?

Despite the extremely hot summer weather, I remained in Jericho for three happy months, which I remember to this day, before returning to the same job at the Governorate in Jerusalem.

SINGER ZAKI MURAD

I met the famous singer Zaki Murad,[165] the father of the famous singer Layla Murad, during his visit to Jerusalem in 1921 through my friends Habib Salem and Ishaq al-Ashqar, who owned the al-Nuzha Café which was located next to Doctor Pascal's property on Jaffa Street in Jerusalem.

Mr. Zaki Murad stayed with some Jewish relatives of his. Their house was located behind the al-Nuzha Café, which Mr. Zaki Murad visited often. We once had an evening party to remember on the second floor of the café. I played the oud for him in the snooker room, while he sang a dawr for us, "The heart is made to love your beauty." This old piece was composed by the well-known composer Ibrahim Qabbani on the maqam Rast Sazkar, and Mr. Zaki Murad's rendering of it on that night was beyond perfection. He also sang a well-known taqtouqa that was new at the time and gaining popularity with Arabs. The taqtouqa was composed and sung by the great musician Sayyid Darweesh—*Zuruni kull sana marra* (Please visit me, be it once a year). It was of the maqam Ajam, and Mr. Zaki Murad sang it with such exquisite beauty, which was no surprise given that he was the pupil of the famous musician Abdul-Hayy Hilmi from whom he learned the art of music, particularly the *layali*. Zaki Murad's voice was of the same type as the late Abdul-Hayy Hilmi's.

After that night, I always kept company to Mr. Zaki Murad, particularly in the Jewish commune known as "the love commune." He really liked to meet friends and go to evening parties there because the people there were Jews from Aleppo who liked unadulterated Arabic songs, and also because Mr. Zaki Murad was originally from Aleppo.

There was a great demand in Palestine for the disc recordings of the dawr "The heart is made to love your beauty," especially since it happened to have been recorded during the victories of Mustafa Kemal Ataturk, who defeated the big nations and forced them, in shatters, to leave Turkey. Other events were also happening at the time which came as a big surprise to the people of Palestine, particularly when they sensed the game that Britain was playing and the secret deal it had struck with international Zionism. Thus, it was rumored that this piece had been written and composed especially for Mustafa Ataturk. Indeed, if you look closely at the lyrics ("kings seek your approval, the moon is nothing but your light"), it would seem that this dawr was composed especially for that hero, or that this is at least what the public was inclined to believe.[166] So the recording was purchased by both ordinary people and cafés at unusually high prices.

Mr. Zaki Murad's sojourn lasted ten days, after which he had to leave Jerusalem. My Jerusalemite friends and I were not able to meet with him. He returned to Egypt, and I still keep some of the books and correspondence we exchanged over a long period of time.

MY GREAT TEACHER KHALIL AL-SAKAKINI

I had the great fortune and honor to have had as my teacher in primary school the great educator Khalil al-Sakakini. Thankfully, my friendship with my greatest teacher remained strong after I grew up. I visited him regularly at his home, known as "the House of the Nation." I was the chief "entertainer" at the evening parties that were held at his place and that were attended by pioneering scientific and literary figures from various Arab countries. It is to my teacher al-Sakakini that I am most indebted for correcting my singing in terms of language, particularly when it came to poems. He particularly liked to listen to me sing Andalusian muwashahat and advised me to sing the finest of it according to his unique and excellent taste in this fine art.

The master appreciated music and played the violin. It was a delight to see him on his feet, holding the violin and playing, with joy and an overwhelming spirit, light pieces including a Lebanese favorite of his, *Abu l'abaya l-beda, feeha sharashibi* (That white abaya with the tassels, are you wearing it to keep cool, or to make me suffer). The song was a waltz of the maqam Rast Nawa and was in the Lebanese dialect. When he sang it, I sang along with him while playing the oud, and it seemed to those who were present that the entire house was dancing!

Those who have known Mr. Abu Sari can testify that it is hard to describe al-Sakakini in words. He was proud, magnanimous, brave, patriotic, and loyal to his people and to his Arab identity. He did not fear the mandate government, for he was loyal and just, and liked everyone to be human in every sense of the word. To this effect, he had the following statement printed on his visiting card: "Khalil al-Sakakini, a human, God willing." He mocked those who led a manipulative social life, and who were many, in his view.

I remember some of his extraordinary, witty jokes about Mu'allim Khalil when his friend and colleague at the school, Mr. Bandali al-Jawzi, returned from Russia. Al-Sakakini made arrangements for some parties to be held in the honor of his dear friend at the homes of other friends in Jerusalem. One soirée would be held at the home of the master, another at the home of the author of this book, and another at the homes of Abdu, Jawzi, Moushabeck, and other families. They were extraordinary evenings in which we reveled until after midnight, singing, playing the oud and the violin, telling jokes, and roaring with laughter.

Once Mr. Bandali al-Jawzi was talking about the different regional dialects of the Russian language. He said to al-Sakakini, "In Ukraine they use the word 'sek' for 'dog.' Interrupting him, the extremely drunk al-Sakakini said, "So, Seksek is a dog and a son of a dog?" By that he was referring to George Seksek who had been nurturing closer ties with the Greek Orthodox Monastery and distancing himself from the community. There was a fit of laughter. Abu Sari despised the arrogant, the vain, and the pompous, and for this reason he used to meet with his colleagues who were men of letters or old students of his on the upper floor of a café situated in front of Jaffa Gate, outside the wall, and smoke the water pipe. This café was called Maqha al-Sa'alik (Vagabond Café).

He was particularly fond of me and of my oud playing and voice. Whenever he introduced me to his friends who were visiting Jerusalem from neighboring Arab countries, he would lecture about me and my brothers and our fondness for art, fun, and humor, saying, "The sons of al-Jawhariyyeh have inherited all this from their late father." On the death of my father, he had written in his memoirs, "With the death of al-Jawhariyyeh, the state of humor has come to its end." He also said this in the eulogy he gave him in Zion Cemetery right after his death. Sakakini's wife, Sultana Abdu, was a relative of mine. Her father, the late Nicola Abdu, was the son of my mother's aunt, and my late father was godfather to her and to her sister Milia, the wife of Doctor De'dis, and also to the late Katinko and Adib.

In the wake of the British occupation, and particularly following the sinister Balfour Declaration which revealed to the people the intentions of His Majesty the King of Britain towards the people of the Arab countries, the master was infuriated and began to bear animosity to all things British. In the end, he even sacrificed his bread and resigned from his post as an inspector at the Education Department in Jerusalem, falling into poverty and becoming in dire need of even one dirham. He remained proud, as a generous soul would. He was secretive about his penury, but men of letters, leaders, and chiefs of the country did not stop visiting him at his humble home out of regard and respect for his great principles. We had evening gatherings that went on until midnight at his home in Maman Allah (Mamilla), which belonged to a Mr. Fleifel of Bethlehem and was located near the headquarters of the Literary Club at the time. He had a Jewish neighbor whom he respected, the lawyer Elias Faraji. At this home, a certain group of al-Sakakini's friends used to meet regularly. Those included Musa al-Alami, George Khamis, Hanna Hamama, Adel Jabr, Tawfiq al-Hallaq al-Baytari, Omar al-Barghouthi, and others.[167] Then, the master moved home to the windmill located near the homes of Moushabeck and Abdu in Ratzbon. He moved there with Sultana and the children, and we spent in this windmill many evenings and good times that I remember with pride and bitterness.[168] Thus, Is'afal-Nashashibi, Ali Jarallah, Amin al-Husseini, Kamel al-Husseini, who was the mufti at the time, and other men of letters and teachers, as well as the neighbors—from the families of Abdu, Moushabeck, Salama, and Hanania—listened to me play and sing until daybreak. My brother Tawfiq and I often borrowed more seats from the neighbors because there were not enough for everyone to sit, God be my witness. The master laughed and joined us in the singing, music, drinking, and festivity. I remember that he once sent for me and my brothers. We came and I brought the oud along, and together we had a long night of reveling. It was an unforgettable night for all those who were present, and he remained the great master, even before the adoption of his first textbook, *Ra's Rus*[169] in the Ma'aref schools thanks to which our master was able to breathe relief, buy a piece of land, and build on it a house to the liking of the late Sultana, where he moved and settled. This house in the Katamon neighborhood became a regular hangout for men of letters and artists, until his life partner Sultana passed away, which prompted the master to write his famous phrase, "Just as we began to live, death came along" and made him bear a grudge towards heaven, earth, and life, saying, "Let us become extinct."

MUHAMMAD YUSUF AL-KHALIDI

The late Muhammad Yusuf al-Khalidi was an honest and just judge in Jerusalem during the British Mandate. He was one of the most famous judges of the criminal court, and he was able to turn heads, particularly since he belonged to the prominent al-Khalidi family that descended from the Arab hero Khalid Ibn al-Walid. There is no greater testimony to the bright and honorable history of this venerable family than the al-Khalidi Library in Jerusalem, which houses a large collection of the finest rare and valuable books and manuscripts. This library remains located in the al-Silsilah neighborhood inside the wall, on the main road leading to al-Haram al-Sharif.[170] Prominent figures of this family played an important role during the Ottoman rule, taking up high positions and together coming to be regarded as a state within a state.

These include the late Badr al-Khalidi, Yusuf Diya Pasha al-Khalidi, Muhammad Ali al-Khalidi, and others. My late father used to tell me stories of these great Khalidi personalities and show me where in Jerusalem this family had been based during its golden age. This large house was located behind the Catholic Armenian Patriarchate, which was founded by Joachim Tomayan in 1886 at the time of Mutasarrif Raouf Pasha, and houses a church named in honor of the sorrows of the Virgin Mary. The family residence of the al-Khalidis is one of Jerusalem's largest houses, comprising rooms, halls, courts, and even a prison, for there had been a time when the prominent men of the al-Khalidi family judged the accused and had them imprisoned inside the house, without seeking the approval of the Ottoman State whose governance at the time was merely nominal. The house stretches all the way to the alley that runs from the house itself to Habs el-Dam—the alley or street that leads to al-Haram al-Sharif. On the eastern side of it runs the alley that separates it from al-Azbakiyah of Sheikh al-Azbaki, opposite the School of the Sisters of Zion, and which also leads to al-Haram al-Sharif.

The al-Khalidi family of Jerusalem was known as the clan of Qays; the other clan, the Yemen clan, was the Husseini family. Qays and Yemen remain part of the people to this day and have been a great blessing, thanks to which justice prevailed and discrimination was rejected so that there was no difference between Christians and Muslims. For example, the town of Beit Jala would be considered to be part of the Qays clan, while Bethlehem belonged to that of Yemen. The remainder of the towns and villages of Palestine were divided between the two parties. A Muslim would come to the help of a Christian village that belonged to his party—Qays, for instance, against a Muslim (Yemeni) village—with the utmost loyalty and fraternity. The symbol of Qays was the color red, while white was the symbol of Yemen. My late father told me that once, one of the two parties was hosting the other, and after the meal the guests were served a dessert called Qays and Yemen[171] which is similar to *haytaliyeh* and is topped with *mawardiyeh*[172] that is poured into the same plate. When the guests started eating, they noticed that the white was under the red, which signifies Yemen being below Qays, knowing that the host belonged to the Qays clan. The Yemeni guests went out of their minds and an infamous fight erupted. Imagine how things were in our country when my father was a youth, just a century ago.

The al-Khalidi family of Jerusalem was a robust supporter and the major assistant to the Greek Orthodox Patriarchate in all things related to its interests. The patriarchate was able to purchase real estate mainly thanks to the al-Khalidi family's influence on sellers in the cities and villages. Woe to anyone who refused to sell willingly to the patriarchate. In order to show appreciation for him and his valuable services to the patriarchate, a picture of the late Sheikh Muhammad Ali Effendi al-Khalidi remains on display at the patriarchate to this day, picturing him in his turban and fur gown, smoking the water pipe. Sheikh Muhammad Ali al-Khalidi was the mufti of Shafiiyah in Jerusalem, as well as the head clerk of the sharia courts at the time. This post was extremely influential in matters of legal documents for real estate sales. For these reasons, the patriarchate considered every member of the al-Khalidi family as its own good son who had the right to visit the many monasteries across Palestine and to eat, drink, and sleep there without any formalities, receiving the full respect of the monks and enjoying wonderful times and hospitality to this day.

To resume telling my memories of Muhammad Yusuf al-Khalidi and his stories, he was an honest judge and, coming from the al-Khalidi family, he had a temper and had been at the center of heated incidents at the courts. He was an amateur musician who particularly liked Andalusian muwashahat and poems. He was addicted to drinking, God bless his soul. He would start drinking in the late afternoon and not quit his party until after midnight. When he got ready to go to his house near al-Haram al-Sharif, he would ride a mare that had got used to him swaying on its back drunkenly, so she would help him by swaying in the opposite direction lest he fall to the ground. On top of that, when getting ready to ride, he would spread her front and hind legs until her back was low enough for him to get on easily. I am not exaggerating when I say that it was the mare who used to take him home.

Muhammad Yusuf al Khalidi liked me a lot, respected me, and liked my art for which he had the greatest appreciation. Woe to Uncle Abu Said (Rateb al-Jaouni) if he spoke while I was playing the oud and singing. He would roar at him. When we left the monastery at night in a car, Uncle Said always sat next to the driver. When the extremely drunk Muhammad Yusuf spat out, where did the spittle land? On the back of Uncle Said's abaya.

He spent his summers in the tents that were set up on his land on the Jerusalem-Hebron Road. We spent wonderful times there. He loved me so much that as soon as I entered the courtroom, he would call me at the top of his voice. The hearing would end, he would send for me, and I would go to his private room where we would agree on a date for a social gathering, or I would ask him kindly to help somebody. He never turned down a request from me, God bless his soul.

The Judge Sentences Himself

It so happened that a prostitute who was well-known in Jerusalem was standing trial before Judge Muhammad Yusuf al-Khalidi, who was extremely inebriated from the previous night. He was infuriated by this prostitute's behavior during the hearing and said to her, in a way that all those present heard him, "*Sharmuta*! Shut up, shut your mouth, you whore!"

The prostitute refused to take the insult and answered, "If I were a 'whore' like you are saying, I would be so at my own home and not in a state court!"

Our friend the judge backtracked immediately and said to her, "True. You are absolutely right." Then, he turned to his chief clerk, Jamal al-Salahi, and told him,

> Lodge the following complaint
> The plaintiff: So-and-so, daughter of so-and-so
> The defendant: Judge Muhammad Yusuf al-Khalidi
> The complaint: Insult
> The verdict: The defendant must pay a fine of five Palestinian pounds.

He reached for the amount in his pocket and gave it to the chief clerk who deposited it in the cash register, brought back a receipt, and handed it to the judge who stamped closed the case he had filed against himself and apologized to the woman. Finally, he moved on to look into the main case filed against the prostitute and take the relevant legal measures. He was prepared to admit guilt willingly and freely.

THE DEATH OF MY MOTHER

My mother, God bless her soul, died of pneumonia during Saint Barabra's week in 1920.[173] She had been bedridden for a week during which our friend Doctor Izzat Tannous watched on her. This was right after the death of her only brother (my uncle) Nakhleh, the son of Andony Barakat, who passed away forty days prior to her death. Her death left me devastated, and I truly realized the meaning of the saying "One's world is one's mother." I was so devastated and upset at her departure that I nearly began to bear grudges against the whole world.

My mother's death brought with it the end of home life for me and my brothers Khalil, Tawfiq, and Fakhri. Dar al-Jawhariyyeh became more like a military barracks. Each one of us lived his own life, coming home inebriated either at midnight or later, just to sleep and then leave again in the morning, until I could no longer tolerate the situation and was obliged to hire an elderly lady named Sultana al-Lengy, through relatives of my mother. However, she was displeased with us and left us after a while, which made each one of us go even further in his irresponsible behavior and bring home at midnight any friends he wanted to bring.

Many historical parties took place in that house. For example, we would party until daybreak with Badi'a Masabni and her husband Najib al-Rihani, and the following evening we would have Fruso Zahran on her oud, and some Jerusalemite music amateurs like Abdul-Hamid Quttaineh, Hamada al-Afifi, Ali Abbas Ja'ouni, and others, until neighbors could not take it any longer; we were disturbing their sleep. I remember with great affection how, when one of us came back home with a bunch of friends, we would wake up my brother Fakhri from his deep sleep—he was a student at the Rashidiya School at the time. Since we no longer had an expert lady who knew all about housekeeping, mezze, and wine, Fakhri had to get up at once and make everything ready. Then he would join in and stay up with us until after midnight.

I could not carry on in this devious path when I was a civil servant at the Governorate in Jerusalem. I felt extremely exhausted and that my health was declining due to the excessive partying, drinking, playing, and singing through the night. So I thought seriously about my destiny and future, and made up my mind to marry.

MY TRIP TO LEBANON AND SYRIA WITH MY BROTHER KHALIL

My brother Khalil had served in the gendarmerie in Beirut throughout the war. After he returned from Beirut, and since I had never in my life left Palestine and East Jordan, he used to share with us the many stories and incidents he had witnessed in Lebanon and Syria, and to describe to us the beauty of these countries, their mountains and their water, while I listened to him eagerly and wished I would be able to visit them one day.

In the summer of 1922 (at age twenty-five), I was able to carry out this plan. At a time when my brother Khalil's finances were in a poor state, I decided to take a trip to these countries and pay for him to come along. I obtained a thirty-day leave from the governorate, and with my pocket money of one hundred sixty-five Egyptian pounds, I traveled with Khalil by car to Haifa. We arrived in the afternoon and stayed in a hotel near the railway station. The two ladies who ran the hotel welcomed us warmly, and we casually ate dinner together. In the morning, we left the hotel and strolled around Haifa. This was the first trip I had ever taken, so I bought some unique showpieces in the stores of Haifa for my future home (at that time, I had secretly made up my mind to marry). I spotted a pair of Italian-made imitation bronze vases, and I liked them. The shop owner promised to keep them for me to pick up on my return from Lebanon.

I checked out of the hotel, and we traveled to Lebanon via al-Nafura. It was indeed a delightful trip, as we were driving along the coast. We arrived in Beirut at noon and stayed in a new hotel overlooking Cannon Square.[174] At the time, Cannon Square was still largely green and had a big café with a fountain at its center, from which water shot out high up before pouring down into a large pond around which were laid all kinds of appetizing food, drink, wine, and water pipes. Each section was independent from the others, and the service was extremely professional. We spent more than five days wandering the city and its suburbs and parks. I bought some silver showpieces from the store known as al-Kaff al-Ahmar (the Red Palm) in Souq al-Tawilah. I still keep this marmalade serving set, which was also partly made of crystal. Like a tourist guide, my brother Khalil took me to the nicest stores around.

We left Beirut and began moving from one village to another, staying at hotels in Aley, Bhamdoun, and Saoufar. I was like a Bedouin in New York. I was charmed by the landscape wherever I went and surprised by the warm welcome I received from café and resort owners, and by the nice way in which they served food to their customers, and particularly drinks and mezze accompaniments to arak. For example, if you ordered arak, it was served to you along with twenty-five different types of mezze in an appetizing and refreshing way. Prices for such dishes were quite low. Only luxuries were expensive. My brother Khalil and I often got along with families that happened to be sitting in the café, and our drinking tables merged, forming a wider circle. Many ladies, and even young ladies, smoked the water pipe, which made me believe what I had heard about these extraordinary cheerful gatherings. I thought of how subdued our ladies were in comparison to the women of this country.

During that time, my brother Khalil and I were drinking quite heavily. We would drink arak for four hours without a break but without ever showing any symptoms of inebriation, possibly because the arak was so well-made. We carried on like this for about two weeks. Then we traveled by car to Zahleh where we stayed at Hotel Kadri which overlooked the valley and was one of the most famous hotels. We spent our time in the resorts and cafés of the Berdawni River. The river flowed marvelously into natural canals, and cafés abounded on both its banks. We spent three days in Zahleh and then headed for Damascus where we stayed in the Hotel Victoria. I was enchanted when I entered Damascus, this city that preserved its Arab character even in its architecture, markets, and lifestyle. I was frankly smitten by Souq al-Hamidiya, where I saw, for instance, someone beating *dondurma* (Arabic ice cream)[175] mixed with mastic, with oriental crockery laid around him—plates, authentic Chinese bowls, wooden Damascus arabesque, and of course, the mother-of-pearl inlaid chairs, seats, picture frames, and mirrors that I am passionate about.

In this souq I bought some beautifully made frames, having intended to use one for the picture of my late father and the other for that of my second father, Hussein Effendi al-Husseini. Indeed, I had the two frames placed as I had wanted in a central location in the hall of the Jawhariyyeh Collection.

We used to spend the evenings in Azbakia. To our luck, the famous Egyptian singer Munira al-Mahdiyyeh was there to enchant us with her old Egyptian singing that was unadulterated by Western frills, under the trees until midnight. I remember that I used to stroll until dawn when I would hear the call to prayer flowing from numerous minarets. My brother Khalil often advised me to spend wisely saying, "By God, Wasif, don't let us run out of money while away from home. We don't know anyone here." I answered, "Don't worry. God will take care of us."

I thus carried on spending, partying, and drinking until one day we woke up to realize that we had almost no money left. The vacation was nearing its end in two days. "How did this happen, Khalil? We must leave Damascus immediately." Khalil became angry and began thundering at me and rebuking me. We got ready, closed our suitcases, carried the boxes filled with Damascene woodwork, frames, a backgammon set, and the like and took the train, traveling via Mzayrib and Dera'a. It was a hot day on which we tasted all kinds of misery. The heat melted the ghee in the sweet boxes bought in Beirut. We also had nothing to ease our hunger as we had not bought any food upon our departure from Damascus, which was particularly tense due to Khalil's anger. We arrived in Haifa just before sunset.

MY MARRIAGE

I met Victoria, the daughter of Saliba Saad, the owner of al-Jiljal Hotel in Jericho during the First World War. I used to watch this young lady as she ran the hotel all by herself when her father Saliba was in prison during the Ottoman times, and also while he was away following the British occupation. She managed the hotel with exceptional competence, which saved its reputation and earned her the respect and admiration of British army leaders like General Bols,[176] Storrs, and others who began to nickname her "Victoria Jericho." After her father returned from exile, she rented the hotel, which they later named the Saint John's Hotel, from the Greek Orthodox Patriarchate. I had remained in touch with Victoria and her family ever since I met her for the first time, until during Easter of 1919 we made verbal promises of marriage to each other. Once we had the financial means to marry, our wedding was administered by Reverend Sutiri Hanania, Reverend Gregory, and Reverend Bastouli at the Nicoforia home on March 9, 1924, and we held a humble party that was attended only by the closest relatives of the bride and groom. I quit the feverish life of being single. I was exhausted and emaciated. Thus marriage marked the beginning of a new life for me.

MY LIFE PARTNER VICTORIA

Victoria's father, Saliba Saad, was from Birzeit, in the Ramallah district. Her mother Hilaneh was the daughter of the late Nicola Naqla who belonged to an old Jerusalemite Greek Orthodox family. The late Reverend Hanna Naqla was her grandfather. Victoria and all her siblings—boys and girls—were born in Jerusalem. Once when she was seven-years-old, she was playing with her brothers and sisters at her father Saliba's house known as al-Marazi, located on Jericho Road, near Khan al-Ahmar, that remains officially known to this day as Khan Saliba after her father who founded it. Patriarch Demianos and his company were passing by in his private carriage. The sight of Victoria captured his attention. He loved her and asked to adopt her officially from her father. At first, her father hesitated and offered that the patriarch might adopt one of his sons, since God had blessed him with four of them. But the patriarch declined and insisted on Victoria until he was able to persuade her father with his usual diplomatic tact. She cried as he took her away with him, and he deprived her of seeing anyone from her family while she was in the care of the head of the Girls School, a lady of Greek descent and great culture. In this way, Victoria acquired the habits of the Greeks and came to regard the patriarch as her own father. The patriarch held an extraordinary session during the Synod in which he publicly and officially announced his adoption of Victoria.

Victoria was fortunate to receive a superior Greek education and lived a quiet aristocratic life, broadening her knowledge of astronomy and classical Greek, while she accompanied the patriarch on his tours outside Jerusalem and Palestine, under the supervision of the school mistress in whose care she had been placed.

When she finished school, she enrolled at the Ramallah Friends School where she learned English in a short time. She also took French lessons with a private teacher. During the First Great War, when Patriarch Demianos was exiled from Jerusalem to Damascus, she had to return to her father Saliba's home at the time when he owned the al-Jaljal Hotel in Jericho. Unfortunately, her father fell out of grace with the Turkish leadership and was exiled to Ankara, along with the late Semaan al-Bayda. Since Victoria had the necessary education and competence, she had to manage the hotel, which she did in the best possible way, while also taking care of all family matters. When the British occupied Palestine, she carried on managing the hotel—which was visited by the English leaders—with all honesty and integrity until her father returned and she handed the hotel's management over to him. She used her relations to rent the Saint John's Hotel which became one of the top hotels in Jerusalem and also passed its management over to her father in order to ready herself (secretly) to marry.

Why Did Patriarch Demianos Choose Victoria to Adopt over Any of Her Brothers?

No doubt, life is all about luck. It was destiny's will that Victoria, rather than any of her brothers or sisters, should have this blessing. Patriarch Demianos came from one of the wealthy families of the city of Samos. He had been a well-known merchant belonging to a family of high social standing, and he married a woman worthy of his name who gave him a baby girl and who died after giving birth. Since he had been smitten with his wife, he lost his mind and was devastated. But such was God's will, so he turned his attention to raising his daughter and loved her fondly. She became the embodiment of the memory of her mother, whose death he had begun to get over thanks to the presence of his doll, until she too passed away suddenly when she was only eight years old. This came as a massive shock to her father, and he made up his mind to retire from worldly life and devote himself to worship.

He decided to spend the rest of his life as a humble monk serving the tomb of Jesus in Jerusalem. He carried out his plan and left his country and homeland and arrived in Jerusalem in his national dress, of which I keep a photograph. He joined the monastic order and was appointed as one of the servants of the Holy Sepulchre inside the Church.

Demianos drew the attention of the monks with his fine looks, the virtue that emanated from his face, his beauty, culture, and education, so that in a short time he rose through the hierarchy until it was unanimously decided to send him to Russia on behalf of the patriarchate in order to promote it and raise funds, a task which he carried out well. He returned from Russia with his head held high, having conquered the hearts of the Russian believers who loved and appreciated him so much that they almost worshipped him. After his second arrival in Palestine, he was ordained archbishop in Bethlehem. It so happened that Patriarch Gerasimous passed away in 1897, and so Demianos was unanimously elected as the Greek Orthodox Patriarch of Jerusalem.

When he first caught sight of Victoria his tears poured out, and he immediately remembered his daughter. He assured Victoria that she resembled his daughter and was like her spitting image in terms of complexion, sense of humor, intelligence, and everything else. He made up his mind to adopt her, having loved her with all his heart, and she became his only distraction after the death of his real daughter. Indeed, many times he wept with happiness as he watched her study or play on the school's rooftops.

This is how Victoria met the patriarch and was able to receive a better education and enjoy a more comfortable life than her siblings. Praise to the Lord, He who distributes people's sustenance.

Patriarch Demianos's Consent to My Marriage to Victoria

For about five years, we kept our verbal agreement to marry without worrying about the families of the bride and groom. I had not even asked her father for her hand in marriage, as was the custom was at the time. We observed the rules of decency, and our love was mutual. We came to greatly trust each other, and with God's blessing we made a promise to be loyal to each other until, with God's help, we met success after going through ordeals and pains.

Victoria was quite worried that the patriarch might not consent to our marriage because he had always warned her against "the cruelty and ignorance of the Arab members of the community" and expressed his dismay about the fact that there were not any "trustworthy Greeks in our country." His best plan was thus to send Victoria to a German university to receive a degree in medicine. After he returned from his exile in Damascus, in the wake of the British occupation, he ordered her to hand the management of the two hotels over to her father and get ready to travel to Germany. Little did he know that Victoria was in love.

In 1924 we both felt that the time was ripe and went to see the patriarch. He was initially surprised, but on hearing that the one who was to be the life partner of his spiritual daughter was the son of Jiryis Jawhariyyeh, he paused a little and said to Victoria,

> I remember his father well. I respected and loved him, and I preferred his company… He was trustworthy and loyal, and I consider him to be a good son of mine and of the patriarchate. I used to visit him at his home in Saadiyeh, where I would look at the spectacular views of Jerusalem from the rooftop. I believe that "like father like son," and if you have made up your mind, you have my blessing.

This was a great joy for Victoria. I thanked the Almighty and was truly proud of my late father and the great reputation he had left for us.

Receiving the Blessing of His Holiness Patriarch Demianos

Victoria and I visited the patriarch together for the first time. It was evening, and he was sitting at his desk. I noticed that he was writing and reading by the light of two candles placed on both sides of the desk. I stood admiring his extraordinary looks, glorious beauty, and lofty stature which he maintained despite his old age, and I said to myself that one rarely sees giants like Patriarch Demianos and Issa Nakhleh Qurt from our community or Sheikh Musa Shafiq al-Khalidi, a Muslim from Jerusalem.[177]

He gave us his blessing, and after our wedding we visited him and he gave us an official reception at the hall of the patriarchate, dressed in his official attire and with the archbishops around him. He presented each of us with a gold chain and cross with a splinter from the crucifix of Jesus, and we thanked him. Then speaking to Victoria he said,

> My current financial situation is precarious. I live on a monthly salary that does not allow me to honor you as I ought to, Victoria. As you know, I would have liked to help you financially with my own money. My brothers gave their consent to my offering you, as my spiritual daughter, the land and house in which you live now. But since the house belongs

> to the Greek Orthodox Patriarchate, my conscience does not allow me to let you, your husband, and your descendants bear this sin.[178] I will content myself with blessing you and your husband in my lifetime. After my death, be sure that my soul will bless you, your husband, and your home, wherever you may be and wherever you go. I ask God to grace you forever with a happy and blissful Christian life. Forgive me for falling short of my duty. I hope that in time I will be able to help with my own money.

He then shed tears of tenderness and affection, and we thanked him and his company.

HONEYMOON

I spent my first night with Victoria at our Nicoforia home. On Sunday morning of March 10, 1924, in unusually rainy weather, we boarded the Cairo-bound train at the Jerusalem rail station. In the afternoon, we arrived at El-Areesh to find that a flood had swept the big bridge away. The train was forced to stop, and we spent the night in it. Since the train was full of foreign tourists, an army force came to guard it from any Bedouin attack. I upgraded my train ticket to first-class and paid the price difference to have a sleeper compartment. So Victoria and I slept to the soft murmuring sounds of water, but remained vigilant after fear had been spread among the staff.

In the morning, the rail management decided that it would be difficult to proceed and that much time might be needed to repair the bridge safely. The train returned to Jaffa with those on board, and all passengers were fully refunded. Exhausted, we headed for the Cliff Hotel[179] which belonged to Salim Barakat and was located in the Ajami Quarter. We stayed there for three days and nights, until we learned that the repair of the railway on the El-Arish bridge had been completed. We then booked new tickets despite Victoria's pessimism and that of my brothers back in Jerusalem who urged me to cancel the trip. We left Jaffa for Egypt, having placed our trust in God, and arrived at around eleven at night.

On the train, between Al-Qantara and Cairo, we met two Greek men who were extremely kind and polite. When they learned that we were Arabs and had never been to Cairo before, they helped when we arrived at the station and took us in a private car at their own expense to look for a suitable hotel. But all was in vain since hotels had filled up with foreign tourists. We were thus forced to stay at the famous Semiramis Hotel located near the Nile Palace Bridge. I had forbidden Victoria to converse in Greek with those Greeks. She understood well everything they said to each other about us, but we spoke to them in Egyptian Arabic. She told me that they only spoke well of us. They also refused categorically to let me pay the driver, and we thanked them profusely.

After the two men left us, Victoria and I stood by the main entrance of this great hotel to discover that the main door was a novelty to us and that we had seen nothing like it before. There were no such doors in Palestine. It was a revolving door with four compartments, where you get into one compartment and push and walk forward until you find yourself inside. We stood, silent and amazed, watching travelers go through the door until we figured it out. I encouraged Victoria to go first, and she got into one compartment, while I entered the second one. We found ourselves inside, thank God, while to ourselves we were both in stitches. The hotel's porters followed us with the luggage. We stayed in this hotel for seven days. It suited us in many ways, and we paid two Egyptian pounds per person per night.

I had the address of Mrs. Froso, Victoria's maternal aunt, the widow of Abu Sawwan, of Jerusalem, but the address was incomplete and merely said Al-Fajjala Street, Cairo. So Victoria and I took a horse carriage and headed for that street where, wandering in the market, I came across Mrs. Froso by chance while she was shopping, with a child in her arms. We were very lucky to have found her, and after exchanging hugs and kisses, we went to the Semiramis Hotel, settled our bill, and went with our luggage to her home where we stayed for about a month, feeling welcome and at home. She was such a virtuous lady and an excellent homemaker in every sense of the word. We still remember this hospitality and miss those good days. Victoria's aunt was married, with children, and her daughter Olga was about to marry. Our joy became complete thanks to our dear Salim[180] who dedicated his time to us. He accompanied us every day around Cairo and its museums, parks, theaters, streets, historical sites, and attractions, all of which we were able to visit paying the right prices thanks to the great experience he had acquired by living in this country for five years, which was, of course, to our great luck.

I was lucky to see the Curlew of the Orient, Miss Umm Kulthum, for the first time at the Opera House theater. At the time, she was only starting her musical career and used to wear the traditional Arab dress, with her braids on her shoulders. I was entranced by her voluptuous, affectionate voice. Her musical ensemble was still basic at the time. Unfortunately, I did not have the opportunity to leave Victoria and visit those friends of mine who were famous artists in Cairo, like Sami al-Shawwa, Zaki Murad, and the others whose songs I had heard from phonograph records.

While we sat with Mrs. Froso and her dear children drinking tea on the balcony of the Continental Hotel overlooking the main street, we saw for the first time the procession of His Majesty King Fuad I on his way to inaugurate the Egyptian Parliament. It was a national holiday, so decorations had been put up, and public celebrations were held all over Cairo until after midnight. We wandered from one place to another, and Cairo seemed to bask in daylight with all those electric lights that were new to us; we had not seen such a thing in Palestine yet.

Our honeymoon was indeed a blessed one in which we were only up to good deeds. We returned to Palestine with wonderful memories, thanks to Mrs. Froso and her good home, as well as to the help of our dear Salim who did his tourist guide job in the best possible way.

THE NICOFORIA HOME AND JERUSALEM IN THE EARLY TWENTIES[181]

The Nicoforia house belonged to the Greek Orthodox Patriarchate of Jerusalem. It was a modest building built in the old architectural style on a piece of land of no more than about two dunums. It enjoyed a privileged location on the eastern side of the Nicoforia mountaintop, with breathtaking views over historical sites. From there you could clearly see the Jaffa Gate entrance, and next to it, along the wall, the historic King David Castle right next to Mount Zion with its prestigious religious institutions. This was the eastern side. The southern side offered views over Jerusalem. One could clearly see Jabal al-Mukabbir and the buildings that were built on it, such as that of the high commissioner and the Arab College, as well as views of al-Thawri neighborhood, al-Baq'aa, and the road to Bethlehem all the way to the Monastery and Church of Mar Elias. I should mention that the King David Hotel and its gardens were to the west of the house, with just an olive grove owned by the patriarchate between them. To the north of the house stood the French Consulate and its marvelous gardens. It so happened that the Church of Saint George el-Khodr, peace be upon him, was located to the southeast of the house whose land belonged to the well-known al-Qurt family.

I remember visiting the house as a youth with my late father during Ottoman rule. At the time, a member of Jerusalem's Greek community was running a café in it, and a man had been killed there while he was drunk, which forced the café manager to close down without paying the patriarchate the due rent. I went there with my father who was employed at the church court at the time and was responsible for the sale of the café's furniture through public auction. I recall that he bought a large antique mirror with an extraordinary marble console which I still keep at this home to this day among the rest of the furniture. I learned from Raouf Lawrence, a well-known Jerusalemite, that his father had rented the house for a long period of time, running a bakery in it and raising pigs in the courtyard.

It so happened that Mrs. Froso and her children had lived in this house during, or shortly prior to, the British occupation. But she insisted on leaving Jerusalem with her children and spending the rest of her life in Cairo following the death of her son George. The house was thus offered for rent to a number of Greek Orthodox families including Semaan al-Khoury Baida and his brother Costandi, Yaacoub Abu Hajar, and others. But they all refused categorically, because the location of the house was quite frightening, as it stood alone on the summit. Nobody lived in that area except for the family of Eid Nakhleh Qurt and his nephews. At the time, 1922, the buildings of the King David Hotel, the YMCA, the French Consulate, and the Jesuit Fathers did not exist yet, nor did even Shama Street or King George Street. The area was simply surrounded by olive trees. Jerusalemites who knew Nicoforia at the time know that it was a hangout for drunkards as well as pickpockets and slum dogs who went there to carouse or to flee the law whenever they had become involved in shameful acts in the city. If you looked at the surrounding shops, particularly those between the house and Jerusalem's Jaffa Gate entrance, you would only find stables, blacksmiths, and the like.

When I learned through Victoria that this house was about to be vacated and became certain of Mrs. Froso's intention to leave Jerusalem, I encouraged Victoria to take it. Since it belonged to the Greek Orthodox Patriarchate, we could marry sooner and save on the rent, being members of the church. As for the frightening location of the house and all those exaggerations, this was not an issue because I was sure of myself, had no enemies, thank God, and was known to all classes, particularly the wretched and the drunkards with whom I had spent quite a lot of time thanks to both my music and my job, through which I used to offer them assistance. The house was to my liking with its old architecture of crossed arches and walls that were no less than a meter thick. Luckily, I was able to persuade Victoria and immediately offered all the help I could give. Since there were no formalities between us and Mrs. Froso, I paid her twenty-four Egyptian pounds in key money, which she accepted with thanks.[182] The house was then handed over to us, and Victoria and her mother moved in, knowing that Uncle Saliba spent most of his time at the Saint John's Hotel running the business. I appointed as a guardian Uncle Abu Salah, a farmer from one of the villages of the Jerusalem district, and he used to sleep outside in the eastern courtyard by the window of the room where Victoria slept while she was still unmarried.

A short while after our marriage, we were able to gain use of the western room that had remained occupied by a Greek family after Mrs. Froso's departure. The father of this family worked as a baker at the Greek Orthodox Monastery. The house thus became entirely ours, and we began repairing it, both inside and out.

I also had an extension built on the top floor as a sleeping accommodation which could be accessed from inside the house. The house remained in my hands from 1922 until the end of the British occupation in 1948, when we left Jerusalem, after which it moved to Jewish ownership. By then it was no longer just a house but had become a spectacular museum.

* * *

On seeing the Arab cross-vault architecture, I had conceived of the idea of collecting antiques—all things oriental and artistic. My family and I saw only good times from when we set foot in it, and every day I spent in it I received more of God's blessings.

While I had no enemies, thank God, one is never safe from envy. In addition to the rumor that was spread among Jerusalemites, in particular among members of my community and even my relatives, claiming that I had received from the patriarch ten thousand Egyptian pounds as a dowry, another rumor was circulated whereby the house had been officially registered in Victoria's name.

God be my witness, neither rumor was true. With regard to the house, I have kept the first, second, and third contracts which I had renewed with those in charge at the Finance Department of the Greek Orthodox Patriarchate and which were certified by the fiscal clerk of the patriarchate who oversaw the management of the patriarchate right after the Israeli occupation.

I do not deny the help I received from the patriarch and other figures of the patriarchate, allowing me to remain at this house for such a long period of time. It is even true that the company that built the King David Hotel had aimed to include the building in the land on which the hotel was built, given its historic appeal in terms of affording a closer look at the King David Castle. But it failed and its request was unanimously rejected by the patriarchate. I recall that I assiduously looked after the properties of the patriarchate at the time, given my job as a financial manager for Jerusalem.

In 1924, prominent individuals at the Finance Department offered to lend me great support, allowing me to claim ownership of this house and take advantage of the absence of any official records of the patriarchate's ownership. But I refused because I knew that taking mortmain money dishonestly would only bring misfortune.

My family and I lived in this house in peace, with nothing to disturb our life. We often left the Persian carpets, and even copperware, out in the courtyard all night without anyone causing us harm.

* * *

I would like to describe the state of the Holy City outside the wall in 1922. When I stood on the rooftop of the Nicoforia home, I could see the old Montefiore commune to the south, as well as the Saint John Eye Hospital, some old houses of the Al-Thawri neighborhood, the railway station, the Kazkhana Building which belonged to the municipality and was located on the road to Bethlehem, the al-Khalili Palace, and the old Baq'aa neighborhood, the neighborhoods of Haririyyeh and al-Wa'ariya, the German and Greek Colonies in Baq'aa, and all the way to the Saint Elias Monastery.[183]

This landscape changed as construction spread, connecting buildings together, starting with a new building for the Saint John Eye Hospital, the building known as the Scottish Memorial Church[184] on the site known as al-Haririyyeh near the railway station, as well as new buildings that began in the al-Thawri neighborhood and continued on both sides of the Bethlehem Road, all the way to the Talpiot commune, then the residence of the high commissioner, the Arab College on Jabal al-Mukabbir, and other buildings, until you caught sight of the astonishing modernization and the elegant adjoined buildings in the neighborhoods of Baq'a Fawqa and Baq'a Tahta.

I could also see to the west of the house the vast olive grove of the Greek Orthodox Monastery stretching all the way to some of the old buildings in the Maman Allah neighborhood and cemetery, and then the windmills near the monastery in Ratisbonne.[185] This landscape was completely transformed when this land was built up with Saint Julian Street, then King George Street, which filled up with famous buildings such as the YMCA, the King David Hotel, the Cardinal Ferrari, the famous Talbieh neighborhood, the Karm al-Ruhban neighborhood, the English Talbieh neighborhood,[186] then Rehavia A, B, and C, all the way to the Convent of the Holy Cross, not to mention the grand buildings erected on this piece of land, which was connected to the lands of Nicoforia that were owned by the Greek Orthodox Patriarchate and were alas sold through a mediator, mostly to Jews at low prices.

From the northern side of the house, you could only see the Jaffa Gate, then the city wall surrounded by the patriarchate's shops, and the Waqf Anabusi buildings standing before it on the Jaffa Gate hill.

A few years later, however, Yusuf al-Shammaa built the Shammaa Quarter, and many famous buildings were erected on the road to Maman Allah, including the famous Palace Hotel.[187] These buildings eclipsed the views we had in the past—the houses of Uwaida and Abu Shaker, and the Armenian land which became one of the finest locations in Jerusalem and counts the Rex Cinema among its buildings.

On the eastern side, you could see the old buildings of Waqf Anabusi, the Maarif Café, and next to it, near the turn leading to our Nicoforia home, some derelict wooden shops which belonged to the Germans at the time, in addition to some wooden sheds used as stables and blacksmith shops. These ruins were removed and replaced with prestigious buildings such as the Tannous Brothers Building, the Halabi Brothers Building, and other buildings of a grandness to match that of Jerusalem's main entrance—Jaffa Gate.

It is truly impossible to describe the scale of the construction that Jerusalem had undergone by the end of the British Mandate. I still recall the scenery I used to see during the British occupation. I still keep some historic photographs that show the state of these very sites between 1880 and 1917.[188]

THE JAWHARIYYEH COLLECTION

I would like to explain to you dear reader the reasons that prompted me to think seriously of collecting artistic objects and antiques, particularly those relating to my dear city of Jerusalem. After succeeding with God's help in collecting a large selection of rare artifacts of historical value that demonstrate the skilled handwork of Arabs and people of the East, I thought of turning this collection into a kind of national museum under the slogan: "This is our legacy that speaks of who we are, so behold it when we are gone." I hope that the Jawhariyyeh Collection and its treasures become a historical and artistic reference.

I love music. At the same time, I appreciate poetry without being a poet, and I can be an art critic, if need be, without being a painter. But there is nothing surprising in that, for all arts are members of one family. In the golden book of the collection, my brother Omar al-Husseini wrote, "To those seeking fine taste in all kinds of art, come to Wasif and you will find without doubt what you are looking for." My home environment added to my knowledge. My late father played the principal role in my musical training, directing me in the footsteps of the old school in playing tarab instruments, performing, and choosing quality music. I often watched him as he showed his friends rare manuscripts in the reception room. I inherited from him some of these documents. He also had two pieces of china which he was proud of and which he displayed on special occasions. Indeed, their rarity piqued the interest of visitors. There were also copper braziers from Istanbul and some coffeepots he was proud to own. The reception room walls were adorned with portraits of influential personalities that added to the elegance of the house and which were also moved around from time to time. He also had an extraordinary snakeskin on display—a snake which had extra teeth in its palate and measured about four meters.

I used to stare at each item my father showed his visiting friends, explaining each one as I passionately looked and listened. When I married in early 1924, I took all these artifacts as souvenirs of my father. But at the same time it made me happy to look at them, and I put them on display in the reception room where they formed the starting point of the Jawhariyyeh Collection.

The house in Nicoforia was an old Arab-style building with cross-vault arches. Living in it with my family, I spent on it generously until it became a decent home in every sense of the word. Its architecture and historical value encouraged me to purchase furniture that fit in with its structure. So for the reception room I bought Cairo-made armchairs, lightly inlaid with mother-of-pearl and with small wooden screens made with the old foot-operated wood lathe. For the curtains I came up with an idea that was suited to the style of the house. I used the long Ibrahim Pasha flintlock rifle (instead of wooden poles) to hang the Persian belt along (instead of silk curtains), and the result was exquisitely beautiful. I adorned the walls of this room with historical pictures and portraits of loved ones such as my late father, the late Hussein Effendi al-Husseini, and others, in oriental Damascene frames, which added to the room's elegance and beauty.

MOVING TO THE REVENUE DEPARTMENT AT GOVERNMENT HOUSE

After my marriage in 1924, one of the employees at the Revenue Department, Yaacoub Baramki, had been absent from work and his backlog had been piling up. I was placed in charge of his work for one month. After Yaacoub returned to work, the head of the department, Mr. Atallah Mantoura, who liked my work, agreed with the tithe inspector Mr. Nakhleh Kutn to keep me. Nakhleh Kutn made me the offer, explaining to me the advantages and benefits of the Finance Department and encouraging me to accept the post. He really meant what he was saying, for he was fond of me. I accepted and was appointed clerk, leaving for good my work at the Registry with all the translation and administrative work. After the British occupation, the person responsible for the Revenue Department was Mr. Abdul-Razzaq Qlibo. His assistant was the late Ahmed Murad, and the late Hussein al-Aranout also worked with him. But when I moved to this department, the highest official, who was known as the finance inspector and assistant to the governor of Jerusalem, was Atallah Mantoura, while the financial secretary was Muhammad Aref al-Costantini, and Ibrahim Shehadah al-Alami was a Werko officer.

The Revenue Department imposed the werko tax on the cities and villages of the country and levied tithes on the crops. These taxes were collected annually by tax collectors on behalf of the governor of Jerusalem, while at the time of the Turks this was done on behalf of the district governor.

These taxation procedures were in place under the Ottomans. The mandate government adopted them, appointing all the department's employees of the Turkish era, for these procedures were wonderful indeed. My colleagues and I continued to work at the department and got to know all its secrets until the end of 1928–1929, when the mandate government devised a new modern plan, namely the property tax that was levied in cities and villages, and which I personally helped to expand.

AT THE WERKO DEPARTMENT

I ended up working as a clerk at the Werko Deparment at the Saraya. It was a modest job which I took up wearily and without any interest. I was in charge of the special registers, including the Werko's check registers and documents, and so I became immersed in accountancy. I would collect the documents showing the names of the taxpayers of the village in question and the total tax due for that village, and once I had done that I would do the necessary calculation to make sure that the tax amount matched that indicated in the summary for each taxpayer.

This job, may God spare us from it, was in stark contrast to my genuine interest. But one is obliged to submit to necessity, and so I did my duty in the best possible way, patiently and enduringly, spending whole nights working in order to finish my tasks meticulously and professionally. I was quite moved when I was transferred from the office and had to leave my colleagues of the earlier days.

From the first day I joined the Finance Department, I noticed that the majority of my colleagues, who were from Jerusalem and good friends of mine, had become distant and only spoke to me about official matters, very reservedly, which made me resent them and feel obliged to treat them likewise for a long period of time. I was surprised by this attitude of theirs as I had done nothing to provoke it. Quite some time went by before things were clarified in a conversation with my friend Muhammad Aref al-Costantini during one festive gathering in which we were all completely enchanted by the oud, and the drinks. He said, God bless his soul, "On the day you started your job, so-and-so whispered in the ear of each one of the employees at the Finance Department that your transfer and appointment at the department were arranged for a purpose. And that Mr. Ronald Storrs, the military governor who trusts you and is a friend a yours, sent you to us at the department so you would spy on each one of us."

When I heard what my friend Muhammad Aref al-Costantini said, it was like being hit by lightning, God be my witness, for I detest the very word "spying" from the bottom of my heart. I was born to be loyal to my friends, my country, and my fine art, thanks to which I have no need to do anyone any harm. Abu Ahmed sensed and felt my innocence, and we recalled the acts of that débauchée, whose depravity was known to all and whom, nevertheless, I had always treated with compassion. As time went by, however, things changed and my colleagues—clerks, tax collectors, and others—grew very fond of me, until the truth was revealed and they learned all about the villain and became assured of my loyalty to them.

Having started out as a clerk, I worked my way around each and every role in this department, big or small, until I had learned all the procedures and became an expert on them, carrying them out with competence and integrity, until I was appointed financial manager for Jerusalem.

MEMORIES OF BEIT JALA

Following the British occupation of Jerusalem, most people spent time celebrating, having put up with suffering, poverty, and disease for the woeful duration of the Great World War, may it never return, particularly the tyranny of Turkey's Jamal Pasha, "the Butcher." My mother was still with us at the time and was very happy about her children's safe return after serving in the Ottoman army. I often tried to cheer her up and make her happy, and so I once took her by carriage to visit my sister Shafiqa who was living in Beit Jala with her family. When I reached the valley that lies between Rachel's Tomb and the Beit Jala hills, the carriage stopped for the horses to rest, and all the passengers got off. I handed my oud to my mother who was wearing her white cover, God bless her soul. I walked a few meters ahead of her, as I heard her say, "For God's sake Wasif, what will people say when they see me holding this oud?" People were approaching my mother, joking with her simply to look at the oud which, I swear, many of them did not know.

We carried on until we reached the house of my sister Shafiqa, which was located near the Maskobiyyeh Building. When my poor mother went in carrying the oud, there was an uproar of laughter. It was an extraordinary night. My sister Shafiqa's home became like a theater to which neighbors, acquaintances, and even strangers were drawn. Some people put ladders up the olive trees and looked on and listened from outside.

Of Beit Jala I would say that thanks to this visit, I gained the friendship of its people. I used to go on delightful picnics under Beit Jala's excellent apricot trees, singing and drinking with Daoud Matar, Beshara Thaljeh, the family of Iskandar and Hanna al-Lahham of Mount Lebanon, and particularly the well-known poet Jumaa al-Shaer. Cheers to those days! We would move from one place to another within the area, such as Bir Odeh, Ain al-Asafir, and Krimzan, each of which had its own share of special gatherings, whose days are now gone.

Later on, the circle of friends expanded to include many of the people of Beit Jala, thanks to my music, my job as financial manager, and my work in the grading of the properties and lands of landlords such as Miklhail Makhluf, Saba al-Aaraj, Saliba Rumman, Iskandar Badr, and many others. During apricot season, we had good times in their orchards, where we visited them and their families, while they also paid us casual visits in Jerusalem. My family and I spent the summer there among them like family.

THE CURLEW OF THE ORIENT—UMM KULTHUM

Umm Kulthum, in the wake of the British occupation, made her first visit to Jerusalem and performed on the stage of the Edison Cinema in Akasha, which was one of the greatest and most famous theaters in

A poster for a concert in Jerusalem by the Egyptian singer Umm Kalthum. From the private collection of Saleh Abdel Jawad.

Jerusalem at the time. The turnout was overwhelming and impossible to describe, with as many standing places as seats sold. Everybody was so swept away they looked like they had passed out. The modesty of her dress and beauty were met with great appreciation, and the night was an unprecedented one the people of Jerusalem would never forget. The Curlew of the Orient was dazzling, and seeing the audience's love and appreciation for her made her sing so marvelously that, unable to contain her emotions, she ended up unknowingly tearing her handkerchief. Neither I nor anyone else could ever forget her song, popular at the time, that began, *Wi haqqak inta al-muna wel-talab* (I swear to your life, you are all I wish for and seek).

I had heard Umm Kulthum for the first time while on honeymoon in Cairo, in 1924. At the time, she sang with her father to the rhythm of the tabla. When I heard her in Jerusalem for the second time, I found that the transformation was massive in terms of artistry and performance, and particularly in terms of the instruments she was now accompanied by, such as the oud and the qanun, which made her even more captivating. One is only stating a fact when saying that she is the queen of Arab music in the entire Arab world, may God keep her and grant her long life.

MUHAMMAD ABDUL-WAHAB

The talented and great musician Muhammad Abdul-Wahab visited Jerusalem for the first time in June 1927 and gave a mesmerizing concert at the humble theater of the Salesian School for Boys, which was located near the Italian Hospital, outside the wall. The demand to see him was not bad at all considering it was only the beginning of his musical career and that only a particular group of the population appreciated his style. As for me, God knows that I had already been one of the first admirers of his voice and his innovative singing style before I had seen him. As the poem goes, "We were conquered by your love before seeing you; at times one's ears are conquered before his eyes are." By 1927 I had amassed a large collection of his recordings, having sensed the beauty and artistry in them. At the time, he still had the voice of a boy.

One of Muhammad Abdul-Wahab's pieces that increased in popularity was Ahmed Shawqi's poem *Ya Jarat al-Wadi* (Oh Neighbor of the Valley), whose music was composed to the maqam Bayati without the slightest pomposity, Western retouching, or any kind of adaptation from the songs of earlier singers. This was the song that made his fame.

Some friends were over at my place, and I played Muhammad Abdul-Wahab's then-famous recording of the song written by Ahmed Shawqi that began

How could you so increase my suffering
And as I plead with you, show no mercy?

He reached the part where the last two verses are sung like a waltz.

This was my as well as your pledge in love,
But you left a sick man without a cure.
Why desert me for so long, why is loyalty lost?
Why must you be cruel and my life matters no more to you?

He sang "matters no more to you" by going across the twenty-four quarters of the Arabic musical scale, from the *qarar* to the *jawab*, in an ingeniously artistic way that we had not seen in the compositions of any of the old classical masters. One of my friends who was present at the time, the learned Mr. Suleiman al-Waari, got up and stopped the disc immediately, thinking that some technical error had occurred after he was disturbed by this innovation. It was indeed an innovation in every sense of the word, but it was too much of a novelty for Mr. al-Waari and some others to appreciate.

I was grateful to the Almighty for granting me the opportunity to hear this talented musician live for the first time. I hoped that he would distinguish himself among other singers and be at their lead, and that he would have a bright future, God hear my prayer.

Abdul-Wahab's Second Visit to Jerusalem

Abdul-Wahab made a second visit to Jerusalem and, being a close friend of the Prince of Poets, Ahmed Shawqi, he stayed at the home of Mr. Isaaf al-Nashashibi in Sheikh Jarrah. This time, Muhammad Abdul-Wahab was already a glowing star, thanks to the wonderful music, art, and singing that he had given the world and which had moved the souls of both men and women, whether music connoisseurs or not, all over the Arab countries. He thus shot to fame and became indeed one of the greatest music masters we know. He pioneered the introduction of more tarab instruments and of Western musical instruments into his orchestra, which added to the beauty and perfection of his music, and people began to savor and appreciate his singing, now that they had become accustomed to his innovative music.

The master decided to give his concert at Cinema Zion on Jaffa Road in Jerusalem. The demand for tickets was so high that there ended up being more people standing than sitting. I was in the front row, waiting impatiently for him to come on stage. The audience received a massive shock with news of the death of the honorable and much loved judge, the late great Ali Bey Jarallah. I thought to myself that, indeed, calamities fall on the calmest nights, while everyone else just froze, for the deceased had been so dear to them. He was an extraordinary person, and his death was a great and irredeemable loss for the people of Jerusalem.

Given the close friendship that joined the deceased with Isaaf al-Nashashibi, poet Ahmed Shawqi, and Mr. Muhammad Abdul-Wahab, a friendship that had grown stronger after a number of private gatherings at al-Nashashibi's palace, most of the audience was certain the concert would be canceled. But soon the curtains were drawn open and Mr. Abdul-Wahab gave a brief speech, fraternally expressing his feeling of loss and offering his condolences to the Jarallah family and the people of Jerusalem. He then announced that he would not be canceling the concert, out of respect for art and for the audience, demonstrating his love and loyalty. And so, he started off the performance looking visibly sad. But strangely, despite the great loss, he and his ensemble excelled in both singing and playing, having sensed the audience's thirst for his voice.

To my great fortune, after the concert Mr. Isaaf al-Nashashibi took me backstage, and I had the honor of being introduced to the master for the first time. I greeted him and congratulated him on his art, and congratulated myself on getting to meet him and listen to him. Mr. Isaaf introduced me and told Mr. Abdul-Wahab about my love for music, my skills in this field, and my fame among the locals. He was impressed and promised me to visit the Jawhariyyeh Collection on another occasion, God willing. So I thanked him and thanked Mr. Isaaf.

MY BROTHER AND FRIEND, MASTER AND PRINCE OF THE VIOLIN, SAMI AL-SHAWWA

I met the Prince of the Violin during his first visit to Jerusalem at the home of my brother and friend, Fakhri al-Nashashibi. It was a great party at which a number of notables of Jerusalem were present. The party had been thrown in honor of Adel Bey Arslan and his uncle Amin Bey Arslan, but Adel Bey did not come that night.

The guests were Ragheb Bey al-Nashashibi, Mr. Isaaf al-Nashashibi, Ali Bey Jarullah, Ishaq Bey al-Bedeiri, Majed Bey Abdul-Hadi, Fayez Bey Haddad, Mustafa Bey al-Khalidi, and others. Mr. Sami played brilliantly, then I accompanied him on my oud, and together we played the Tanios Bashraf in Rast. When I sang solo, he liked it and was very impressed with me, and through the fine art of music, a strong friendship grew between us. He became like a member of the Jawhariyyeh family. So whenever he was in Jerusalem, he would stay with us, as though he was one of us. He and my brother Tawfiq were inseparable, day and night. We had the most wonderful times with Sami at many homes in Jerusalem, particularly in the village of Ain Karem, of which we have special memories. Many nights we kept going until dawn, while Sami unleashed his creativity on the violin, as though he was speaking through it.

Whoever nicknamed him the Prince of the Violin was right, for it is impossible to describe his playing, particularly of *taqasim* and what is musically referred to as the *qafla* (melodic cadence). He was one of a kind in this respect and was able to make one feel deep sorrow when he played a melancholic piece, which he would then connect to another piece which, amazingly, made you leap with joy.

He was a talented artist and a virtuosic player, and had a great knowledge of Arab music, for he was a master of Andalusian muwashahat, being from Aleppo, the city which to this day is the bastion of this type of music and where one is constantly exposed to it. Music had been in his blood since his youth. His father, Anton al-Shawwa, was one of the most famous players of this instrument at the time and had made private recordings, of which I kept one disc in the Jawhariyyeh Collection. Furthermore, Sami had become familiar with the music and singing of famous classical singers such as Abdu, Salamah, al-Manyalawi, Uthman, Abu al-Alaa, Abu Daoud, and others, until the arrival of the music of Sayyed Darwish. Sami's extraordinary playing was enchanting and was not based on the Western musical notation which, as far as I know, he did not know. Yet, he was a reference on music and the classical Arabic science of maqam, and on the oriental musical scale and rhythm, just like classical musicians.

One incident, dear reader, shows Sami's true merit despite his lack of knowledge of musical notation. I once took Sami to the Hebrew Music Institute in Jerusalem at the time when my friend, Mr. Hausen, the violinist, was its president. The institute was known to be home to the finest musical geniuses and musicians, particularly violinists, most of whom came from Germany. They had all heard of Sami al-Shawwa's fame and were keen to hear him play. I acted as the translator. Sami grabbed the violin and started playing pure Arabic maqams with quarter tones of the maqams Saba, Sikah, and Bastinkar. No sooner had he started playing than they were holding their heads with their hands and shaking with tarab. They were truly amazed and just turned wild, complimenting him profusely. When Sami realized how much they liked his playing and natural artistry, he became more enthusiastic and whispered in my ear that he would play for them a historical piece of his own composition that represented the exodus of the people of Israel from Egypt. I translated what he said, and they all became excited to hear this piece, thanking him in advance with smiles on their faces. Sami began to play different but harmonious movements and pieces on the maqam Yakah, going from the qarar to the jawab with such creativity that the listener could picture the crowds fleeing the horrors in a massive flux. Sami carried on before slowing down again to symbolize their arrival to safety. They remained silent, looking amazed and entranced. In the end they showered him with compliments, thanks, and words of appreciation and admiration. It had seemed to them that they actually had been among the crowds exiting Egypt. They asked him to play it once more so they could transcribe it, in case Sami did not have the transcription with him. But Sami managed to get out of it with his usual tact, fooling the musical geniuses who did not realize that Sami could not read music. This long piece was in fact an improvisation of the moment, and were Sami to play it again, I believe each phrase would come out differently. Sami and I then left the music institute and made our way back, bursting with laughter.

LISTENING TO THE RADIO IN JERUSALEM FOR THE FIRST TIME[189]

When the radio first appeared in Jerusalem, its use spread rather slowly in the homes of the rich, as it was expensive at the time. Since this magic invention was unique, I longed to see and listen to it. My brother and friend, lawyer Aouni Bey al-Hadi,[190] who lived in Musrara at the time, bought a set, and we agreed to have a party at his place in the company of my dear teacher Khalil al-Sakakini. It was a family party at which a number of friends were present. When Aouni Bey tried to turn on the radio set, not knowing much about mechanical things, he pressed too hard to get the sound, and the set started emitting annoying, incomprehensible noises which were a mixture of music and shouting. Some of those present tried in vain to fix it using keys. We bemoaned our luck, left the radio set alone, and spent that evening as usual, with me on my oud and Mr. Aouni and Mr. al-Sakakini engaging in cultural debates.

I had another opportunity to listen to the radio at the home of His Excellency the Archbishop Ephedoros, at the Monastery of Abu Tor, at the time when he was the head of the monastery and its church. We were lucky to be able to listen to songs and music broadcast from Athens and Cairo with perfect clarity. I was pleased and enchanted by this invention, and I thanked the Lord for giving me the chance to listen to it. The radio spread slowly to shops, cafés, and homes in the majority of Jerusalem's neighborhoods. Through my brother and friend Assad Tombo, I bought my first radio. To match the oriental furniture of the Jawhariyyeh Collection, I placed this set inside a tall frame that resembled the Taj Mahal and was inscribed in gold with the phrase "This is Jerusalem."

MR. BOWMAN'S PARTIES

Mr. Bowman arrived in Palestine with the first campaign of the British occupation army. When the mandate government established a Civil Administration, he was appointed director of education for the Arabs. Mr. Bowman was well-known and had spent the greater part of his life in British colonies as well as in our Arab Orient. He came to know the Arabs and our customs and traditions quite well, and became fluent in the language, which enabled him to endear himself to Arabs and Arab civil servants in Palestine. Since he was also an excellent scout, he became fond of my brother Fakhri, who was a born scout, and trusted his work and liked to enjoy his company, as well as the company of his colleague, Fawzi al-Nashashibi, at scout camps. Together they were the subject of many amusing incidents.

Mr. Bowman lived in the house of the German engineer Frank (the Frank House), on Thawri Mountain, overlooking the city and Temple Mount with breathtaking views that made it one of the best locations outside the wall. Mr. Frank, a world-renowned German engineer known for his fine taste, is credited with its construction. Frank had come to Jerusalem during the Ottoman time and drew the plans for Wadi Musa Road and the slope leading to the village of al-Qastal. His work on these two roads testify to his genius in the windings he designed, which made it easier for horses to pull carts up the slope. Ownership of the house later passed to the Barakat family.

Mr. Bowman held many parties at this home for the teachers in Palestine. On many occasions I myself took charge of entertainment at these parties, playing the oud and singing. Mr. Bowman liked to listen to Arabic music, which he savored and truly appreciated, along with Mr. Stewart, the Education Department inspector and a famous artist and painter at the time.

A number of my best friends used to come to these parties, such as my brother and friend Mr. Ahmed Sameh al-Khalidi, the director of the Arab College, Mr. Habib al-Khoury, Mr. Sharif al-Nashashibi, and other dear compatriots. Each one of us at these parties was pleased with, and proud of, the presence of the cream of humor, the extraordinary Mr. Talaat al-Sayfi. No sooner had a musical piece, or a muwashah, or a poem ended than everyone was roaring with laughter. Such was Talaat's acting ability, which words cannot describe. He was talented, and his humor and wit were beyond competition. And so, this beautiful house left each of us with memories to remember, fondly.

MASTER MUSICIAN AND OUD PLAYER SISAQ

My friend Doctor Hagob Karakozian once came to see me at the Saraya in Damascus Gate, bringing me good news of the visit of an international oud player whom he had met one evening in the Armenian Quarter. He invited me to a party at his place where this musician would be present, and I accepted gratefully. In this way I got to meet an extraordinary artist on that unforgettable night. I had never heard anything quite like it. He played with exceptional virtuosity and style that exceeded what I had heard from the finest players, whether Egyptian or Turkish. Sisaq was naturally inclined towards the Turkish style in playing, and his ability to read music gave him a firm foundation for mastering the instrument. He was gifted without a doubt. He stayed in Jerusalem, and we met constantly for a week. Every day, after work, I would go to join him wherever he was. We have great memories of our times together in the Armenian Quarter. I invited him once to my home in Nicoforia, where we had a great party. He liked the musical atmosphere he sensed, as well as the Jawhariyyeh Collection. He presented me with a copy of his book on music, which has his photo and signature on the cover and which I will keep as long as I live. After this party, at which my brother and friend al-Nabulsi and Judge Muhammad Yusuf al-Khalidi were present, Sisaq agreed to spend the night at our place. He lay on the other bed next to mine, and we chatted about art and music until daybreak. He told me that he had a friend who played the Indian violin, an instrument made with a coconut, and I took note of that. When he left Jerusalem, we were extremely sorry to part with him. May God grant him success and longevity, and may He bless art with more of his likes.

FAHIM NASIBA AND HIS MISTRESS KYRIAKI

The late Fahim Nasiba's sense of humor, loyalty, and wit made him the partying companion of many of Jerusalem's young men. He was extremely passionate about music and listening to singers, so he cared little about how much he spent in this regard. He had a mistress called Kyriaki who lived in one of the houses of the Nashashibi Waqfs in Aqabat al-Mufti, right by the residence of Salim Bey Tahboub, which had a spacious hall with a very high domed ceiling. Fahim Nasiba once threw a party at Kyriaki's place, to which he invited friends, of whom I recall Munir Darwish, Ragheb al-Afifi, Abd al-Qawwas, Abdul-Salam al-Nashashibi, Hassan Qlibo, Fuad Nasiba, Ali Abbas al-Jaouni, Ahmed Totah, Ahmed Jamus Shatiyah, Mustafa al-Hindi, Hussein al-Nashashibi, Abdul-Latif al-Nashashibi, and others. It was indeed a festive party in which I took charge of musical entertainment with my oud, while Uncle Abu Musa (Jamus) took charge of comic entertainment, excelling in his enactments that made all those present nearly pass out from laughing.

Our host was Abu Nu'man, who used to dress in light-colored Arab attire, always preferring that gombaz which all his acquaintances recognized by its shine, particularly in the sunlight which reflected on his weary, or rather crusty, eyes. He was nicknamed "the fox" because of his eyes. That evening Abu Nu'man kept cajoling his mistress, until we decided to set him up beside her as a bridegroom, and then we were able to really see Abu Nu'man's fondness for the honorable lady and his love for her. In the meantime, we cheered for him as one would cheer for a groom, while everybody sang after me in a fascinating spectacle, "Come on flauntingly, O beauty, O rose of the garden." I should mention that we were all extremely inebriated, while Abu Nu'man humored us by drinking red pop and seemed to be more drunk than any of us.

On the large table in the room, we placed a small table and a high wooden chair on top of it. I climbed up this lighthouse and stood on the chair, holding on with my left hand to the ceiling ring that hung high in the middle of the dome, at the highest point of the house. Then, I grabbed the oud from my friends and began to play and sing from my lofty platform, "O Darling, I want to go back to my country," while everybody sang the famous chorus after me. It was an extraordinary scene and an innovation in the science of inebriation. Then, we moved on to the song "O, my darling tanned boy," and it seemed to us that the entire building was dancing with joy. We carried on like this until daybreak. Far from feeling content with what we had already been up to, we left the building and set off on foot, with everyone who had been at the party walking around or behind me as I played the oud. We went up to the Austrian Hospice, then on to the road leading to Damascus Gate, down the alley leading to Musrara, and sat down to sing in the sesame press which at the time belonged to the late Omar al-Dajani and stood next to al-Zawraq Bakery. Then our convoy proceeded, while Jamus, Fahim, and others ululated and cheered exactly like in a wedding, until they brought me to my father's place in Saadiyeh. Along the way, many people woke up and looked at us through the windows. It was a night our acquaintances, neighbors, and residents of those neighborhoods, from Aqabat al-Mufti to Sheikh Rihan, remember to this day.

Such were our parties, and this is but a modest description of what we used to do. The reason is simple—people's longing to celebrate and be joyous after the humiliation, disease, hunger, and separation suffered during the First Great War, under the rule of the tyrannical Turkish state. When Britain occupied the country, we were able to breathe relief briefly. But this was soon to end as we found ourselves facing a bigger and more catastrophic ordeal than we did under the Turks—the total loss of our dear country at the hands of the British occupiers, may God strike them, for He is the All-hearing, the Responsive.

AL-ARAB CAFÉ

The café of Abu Abd al-Arab of Ain Karem was located near the village fountain and was a meeting place. You could see friends and acquaintances sitting there on Sundays, listening to the new discs which Abu al-Abd was happy to buy immediately upon their release and play for his customers. Since the water of Ain Karem was famous in Palestine for its purity, many rich people and bishops in particular traveled there just to sit at this beautiful café and drink a glass of the fountain water.

Ain Karem was a summer destination for Jerusalemites, particularly for families and civil servants who were drawn by its breathtaking views, the quality of its climate, its fruits, and water, and its proximity to Jerusalem.

MR. JAMES EDWARD CAMPBELL

In the summer of 1922, when Mr. Campbell was assistant to the governor of Jerusalem and Jaffa, he used to visit Jerusalem to head a special military tribunal that looked into cases of infringement by farmers on the property lines of lands that were still being used by the British army, and issued compensations for the owners.

Mr. Campbell was one of the kindest Englishmen who had arrived in the country with the campaign from Egypt, upon the occupation. He was good-natured, humble, and humane in every sense of the word, so much so that it became clear to us, his subordinates, that he was a conscientious man and an opponent of the policies of the British Empire and the idea of a Jewish national home in Palestine. He was fair in his judgments and compassionate towards Arabs and their rights. He resigned from his post in 1931 as the Arab struggle intensified across the country in the wake of the Balfour Declaration. When he handed in his resignation, he wrote, "I do not wish for Mrs. Campbell to become Widow Campbell in Palestine because of wrong policy." So he left and returned to his country with his head held high and his conscience clear.

My colleague Daoud Yasmina was the translator at this tribunal and wrote about him many times in the course of his translation work which he carried out in the first big hall after the entrance to the Saraya in Damascus Gate, which was owned by the German Schmidt.

One Hundred Egyptian Pounds, and a Diamond

One incident that testifies to Mr. Campbell's fairness took place when he was governor of Jaffa. This amusing incident was related to me by the late well-known journalist, Issa al-Issa.

Once, in one of Jaffa's quarters, a man sat smoking a water pipe at the harbor's café when his daughter suddenly came and told him that he was needed urgently at home because her mother had just given birth to a baby girl. Since this man was in a precarious situation and was providing for a large family, he put his water pipe down with a sigh, and said, "There is no power or might except with God." Then he left the café and went home thinking that his wife and those with her were waiting for him to do and provide what is necessary in this situation. As he walked alone in the old alleys of Jaffa, he spotted a purse on the ground. He grabbed it, opened it, and found a one hundred Egyptian pound note. Overjoyed and unable to believe his eyes, he rushed to one of the money changers to change the one hundred pound note into smaller notes and spent ten pounds to pay the costs of the birth, thanking the Lord for this gift. Then he hid the purse with the remaining ninety pounds in his shirt and went back to the café, as he used to do.

While this sailor was sitting at the café, he heard the town crier call, "O good people, you who will return what has been entrusted to you to its rightful owner, and who will answer a plea, if you find a purse with one hundred pounds in it, ten pounds of the money will be yours."

Since this sailor was honest and good-hearted and had the fear of God, he accompanied the crier and the owner of the purse to the police station where he related what had happened to him and how he had already spent the ten pounds as he was in dire need of money. But the purse's owner was overcome by greed and wanted to save the ten pounds he had promised to give as a reward to the person who found his money. He said, "Brother, I do not care for the one hundred pounds. What's important is the diamond that was with the money." He swore that he was speaking the truth.

The sailor was dismayed and also swore that all he had found inside the purse was the one hundred pound note. But the owner was not convinced, and so the case was referred to the governor, Mr. Campbell.

On looking into the case and realizing what mischief the owner of the purse had been up to, he was fully convinced of the version of events told by the sailor and that the latter had only found the one hundred pound note. For had he gone against his conscience, he would not have admitted to having found the purse in the first place because he was alone when he found it and was seen by no one. The following strange verdict was issued.

Mr. Campbell took the purse with the ninety pounds in it and gave it to the sailor saying, "Take this and the money in it. It is yours, for God the Almighty sent it to be yours rightfully. But please, if you ever find a purse containing one hundred Egyptian pounds and a diamond, do bring it to us so we can return it to the owner here." The owner of the purse was infuriated and regretted, when it was too late for regret, his bad faith and his greed. The sailor then took the purse with the money in it, having acquired ownership of it through an incontestable court verdict.

This anecdote spread quickly and enthusiastically among the people of Jaffa and of most cities in Palestine, testifying to the just governance of Mr. Campbell.

THE END OF SIR RONALD STORRS'S MANDATE IN JERUSALEM

Sir Ronald Storrs, an extraordinary personality of the British Empire, played an important role in serving the empire's interests and was one of the foundation stones for the Jewish national home. Storrs was the first player to draw up the policy adopted by the Civil Administration that evolved out of the military front that occupied Palestine. It was Sir Ronald Storrs who created parties in the country, with the parties known as "al-Husseini" and "al-Nashashibi" being the main ones. Together with Sir Herbert Samuel, he paved the way for the return and pardon of Hajj Amin al-Husseini, and his appointment as the Grand Mufti of Jerusalem and later as President of the Supreme Muslim Council in the country. He then gave his support to the National Defense Party that was led by Ragheb Bey al-Nashashibi, and this action was pivotal in achieving division among Palestinians. He tried all he could to sow division between Christians and Muslims, but fortunately—and a million thanks to God—the Muslim-Christian Association was stronger than Britain and Zionism.

Sir Ronald Storrs was one of the most cunning colonists, and many incidents testify to this. On special occasions, he presented himself as a loyal friend of the Arabs, but at the same time he presented himself to Jewish settlers as a keystone of Zionism. I still recall the following bizarre incident.

In 1920 the first Arab uprising had begun in Jerusalem during the Nabi Musa festivities, when the people of Mount Hebron rose up on their arrival at Jaffa Gate while on their way to the Temple Mount inside the wall, following the tradition observed in Palestine. The Arabs indeed attacked Jews who were living along this road, causing a significant death toll and material damage, which infuriated the Zionists. The attack also affected the image of the country's British military rulers, so the occupation government made sure it was fully prepared for the day the Mount Hebron convoy was to enter the city, which coincided with Palm Sunday for Eastern Christians.

I also witnessed the uprising of 1921 (at age twenty-four). The army stationed a huge defense force at the opening in the city wall that was made especially for the visit of the German emperor, near the main entrance of Jaffa Gate. This force, which was reinforced by heavy artillery, tanks, and fully armed military forces, was led pro forma by Jerusalem's military governor, Sir Ronald Storrs, who was on horseback and in military uniform. It was stationed there especially to intercept the massive convoy and the heroes of Mount Hebron, or Jabal al-Nar (Mountain of Fire), as it continues to be called, and prevent them from walking down the road leading to the Temple Mount lest they might attack Jews again.

On this occasion the British army had brought a special "knight" who was trained to arrest any rebel by using a rope that he held rolled around his hand and could throw around the rebel's neck, then easily pull him towards him. As far as I know, he had been brought over from Senegal.

On Sunday morning, the convoy arrived at the bridge which lies between the Sultan Pool and Wadi al-Rababa (the Valley of Hinnom), where it began to slow down, proceeding step by step as the young men danced with their swords, old men chanted religious hymns, and another group formed dancing circles in the street and sang patriotic songs. The flags of each village and locality of Mount Hebron hovered above, and the Arabian horses marched to the sound of the drums and flutes in a joyous sight, until the convoy arrived at two in the afternoon, having taken more than six hours to cross the archway between the Sultan's Pool and the edge of the wall at the Jaffa Gate entrance. British soldiers, policemen, and security officials had a very rough time, beaten down by thirst. It so happened that the weather was unusually warm, which made the crowds feel more enthused and empowered. Onlookers watching this convoy from both sides of the road, balconies, cafés, and shops could see the thirst for blood in people's eyes. They were definitely going to be up to something.

The onlookers' predictions turned out to be true. For when the front of the convoy reached the top of Jaffa Gate slope, also known as al-Quds al-Tallah (Jerusalem hilltop), they found that the gate was closed and the well-known opening in the wall also completely blocked by artillery, tanks, and fully armed soldiers. On a command from Governor Sir Ronald Storrs, the front of the convoy turned west, heading for Jaffa Road, joined by approximately half of the people in the convoy. In the blink of an eye, the first half of the convoy went back, joined the other half, and winded in the direction of the wall opening, attacking the British forces and defying the artillery, machine guns, tanks, and all the security forces. It was indeed a frightful sight.

What did Sir Ronald Storrs do then to save Britain's image? He cunningly transformed into a Qahtanite Arab and began welcoming the convoy in Arabic with the warmest words saying, "Welcome, welcome, to the heroes. Yes, please come this way. You are right to keep up the tradition and walk to Temple Mount inside the wall. Come on this way." In this way he was able to save the day, prevent the spilling of blood, and spare the lives of the British soldiers. When the convoy saw Storrs welcoming them in this manner, they refrained from attacking anybody as they had intended to do when they decided to walk inside the wall rather than down Jaffa Road, and proceed via Damascus Gate, and perhaps Bab al-Sahira, before entering Temple Mount via Lions' Gate.

I saw with my own eyes how a hero from this convoy who people recognized by his braids that went down his shoulders, a Qaysi, or farmer, from Mount Hebron, attacked the knight on his horse, grabbed the gun and rope from him, then heroically went back and handed them to Storrs on his horse. Storrs accepted them with pleasure and admiration, and was fascinated by his extraordinary bravery. But I am embarrassed to say that this fearless hero signed his soul away and forgot about his Arab identity, joining the Jerusalem police force and becoming a subject in the hands of the rulers, whom he served loyally and faithfully.

This is a brief story from my memories of Sir Ronald Storrs and the cunningness he showed in Palestine, and it is but one of hundreds. This man truly deserves most of the credit for his behind-the-scenes work in establishing a Jewish national home.

* * *

A decision was issued terminating his assignment and appointing Storrs as governor of the colony of Cyprus. Since I had been a civil servant during his mandate, from the beginning of the British occupation, I went to a farewell party that he held for first-grade and second-grade employees at his home on the rise of the Italian hospital.

I remember that Storrs had acquired the title "Sir" upon his marriage to Lady Storrs. This lady, along with her three daughters, served us sweets and tea themselves, proving with this humility of theirs—and by not letting any of the servants attend to the party guests—that they were one of the most prestigious English families. They showed even greater kindness towards us when they organized some games for our entertainment. They all sat on the floor, and so did the employees. Then we all held up a bed sheet by tucking its edges under our chins, after a small bird feather had been placed in the center. When one of her daughters counted to three, each of us had to start blowing the feather as hard as we could to prevent it from landing on our face. When it did land on someone's face, there was a roar of laughter, and that person had to leave the game.

I recall the following incident which caused quite a stir among the employees. When we sat on the carpeted floor, Lady Storrs and her three beautiful daughters sat with us without the slightest formality. But one colleague, Sami Haddawi, apologized, saying he was not used to sitting on the floor, and remained standing, while everyone looked at him with surprise and bewilderment. Those who have known Haddawi, how he had lived since he was born, and what his youth, his home, and his lifestyle were like, would look down at him for what he did. For how is it possible that Lady Storrs and her daughters could sit down in all modesty, just out of humility and to entertain the employees.

For a long time afterwards, Sami was not spared the biting Jawhariyyeh comments for his shameful behavior.

Storrs bid us farewell in his office, where every employee received a photograph of him. I still keep mine in the Jawhariyyeh Collection, signed in the red ink that Storrs used to sign with at the time. Mr. Cast, Mr. Macintyre, and Mr. Bailey were among his inner circle and closest friends. In the morning, he boarded the train at Jerusalem rail station. When he placed his foot on the first step, he looked back at the crowd that had come to bid him farewell, a large crowd that included ambassadors, clergymen from all sects, diplomats, jurists, government leaders, and Jewish and Arab figures and notables, and said, "I hope to see you all in Cyprus."[191]

THE SARAYA OF THE JERUSALEM DISTRICT

Upon the occupation of Palestine at the end of 1917, Britain took possession of the properties of the German enemies, including the building known as the Saint Paul Hotel which was located approximately a hundred meters to the north of Damascus Gate and was owned by German Catholics. Its construction began in 1902 and ended in 1908, and it was used as the headquarters of the military governor of Jerusalem. Later on, the building became home to Schmidt's Girls College.

When Mr. Keith-Roach was appointed governor of the Jerusalem district in 1926, he left this building to rent the one known as the hospital of the Greek Orthodox Monastery, which was located on the way leading to the Latin Patriarchate, inside the wall. The building was divided into two sections. The northern section, whose entrance faced Saint Dimitri's School, was used as his family residence, while the southern section, which was accessed from the street that led to the Latin Patriarchate, was used as the government building, or *Saraya* (palace in Turkish). Back at the Damascus Gate German Building, we were replaced on the first floor by the treasury, which was headed by Mr. Davies. Given the immensity of this Jerusalem building and its solid construction, he had the lower part of it redesigned and dedicated to the storage of Palestinian currency banknotes, whose countrywide circulation was then about to begin. Official celebrations were held at the residence of Keith-Roach, and the guests used to enter through the northern door facing Saint Dimitri's Orthodox School for Boys.

During our Muslim brothers' celebration of the national feast of Nabi Musa, and following the tradition that had been in place during Ottoman rule whereby the celebratory convoy received the flag of Prophet Moses from the mutasarrif of Jerusalem, the Muslims came when the flag was brought down and received it at this door from His Excellency the Governor of Jerusalem, Mr. Keith-Roach. At that moment, Mr. Keith-Roach stood there, proud as a peacock.

We watched the celebration unfold at the Orthodox Monastery hospital only once, after which the Muslim community fortunately realized what a grave mistake this had been and from then on refused to be handed the flag within a religious ritual by a foreign colonist, arguing that at the time of the Turks the mutasarrif was a Muslim. Their pain was made worse by the deception and great betrayal that the British committed by giving Jewish settlers a national home in the heart of the nation of the Arabs and the Muslims. It was Mufti Hajj Amin al-Husseini who put an end to this by ordering that the flag be handed to the Nabi Musa convoy by the Supreme Muslim Council, thus delivering a masterstroke, as they say.

A BRIEF NOTE ON THE LIFE OF MR. KEITH-ROACH, GOVERNOR OF JERUSALEM

Sir Ronald Storrs was beyond all doubt one of the greatest men of the British Empire in the East, in his cunningness, political maneuvring, and the long time he spent mingling in Arab countries, observing the traditions and customs, and learning the language. There are many stories about him and Lawrence while they were in the desert, and about Britain's arrangement with the Arabs, and with King Hussein I in particular. Whatever Storrs undertook, he carried out to perfection. Despite his selfless dedication to British interests, his actions were received by Arabs with pleasure and good faith. Such was the extent of his discreet cunning.

When Mr. Keith-Roach was appointed as his successor to the post of governor of Jerusalem, we noticed that Roach wanted to emulate Storrs's ways, but his attempts came across as a fake imitation in every sense of the word. I do not mean to belittle Mr. Keith-Roach's knowledge. On the contrary, we thought of him as having a kinder heart and better intentions than Sir Ronald Storrs. But the way he carried out his business was the mockery of both employees and customers. I learned that he had been an actor earlier in his life and had a wide experience in this art, as did his colleague, Mr. Elmer Hirs, the grading inspector who was well-known in Jerusalem. Here are some examples of his behavior.

At the time when we were still based in the German Building in Damascus Gate, Mr. Keith-Roach once came across a customer, Iskandar Daadas, a Greek Orthodox who had the reputation of being a brave man, smoking a cigarette in the hall. So he went up to him, slapped him on the face, without a warning or a single question, left him, and went to the governor's lounge. Iskandar Daadas started roaring and shouting at the top of his voice, promising revenge. We came over and consoled him, and some went to see Mr. Keith-Roach. After some discussion, he issued his order, and we took Iskandar to him. He stood up and received him respectfully, invited him to sit on the chair facing him, offered him coffee and a cigarette, and apologized.

This incident, which kept both civil servants and ordinary people talking, highlights the arrogance and conceit Mr. Keith-Roach showed following his appointment as the governor of Jerusalem. But at the same time it shows that he was kind-hearted and capable of remorse.

Mr. Keith-Roach was living in a section of the Saraya, in the building of the Greek Orthodox hospital. He used to surprise employees during business hours and in the presence of customers by visiting different departments in the morning while still in his pajamas.

Many times he came in early, in his pajamas, and took attendance on the register at seven in the morning. Employees who were late had to face His Excellency and receive their share of rebuke. Even first-grade employees were repeatedly subjected to this treatment. This responsibility ought to have been passed on to the head clerk, as Keith-Roach should have been above these little formalities, being the governor of the district of Jerusalem.

He liked to be in the public eye and to be famous. When he walked, the Qu'ranic verse came to mind: "And do not walk upon the earth exultantly." God Almighty speaks the truth. Add to this that he liked to have his hands kissed by the people, particularly by poor farmers, so that if one of them kissed his hand, his business was done immediately, however complicated it was. It reminds me of that period of the Great War when I worked in Jericho playing the oud for the governor of Jericho known at the time as Murjan Bey. Murjan Bey was a dwarf. I believe that he was a Turk who had been born in Greece because he spoke Greek fluently. Mikhail al-Qazzaz, Mina Halabi, myself, and others, too, used to kiss his hand to obtain a two-week leave to spend in Jerusalem away from Jericho's damned heat.

On top of that, Mr. Keith-Roach liked to be glorified and called "the Pasha." He often said to people while talking to them, "Do you realize whom you're talking to? You're talking to the Pasha." There are many funny stories and anecdotes about him in this regard.

Mr. Keith-Roach made sure in person that no cars were allowed to park in the street leading to the patriarchate. He used to argue with shopkeepers on the left side of the street, who were mostly from al-Ladd, and try to stop them from leaving any goods out on the street, until they moved them inside. They used to brace themselves whenever Mr. Keith-Roach stopped by. Once it happened that an egg carton was lying outside the door of one of those shopkeepers, Mr. Batshon. So Mr. Keith-Roach got out of the car and trampled on the eggs, crushing them in a terribly funny way until his trousers were splattered with eggs all the way to the top. Then he left them and went inside the Saraya in that state, while everybody looked on.

He liked to exercise in the morning, and so, still in his pajamas, he would take the bicycle and cycle around for quite a long time on the rooftop of the Saraya in plain view of the Greek Orthodox School, the nearby Morcos Hotel, and all the neighbors who lived around the Saraya building.

He had a black cat named Good Luck which he absolutely loved. Many times he ordered all the windows shut at his residence, and even at the Saraya, for fear that the cat of the owners of the Morcos Hotel would come in and fall in love with his black cat. This reminds me of a *Karakoz and Iwaz* act in which Karakoz shouts at the top of his voice, "What a scandal, what a dishonor. The neighbors' cat has jumped on ours."

I still remember with exquisite pleasure the Pasha's yearly invitation to his neighbors at the Saraya, such as Basil Fattalah, an olivewood carpenter, Hanna and Isbir Boullata, both carpenters, Minas, the famous barber, and other shopkeepers from the area around the governor's headquarters. They would come dressed in their best garments to show their respect and esteem for the governor, and they would humor "the Pasha" with some chit-chat and good wishes. The Pasha, with his conceited pose, his attire and decorations, was an extraordinary sight. So cheers to those days, and, as they say, God works in mysterious ways with His creation.

Time and again, I was able to avert the Pasha's visit to the Jawhariyyeh Collection, for I feared he might feel hurt on seeing the precious artifacts and think that I am a pasha like him, God forbid.

After the end of Sir Ronald Storrs's service, Mr. Keith-Roach made a lot of changes to the administration. We, the employees of the Revenue Department, noticed that he picked on all those he knew to have been loyal to Sir Ronald Storrs. Even our boss, financial inspector Atallah Mantoura, fell out of favor and was ordered to work in the same room as the clerks, the second-grade employees of the revenue office, for quite a long time, on the pretext that he was responsible for verifying the records and registers of the tithe and werko. Mr. Keith-Roach came into the room and personally designated a desk for Mr. Mantoura by the main entrance, which we, the employees, found quite disturbing since Mantoura was our capable boss. But there was nothing we could have done, powerless as we were.

This is what I am able to write about the life of Mr. Edward Keith-Roach, and it is brief. I admit that he was kind-hearted and liked to help his subordinates. But he also proved to us that he preferred Zionists to Arabs, just like all the other Englishmen who had come before. They all seemed to have come from the same school. They went along with the establishment of the Jewish national home in Palestine and subscribed to Britain's treacherous policy in our country, may God punish them for their deeds.

THE REPLACEMENT OF EGYPTIAN CURRENCY BY PALESTINIAN CURRENCY IN 1927

"What to do, when my enemy is my ruler?"
—Sheikh Ahmed Hassanein

Under the Turks, werko tax accounts were closed down on a yearly basis. This we did by verifying the amount of tax paid by each taxpayer for the current year and rolling the outstanding amount over to his account for the following year. Mr. Keith-Roach put an end to this practice so that accounts were to be closed on a quarterly basis, which hardly left the employees any time to breathe. It was as though they were condemned to forced labor all year round, and the financial inspector, Mr. Mantoura, had to force the employees of this department to work an extra three or four hours beyond the official business hours every afternoon and quite often at night, too. God be my wintness that we spent many Sundays and major public holidays at the department, registering, adding, subtracting, dividing, and rounding up the taxes due on each taxpayer until the numbers matched the amounts entered in the daily register, not to mention the reductions and exemptions, which were issued in a special revenue and outgoings record. All accountancy done one day was then kept in a special envelope for that day.

It so happened that the new Palestinian currency was released, which was a great ordeal. The Palestinian currency which was coined especially for Palestine, and issued both in banknotes and coins, had the phrase "the land of Israel" written on it in Hebrew. Despite this hint, we accepted it, and the Arabs of Palestine dealt in it in what was almost an acknowledgment that Palestine was the land of Israel.

This currency remained in use until the end of the British Mandate. We did our job quickly, exchanging the Egyptian currency that the public had with the new Palestinian currency. I did this laborious work for a considerable amount of time, with the help of my colleagues—Tawfiq Manawil, Emile al-Kurdi, Anis Haddad, and others, under the supervision of Mr. Atallah Mantoura.

Since my inclination had always been for music, I was worn out by the amount of problems at this department to which I had been forced to belong. The job obviously did not go with my likings and the talent I had been born for. So I composed a *zajal* poem about our tasks.

It was well-received by the employees who began to sing it. I also sang it on my oud on many occasions and cheerful evenings with the boss, Mr. Atallah Mantoura, particularly during the Ramallah nights, at the time of subgovernor Mitri Farraj and the late Doctor Saadallah al-Qassis. When Mr. Mantoura asked me what had prompted me to compose this *zajalia*, I said to him, "I could teach it as a musical piece to anyone who wishes to apply for a job at our department instead of making him take the examination."

AN EARTHQUAKE HITS PALESTINE

At around two o'clock on July 14, 1927, while I was lying on the bed taking my siesta, we heard a terrifying noise, like distant thunder. Then we felt the earthquake. It was extremely frightening because it was powerful and lasted for quite a while during which everything was shaking, and the house, furniture, and vessels were trembling, may God help us. Victoria, my life partner, had only just left bed on that day after having given birth to our daughter Layla on the twenty-ninth of June. All of us at home were disturbed by this. But we thanked God that none of us were harmed and that the earthquake did not cause any damage to the walls or the roof of the house, despite the building being very old. Praise the Lord for looking after us and His people.

Immediately after the earthquake, I left the house and went out to find that many buildings, particularly inside the wall, had been damaged and that some of them had been knocked down. Even the higher parts of the wall had suffered in many parts of Jerusalem. This earthquake affected the most important famous buildings in Jerusalem, in particular the Church of the Holy Sepulchre, the al-Aqsa Mosque, the Dome of the Rock, and even that German-owned building known as the Augusta Victoria Hotel, which was located on the Mount of Olives.

From that day, Britain, with its colonial intentions, went into action, claiming that buildings had become dangerous and that Britain was now the main party in charge in the country. British engineers were brought over who unanimously agreed that the Church of the Holy Sepulchre was in danger of collapsing. Despite the objection voiced by all concerned parties from the various confessions based in this church, particularly by the Greeks, they removed all icons, lamps, and chandeliers that decorated the church and the Holy Sepulchre, and iron, wood, and armed concrete scaffolds were put up along the columns and walls inside the church, while a massive iron and armed concrete scaffold was built on the southern wall, above the main entrance, which ruined the view of the Church of the Holy Sepulchre and remained standing.

It turned out that the country had not seen an earthquake for over one hundred years, when the northern provinces were hit and Nablus and its suburbs sustained significant damage. The earthquake then winded east towards al-Ghor, the Dead Sea, and Jerusalem via al-Aizariyeh and al-Tor, causing immense material losses. I recall that an inspection of all buildings in Jerusalem, particularly those inside the wall, was carried out immediately by engineers and architects, during which our neighbor, Issa Nakhleh Qurt, demonstrated his valuable knowledge on the subject. Based on his reports, many buildings were knocked down by the municipality and the workers of the Public Works Department, for fear that the buildings might collapse on the residents.

I have a valuable collection of the photographs of the knocked down and damaged houses in many parts of Palestine, but mainly in Nablus and Jerusalem.

KHAIRIYYEH AL-SAQQA

In September 1928, singer Khairiyyeh al-Saqqa and her musical ensemble visited Jerusalem where they gave concerts at the theater of al-Maarif Café, outside Jaffa Gate. There was a great demand to see her in Jerusalem. Her ensemble consisted of a Jewish violinist, a qanun player, an oud player, and an elegant young man who played the riqq with extraordinary virtuosity. Her voice was voluptuous and affectionate, and the modesty and innocent smile with which she sang made everyone who was watching and listening feel overcome with joy. She was, indeed, a capable artist, particularly when it came to singing poems.

I used to sit in the first row with some of my musical friends, such as Taher Younis, Hassan al-Azhari, Kamel Younis, Hamada al-Afifi, Abdul-Hamid Quttaineh, Hussein al-Nashashibi, Abdul-Halim al-Tabji, and last but not least Ali Abbas al-Jaouni. Together we would ask for a repeat of every phrase sung or played which we liked. One night the police superintendent of Jaffa Gate, Ibrahim Bey Istanbuli, arranged for us to stay alone with the singer and her ensemble at the back of the café beyond the time agreed for the concert, until three in the morning. Khairiyyeh was outstanding that night, and her singing was marvelous. This, to tell the truth, was thanks to the presence of this eclectic group of Jerusalemites who were well-known for their artistry and their appreciation for music. That night was one to remember.

I encouraged my friend Ragheb Bey, the mayor of Jerusalem, to meet and listen to her. We had a party at my place in Nicoforia, which was attended by Ragheb Bey, Ali Bey Jarullah, Ishaq al-Bedeiri, Majed Bey Abdul-Hadi, Hamada al-Afifi, Fakhri al-Nashashibi, Hassan Sidqi al-Dajani,[192] and others. That evening is impossible to describe. I presented the riqq (tambourine) player with a beautiful riqq from the Jawhariyyeh Collection, as a souvenir. I still remember the poem of the maqam Hijaz Kar, which Khairiyyeh sang exquisitely.

O Pigeon of the winding valley, your tears broke my heart.
For the sake of he who made you weep, tell me what makes you weep.
As for me, I weep from the pain of love and my separation from my beloved.
Do you, too?

I learned the music of this poem from Khairiyyeh, and I sang it at many parties that followed our meeting with her.

At the start of the party at my home, we preferred to be in the courtyard of the house, in the shade of the leafy vine that spread above the fountain and the flowers. But when the ensemble started playing and Khairiyyeh started singing, different people gathered around the house's fence on all sides, which we found a bit surprising and disturbing. And so, we went into the museum,[193] and Khairiyyeh was astonished by the marvelous artifacts she saw, particularly the photographs of the old pioneering singers, composers, and musicians adorning the walls of the music room that led to the entrance of the antiques room.

FIELD MARSHAL PLUMER SUCCEEDS HERBERT SAMUEL

The Zionist Sir Herbert Samuel had been the first high commissioner for Palestine, serving from the summer of 1920 to the summer of 1925.

Many considered him to be the founder of the Jewish national home and to have laid the foundation stone for it by investing all his efforts, along with the Zionists, in obtaining that sinister declaration from Balfour on behalf of Great Britain, before the British occupation of Palestine.

Sir Herbert Samuel did his best to win the Arabs' trust during his rule and resorted to all kinds of measures, both harsh and lenient. He put money in the hands of the people who had been longing for it after suffering from tyranny, humiliation, despotism, poverty, and ignorance under the Ottomans for hundreds of years, until they ended up having to fight in that famous battle alongside the Turks during the First Great War, and lost their dearest and most loyal sons at the hands of Jamal Pasha, the Butcher. The people had come out of the First Great War exhausted, with their willpower weakened, and they contentedly resigned themselves to the British occupation, loyally helping the occupiers, as proved by the treaty signed by King Hussein I.

The parties of Sir Herbert Samuel were much like the nights of Harun al-Rashid and used to be held in the vast halls of his headquarters, in the well-known German-owned Augusta Victoria Building which stood on the Mount of Olives. The country's notables and the greatest public figures who belonged to the most prestigious families would gather in this palace. After all this, Sir Herbert Samuel lived to feel the pain and realize deep in his heart the magnanimity of Arabs, despite the existence of a minority of hypocrites among them. In the end he left the country alone, after he had done all he could for the establishment of a Civil Administration committed to the establishment of a Jewish national home.

According to a plan laid out by Britain and the Zionists, Field Marshal Plumer, a powerful military figure, was appointed as his successor in the summer of 1925.[194] Immediately upon his arrival in the country, he fully maintained a military-style government and abstained from having any relations with the people, whether distant or close. He did not give parties or side with any of the country's groups, but remained aware of his military status. As a result, the country plunged into a sleep and did not lift a finger throughout his rule of Palestine, until his time on stage ended in the autumn of 1928.

Field Marshall Plumer only made an appearance at official state celebrations, particularly at army parades which, according to the plan drawn by His Majesty, and given the needs of the country at the time, were his major preoccupation.

THE URBAN PROPERTY TAX IN JERUSALEM

At the Saraya the government decided to replace the werko (house and land) tax that had been in place since the beginning of the British occupation with a new tax known as the urban property tax, beginning March 31, 1929. Planning for this tax began in 1928, and I was one of the civil servants involved in this process.

I was the head of one of the first six grading committees formed and remained in this role throughout the mandate period. In this way I came to know by heart the lands and the units of the city of Jerusalem and its quarters. I have such good memories of those times. As part of my work, I visited the majority of Jerusalem's homes outside the wall, which belonged to people from all communities. I would go from the quarters of al-Najariah, Mea Shearim, and Nahlat Siqi, among others, to Rahavia, Katamon, and Baq'aa, then to Musrara, Bab al-Sahira, Sheikh Jarrah, and al-Thawri. I would meet and visit with the landlords, get to know them, and learn a great deal about their businesses. They also came to know and like me. I acquired invaluable knowledge thanks to my mingling with people in this way for over twenty years. More blocs were included in 1932, and then larger blocs in 1935, bringing the number of the city's blocs to 168.

Under the property tax law, it was enough for us to register the name of the person known to be the landowner, that is, the owner known by the government to be managing the property and receiving its income. The official owner did not matter, even if there was a valid tapu document proving ownership. Even worse, the person who had to be registered in the land property tax records as being the landowner was whichever person happened to be the most prominent within the relevant family, whether for his social status or his income, in order to make it possible for the government to collect the tax from him more easily. Indeed, if this person took his partners to court, the government helped him in collecting the monies he paid on their behalf.

This article was specifically designed to sow division within families—even between brothers—so that as a result of this falling-out which the mandate government created, partners felt compelled to gradually sell everything they owned to Jews, in order to end the squabbles and family disagreements. This reinforced the foundations of a Jewish national home in the country, ensuring that the majority of the land was owned by Jews, and was but one of many examples.

Many pieces of agricultural land that belonged to the villages surrounding the city became subject to property tax, such as in the villages of Beit Sahur, Sharafat, Beit Safafa, al-Malha, Sur Bahir, al-Salib, Ain

Karem, al-Walajeh, Qaluniah, Deir Yasin, Lifta, Nabi Samuel, Shifat, al-Tor, al-Aizariyeh, Silwan, and others, provoking complaints from farmers. But their complaints fell on deaf ears. Although farmers suffered an injustice when they were forced to submit and pay extortionate amounts for these lands, they did not betray their country and rush to sell their land, as it is said. None of the properties inside the wall were subject to this law. They had been exempt from tax since the Ottoman times, thank God.

Since the enforcement of the property tax in Jerusalem was successful, the practice spread to the various cities of Palestine.

THE ARAB UPRISING IN PALESTINE IN 1929

My sister Shafiqa and I were once swimming in the Dead Sea. A week into my leave, news spread of the 1929 Arab uprising. Following the massacre of Jews in Hebron, a curfew was enforced all over the country, both day and night. Traffic between cities and villages ceased, and we were anxious about our families whom we had left behind. News became inflated before it reached those who were far from the action.

We made up our mind to leave. So we rented donkeys from some Arabs (Bedouins)[195] and headed for Jericho. My sister Shafiqa had not left Jerusalem all her life. It was as the proverb goes, "When the unlucky woman went to the city, the city gates closed." In Jericho all my friends advised me not to proceed to Jerusalem. But I insisted and rented a car with my sister from the children of Ereikat for a large amount of money, and we entered Jerusalem through Saint Stephen's Gate. Our families were well, thank God for that. But there had been some bloody incidents between Arabs and Jews near our house in Nicoforia.

Early in the morning of the following day, while I was smoking the water pipe on the patio among my family, including the children and my brother Khalil, British soldiers surrounded the house on all four sides, which terrified us. They entered the house—which resembled a museum—and started roaming around in it with expressions of amazement on their faces. Then they asked me a few questions and made me sign a statement declaring that I was not keeping weapons of any kind in the house. After they learned that I was a well-known civil servant at the Saraya, they went off, never to return.

Later, I secretly found out from some loyal friends who worked at the Intelligence Department that this inspection by the army was carried out because the car I had rented from the Ereikat family in Jericho was being used to transport weapons to the Arab rebels, and upon our entry through Saint Stephen's Gate, an official report had been submitted stating that Wasif Jawhariyyeh was in the car. The army had made inquiries and searched the house until it became certain that the tipoff was false one. Although I wish I could have helped the rebels for the sake of my beloved country.

The Causes of the 1929 Uprising

In Zurich the Zionist Organization became the Jewish Agency—an agency for all Jews whose aim was to support the establishment of a national Jewish home in Palestine. The Revisionist Zionist Party, led by Vladimir Jabotinsky, began to actively call Jews to arm and resort to force, and publicly demanded the takeover of the Wailing Wall in al-Buraq.[196]

In August of 1929 Jews demonstrated, demanding to take over the Wailing Wall. They attacked families living near al-Buraq, as well as individuals in Jaffa. Arabs grew more fearful when they learned that the British director of public security had ordered that Jewish settlers be given weapons and that he had recruited a number of their youth into the police force.

On August 23, after the Friday prayers, Arabs peacefully demonstrated to express their unity against the government's stance and the attacks by Jews. The English fired on the demonstrators, and a clash ensued. For a week the uprising flared up and spread all over Palestine, forcing the government to seek British military assistance from Egypt and East Jordan before it was able squash it. Arab losses reached three hundred fifty dead and fifteen hundred wounded, and those of Jews and the armed forces one hundred thirty dead and two hundred forty wounded. Then, in Hebron, Arabs massacred Jews of that area.

Following these events, the mandate government executed Fuad Hijazi, Ata El-Zeer, and Muhammad Jamjoum.[197] It also sentenced twenty-three fighters to life imprisonment and one hundred eighty-seven Arabs to prison for periods ranging from three to fifteen years. Extortionate fines were also imposed on a number of villages, and a number of the leaders of the National Movement were placed under house arrest in remote areas, away from Palestine. I recall that the high commissioner at the time, Sir John Chancellor, who had been away from Palestine, returned and immediately upon his return broadcasted a strong statement in which he hurled insults at Arabs, describing them as "bloodthirsty." But when the Arabs responded in rebuttal to his arguments with a strong and harsh statement, accusing him of backstabbing and betrayal, he was forced to broadcast his second statement, which was considered an apology to the Arabs.

The Arabs persisted in their demands for a national government. After the uprising of 1929, and the report of the British parliamentary mission of inquiry chaired by Sir Walter Shaw, Britain issued a white paper in October 1930.

> The time has arrived for a further step in the direction of the grant to the people of Palestine, of a measure of self-government. His Majesty's Government accordingly intend to set up a Legislative Council generally on the lines indicated in the statement of British policy in Palestine in June 1922.[198]

The Arabs wanted to show their good will and cooperate with Britain, so they gave their consent. This paper became known as the Passfield Paper, after Lord Passfield (Sidney Webb), then secretary of state for the colonies of the Labor government. This infuriated Churchill, Amery, Chamberlain, Baldwin, and others who demanded that it be annulled. Jews around the world were outraged by it and opposed it. Prime Minister Ramsay MacDonald sent a letter to Doctor Weizmann on February 13, 1931, in which he assured him of Britain's commitment to the establishment of a Jewish national home, leading the Arabs to nickname this letter "the Black Paper."

Thus, the government withdrew its paper and carried on with its dictatorial and twisted rule in Palestine. Weizmann was reassured by this and withdrew his resignation from the presidency of the Jewish Agency. Lord Passfield later had to resign from the government and quit politics.

THE MANDATE GOVERNMENT'S AUDACITY TO ARM JEWS AGAINST ARABS, IN SECRET AND IN PUBLIC

In the wake of the 1929 revolt, the mandate government set up an armed force made up of young Jewish men, which it called the Settlement Police, adjoined to the public security administration. Jews were given a license to form military groups that would be attached to the Jewish Agency on the pretext that these were necessary to defend the Jewish people in emergencies. Mandate officers and military experts themselves trained the members of these Jewish groups, and worst of all, the government provided the Jewish settlements with weapons in sealed boxes, saying that these were only to be opened on the government's orders and under its supervision. These groups formed the foundation of the Haganah organization, which was set up to later become the regular army.

A NEW MUSICAL INSTRUMENT KNOWN AS THE CÜMBÜS

In 1930, a string ensemble from Turkey visited Jerusalem and gave a family concert at the Zion Cinema theater. My friend Hassan Sidqi al-Dajani met the band leader and invited the band to a party at his home, where a number of the finest Jerusalemites took part in an atmosphere of inebriation and exhilaration. Among those present were Ragheb al-Nashashibi, Ali Bey Jarullah, Majed Abdul-Hadi, Ibrahim Haqqi, Hamadeh al-Afifi, Ragheb al-Afifi, Thuraya al-Bedeiri, Daoud al-Fitiani, Tahsin al-Khalidi, lawyer Farraji, lawyer Ammun, Fakhri al-Nashashibi, Hussein al-Nashashibi, Ishaq al-Budeiri, and others.

Our attention was drawn to a weird-shaped instrument that a member of the band had been playing skillfully. After we inquired about it, we understood that this was a new creation in Turkey. It was similar to Nashaat Bey's well-known instrument, the nashaat kar, which was adapted from the oud but had a neck twice as long as the oud's in order to allow for higher notes and maqams that are not possible to play on the oud. The instrument, called the *cümbüş* (which means "fun") had a powerful, voluptuous, resonant tone. It consisted of a bowl made of spun aluminium and a body made of fish skin or rabbit skin which was fitted in an ingenious way that allowed the player to tighten it using special machine heads fitted around it, should it loosen due to humidity. In other words, it was possible to tune the body. The long neck resembled that of a guitar, and the machine heads were made of iron and also resembled those of the guitar or the mandolin, while the strings were made of steel. The neck could be detached from the bowl using a large key that was conveniently fitted behind the neck so that during travel each part could be placed separately inside the travel bag through a meticulous manual process. The instrument comprised five double strings that could be tuned just like oud strings and were played with a plectrum like the one used to play the guitar or mandolin. It also had a soft leather case to protect it from the cold and the heat.

With the permission of the owner, I took the instrument and tuned it a little, then played it with great care, as though it was an oud, which surprised both musicians and guests. The next morning, my friend Hassan Sufi, Abu Omar, came to my home and gave me the instrument, saying that Ragheb Bey had bought it for me as a present. So I thanked him and thanked Ragheb Bey later.

This instrument became widespread, particularly in Jaffa, and was known as "Mustafa Ataturk's modern oud." I have kept it in my collection of musical instruments and played it often at parties, gatherings, and picnics. I forsook the oud for a while, as I was too keen to play the cümbüş. But I still believe that no instrument is more entrancing, or closer to a man's heart, than the oud that is made of wood and real leather strings, and is played with a genuine eagle's feather. But then, different people, different tastes.

LEBANON AND MEMORIES OF DUHUR AL-SHUWEIR

I got my yearly one-month leave and made up my mind to travel to Mount Lebanon. We were lucky to have Khalil as our neighbor, as this put our minds at rest regarding the house, and we left Yusra and Layla in the care of their grandmother Hilweh and under the supervision of Khalil and his wife for the duration our absence. I set off with Victoria via Haifa. I had taken with me the cümbüş, which is indeed travel-friendly, for it is small and easy to carry. On the first day, we visited our friend Victoria Said, the wife of our friend Pascal Hanania, in Mount Carmel, where we enjoyed this mountain's breathtaking views over the sea. We spent our first evening there playing the cümbüş. The presence of Victoria and Pascal's friends made this a joyous party, so much so that I nearly decided to discontinue the journey to Lebanon.

However, we resumed our trip the next day via al-Naqoura and made it to Beirut. Unfortunately the weather was so hot that we did not sleep a wink all night. We headed for Duhur al-Shweir, where we stayed at Al-Rawda Hotel. It was the first hotel to the right as you entered the town and belonged to Edward Merhej. Here we found many of our friends, such as lawyer Ragheb al-Imam of Jaffa, Jameel Tannas al-Halabi, Shukri al-Harami, Khodr Sheheiber and his uncle from Gaza, and others. Once those friends had seen the cümbüş, they went wild. That first night we played and sang until midnight in the hotel's vast hall and dining room, and all of the hotel's residents were happy. We got along so well together, men and women, and were extraordinarily cheerful. Everyone kept asking me for repeats or requesting particular songs, especially the Yazbek family, whom I was meeting for the first time, and also a judge from Cairo. The latter had a passion for singing and music, and had an affectionate voice, so he joined me in some easy pieces. On listening to it for the first time, everybody liked the cümbüş, whose loud, deep tone made it like a music band in its own right.

We remained in this hotel, celebrating and singing day and night, until one day Mr. Edward Merhej came to me and begged me to accept his request for me to be the godfather of his first child, having sensed my love for his children. He was Greek Orthodox, and I could not refuse. So we took the child to a very old church known as Saint Elias, situated some way from Duhur al-Shuweir. In this historical church we christened the boy in the name Michel and wished him a long life. Then, when we returned to the hotel in the evening, Mr. Merhej gave a party in the hotel's hall in honor of the godfather, on the occasion of the christening of his eldest child, and traditional Lebanese generosity was put on full display as dinner and drinks were served at his own expense to every resident in the hotel. We went on drinking, playing, and singing all kinds of songs on the cümbüş until after midnight, and to this day this is remembered with passion and nostalgia by all those who were there.

Thanks to the christening, I became like one of the hotel's owners and a member of the good Merhej family. Victoria would visit the kitchen and oversee the cooking of food we ordered or liked to eat. In fact I really got along with this good family, Edward Merhej's wife, and particularly his sister Marie.

It so happened that a beauty pageant was organized at this hotel, and I was appointed a member and an expert at this event. This was a source of hilarity, particularly to my Palestinian acquaintances. I was overjoyed and drunk.

We enjoyed this atmosphere for about nine truly memorable days. My brother Merhej refused to take payment for our bill, but I insisted. After great efforts, I accepted being treated to just three days and nights of Arab hospitality—including drinks.

So we now had a family in Mount Lebanon, and we continued to be friends, exchanging letters and presents to this day. We left the hotel and spent the rest of our holiday in the hotels of Baruk, Nabaa al-Safa, Shaghur, and Hammana where we met Fakhri and a friend of his from Cairo, Saba and his wife. We were very pleased to make this acquaintance.

Our friend Doctor Saliba Said happened to be in the North. So we telephoned him and all met together and returned to Jerusalem via Syria in a private car. We laughed and joked so much that we did not notice the journey to Sheikh Jarrah. For as soon as I had finished telling a joke, Fakhri would start another. When we arrived in Jerusalem, the car broke down near the house of Ragheb Bey al-Nashashibi. We waited for the driver to fix the tires and thought, Good Lord, even the car did not want to return and had to be forced to.

WORKING AS A PREFECT DURING HOLY WEEK CELEBRATIONS

I have written about the religious celebrations held in Jerusalem during Holy Week, giving an idea about each Muslim and Christian celebration, particularly under Ottoman rule. During the British occupation, Britain and the mandate government were pleased to watch these celebrations, particularly those held during Holy Week in the Church of the Holy Sepulchre, which are rarely seen in other countries. For these celebrations are more like acts that are organized by the heads of the religious communities and take place in the actual location where Christ suffered, was crucified and buried, and ascended into Heaven. Since the occupation, and given that neither the English nor any of the Protestants owned any properties in the Holy sites, and particularly in the Church of the Holy Sepulchre, and that the English had become the rulers of the country, the celebrations became to them like theatrical shows which they could watch with their families. Since I was a civil servant in the administration of the governor of the Jerusalem district, I used to carry out the duties of "supervisor," along with many of my colleagues, in order to ensure the safety and well-being of the families of the English notables and rulers, and to entertain them, particularly inside the church.

We, the civil servants, of whom I recall Matiyya Marroum, Daoud Yasmineh, Anis Haddad, Rock Sabilla, and Issa Bayyuk, worked under Mr. Atallah Mantura, who was an arbiter on disputes between Christian denominations and had been appointed to this hard job for many years during the occupation. I used to assist him myself, given that I had mingled with both the people and the clergy. I was of great help to him, being one of the well-known members of the community in Jerusalem. When the Greek Orthodox held Maundy Thursday celebration early in the morning outside the gate of the Church of the Holy Sepulchre, my colleagues and I were there along with a police force at five-thirty in the morning securing the spaces allotted to the British families who came to view this holy celebration from the windows of the Greek Monastery of Abraham, and from the wooden benches which were set up especially for this day in the garden of the home of the Virgin Mary opposite the door to the Church of the Holy Sepulchre. Britain tried to have the English archbishop take part in this celebration by having him stand next to the patriarch during the mass service, then wash the feet of every Greek and Arab Greek Orthodox priest like Jesus Christ had washed the feet of his disciples.

Many times, when the English archbishop attempted to read the Bible in English alongside the late Damianos, I saw the latter stop him abruptly. But he was allowed to watch the celebration and listen to it, and then listen to the patriarch reading the Bible, in several languages, from the platform that was suspended on the wall of the Monastery of Abraham.

Holy Saturday at the Church of the Holy Sepulchre

In Ottoman times the rituals of this celebration, the old tradition, remained the same. But I got to know aspects as a civil servant during the British Mandate. We used to secure the seats of the English families invited to attend the Holy Saturday ceremony in various parts of the church. The most important of these were ones allocated to the highest government officials in the the elevated balcony, in that part of the church known as the katholikon, located opposite the Edicule[199] on the eastern side, and in the Calvary,[200] which overlooks the courtyard of the church on the entrance side and is accessed via the Greek Orthodox Calvary,[201] as well as ones in the courtyards adjacent to Golgotha which also overlook the door of the church from the inside, above the stone of unction. There are also three windows for the use of the Armenian community that overlook the Holy Sepulchre, of which we would use two, while the third one was reserved for the Armenian patriarch and his company of bishops.

The government used the seven windows reserved for the Latin community, overlooking the Holy Sepulchre (the tomb of Christ), for a few years after the beginning of the British occupation. These vast windows were like a blessing for the families of the British chiefs of Palestine's districts. However, during the time of Patriarch Barlassina, the Latin community for some reason categorically refused to offer them to the British. Since I was witness to both eras, I was able to see these celebrations at the time of the Turks, then at the time of the British. I will frankly say that the Ottoman era, and particularly the government chiefs, showed much respect and empathy towards the people, whatever their religion, rites, traditions, and customs, compared to the chiefs of the mandate government who gave preference to the British, and only the British, over the rest of the people who came to the celebrations. I used to see, alas, the director of the British police whipping the Egyptian Coptic pilgrims when they tried to enter the church. How is that possible when they have traveled and sacrificed all things dear to come on pilgrimage to Jerusalem, sleeping in the streets and the souqs of the Christian Quarter in humiliation, but with faith and endurance, waiting impatiently to see the celebrations marking the end of Holy Week?

THE GERMAN AIRSHIP ZEPPELIN GRAF VISITS JERUSALEM

Once I was working as an inspector inside the Church of the Holy Sepulchre during the celebrations of Holy Saturday. Despite the clamor that the congregation was making, we heard a boisterous noise and a roar that shook the corners of the church. Since the church door was shut as usual and could not be opened except after the pouring of Holy Light, I gazed up from one of the windows of the Armenian Monastery, which overlooked the rooftop of the Church of the Holy Sepulchre, and I saw that amazing massive airship, the Zeppelin Graf, in the skies of Jerusalem. It was a bewildering, terrifying sight. Such was the greatness of this invention that I thought to myself that it was like a country up in the sky. At the same moment, I saw my family, Umm George,[202] Yusra, and Layla, who was still a little child at the time, so I waved at them. Later on I learned that dear Layla became upset when she saw the Zeppelin and thought I was in it. She started screaming at the top of her voice, "Daddy, Daddy. Up there! I want Daddy," pointing to the Zeppelin. Her mother tried to convince her that her Daddy was in the church and pointed to me. But it was all in vain, and she had to take her and her sister Yusra home before they could watch the pouring of Light.

THE TREASURY OF THE HOLY SEPULCHRE AT THE GREEK ORTHODOX PATRIARCHATE IN JERUSALEM

From the time I was young, when my father was alive, I used to hear a lot about the treasury of the Holy Sepulchre, its value, its historical worth, and its greatness. So I grew up wishing I would one day have the chance to look at these jewels, until one day I got lucky and my wish was granted.

As I mentioned, I used to work with Mr. Atallah Mantura at the Saraya in Jerusalem, where in addition to my work at the Revenue Department I helped him with his responsibilities in sorting out disagreements between the different Christian communities—the Status Quo. It so happened that I was to accompany High Commissioner Sir John Robert Chancellor, who was passionate about antiques. I shopped and bought rare pieces from all parts of Jerusalem, particularly from the Byzantine icon collection of our friend, the great painter and artist Nicola al-Sayigh.[203]

After we made an appointment with the Greek Orthodox Patriarchate for the visit of the high commissioner, I accompanied His Excellency, on his orders, for he was very fond of me and was aware of my talent and the fact that I owned the largest collection of oriental antiques in Palestine. After we had coffee in the administrative offices of the Church of the Holy Sepulchre, we went up the stairs leading to Golgotha, where an iron door in the church's ceiling was opened for us. Climbing the iron stairs, we got to a small area that overlooked a rectangular hall that led to the treasury. It contained all kinds of the greatest and most extraordinary, unique, rare gems, inlaid into the crowns of the Orthodox patriarchs who had served since ancient times, as well as into "the mace"—crosses, ornamented golden chains, breathtaking decorations from a number of countries, lamps, and the vestments of the patriarchs, endlessly ornamented with silver, gold, and pearls.

Even the high commissioner himself was not allowed to enter this grand room. We looked at it from the hall, which was like an entrance to the room. The *rais* (principal) of the church alone would hand the pieces one by one to the deacon, who would hand them in turn to the monk who was in charge of showing them to us. After we had looked at an item, he would hand it back. If these antiques were to be sold, they would raise enough money to buy the whole of Jerusalem. So many are the jewels and gems they contain that it is not possible to describe them here. I am sure that these treasures, or most of them, particularly the large crosses, crowns, and maces, must have been sent to Jerusalem as presents by the Russian czars before the 1917 revolution. In addition to diamonds, there were turquoise, Russian rubies, and more importantly huge and incredibly dazzling emeralds that could not be counted, for there were so many of them inlaid next to one another.

After visiting this valuable collection, which I will never forget, I understood that only those few who are very close to the patriarchate are allowed to see it, and only with great difficulty. I learned from my friends the archbishops and the patriarch that neither the patriarchate, the monastery, nor the church were allowed to resort to this "treasury" even if the monastery were to fall to dire need. After seeing what I saw, I began to hold monks and monkhood in high esteem, for monks work hard to preserve this valuable legacy which is without a doubt a great responsibility for the principal of the Church of the Holy Sepulchre who did his utmost to preserve it and never tried to sell even one precious stone from a crown or mace.

MY APPOINTMENT AS FISCAL MANAGER FOR JERUSALEM

When the mandate government realized that its plan to impose a property tax in cities had been successful, and that it had succeeded in getting rid of the werko tax which had continued from the beginning of the British occupation until 1929, it started broadening the scheme. It pressed ahead with a new plan for the villages of the Jerusalem district, setting up a village tax, more or less according to the model of the tax levied in the cities but with some inevitable modifications regarding rent and agricultural lands. In the end it was forced to restructure the original Revenue Department and reallocate us, the staff.

Under the supervision of Mr. Atallah Mantura, I was appointed fiscal manager for Jerusalem and became personally responsible for the department's management, in addition to being the head of the property committee and a member of the Property Tax Appeals Committee. Of the old staff members, Yaacoub Baramki, Yahia Hammoudah, Suleiman Farraj, Ibrahim Barkan, and Ashur Ashur remained with me.

The late Muhammad Aref al-Costantini became fiscal manager for the department that dealt with the village tax and with what remained of the werko and tithe taxes that continued to be enforced according to the Turkish framework under the supervision of Mr. Nicola Saba, the district governor of Jerusalem. The clerks were Ibrahim al-Alami, Suleiman Farraj, Musa Murali, Said Mukhtar, and Sheikh Shehada Abu al-Suud.

This department was moved from the building of what was formerly the hospital of the Greek Orthodox Monastery to the Russian Building located on the street of Notre Dame de France, on the corner leading to Musrara and on to Damascus Gate, and which used to be known as the Russian Consulate during the Ottoman rule, before the communist revolution. With God's blessing I was able to reach this high position of fiscal manager for Jerusalem, thanks to the knowledge and broad expertise I had gained in the field of properties and lands, and the relevant paperwork according to the Turkish and British frameworks. I became a senior official—given the responsibility that this job involves towards both the government and the people—until the end of British rule.

THE GERMAN ORIENTALIST, DOCTOR LACHMANN

I made the acquaintance of Doctor Lachmann, a doctor of music, through my friend, the Western artist Mr. Stuart, one of the inspectors of the Education Department of the mandate government in Jerusalem.[204]

First I should tell the reader about Mr. Stuart, an artist who lived in one of the houses of the al-Nimri family in Mahallat al-Namamira in Baq'aa in Jerusalem. On seeing this house, and as soon as you set foot in it, one could be sure beyond doubt that it belonged to a great artist. The unique oriental furniture and antiques testified to their owner's fine taste, particularly when it came to furniture of the old Egyptian style, which was made of precious untanned wood, with marvelous engravings and patterns made with immaculate precision, beautiful artistry, and infinite grandeur. At his home I really enjoyed admiring oil paintings of natural landscapes, flowers, and roses which he had painted himself and which showed that he was a skilled painter. He often visited me with his friends to look at the Jawhariyyeh Collection and its treasures, and he used to compliment me on having one of the finest tastes he had encountered in the Middle East, particularly as I was not a wealthy man, but a simple civil servant.

He was fond of me, and so he gave me a lot of guidance regarding these antiques, their age, and value. I gained from him a good deal of knowledge which I would never forget and for which I will always be grateful. He often took me along to Tel Aviv where we had good times all over the city. Once when we were there with my brother Tawfiq, he introduced me to a lady who was running dance and rhythm classes in a big hall located in a basement in which a number of beautiful oriental Jewish young ladies were learning uhzujas and dabkeh. We visited again and this lady learned from me the dabkeh, songs, and uhzujas that I knew from the times I used to play the rebeck and the tanboor as a youth, and she was very pleased with me.

Mr. Stuart introduced me to Doctor Lachmann. The first meeting happened at my place, at the Jawhariyyeh Collection. Lachmann spoke Arabic well, so we talked about art and music. Then I made him listen to a large collection of songs I knew from a variety of genres, from peasant songs to the urban songs of Egypt, Syria, and Palestine, to Andalusian muwashahat, mawwals, taqtouqas, and qasidas, and I played some instruments for him such as the rebeck, the tanboor, the Indian tanboor, the cümbüş, and finally the master of all these instruments, the oud. He was very pleased and nicknamed me, in Mr. Stuart's presence, "the encyclopedia of Arabic music."

Doctor Lachmann remained in contact, coming to see me at my place and continuing his research on music with my help. He learned a lot from me about oud playing and modern Arabic music scale and rhythm as I had been taught them by the old masters who could not read music. The way in which I picked up this art from them remains imprinted on my mind, and I have not forgotten to this day. This conversation was exactly what Lachmann had been looking for; it was like I was quenching his thirst. He took me along to a lot of the academic musical events of the Hebrew Music Institute, and also to Hebrew University, and even the Arab College. He used to lecture, referring to my singing and playing, and say, "This is the art and methodology that I would like to see adopted and followed by the Arabs; in fact, by the East as a whole." He would add,

> Arabic music is emotional and cannot in any way go together with Western-style musical notation. I can assure you that an Arab musician who adopts Western-style musical transcription and follows it cannot be considered a musician. For his singing and performance of complex Arabic compositions cannot be reflected in Western musical notation. His art would come out rather wanting and lacking in purity. For in my belief, should it be based on the rules of Western notation, the presence of the quarter tone in the Arabic music scale, which is made up of twenty-four quarter tones, would clash with the Western scales's twelve quarter tones, and the result would be a terrible one in which the purity of Arabic music would be lost.

I also remember that he gave a lecture about rhythm in Arabic music and the huge difference between it and rhythm in Western music, where there are no more than eight rhythms, pointing out that in Arabic music there are over seventy-two different rhythms upon which the classical style known as muwashah is based. He also touched on the many airs based on the quarter tone, such as the Saba, Bayati, Sigah, Bastanikar, and others, explaining that they did not exist in Western music and that it was impossible to play them on classical Western instruments. His lectures were valuable, and he gave them at many venues, such as the Arab College, at the time of great master Ahmed Sameh al-Khalidi. I played my oud and sang, as a demonstration of Doctor Lachmann's theories, for students and professors at the college, and Mr. Stuart; at the Hebrew University, on Mount Skopas, in the presence of orientalists and foreign musicians, particularly Jewish German musicians; and at the Jewish Music Club, where we had many meetings to discuss such issues.

Whenever Doctor Lachmann started his speech by having me play and sing in order to prove his point, he never forgot to mention and remind the audience of the necessity to learn Arabic music the way Wasif had learned it, and that way only. In other words, the musical pieces should be taught to the pupil one by one. The teacher should keep repeating them, piece by piece, until the pupil has learned them, and he should clap his hands to teach the rhythm of the muwashahat. But one day, I interrupted him in the presence of some of the elite musicians.

> Doctor Lachmann, I agree with you that Arabic music is more about feelings and tarab than Western music, which is why, when the listener reaches the state of tarab, he cannot contain himself and must sigh and let out an "aah… aah…" and then request a repeat of a small piece that consists of just a few vocal notes which have nothing to do with Western harmony and philosophy. After the rise of Islam, the Prophet Muhammad allowed Arabs to recite the Qu'ran by singing. At the same time, because of his understanding of these feelings, he allowed the listeners of religious recitation to cheer the *muqri* (reciter) with "Allah… Allah… Allah…" in order to nurture their souls and love for tarab, even in religion.
>
> You are also right about the Arabic oriental scale known to the old Arab musicians, which consists of twenty-four quarter tones, beginning with Kaba Nim Hisar and ending with the Nawa string, then with nim Hisar and ending with Jawab Tik Hijaz of the second diwan, as I explain in my book *The Jawhariyyeh Selections of Arabic Music*, with illustrations showing for each tone the corresponding position of the fingers on the strings of the oud.
>
> But who can memorize all these complicated facts and apply each quarter tone correctly just in his head for his entire life? Don't you agree with me that there cannot be more than one person in every twenty thousand who actually masters this art, which means that if Arabs stick to this difficult way of doing things, it will not be long before there is hardly one remarkable musician left?
>
> Having said that, why do you oppose the principle of learning Arabic music using Western-style musical notation? I am sure that it would be possible to find, in every ten houses, a person who can play very well according to fixed rules that are not under threat of disappearing. A symbol for the quarter tone you have mentioned has been added to the Western-style transcription at the conference on Arabic music which was

held in Cairo in 1931, and in which you took part yourself. Isn't it so?

My experience in this fine art makes me certain that today's musicians who learned music after that conference can play the long complex pieces which are full of quarter tones by following Western-style musical transcription, as is the case in Egypt and the various Arab countries. These are the musical symbols for the quarter tones which it was decided to adopt at the music conference.

Flat	𝄳̸	to lower the pitch by three-quarters of a tone
	♭	to lower the pitch by a half tone
	𝄳	to lower the pitch by a quarter tone
Sharp	𝄲	to raise the pitch by a quarter tone
	♯	to raise the pitch by a half tone
	♯𝄲	to raise the pitch by three-quarters of a tone

I am sure that Arab musicians have the courage to learn music. In this way the number of Arab musicians would be in the hundreds, just as it is in the West where there is a musical instrument in each and every house. Look at Muhammad Abdul-Wahab's musical orchestra today. There is also the orchestra of the Queen of Hearts, Umm Kulthum. Listen and see for yourself how they are able to play with exquisite skill sophisticated musical pieces that are crammed with quarter tones.

So, allow me to tell you, Doctor Lachmann, that if you still insist on your opinion, it is from a Zionist, anti-Arab, and somewhat sly point of view that aims to prevent Arabs from spreading their music and from ever evolving beyond what they have already achieved, and that is all there is to it. By God, do you really believe that my children, let alone strangers, would be able to learn what I learned in terms of uhzujas, dabkehs, folk songs, Egyptian songs, Andalusian muwashahat, in addition to playing a number of musical instruments and investing the best part of my life in the task? No, and a thousand times no.

Doctor Lachmann went mad. He insisted on his opinion, saying,

No, this is wrong. I'd rather there was among every twenty thousand Arabs only one Wasif Jawhariyyeh who masters the old-style music and performance. There is nothing political to this because in everyone's eyes, art is art, and this is especially true for music.

I used to visit Doctor Lachmann at this home. He had many books on music, such as Shihab al-Din's *Safinat al-Mulk*, Kamel al-Khulai, *Kitab al-Aghani* (*The Book of Songs*), and others. His valuable collection included a number of Moroccan folk songs recorded on small aluminium discs. It was a truly valuable collection. He recorded about seventeen discs of me singing taqtouqas and muwashahat, and playing the oud, the rebeck, the tanboor, and the cümbüş, solo. He played these discs to foreigners, particularly German Jews, on many occasions and in various part of Jerusalem.

When Doctor Lachmann passed away, I was very saddened by his death, may God bless his soul. I learned that his recording equipment and all his disc recordings of pure Arabic musical pieces, including those of me singing and playing, were moved from his home in Jerusalem to the Hebrew University where they are now kept. I will not forget the times I spent with this great artist, orientalist, and oriental music specialist, so cheers to those days.

He told the head of the Jewish Music Institute that I must be appointed a teacher of Arabic music there, and indeed, I was appointed an honorary member. I struck up a friendship with the director, the great German Jew Mr. Hauser, as well as with Mr. Ebelia. But I did not stick to this job given all the fighting that had broken out between Arabs and Jews in the wake of the British Mandate.

Speaking of Mr. Hauser, the well-known musician and violinist, he married a lady who might have been older than his own mother, but she was a virtuous lady who married him for his art. This lady was a doctor, the famous pediatrician Doctor Kakan, of Jerusalem, and she was the pediatrician of all my children. I will not forget her kindness to the children, or the loyalty, love, and selflessness she showed towards them.

And so, our home in Nicoforia was like a pilgrimage destination for artists of all kinds, for art is for everyone. This helped develop my children's appreciation for music and their understanding of fine arts from when they were little. This is particularly true for Yusra, who grew up between Arabic music and Western music, and who earned the admiration of everyone for the great deal of knowledge she acquired on the subject. I am sure that in the future she will be one of those ladies with an international reputation in the world of music. God is capable of anything.

Karshat song: Musical notation of the karshat (lamb intestines) song. From a book by Wasif's daughter Yusra in Arabic entitled ***Popular Arts in Palestine*** (Beirut: PLO Research Center , 1968)

THE STRUGGLE OF THE ARAB POPULATION AGAINST THE MANDATE GOVERNMENT

When the British government withdrew its white paper of 1930, the Arabs unanimously decided to consider the British alone, and not international Zionism, as the enemy of Arabs, and that it was necessary to arm against the mandate government and not attack Jews. Thus, when a demonstration against the government was organized in Nablus in 1931 under the leadership of Sheikh Muhammad Sabri Abdin and Mr. Akram Za'aitir, the crowd clashed with the government forces. The seventh congress was then called for and held in Jaffa in 1933, and in it the decision was taken to boycott the government and abstain from paying taxes.

On a Friday in October 1933, all the cities of Palestine went on strike. A demonstration took off in Jerusalem under the leadership of the late Musa Kazem Pasha al-Husseini and clashed with the government forces at New Gate. We had been following the course of the demonstration from the Saraya, which was housed at the time in the hospital building of the Greek Orthodox Monastery. The demonstration was followed on the twenty-sixth of October by another one in which women took part for the first time. Led by Musa Kazem, this demonstration proceeded with the participation of members of the committee as well as young people, despite the government's failed attempt to stop it. The demonstration clashed with the army and the government fired on protestors, wounding thirty-five of them. Following a decision taken at the home of Musa Kazem Pasha, a demonstration took place in Jaffa, and the whole country went on strike against the mandate government. The latter reacted by arresting a number of protesters in Jaffa, at the Muslim-Christian Association, and transferring them to Acre. More protests took place in Ramla, Jerusalem, Nablus, Haifa, and Acre and were dispersed by force, again. So Palestine went on strike for an entire week, declaring its anger against the mandate government and its actions. No Jews were attacked in any of these protests which were aimed directly against Britain. Musa Kazem Pasha suffered serious injuries when he was leading the Jaffa protest and became bedridden until his death in 1934.

In the midst of this crisis and the hard times the country had been going through with all the uprisings, struggle, tragedies, and strikes, the Lord blessed us with a baby boy on November 3, 1933. As they say, he came to us like a hero at a time of revolutions, and I hope that he will be one of the great men of the future and that he will serve his people and his homeland, God bless him.

THE DEATH OF MUSA KAZEM PASHA AL-HUSSEINI

Musa Kazem Pasha al-Husseini, God bless his soul, passed away on March 26, 1934, at his home in Sheikh Jarrah in Jerusalem, at around eighty years of age. All major Palestinian cities declared mourning, and delegations from all over the country came to Jerusalem to be at the funeral.

It is impossible to describe this Jerusalem funeral. People came in their thousands and walked in a grand procession from Sheikh Jarrah to Temple Mount in one uninterrupted flow. There, after the funeral and the eulogies given by the country's greatest men of letters, scholars, and leaders, he was buried in the court of Temple Mount as a sign of appreciation for his efforts, his struggle, and the loyalty he had shown in his lifetime, particularly his noble and patriotic stances towards his dear country. I recall the late Musa Kazem Pasha al-Husseini as being the only member of this family to be buried in the court of Temple Mount.

Musa Kazem Pasha was a man of morals and a true human in every sense of the word. He obtained various senior posts during the Ottoman rule until Istanbul granted him the title of pasha. When his brother, the late Hussein Effendi who had been mayor of Jerusalem during the British occupation, passed away, the mandate government appointed him to succeed his brother as mayor. After the Balfour Declaration that revealed to the Arabs the malicious intentions of the British towards Arabs and the country, Musa Kazem Pasha al-Husseini was asked to sign municipal administrative documents in the three languages—English, Hebrew, and Arabic—according to the mandate government's decrees.

However, despite his need for his mayor's salary, he refused to abide and acknowledge the Hebrew language, and insisted on his stance, resigning from the mayorship of Jerusalem, which was a good gesture that was extremely appreciated by the people. May God rest his soul in heaven.

After the resignation of the late Musa Kazem Pasha from the mayorship, the British had the governor of Jerusalem, Mr. Ronald Storrs, ask Ragheb Bey al-Nashahibi to step in. He agreed with pleasure to acknowledge the Hebrew language and was thus appointed to succeed Musa Kazem Pasha al-Husseini as mayor of Jerusalem.

THE FIRST ARAB EXHIBITION

The steps taken by the national Palestinian leadership were meant in their totality to link the Arab economy to the Palestinian one and find Arab substitutes for Zionist and foreign goods and products, wherever possible. In order to reach this aim, the late Palestinian leader Musa Kazem Pasha el-Husseini launched the First Arab Exhibition in Jerusalem on July 7, 1933, in the new building of the Muslim Religious Trust in Maman Allah, which later became known as the Palace Hotel[205] and was let to Jews.

In this exhibition, and later in the Second Arab Exhibition, Arab industrial and agricultural products from the various Arab countries were displayed, and large numbers of Arabs—Palestinians in particular—visited both exhibitions. The Second Exhibition saw the participation of one hundred eighty Arab companies from Egypt, Syria, Iraq, East Jordan, Morocco, and Saudi Arabia. The mandate government was manifestly opposed to this Arab Exhibition and banned Egyptian aircraft from flying over Jerusalem on the launch day of the Second Exhibition, as well as the use of the exhibition's postal stamps, while British consulates in Arab capital cities refused to grant entry visas to thousands of Arab visitors.

The Jewish Agency was infuriated by the success of the first and second exhibitions and thus held an exhibition in Tel Aviv in May 1934. The high commissioner went there from Jerusalem specifically to attend the inauguration, and the state musical band played at the party. The British authorities allowed tens of thousands of Jewish migrants from all parts of the world to enter the country under the pretext of visiting the exhibition, and the majority of them remained in Palestine.

The manager of both Arab exhibitions was the Syrian, Mr. al-Azama, of Damascus, who was indeed capable, competent, and extremely organized, which enabled the Arabs to take pride in the management of the two Jerusalem exhibitions. Mr. Tabbarah worked very hard to introduce some entertainment in the form of beautiful, unforgettable fireworks that illuminated the ground and the skies of Jerusalem with all sorts of extraordinary firework patterns and designs. I purchased many things at the first and second exhibitions, which I still keep in the Jawhariyyeh Collection—oriental vessels, textiles made in Homs and Hamah, Egyptian ivory-encrusted frames, and more importantly water pipes that resemble the stem of a lily, with skillfully crafted leaves that looked real.

THE MUFTI, SHEIKH AHMED HASSANEIN

On December 3, 1935, the renowned Egyptian mufti Mr. Ahmed Hassanein visited Jerusalem with his musical ensemble which was made up of a qanun player, a violinist, a riqq player, and the Prince of the Buzuq, Mr. Abdul-Kareem. We had seen him and listened to his singing for the first time in Jericho, at a café that belonged to Musa al-Ragheb al-Husseini. He gave an excellent, marvelous performance on that occasion. I made his acquaintance, and we both liked each other. Mr. Hassanein was one of the most handsome singers I have met. He was tall, with a handsome, ever-smiling face, and he was elegant with his authentic Egyptian dress and turban that drew looks, particularly when he was singing, adding to his wonder and pleasantness.

At the lead of the audience was Uncle Muhyiddine Effendi al-Husseini, who displayed great generosity by paying for the tickets of a great number of people that night. Sheikh Hassanein sang many of the famous poems of his which I liked, such as *ala za'amat Layla*, which he sang brilliantly. When he reached the verse *faddaltu Layla,*

(I choose Layla over all others, just as over a thousand months, I would choose the Night of Measures), the audience went wild. So the sheikh repeated the verse on their request, and particularly on the request of Uncle Muhyiddin Effendi who made him sing it four times. Then, on my request, he sang the telephone dialogue which I had been singing myself at my parties, and which I had picked up listening to the sheikh's recording of it. Indeed, the dialogue was a nice one and funnily criticized the telephone company, particularly the young ladies employed to provide phone numbers, and the music suited the content well.

After this concert, Mr. Hassanein and his ensemble visited me regularly to look at the Jawhariyyeh Collection. I made my friend Artin, the santoor player, play with the ensemble, and we spent great times together, both at home and elsewhere. The sheikh became one of my dearest friends, and he liked Jerusalem and stayed. I always got my friends at the Immigration and Travel Department to help him renew his residence permit, until the Broadcasting House was opened in 1936 and he and his ensemble were appointed there and ended up staying with us for a long time. He presented me with a photograph of him and his ensemble.

Mr. Hassanein and his ensemble performed at the café of Uncle Abu Zuhdi Zuhayman in Damascus Gate. He was one of the finest chanters of poems. His voice was affectionate and voluptuous, and the way he sang was excellent, which is not surprising given that he was a Qu'ran reciter. We spent long nights with him in Jerusalem, nurturing our souls with the purity of his singing.

THE 1936 COUNTRYWIDE STRIKE

Nobody who understands the Palestinian problem could deny that Arabs, both Muslim and Christian, did not shy away from their sacred struggle throughout the British Mandate of Palestine, from the beginning of the British occupation until the end of the mandate on May 25, 1948. They persistently fought, not just against Zionists but also against the mandate government and its army, despite their own weakness, lack of weapons necessary to stand up to the enemies, and lack of support. The great strike of 1936, which was unprecedented in the entire world and lasted for more than six months is irrefutable proof of the heroism and genuine patriotism of the Arabs. British Secretary of State for the Colonies Mr. Thomas acknowledged on the twenty-third of April that it was Jewish settlers who had begun the hostilities in Tel Aviv by attacking peaceful Arab citizens and the indigenous population. All the Arabs had done was to unite officially against the influx of Jewish immigration, which was invading the country on a terrifying scale, and the sale of land to settlers.

The revolt continued throughout the strike and the Arabs showed great heroism, particularly in the face of the British army, which was the direct cause for the country's ruin. Fawzi al-Qawuqji was leading the volunteers who came from Iraq, Syria, Lebanon, and East Jordan to help the Arabs. The British leader was General Ritchie, who was succeeded in his role by General Dill,[206] the head of staff of the armies of the British Empire. By September of that year, the British forces had four legions stationed in Palestine—around seventy-two thousand soldiers. The patriotic rebels were led by Mr. Abdul-Qader al-Husseini, who was the son of the country's great leader, the late Musa Kazem Pasha. On the mandate government's orders, its famous agent Nuri Pasha al-Said came from Iraq to act as a mediator, but that was in vain.[207]

On the seventh of September of the same year, it was decided that a Royal Commission on Palestine would be dispatched to Palestine to demand an end to the revolt and an inquiry into the strike. On October 11, 1936, the Higher Arab Committee held its famous meeting in Jerusalem, and following a call from Kings Saud, Abdullah, and Ghazi, the decision was taken to halt the revolt and end the strike, which had been ongoing for one hundred and seventy-five days. As for the losses, there were twenty-five hundred martyrs, seven thousand wounded, eight thousand civilan deaths, and over nineteen hundred seventy arrests. In August 1936, the senior Arab officials of the British Mandate government in Palestine, both Muslim and Christian, sent the government a harshly toned memorandum in which they threatened to abstain from work should the government continue with its twisted policy that brought the country to the brink.

MR. ANDREWS AND THE CANARY ON THE OCCASION OF HIS WIFE'S BIRTHDAY

In 1936, Mr. Andrews was solely in charge of the administration of Jerusalem as governor. He was without a doubt one of Britain's most knowledgeable figures about the East, the Arabs, and their customs, and he was well-versed in Arabic which he spoke with the greatest fluency and on a high register. He extremely hated the Arabs and was biased toward Jews, as far as I know. He was the supreme leader, and all political matters lay in his hands.

Once, on the occasion of his dear wife's birthday, he wanted to offer her a canary. And who could have seen to this but Wasif Jawhariyyeh? When my friend Matia Marrum entrusted the mission to me, it was accomplished immediately. The man who dealt in the purchase and sale of canaries—a Jerusalemite called Hassunah who was known for his magnanimity and swift manual skills—came and brought with him an exquisite yellow canary in a beautiful ornate cage. I asked Mitia to inform the governor that he could come to see the canary. The governor, who did not know me at the time, came and liked the canary when he saw it, and then said to Hassunah, "Can this bird sing?" Hassunah answered, "Yes, sir, he does." But the governor wanted to be mocking and went on. "What does he sing? 'Muhammad's Army Came with the Sword?'" He said this while looking at Hassunah with contempt, then turned to Matia and me and smiled. I said to myself that he was in need of a Jawhariyyeh-style reply, particularly since Hassunah was too scared to answer. So I said, "Your Excellency, he is singing 'O darling, I want to go back to my country.'"

At this he remained silent and seemed bitter. Then he said to me, "Could you keep it and feed it until the morning of my wife's birthday?" I answered, "With pleasure. I will even give him a glass of arak to drink." Then, he went back to his room while staring at me, drinking my face in. I learned later from Matia Marrum that the governor asked him a lot about me.

Speaking of Andrews, the rebels assassinated him in Nazareth on September 29, 1937, because he was one of the supporters of the partition plan and was set against the Arabs of Palestine when he was appointed governor in the North. I had been lucky to obtain a document signed by him on the very morning of his assassination, for he had stopped by the office and signed the document before setting off for church to pray and being assassinated by the rebels.

THE HEADQUARTERS OF THE GOVERNOR OF JERUSALEM IS MOVED OUTSIDE THE WALL

In the wake of the 1936 revolt and the strike that paralyzed the administration of the mandate government, Jewish customers did not dare come to the Saraya, which was located in the former Greek Orthodox hospital inside the wall, on the road leading to the Latin patriarchate, as they were afraid of the Arabs. So it was decided to move the Saraya to Jaffa Road, which was on the borderline separating Arabs and Jews in Jerusalem. The new Saraya was based in one of the Russian-owned properties, at the corner leading to the Ammail properties. These properties also housed the Immigration and Travel Department and, next to it, the Public Works Department, in addition to the many Russian properties of that neighborhood.

We have wonderful memories of the great times we spent at the former Saraya during the 1936 strike. Since Jews were not able to visit to do their business, we were able to have good times with friends at the café of our brother Issa al-Toubbeh, the mukhtar of the Greek Orthodox community, which was located almost opposite the Saraya. There, on the sofa, with our brother Abu Michel, we would discuss among friends the state which the country had got into, and our discussions were always shot through with humor and innocent jokes, until the strike came to an end. In the new Saraya, we felt like strangers and recalled the old days with bitterness.

THE PALESTINE BROADCASTING HOUSE—"JERUSALEM CALLING"[208]

The Broadcasting House in Jerusalem was launched in 1936, employing many art lovers such as Ibrahim Abdul-Aal, Muhammad Ayta, Iskandar al-Fallas, Yahiya al-Saoudi, Jaleel Rakb, Ramez al-Zaghah, Kazem al-Sibasi, Fahd Najjar, Milad Farah, Tawfiq Jawhariyyeh, Rouhi al-Khammash from Nablus, Artin Santurji, Bassil Tharwat, and Abdul Karim.

The Arabic section was headed by the late Yahiya al-Lababidi and the talented poet Ibrahim Touqan. The late violinist Jamil Uways was brought in later and tried to teach those amateurs to play according to Western-style musical transcription, and indeed succeeded to a certain extent, until the arrival of the famous pianist Yusuf Batrouni, to whom credit is due for putting order into the ensemble.

The famous Jewish Iraqi master musician Mr. Azzuri[209] was one of the first musicians to join the radio. But given the political tension between Arabs and Jews, the government had to split them apart so that each group was singing and playing separately from the other. Mr. Azzuri, who had represented Iraq at the 1931 Arabic music conference in Cairo, came up with an innovative but malicious idea that consisted of replacing the lyrics of the authentic Arabic Andalusian muwashahat with Hebrew lyrics. But his attempt was doomed to failure, and he soon became the joke of the other musicians.

The musical ensemble of the famous singer Amin Hassanein happened to be visiting Jerusalem at the time and was leading the singing and playing at the launch celebration. Indeed, with my mediation,

Sheikh Hassanein continued to work at the radio for a long time, along with his brother who sang some monologues and dialogues, until they quit and returned to Cairo. Of his ensemble, as I recall, my brother Abdul Karim, the Prince of the Buzuq, remained with us and excelled in his work. There was no doubt that he was a talented artist and that he was truly the prince of this rare oriental instrument.

As for Ibrahim Abdul-Aal, the excellent qanun player, he was a friend of mine, and his wife was the daughter of my brother and friend Omar al-Batsh of Aleppo. This great musician had taught me the Andalusian muwashahat when I was sixteen, and from him I learned a huge number of muwashahat which were sung on the radio in Jerusalem thanks to my brother Tawfiq who introduced them to the musicians there. I wrote a lot about Omar al-Batsh. The violinist Abboud was the son of Ibrahim Abdul-Aal and an old friend of mine. Speaking of Mr. Ibrahim Abdul-Aal, I should say that he successfully taught my son George to play the qanun. He was then taught by Mr. Abdul-Fattah Mansi and showed even more progress. But unfortunately the latter left Jerusalem in 1948 before our son George had mastered the qanun.

There was also Mr. Muhammad Atiyah, the Egyptian qanun player who excelled in Jerusalem and never stopped visiting us. As for my brother Yahiya al-Saoudi, he was without any doubt a talented young man who had taken up music as a hobby in his older years. Earlier he had been one of the most famous shoemakers in Jerusalem. But the purity of his voice and his love for music made him give up the profession and specialize in art, learning the oud and managing to achieve fame within a short while, until he took the leadership of the string music band at the radio. He is credited with the success of violinist Jaleel Rakb, oud player Ramez al-Zaaa, percussionist Basil Tharwat, and oud player Iskandar al-Fallas, in particular.

My brother Tawfiq was talented in all fields of art, particularly in painting and playing the nay. For the first time in his life, he worked for a monthly salary as a nay player at the radio, and indeed, he excelled and did brilliantly. He only worked out of love for music and because both his superiors and subordinates appreciated him and liked him. Otherwise, he would not have been able to bear up, for he had no patience with regular jobs.

Brother Kazem al-Sibasi had a fine, affectionate voice and was able to master melodies. But in general he lacked discipline, so when he sang, he would forget some of the lyrics as he had no patience to invest in learning them properly, careless as he was, may God fogive him. I only say this out of my respect for art, for Kazem came from an artistic family. His uncle, Muhammad al-Sibasi, had an amazing success in Jerusalem where he became famous for decades as a great amateur singer. His father, Musa al-Sibasi, whom I met towards the end of his life, was a percussionist known as Musa the instrumentalist, and was a friend of my father's.

The Jerusalem Broadcasting House was a blessing, for it turned Jerusalem into a top destination for musicians from the various Arab countries. In this way I was able to make the acquaintance of Amal Hussein and her husband, a composer. They used to visit, and we would talk about music. The late Jameel Uways never stopped visiting us, nor did Yusuf Batruni to whom we are grateful for teaching our daughter Yusra to play Arabic quarter-tone-free musical pieces on the piano. I also recall Fadel al-Shawwa, the brother of the Prince of the Violin Sami al-Shawwa, and others who came to the Broadcasting House on music-related business. A visit to the Jawhariyyeh Collection was mandatory after the collection became nearly one of the departments of the Broadcasting House. On more evenings than one could count, and sometimes even during the day, we hosted all the radio musicians and their visitors at our home.

Before the Broadcasting House was opened, a suggestion was discussed to appoint me head of the music section, given that I was an Arabic music expert from Jerusalem. Indeed, once at a party at the home of Mr. Ihsan Hashem, Mr. Keith-Roach asked me before he left Jerusalem to take the post on the condition that my civil servant post would be moved to the radio. But for personal reasons, I declined the offer, preferring to remain in administration rather than becoming a professional artist. I decided to consider art as a religion, which I would follow solely for the love of it, just as I had been raised to.

I did not backtrack, even when my name was published in the official gazette as one of the artists who were joining the Broadcasting House on the day of the launch. But I declined and categorically refused to accept. I did not regret my decision to turn down the post at the radio. A true artist demeans himself as an artist when he turns his art into a source of income, particularly in the East. For in this way art becomes a job and stops being true art. Once, my brother Kazem al-Sibasi came to me with a petition signed by well-known Jerusalemite figures, demanding that the Broadcasting House pay him more than once a week because they found his songs particularly likable. He asked me to sign this petition since I was a well-known expert in this field. Does an artist need to knock on doors like this when he decides to take up art as a profession?

The Broadcasting House never stopped consulting me on various artistic matters. After Yahiya al-Nashashibi became head of the music section, he started calling me "the retired artist." I used to transcribe my own compositions at home and have Ruhi al-Khammash take the transcriptions to the Broadcasting House where they were sung by some singers, in return for just a few pounds per composition.

THE ROYAL COMMISSION'S DECISION TO PARTITION PALESTINE

I mentioned the revolt and the 1936 countrywide strike, as well as the forced exile imposed by Britain on the patriotic leaders of the country. After that, the strike was brought to an end, and the revolt was halted with the arrival of the Royal Commission.[210] The commission took the extraordinary decision to partition the country. Its decision was rejected by the Arabs of Palestine and by the people and governments of the Arab states, with the exception of Prince Abdullah.

The Arabs resumed the revolt against the British under the leadership of the hero Abdul-Qader, the son of Musa Kazem Pasha al-Husseini. When the government failed to quash it, it was forced to announce its willingness to relook into the partition plan and sent a technical British committee known as the Woodhead Commission, which decided that the partition plan could not be implemented unless the revolt came to a halt. However, the rebels would not be defeated, and they upped their struggle across the country, inflicting humiliation on the colonialist forces in many sites such as Bab al-Wad, the villages of Balaa, Yabad, Silat al-Dahr, Silat al-Harithiya, Beit Umrein, Jaba, Deir Sharaf, and Zayta, and in the Nablus and Tulkarm areas where Abdul-Raheem al-Hajj fell as a martyr, as well as in Halhul, Beit Mahsir, Beddu, and other villages in the Jerusalem hills.

During this uprising, at the battle of Bani Naim that was led by Abdul-Qader, the heroic Ali, who was the son of the late Hussein Salim al-Husseini (Abdul-Qader's cousin) fell as a martyr. When Britain realized that it had failed in many battles, the secretary for the colonies, Mr. Malcolm MacDonald, came in person in August 1938 to try to bring the revolt to an end, but also failed. This forced a complete British withdrawal from Hebron, Bir al-Sab' (Beersheba), Jericho, Bethlehem, Ramallah, Tabariyya (Tiberius), and Old Jerusalem, and the Arab flag was raised over the Tower of David.

The country had never witnessed anything harsher, crueler, or fiercer than the 1937 revolt. Speaking of the British withdrawal from

Old Jerusalem in particular, and as someone who was living opposite Jaffa Gate, I recall that when the British government decided to reclaim Old Jerusalem from the Arab fighters, the battle that ensued that night between the two parties was so ferocious that it is impossible to describe in words what we heard and saw throughout the night—the incredible sound of missiles, bombs, and bullets. For during the first occupation of the city with the British conquest in 1917, we did not hear or see that which we heard and saw on this night, a night which was, without a doubt, a mark of shame for the British state. Inside the wall there were just a few men armed with antique weapons, who managed to stand their ground in the face of the British army for many days and nights, and this was only possible because justice always prevails.

THE ATROCITIES COMMITTED BY THE BRITISH AGAINST THE ARAB POPULATION

"He could not get on the donkey, so he got on the saddle."

This proverb applies perfectly well to the terrible atrocities and crimes committed by the mandate government in 1937–1938 against peaceful citizens, when it was unable to pull the fight with the Arab rebels.

Should the sniffer dog tracking mission lead them to a certain village, this was considered sufficient reason to shell and destroy the entire village with dynamite and explosives, and the residents were left without shelter or compensation. Here are some of the shelled villages: Kawkab Abu al-Heija, al-Maghar, Sha'ab, al-Birwa, Jaba', al-Tira, Lubya, Balad al-Sheikh, Hawwasa, al-Mjeidel, 'Arab al-Sakhinah among others in the North; al-Mazar, Sila, Rummana, Umm al-Fahm, Qabatiyya, Jab'a, Yaabud, and Baqa al-Gharbiyya among others in the Jenin area; Asira al-Shamaliya, Deir Sharaf, Barqa, and Hawwara among others in the Nablus area; Zayta, Bal'a, Beit Umreen, Dhannaba, 'Atlit, and al-Taiba in the Tulkarm area; Beit Rima, Shu'fat, Rammun, Qalunya, and Beit Surik among others in the Jerusalem district; and el-Khader, Husan, Sureef, Yatta, Halhul, and al-Dawaymeh in the Hebron and Bethlehem areas.

Countless residential homes in this area were shelled in order to extinguish the revolt, but it was all in vain. The British forces shelled the main street in the city of Jenin and a large part of al-Lydd (Lyddah) after the fighters had shelled a military train in the station of Kafr Jinnis.

THE SHELLING OF JAFFA'S OLD QUARTER

This quarter contained around two thousand houses in which around twelve thousand people lived. They were constantly and publicly at the lead of the struggle against the British forces. So the army decided to shell the Old Quarter in its entirety and issued a warning for residents to evacuate it within twenty-four hours. Then they destroyed it, and not one stone was left upon another. The government claimed that this mass shelling was carried out with the intention of rehabilitating the city.

One of the residents filed a case against the government for shelling his house. The case was looked into by the British chief justice, Sir Francis McDonnell, who passed a categorical and fair judgment indicting the government and condemning its criminal acts, saying, "The government wanted to mislead people, claiming that it shelled the quarter in order to improve the town. But this statement is actually a lie. The government ought to announce frankly that the shelling was intended to fight the rebels."

For this he was punished by being removed from his post and relocated to another British colony within a few days of the issuing of the judgment. Such were the actions of the British Mandate in Palestine. But numerous British officials, such as the chief justice, were saddened as individuals by the government's actions and were opposed to its barbaric policy in the country. Many of them quit their posts of their own accord, while others were relocated or fired from their jobs, just to please the Zionists.

JAMAL BEY TOUQAN

In 1938, Jamal Bey Touqan joined us at the Saraya, located at that time on Jaffa Road. He became temporarily based in the office of Mr. Mantura, the financial inspector, while remaining without work for a considerable amount of time. For this reason, a rumor circulated among the employees that he was to become Mr. Mantura's assistant, particularly in the Revenue Department's work now that the urban property tax area of Jerusalem was expanded to include thousands of dunums of the surrounding villages, bringing the total number of blocs outside the wall to one hundred sixty-eight.

The arrival of Jamal Bey was no surprise to us. We had already welcomed a good number of newcomers such as Nazif Bey al-Khairi, Naim Bey al-Hadi, Mr. George Qurt, and others who picked up management skills from Mr. Mantura. We were astonished, however, by the surprising appointment of Jamal Bey Touqan as assistant to the governor of Jerusalem. Indeed, he took over all of Mr. Mantura's responsibilities that had to do with the Revenue Department, including auditing and rounding up accounts, verifications, collections, exemptions, evaluations, the supervision of evaluation committees, the yearly review of evaluations, objections, and all the way to appeals. In addition to this exhausting job, he also took charge of managing the affairs of the Muslim community in Jerusalem and all relevant issues, which had been previously the responsibility of Nasuhi Bey Baydun. In this way, Jamal Bey became overnight a man of broad powers, or rather an independent governor of the affairs of the city in its entirety.

Jamal Bey started his work by turning the administration upside down and adopting a new, modern managerial approach, assigning to each one of his subordinates a particular task which they were able to perform and about which they reported to him directly. Woe to those who overstepped their bounds and interfered in the business of others. He abandoned the old management style followed by his predecessors, which to him was just "chaos." To his subordinates' joy, he even issued a written order banning all employees from entering the Saraya offices outside official business hours. This was indeed the right thing to do because we used to spend the majority of our time at the Saraya, investing long nights and official holidays among records and registers in order to get our exhausting work done.

Within a short while, it became clear to all that Jamal Bey had done this momentous work on his own in the best possible way and demonstrated great abilities and an extraordinary competence, thanks to which we were able to work in a better-paced, more orderly fashion. His wise managerial style soon became an example to follow for many of the district's department managers. When Jamal Bey arrived at the Saraya, I was financial manager for the city, and I remained in this post throughout his time there until the end of the mandate. But in the summer of 1939, I was involved in an incident that affected my health, and so Jamal Bey appointed my friend Anis Abu Rahmah as a head clerk, thereby relieving me of a heavy workload.

UNCLE HAJJ KHALIL AL-RASASI

Hajj Khalil al-Rasasi had a glorious past. He had been a gendarme under the Ottomans, and his loyalty, God bless his soul, was such that his name and bravery were known to all, particularly during the First Great War. He did not fear his Turkish superiors and dared to defy them, and he showed compassion for the members of the Arab community and defended them. There are extraordinary incidents in this regard which are too many to relate. I had the greatest respect for him when we worked together on the Jerusalem property evaluation committee.

THE ECONOMIC SITUATION IN THE COUNTRY DURING THE SECOND GREAT WAR

Since there was an emirate in East Jordan at the time of the Second World War, the country's Arab traders had an unprecedented amount of business, importing goods, textiles, and even carpets for no or little customs fees. In this way, the black market flourished, and many citizens became terribly rich. This meant that the civil servants of the first and second grades (heads of departments and clerks) became the wronged party, as their fixed salary was no longer sufficient to cover an employee's needs with the prices of all and any goods going up.

Before the start of the Second Great War, we used to buy the following goods for these prices:

olive oil: 3 kilograms for ten piasters
ghee: 120 piasters per canister
premium quality flour: 96 piasters per sack
Johnny Walker whiskey: 40 piasters per bottle
a prêt-a-porter suit made of fine wool: five Palestinian pounds

But these prices went up as follows:

olive oil: 3 kilograms for 110 piasters
ghee: 18 Palestinian pounds per canister
premium quality flour: 9 Palestinian pounds per sack
Johnny Walker whiskey: 4 Palestinian pounds per bottle
a prêt-a-porter suit made of fine wool: 25 Palestinian pounds

Once, during the war, I entered the shop of the Abu George Deeb Shukri, where my master Khalil Sakakini was smoking a water pipe. Abu George Pasha welcomed me and offered me a cup of coffee. I said, "No, thank you. But perhaps you could offer me a cup of that pure ghee I used to buy from you before the war." We all started laughing, for I used to buy from him pure Eastern ghee for one hundred ninety piasters a canister.

The price of onions also went up beyond imagination, so I displayed in the Jawhariyyeh Collection three onions among the rosaries, the precious stones, and the red and yellow carbuncle stones. This piqued the curiosity of visitors who wondered why the onions had been displayed among the carbuncle stones. I answered them that this was because they nowadays cost the same, for God gives in wondrous ways.

PALESTINE BECOMES THE LAND OF THE PIGS

God bless the soul of he who said, "The worst misfortunes are those that make you laugh." As I write, I can still picture before me citizens in large numbers, busying themselves talking and discussing pigs and pig farming at home gatherings, markets, and evening parties.

Many people of all confessions and professions, regardless of their level of education, engaged in a battle about which they were clueless—pig farming in Palestine in the Second Great War. There was seldom an old stable inside the wall, or an abandoned basement room in a house, or a house in one of Jerusalem's villages and towns such as Bethlehem, Beit Jala, Beit Sahur, Ain Karem, Beit Safafa, Ramallah, and its villages, or a private farm that did not breed pigs of some kind. Female pigs became so venerated that the owner of one would sacrifice his dearest possessions to bring her a doctor in the winter nights or freezing cold, to give her an injection if he sensed that she was not in a good mood. He would pay the doctor an extortionate honorarium on top of the cost of the injection, whose price was known to be one Palestinian pound, only after which was the owner able to enjoy a good night's sleep. I can say without any doubt that among those people were some who would not have dared to call the doctor to check on their wives—the mothers of their children—in a similar case.

So, what caused this excessive compassion towards pigs and this great care for them? It's a fact that during the war, the price of a she-pig exceeded one thousand Palestinian pounds, which is obviously a fortune that could buy a house and is almost equivalent to the capital of many traders.

Pig farming and trading became a trend, perhaps like fashion, in the country, a contagious disease that hit hundreds of well-known families. Some of these made some profit initially, as they were lucky to buy and then sell as soon as Lady Piggy was pregnant. But in the end they were bankrupt, may God help us all. Many of those went bankrupt after pawning or selling their properties and their wives' jewelery.

The mandate government, and particularly the head of this government, His Excellency the High Commissioner, were directly responsible for encouraging the population to breed pigs, for the allied forces had thousands and thousands of soldiers who were keen to buy pork. Alas, everyone had their share of this dirty trade which was built on a perfidious British policy that ended up wiping out everything in its path.

Here is an example, dear reader, of the astronomical prices of pigs during the Second Great War. I was told by my brother Foteh Daadush, my school and work colleague who worked in this trade, that he once bought a female pig called Jaabura, from Mr. John Weinbeck, an American gentleman living in Jerusalem, for nine hundred Palestinian pounds. He refused to buy her six female piglets because they were going for six hundred Palestinian pounds a head. He then bought two female pigs from the Bastuli family for one thousand three hundred Palestinian pounds.

When the government's farce came to an end, they stopped distributing pig feed to pig farmers all of sudden, and so the price of pigs dropped abruptly and poor Foteh Daadush had to sell his pig for twenty-nine Palestinian pounds. The price of male pigs went down sixty piasters per five kilos. The government's trick with the pig farming trend simply boiled down to the fact that the government was selling pig feed to farmers for thirty to sixty Palestinian pounds per ton. The average daily cost of a female pig's feed was twenty-five Palestinian piasters.

THE STRIKE BY THE MANDATE GOVERNMENT'S CIVIL SERVANTS

The prices of all goods went up to astronomical levels in comparison to prices in prewar times, and civil servants—particularly second-grade employees—were stuck in a very bad financial situation. No matter how hard they tried to be economical, their monthly salaries only lasted a few days each month, and in the end we could no longer take it. For we had repeatedly asked the government to pay us proportionately with the changing cost of living, but it was all in vain.

After some communications between senior civil servants in all the cities of Palestine, the civil servants' committee reached the decision to go on public strike, on the condition that civil servants leave their departments and head for the mosque, church, or synagogue in a special convoy in order to show their plight to the government of His Majesty. But it was all in vain. The committee then made another decision that civil servants should stand outside their respective departments to draw the attention of the customers and the people to their plight. We did, but alas, in vain.

A decision was finally taken for the civil servants to stand in their respective departments during business hours and totally refrain from all work as well as from talking to customers or government officials. The decision was carried out, and after a lot of effort and procrastination, the government caved in and granted us a pay raise in view of the inflation so that the poor civil servants were able stand on their feet and live decently, to some extent, among their families and friends.

THE TIMES OF THE TARBUSH

The oriental headgear known as the *tarbush* came from the Maghreb, North Africa—Tunisia, Marrakesh, Algeria, and Lybia, and that is why in foreign languages it is referred to as the fez. But the word tarbush itself is of Turkish origin (*ser*: head; *push*: cover), and with time it changed and became "tarbush" after reaching the Arabs.[211]

The tarbush had been known of old to the people of Palestine, particularly farmers and villagers. Farmers on all sides of Jerusalem—west, south, and north—wore the Moroccan tarbush. When they reached manhood, after the age of thirty, they would also put on the traditional dress of their district or village, and the costume became known as the *tabaziyah*. There were dozens of tabaziyah costumes in the Hebron district, Bethlehem, Beit Jala, Beit Sahur, and al-Khudr in the South. Each village had a special cut and color for its tabaziyah, and this was the case for neighboring villages, as well. There is a great difference between the tabaziyah of Bethlehem and that of Beit Jala. Likewise, in the North, Ramallah's tabaziyah was quite distinct from that of al-Bireh, which was right next to it. The cloth that was wrapped around the tarbush was ornamented in red, yellow, and green patterns, and for religious Muslims it was just plain green or dark red. Some farmers used the Damascene fabric known as *nabani*. White was normally worn by Sheikhs who recited the Qu'ran.

No doubt the tarbush is not a healthy headgear. But it is beautiful and generally suits one's face, for its maroon color makes the face seem more handsome and goes well with menswear of all shapes and colors. The tarbush gives one a more respectful, dignified look. This is particularly true for civil servants, as the custom of wearing this elegant headgear dictates that, unlike hats, it may not be taken off at official meetings or at governmental buildings or at homes. I still recall the Ottoman era in our country, the era during which the tarbush was worn by the pasha, the commissioner, civil servants, soldiers, gendarmes, policemen, and the rest of the population. Even workers wore it, along with their uniforms and whether their dress was Eastern or Western.

I recall that the indigenous Jews of our country were also proud to wear it, such as the Jerusalemite families of Eliasher, Ezqiel, Mani, Abu Al-'afiyah, Bengil, Valero, Mer'esh, Kukia, Eintabi, Hazzan, Samha, and Yelin.

Some wore the old tarbush known as the Moroccan tarbush, such as Hanna Boullata, Foteh Zakhariya and his father, and Issa Nakhla Qurt. Others wrapped a piece of cloth around their tarbush, such as Nicola's father "Abdu" (who may have been called Semaan), Banayot al-Sawabini, and others.

There was also a kind of innovation among the workers, namely the black tarbush. Many Arab Greek Orthodox people, as well as Armenians, wore it, but I do not know why they chose this color. It could have been imposed on their ancestors given that they were Christian.

Wearing the tarbush was an obligation for all. During the Ottoman rule, no one was seen without headgear. Rulers, blacksmiths, carpenters, writers, bakers, porters, and even school pupils all wore the tarbush. At the time, the tarbush was plain, with no lining, and was known as "the Azizi," after the Ottoman Sultan Abdul-Aziz. It was so supple that it was weighed down by the tassel. Young men, particularly those who dressed in authentic Arab dress—the qumbaz or the shirwal—also wore the tarbush and called it the *nekl*. It only differed from the other types of tarbush in terms of color. I recall that some men who had a rather fair complexion preferred the light red color, but in general, there was one predominant color.

At the end of Ottoman rule some improvements were introduced to the tarbush. The idea had come from Egypt, where the tarbush was lined with soft straw, and its shape was modified so that it was more in line with our time. Some had three holes on the top in order to allow some air in, a great idea that proved very popular with the people, who also liked how the straw lining at the bottom was fitted with a strip of soft leather or organza that protected the tarbush from sweat.

The doctors of Jerusalem, including the foreigners among them, such as the Greek doctors Foti, George, Barnaba, and Nicola, also wore this beautiful headgear. The Azizi tarbush died out with its contemporaries, and the only person to have carried on wearing it until the end of his days, even after the Nakba, is the late Ragheb Bey al-Nashashibi, who was indeed a handsome man who turned heads, and continued to wear the tarbush without a lining.

Since the tarbush was a national Arab gear, people continued to wear it during the British Mandate, from the end of 1917 until 1936. Given the clashing political ideas of the country's six political parties, the mufti's party, the largest party in Palestine, denounced the wearing of the tarbush, preferring that it be replaced with the authentic Arab dress, namely the *kaffiyeh* (scarf headdress) and *agal* (cord).[212] The people thus embraced the Arab dress, either willingly, or following threats of violence or even assassination, and thus the tarbush was abandoned in our country after the strike of 1936, except by a few members of the National Defense Party. The mufti's ambition to kill it off was fulfilled during the 1937 revolt, as the people began to wear the kaffiyeh and agal, and even the Iraqi *Faisaliyah cap* in honor of King Faisal the First who created it for himself and the people of Iraq. In this way, the use of the tarbush was eradicated in the country. Only very little of it remained, and we lost, alas, this beautiful headgear. However, some people, including the author of this book, went back to it, particularly after the tragic events of the Nakba in Palestine.

The majority of the population gave up headgear altogether and started going about bareheaded, in summer and in winter, day and night. They carried on like this to this day, although this custom, God preserve us, was resented and regarded as unacceptable, particularly during the Ottoman rule when it was totally shameful for one to walk the streets bareheaded.

As for those who used to work in the sale, manufacturing, and ironing of the tarbush in Jerusalem, I recall Faraj and his brothers, in the Christian Quarter, under the arch of the Orthodox Monastery, on the way to the Church of the Holy Sepulchre; Dawud Abu Jadam, who was later joined by his brother-in-law Philip Aqruq and his brothers, in the Christian Quarter, near the Pool of the Patriarch (Brother Philip was famous for his skill at this elegant art all over the country, becoming the ultimate reference on it and attracting customers from the neighboring Arab countries); Abdul-Qader al-Muhtadi in Jaffa Gate, opposite al Qal'a the Citadel; Nicola al-Khoury (al-Bayda) in the spice market, and after him Shukri Rasas.

So cheers to the days of the tarbush! They were days of blessing and brotherliness. On this occasion, what Abdu al-Hamuli said in his dawr comes to mind: "I lived through years and years, and he who lives gets to see wonders."

OUR ACQUAINTANCE WITH FARID AL-ATRASH

When Farid al-Atrash[213] visited Jerusalem, our friend Talaat al-Sayfi al-Tabgha, who was loved by all, invited him to his place. A number of Mr. Talaat's Jerusalemite friends, myself included, were present. Mr. Talaat invited the heads and musicians of the Broadcasting House in

Jerusalem, including Mr. Ibrahim Touqan, Mr. Yahia al-Lababidi, Jamil Uwais, Yahia al-Saoudi, the Prince of the Buzuq Abdul Karim, and the radio's musical ensemble. As the host he showed exceptional generosity, serving all sorts of wine and artistically decorated mezze. But Farid refused to sing even a single piece, which caused the resentment of all those present, particularly since they had been begging him to. He just continued to play hard to get, until we finally tried to spare our host the offense and started playing, singing, and telling jokes to cheer him up, while the agha—al-Atrash—remained silent as though he was mute. Finally, though, he grabbed the oud and played a Bashraf Shadd Araban of the maqam Hijaz Kar, while Mr. Abdul Karim accompanied him on the buzuq, and that was all. I remember that at the time, Mr. Yahia al-Lababidi had just composed the song *Ya retni teir*[214] (I wish I were a bird so I could fly around you), and that its rhythm had provoked a heated debate among the radio's musicians.

I still love al-Atrash's compositions, particularly some of his taqtouqas, but I have always disliked listening to him, and I'd rather hear his songs from someone else. When Umm Kulthum was asked what she thought of his voice and singing, she was right to answer, "I wish he were *akhras* (mute) instead."[215]

DANCER TAHIYA CARIOCA

We never wasted an opportunity to enjoy ourselves. Our life, thank God, was always elevated by the fine art which occupied the best part of my life despite the disturbances and uprisings that shook the country during the mandate period. When the widely famous dancer Tahiya Carioca visited Jerusalem, we agreed with some friends to have a party at our place in Nicoforia. Dancing and flirting, Carioca shone like a star among the Jawhariyyeh Collection. It was indeed the party of a lifetime, going on beyond midnight. Having had too much to drink, Carioca started joking with my friend Sami al-Shawwa, the Prince of the Violin, and swearing at him, "May your father be cursed." But Sami would only swear back at her on the violin, and the partiers were amazed by how his interpretation of swearing came out on the strings.

The party was attended by a number of notables—Jerusalem's politicians and their families, the Iranian ambassador and his wife, the Turkish ambassador and his wife, Ragheb Bey al-Nashashibi, Majed Bey Abdul-Hadi, Aouni Bey Abdul-Hadi, Ali Bey Jarallah, Jamal Bey Touqan, and others. A number of the finest radio musicians played string instruments under the temporary leadership of Mr. Sami al-Shawwa who happened to be in Jerusalem at that time.

THE DEATH OF MY BROTHER TAWFIQ

On March 10, 1944, my brother Tawfiq passed away at the home of our brother Khalil, which belonged to Youssef or Ata Sbeih in al-Katamon in Jerusalem. Family and friends were thunderstruck by the news of his death, for the deceased was appreciated for his humor and his art. His funeral testified to this. It was a great procession in which hundreds of people from all denominations and confessions took part, including various personalities and notables, civil servants, and people from the middle, and even lower, class. Here one saw the great leader Yaacoub Farraj, Mr. Ajaj Nuwaihid, and some sheikhs and church ministers, and there one saw Frusu Zahran crying bitterly along with her daughter over the loss of dear Abu Nader.

He was indeed sociable in every sense of the word. For he dedicated his life to art and lived and died for the sake of art, making no fuss about money or life, and spending his life celebrating and enjoying evening parties and picnics, staying in Jericho in the winter, and moving to the mountains in the summer. He lived a bachelor, but did better than married men. His artist's room on Maman Allah Street was famous for being packed with paintings of beautiful women and artists, which he had painted himself, God bless his soul. He was a true artist, and he played the nay. He worked with the radio's musical ensemble in Jerusalem at the time of the late Ibrahim Touqan, al-Lababidi, and al-Saoudi, and died at the time of Mr. Ajaj Nuwaihid who loved him, appreciated his authentic art, and wrote a wonderful eulogy for him in the papers of Jerusalem.

Abu Nader died young at around fifty years of age. His funeral took place at the Greek Orthodox San Simon Church in the woods of Katamon. We had to assist the guests by carrying them in cars to his final resting place in Zion cemetery, where he was buried by my father's side.

JEWS THREATEN TO BLOW UP THE GOVERNOR'S HEADQUARTERS

I was financial manager at Jerusalem's Revenue Department and was based in a room on the second floor of the Russian Building, known at the time as the governor's headquarters. A messenger came to me and whispered in my ear that Ragheb Bey al-Nashashibi wished to speak to me over the telephone. Since there were too many customers and employees in the room, and given that I was a good friend of Ragheb Bey, I went up to a secluded room on the third floor and called him. Our chat lasted a while, as we were discussing business related to the properties of Ragheb Bey and which he was asking me to help him with.

Since it was summertime, I was without my jacket and my tarbush, as usual. After the call ended, I left the room to find that everyone had left the hall and that the entire place was empty and quiet. I went down to the second floor and was gripped by fear when I saw the hall there also empty. There were no customers, or a single employee, in any of the rooms on that floor, so I panicked and hurried down to the ground floor, heading for the Saraya's main entrance.

There, I was met by soldiers in iron helmets who drew their weapons at me and ordered me to stop and surrender. I was mortified and walked towards them. After talking to them, they were reassured that I was one of the Saraya's employees, but they ordered me to leave the Saraya as fast as I could. I obeyed and left running, only to find there were no people on Jaffa Road which was opposite the Saraya, and that it was packed with soldiers.

I ran in despair from one place to another like a mad cat when a colleague shouted to me at the top of his voice, "Hey, Wasif, don't be scared. Go down Ben Yehuda Street. The Saraya is rigged with explosives." So I moved away from the building and ran down Ben Yehuda Street, where I entered the café of my brother and friend Yaacoub Zakharia and his partners, near Cinema Rex. There he came to my help and offered me some pop. I was in a deplorable state, for I was extremely terrified when I saw all the employees and the people on the pavement waiting for the explosion to go off.

I was standing with my friends at the café's entrance when all the employees of the post office, which at the time was based in the new three-storey building, came running. Men and women tried to overtake one another and rushed, one flock after another, to leave the building and reach the street. For they had received a similar warning that an explosive had been planted inside the building and was about to go off. They joined the Saraya's employees in what was a worrying, terrifying sight.

AREAS WHERE ENTRY WAS FORBIDDEN EXCEPT BY MEANS OF A SPECIAL ID

As Jewish attacks against the army and the mandate government's employees increased, the mandate government had to resort to classifying the areas occupied by government departments, employees, and their families, dividing Jerusalem into three zones.

Zone 1 comprised the Russian compound known as the Maskobiyyeh Building, in which most governmental departments were based, like the Justice Department, the police, the Intelligence service, the prison, the Public Works Department, state hospitals, state birthing houses, the Saraya, and the Immigration Department, among others.

Zone 2 included the Tapu Department, the YMCA, the King David Hotel, the house on Nicoforia Mountain, the French consulate, the Jesuit Monastery facing the King David Hotel on the northern side, and other well-known buildings.

Zone 3 included the greatest residences of the families of the British heads of departments in al-Baq'aa al-Tahta and the Greek Colony, among others. The residents of each one of these areas were given IDs to produce in order to be allowed entry into their respective areas.

Despite all the precautions, losses, and destruction, the mandate government was not successful against terrorism, which increased day after day. The following departments were blown up, most of which were located inside the most secured areas, and so we said to ourselves, "Wheresoever you may be, death will overtake you, even if you be in strongly built towers." God Almighty has spoken the truth.

The Tapu Department was based in the building owned by Isaac Cohen in the square of Maman Allah Street. An explosion destroyed the records and documents belonging to the citizens.

The Police Department in Ma'amanallah, time and again.

The Immigration and Travel Department near the Maskobiyyeh Building. The building was the property of 'Ammail al-Yahudi.[216]

The Police Department central, time and again.

The post office on Jaffa Road.

The prison in the Maskobiyyeh Building.

The headquarters of the intelligence service in the Maskobiyyeh Building

Most importantly, the King David Hotel which housed the office of the mandate government general secretariat.

Other departments were also blown up which had great significance for the mandate government. Thus, commercial activity in the country ceased, and many stores shut down, while activity and traffic came to a standstill in many of the main streets. British heads of departments, such as the governor of Jerusalem and his assistants, the director of the police, the directors of the Tapu Department and the Travel and Immigration Departments, and others, preferred to work from home, inside the secured areas, fearing Jewish attacks. Many times

I personally went in a tank to deliver official documents from the Saraya to a home, and then went back in the same tank.

THE BOMBING OF THE KING DAVID HOTEL

At eleven o'clock on the morning of July 22, 1946, when I was with my boss Jamal Bey Touqan on an assignment to inspect and value a small piece of land near the tunnel of Zion Cinema on Ben Yehuda Street, one of Jerusalem's most prestigious streets, we heard a big explosion, followed by another, bigger one. Passersby were surprised, and they all stopped, taken aback by the power of the two explosions. No one knew where the explosion had happened, so Jamal Bey and I returned quickly to the Saraya. After some search, we found out that none of the employees of the Saraya and its departments, or even the governor himself, knew the location of this terrible explosion that shook all parts and corners of the city.

On top of that, when the governor's administration contacted the police, the police did not reveal where the explosion had happened, which we thought was quite curious. After a short while, my daughter Yusra told me on the phone, almost choking from shock, that the King David Hotel and the offices of the General Secretariat of Palestine in it had just been blown up. She added that debris had hit our house and that the house was shaken by the powerful explosion, which affected some of the pieces hung on the walls, particularly the china.

Yusra, her mother, and her siblings were quite upset and scared. So they left the house and went to the house of our neighbor Ibrahim al-Hazina to rest. After this phone call, I went to the office of Jamal Bey and informed him that the location of the explosion was the King David Hotel. In his turn he went to inform the governor.

The terrible news spread. We learned that this was the most horrifying bombing the country had ever witnessed. It also turned out that the entire north wing, from the hotel's ground floor to the sixth floor, was blown up, knowing that the most senior personalities of the mandate government, both British and Arab, were based in it—one hundred ten victims. There was not a single Jew among the victims, for the Jewish gangs would inform Jews not to show up at work when they carried out these barbaric acts.

It turned out that the explosives had been transported in milk buckets which were usually delivered each morning through the hotel's northern entrance that led to the kitchen and the facilities. These buckets were brought in by fully armed criminals who, upon arriving on the ground floor, ordered all the waiters, servants, cooks, restaurant, and ironing workers to stand facing the wall, and once their order was obeyed, placed the explosives in designated corners of the building. The explosion happened at the fixed time.

Ibrahim, the son of the priest Zakharia al-Qassis of Ramallah was an ironing worker there. This young man grew up at our house, and he came to our place after the incident and told us the details, his face paralyzed by terror.

Jerusalem turned into a massive funeral. This horrid criminal act became the main conversation topic for the people, who cursed the day Britain occupied our country and allowed Jews to immigrate, keeping its promise to them to establish a national home. As I write about this event, its painful memory makes my hands tremble, for my house was situated to the east of King David Hotel. So, we listened with sadness to the engine sounds of the machines that the government sent to remove the rubble and retrieve the bodies of the victims. Some of the victims were still alive and screamed for help under the rubble, such as Atallah Mantura and his colleague Mr. Erason who was also under the rubble and survived by a miracle. This broke the hearts of his wife, sons, and daughters, and still does to this day.

For a week, we lived on our nerves at our home in Nicoforia, watching every funeral go by from Jaffa Gate to Mount Zion Cemetery. Sadly, we could smell the bodies of the victims at night, until they were all retrieved. About two weeks after this painful incident, since some of the hotel's corners posed a risk, the government had to demolish them with dynamite, so we were warned, along with the other neighbors of the hotel, to leave our homes. I went with my family to the house of sister Umm Salim, the widow of the late Hussein Hashem al-Husseini, which was in al-Baq'aa al-Fawqa on the road to Bethlehem, and from there we watched the demolition and heard the frightening explosions that brought down the unstable corners of the building. Then, in the evening, we went back home.

THE TREASONOUS DECISION TO PARTITION PALESTINE

When I woke up on Sunday morning, November 30, 1947, my gaze fell on our son George, who was awake in his bed on the upper floor in our house in Nicoforia.

I turned on the radio that was next to me and was shocked to hear the news of the decision to partition Palestine that had been made in Lake Success, in America, on the evening before. My son George and

I did not utter a word. We just stared at one other. Never will I forget that moment.

I left the house and went to Maman Allah Street where Arabs had gathered to talk about the partition and share their worries about the future of the country, wondering whether, God forbid, this sinister news would become a reality. Would we see Palestine, particularly the fertile part of it, become the Kingdom of Israel? Could Arabs and Muslims make no reaction to this unjust decision? Would they just accept the humiliation and shame inflicted on them by the colonialists and the Zionists?

To speak of the Arabs, who were devastated by this unexpected decision, without a doubt we had been wronged, and the country was ours. There was no way to accept that, under any circumstances. The wiser ones now understood the story of the Jewish national home in Palestine and all that had ensued from it over the thirty years of British Mandate. Britain had helped implement this decision through its political tactics—allowing Jewish settlers of the world to flood into Palestine, helping them to buy as much Arab land as possible, maltreating Arabs—until Zionism was able to get what it wanted in the form of the unjust partition decision. Alas, they considered this to be the final chapter of the story.

As for Jews of Palestine, they held celebrations on the occasion and indeed went out on the nights of the 29th and 30th November of 1947, to dance and cheer through the night, drinking with British soldiers in the streets, knowing that before the partition decision the British army had been the sworn enemy of Jewish settlers who had fought against it all over the country, in secret and in public.

JERUSALEM AFTER THE PARTITION DECISION

In the wake of the partition decision, a poisoned atmosphere prevailed across the country. In Jerusalem, we saw wonders as Jews joyfully held public national celebrations in the streets, which offended the Arabs who grew to bear grudges against Britain and Jewish settlers.

On the morning of December 2, 1947, tragic incidents took place, with both parties attacking each other. While on Princess Mary Street on my way to the Saraya, I saw the Jewish buses number one and three returning after their windows had been smashed by stones that Arabs had hurled at them on Jaffa Road. I thought may God help us, this is but the beginning.

The Arabs decided to go on strike for three days, in compliance with the decision of the Arab Higher Committee. Indeed, the strike went ahead starting on the morning of Tuesday, December 20, 1947, in order to show the world the anger and resentment of the Arabs at this unjust decision to partition Palestine. There were demonstrations in which, as I remember, a lot of young men took part who then attacked the Jewish commercial center known as al-Shamma'a, located between the road to Maman Allah near Joret al-Nasnas and the Nicoforia mountain where I lived.

They attacked this market which was packed with Jewish merchants, and Jews were forced to leave it since they feared the Arab demonstrators. They then attacked some shops and burned them down, looting whatever contents they could get hold of. The demonstration then proceeded to Jaffa Road, where Jewish shops were set on fire, before the crowd finally reached the location of Barclays Bank.

At the same time on Tuesday, while my colleagues and I were at work at the Saraya on Jaffa Road, wc saw through the windows a massive Jewish gathering of members of the Haganah, and others. They were extremely agitated and were heading east to attack purely Arab areas, but they were stopped by their leaders and the British army. They did attack some Arab places and properties there, burning down Rex Cinema on Princess Mary Street and some of the shops there, which included a carpentry workshop situated behind the building of Mikhail Makhlouf, of Beit Jala. This prompted all the employees to leave the Saraya for fear that the fire might spread and that an attack was imminent. Nobody remained in the Saraya except our boss Jamal Bey Touqan, who kindly took me along in his car that had the British flag raised on it. So the car frayed its way among the gathered crowds on Ben Yehuda Street, and I was brought to the secured Zone 2 where I lived. I thanked him and went into the house in a deplorable state of fear, anguish, and terror.

I rested a bit after lunch. Then, in the afternoon of that Tuesday, we noticed that the wall of our home, particularly the eastern side of it which overlooked the hill of Jaffa Gate, was surrounded by young Jewish men and women. Although not dressed in any official uniform, it was clear that this group was organized in military fashion. They had come from the southern side known as the Montefiore Quarter, or commune, and belonged to the Haganah. They had bludgeons, spades, and buckets, and they forbade all the family to stand on the wall.

They were watching a massive Arab crowd marching in an uproarious demonstration on the Jaffa Gate hill, on the outer side which overlooked the Sultan's Pond and Montefiore to the south, and Maman Allah Street and Jaffa Road to the west, while I secretly watched them all from a window of the upper-floor room. The Arab crowds that were in Jaffa Gate got larger and more equipped, spreading all the way to Mount Zion and Hebron Road, until they filled the whole area, sowing fear in the heart of the enemy who was lurking near our house. In the evening, when we learned of the curfew imposed by the army, the settlers returned to the Montefiore commune, while the Arabs dispersed and retired to their homes.

Since our home had a strategic location, we had an extremely good view of the entire area. So we were able to see in the quiet night how the British army and a unit of the mandate's Jewish police, under the leadership of officer Mr. Linker, brought young Jews and helped them to open the shops of Arab merchants in the commercial center, such as the shops of Rashad Barakat, Michel Manneh, and others, allowing them to loot silk and wool fabrics, before burning down whichever shops they wanted to burn down. I recall that on seeing them unashamedly committing these aberrant acts with the help of Britain, its army, and its police. My wife shouted in English that these goods and shops were the property of Arabs and that they were doing this during curfew. So they threatened her and told her to get off the wall, pointing their rifles at her in case she disobeyed their orders.

The battles went on. At home we went through hell, sleeping to the sound of explosions, machine guns, rifles, and fires around us day and night, until we came to the conclusion that life at home had become unbearable. We were somewhat lucky to be inside secured Zone 2. There was a military base at the northeastern corner of the wall of our home, alternately opening fire on the Arab area and then on the Jewish Montefiore neighborhood.

THE BOMBING OF THE SEMIRAMIS HOTEL IN AL-KATAMON

My friend Lutfi Abu Sawwan and his family were living in the al-Halabi building which was located near our home in Nicoforia. This building, which stood right near the entrance to the commercial center, became more like ruins. He could not bear to continue living in it and decided to leave, taking his family to the al-Katamon neighborhood where he stayed with his cousins and brother-in-law Raouf Lawrence at the well-known Semiramis Hotel. But it was God's will, alas, that Jewish settlers should blow up this hotel on the night of January 5, 1948, killing fifteen people, among whom was Lutfi and his family—his wife, her sisters, and her brother Raouf Lawrence and his wife, may

God rest their souls. His wife had advised us to accompany them to this hotel to get some relief after our neighborhood had become a battlefield. We were extremely saddened by their deaths with which we lost good neighbors whom we shall never forget for as long as we shall live.

JEWISH EXPLOSIVES IN DAMASCUS GATE

On December 29, 1947, Jews were able to plant in Damascus Gate a canister filled with explosives which went off killing fourteen Arabs and wounding thirty. This day was a great tragedy for Arabs, particularly for the people who appeared at the funerals of the martyrs.

THE BLOWING UP OF BUILDINGS ON BEN YEHUDA STREET, INCLUDING THE *PALESTINE POST*

On February 1, 1948, the Arab *fedayeen* were able to enter the Jewish area of Ben Yehuda Street in Jerusalem and plant some dynamite explosives. When they went off, they shook every corner of the city. Ben Yehuda Street was devastated, particularly the building of the *Palestine Post* newspaper which was one of the most sworn enemies of Arabhood in the country.

THE BOMBING OF THE JEWISH AGENCY BUILDING

Jewish Zionists and the British stationed a strong guard force at the Jewish Agency building and closed the main and side streets leading to the building so that it was impossible for an Arab to reach it.

The hero Anton Daoud of Bethlehem was the chauffeur of the American consul in Jerusalem and was continuously in contact with the great hero Abdul-Qader al-Husseini. The consul had assigned to Anton the task of delivering the *Post* in an American diplomatic briefcase to the agency. So Anton went to the agency every day in the consul's car with the American flag flapping on it. The Jewish and British guards were reassured and grew to trust their daily guest. Anton went with the car to the leadership headquarters of Abdul-Qader al-Husseini in Birzeit.

Abdul-Qader himself took charge of preparation of the necessary explosives; he was one of the most skilled Arabs at this job. Anton drove the rigged car to the agency's building in order to deliver the *Post*. While the guards were carrying the bundle to the agency's offices, Anton drove and parked the car in front of the agency's offices, near the large reception room, and set the timing device so that the explosion would go off five minutes later. Then he slipped out of the car and tried to leave on foot.

At that point the Jewish guards grew suspicious and shouted at him to stop. But he threw himself onto the ground and started shooting at them with two guns he was carrying, and was able to slip out across the barbed wire.

Ben Yehuda Street after the bombing on 1 February 1948. From the private collection of Issam Nassar.

The explosives went off with the loudest sound Jerusalem had ever heard, destroying a large part of the agency and setting its offices on fire. A number of those in it were killed, and Anton, who did not lose his nerve, was able to make his way through the Jewish area and get to the Arab one. From there he was carried on shoulders to the Old City where he received treatment and eventually recovered.

THE MARTYRDOM OF ABDUL-QADER AL-HUSSEINI IN THE FAMOUS BATTLE FOR AL-QASTAL

In the afternoon of April 7, 1948, leading the fighters, Abdul-Qader marched on the Zionists' strongholds around al-Qastal which was in their hands. He had only arrived from Damascus a day earlier and had failed to obtain the weapons he demanded there. A ferocious battle ensued in which Abdul-Qader fought with his life and was able to purge the areas around al-Qastal so that the fighters finally entered the village to the crowds' cheers and chants of "God is Great."

Once the village was purged, and while the rapture of victory still filled the air, the fighters noticed that their leader was missing and started looking for him. They found him in a house, his weapon in his arms and his hand on the trigger. He was leaning against the wall and bleeding heavily. He turned his head toward them and asked, "Did you take the village back?" They said, "Yes," and he said, "Thanks be to God. We have purged the shame," and then he fell dead. May God have mercy on his soul.

Al-Qastal Village

The village of al-Qastal, the highest village in that area, was located in one of the most strategic spots overlooking the Jerusalem-Jaffa Road, and I have good memories of it. The village, in fact, consisted of just one extended family known as Matar and sometimes Mteir. I often stopped by this village with my late father and my second father Hussein Effendi al-Husseini when we went to spend the summer in Deir Amr.[217] It was accessed from the west side via a special road known only to a few. It was a wide Roman road built in the rocks, and one could see on it the traces of the wheels of Roman carriages. The road led to the border of the village of Suba to the west of al-Qastal, and I took it many times with my late father, riding on donkeys. I also recall spending two nights in it with Hussein Effendi al-Husseini after being invited by its residents to do some important business.

MY LAST DAY OF WORK WITH THE BRITISH MANDATE GOVERNMENT

The funeral of the late leader Abdul-Qader al-Husseini took place on April 9, 1948, while I was working at the new Saraya in the Selwees Building. I had been in a hopeless state both in terms of my health and my state of mind since the decision to partition Palestine, which was the direct cause for the ruin of Jerusalem. Thus, with the help of my boss Jamal Bey Touqan, I left the Saraya at eleven o'clock that morning, went home, and did not go back to my job, although no civil servant was to be absent before May, 15 1948, the date set for the end of the British Mandate. I stayed at home with my family, trying to work out what would be the best thing to do in these difficult circumstances.

MY FAMILY'S REASONS FOR LEAVING

In the dangerous location of our home, we were living in agony, anguish, and fear because of what was going on around it on all sides—explosives, bombs, and battles, starting with the bombing of the King David Hotel, the Montefiore neighborhood, the buildings of al-Halabi and Tannous, and tens of buildings in the Jewish commercial center.

Our house was in Zone 2 which had been encircled with barbed wire. A military base was set up on the eastern side of the wall around our house. We did not like the presence of the army. They were watching the Arabs on the side of Jaffa Gate and the Tower of David, and Jews in the Montefiore neighborhood. They never stopped firing day or night, and our home became but a target. It was also hard to reach our home from the Saint Julian's Way entrance to the zone. None, not even doctors in emergency cases, were allowed in through this entrance except with a special permit. More importantly, this wall secured the protection of our home. But what would happen when the mandate ended? Would it remain? And if it did, would it be under the control of Jewish settlers or the Arabs after the troops withdrew?

For any of us to get to the house once inside the secured zone we had to walk past the King David Hotel, which posed a risk as this area was exposed to fire by Jewish settlers of the Montefiore neighborhood who shot at anyone who walked there. They often shot at us and at our son-in-law Zuhdi. We only survived these battles by a miracle.[218]

The situation in Jerusalem deteriorated. Bloody battles between the two parties, bombings, and explosions continued day and night, until buildings were deserted or turned into rubble. This was worsened by the invasion of crows (ravens) which returned every day and let out their horrid croaks on the rooftops of the destroyed buildings, moving on to the French consulate and then to our own rooftop. They croaked morning and night, and this truly instilled an ill feeling in all of us, for I had not seen such a thing throughout my residence in Nicoforia. Without electricity or anything of the kind, we were living in the darkness.

My body became extremely sensitive. I was not able to cope with all these difficulties, and my health deteriorated. The doctor advised me to leave the area and go somewhere quieter until God's will was done. It rained heavily that year, and we struggled to cope with the cold, as the windows had no shutters after these had been removed because of the explosions. Some of them were filled with sandbags.

As for the Jawhariyyeh Collection, which for thirty years was the main object of my attention and diligence, my family and I started taking down all the valuable pieces hung on the walls and kept as much of it as possible in wooden and iron coffers. We thought about transporting the more precious pieces, particularly the china, which was a great and rare collection in the East. But this would have been difficult to do in that dangerous situation. We thought out many solutions, but finally decided that everything should stay in the house, and made up our minds to leave the house never to return, in order to save our lives and those of our beloved children.

It so happened that our neighbor, His Excellency the French consul Mr. Neuville, came to visit us. He was a friend of ours, and at the same time he appreciated oriental art pieces of historic value. The consul said to me that the French consulate was already filled by French families, most of whom had come with their furniture, particularly valuable furniture, which they placed in the consulate's safekeeping. So the consulate could no longer house any more people or furniture. He added that a force of French North African soldiers would soon come on the government's orders to protect the consulate after the end of the mandate on May 15, 1948. He pleaded with me to permit this force to be based in the courtyard of our house, on condition that he would personally and officially take charge of the entire house and then hand it back to me with all its furniture and art pieces once the dust had settled and the Palestine problem was resolved.

I considered his request carefully and thought that it had come as a blessing for the valuable Jawhariyyeh Collection at this difficult time. So we made it a deal. But I said to him, "I think it would be necessary for Your Excellency to write two letters—one to the Arab Higher Committee and the other to the Jewish Agency, asking if they would consent in principle to this idea so that we are not under threat of attack from either party after the end of the mandate." After a short pause, His Excellency looked at me with a smile and said, "It's a wonderful idea. I'll do it right now." The consul wrote to the relevant parties, and six days later he invited me to see him and read out to me the consent of each party to our request.

After the balance tipped in favor of the settlers, and our house was included in the area which was to be the share of the Jewish state, the Haganah forces tried to enter and occupy our house, take possession of its contents, and turn it into a military base, given its strategic location. But they were stopped, as the consul informed us, when he showed them the Jewish Agency's letter which was dated before the end of the British Mandate and gave the agency's consent to the house being taken by the French Consulate.

We agreed to hand the house, with all its contents, to our neighbor the French consul when we left Jerusalem. We thought a lot about where to go, hoping that we would not be away from home for longer than two weeks. For we knew that Palestine would certainly return to its rightful owners, the Arabs. How not, when very soon the armies of seven Arab countries would come to occupy it and hand it back to the people to whom it belonged?

We thought it would be difficult to go to Bethlehem or Beit Jala, or to live in a monastery near Our Lady Mary. My dear wife Victoria feared for our safety and for the children's. Finally, we agreed to go to the Monastery of Quruntal, which belonged to the Greek Orthodox Monastery of Jericho and provided a safe shelter from which we could watch the destiny of the nation unfold, in peace and out of reach, and have some respite after all we had gone through and witnessed.[219] This happened during the time of Patriarch Timotheos, who was ill then. He offered Victoria the small official reception room of the patriarchate to stay in with our family. We thanked him and took a letter from Patriarchal Qaim Maqam Bishop Athenagoras to give to the head of the Monastery of Quruntal.

These were long days and nights for me, my family, and two families from the city of Hebron who lived outside our house, inside the house's wall. We worked together, organizing, hiding, and keeping as many as possible of the pieces of the Jawhariyyeh Collection in hiding places, safes, and wooden and iron coffers. We also tried to store the rest of the furniture, and even our clothes. We had decided to leave, thinking, "Save yourself, should you suffer injustice, and leave the house behind to mourn its builder."

On the morning of 18 April 1948, we left in tears, praying for God to protect the house and its invaluable contents from any harm, criminal hands, and evil eyes, and to grant that we may one day return to it safely with our children. Someone came on behalf of the consul to offer us one of the French consulate's massive cars. He raised the French flag on the rooftop of the house which we handed to him, along with the keys for each one of its rooms, on the condition that our son-in-law Zuhdi and Salvo would remain in it temporarily until their governmental work with the YMCA ended with the mandate. He agreed to this, and we got into the car—myself, my wife, Yusra, the little child Shadia, George, and Ayah—and set off for Jericho, then for Quruntal.

THE MONASTERY OF QURUNTAL

We asked the gardener to tell of our arrival, and my brother Khalil and our friend and neighbor Ibrahim al-Hazina accompanied him. But the head of the monastery did not agree in principle to receive us because this was a historic monastery reserved solely for the residence of some Greek Orthodox hermits, and particularly because women were not allowed to stay in it under any circumstances. But after he and the monks met Victoria, they apologized and the monastery's main gate was opened. So we all went in, except Yusra who remained with Shadia at the home of our brother al-Hazina near Ain Al-Sultan, for she was still in her postpartum period and was not able to walk up to the monastery.

The head of the monastery reserved for me and my family the two rooms on the upper floor of the monastery's hall, which were always prepared for the patriarch's stay on special occasions. He also reserved a special room for Zuhdi and Layla, and another for Salvo, Yusra, and Shadia.

We were in need of rest after spending days and nights among bloody battles since the partition. We could not believe that we were able to sleep on our first night at the monastery. The atmosphere was calm and wonderful, and the silence of the night had something blissful to it, for it transported us away from the orchestra the bombs, explosives, and whizzing bullets that we had had to live with for about four and a half months. We thanked the Lord for his blessings and for guiding us to choose this safe place where we could stay until things had eased and the situation regarding the Palestine problem had become clear. We were also in a somewhat poor financial situation. We later realized that those who sought refuge in Syria, Lebanon, and Egypt had spent all their money at hotels and nice summer resorts and ended up penniless.

When we entered the monastery, we decided to fast for three days. After the fast, we received communion in the monastery's historic church, and we thanked the Lord for delivering us from the insufferable hell that Jerusalem had become. We were told that a few weeks before our arrival, some armed Bedouin robbers had entered the monastery at night through the back gate on the western side, which leads to the top of Quruntal Mountain. This had prompted the monks to reinforce this gate and obtain some rifles and weapons in order to protect their lives and the precious valuables they had, particularly in the church.

We felt we had to be cautious and hid our jewelry and money, which came to a negligible amount. Layla and her husband were staying in the monastery's big hall whose corners were laid on three sides with wooden platforms in order to receive Russian tourists who in the past used to sit and sleep on them. We secretly hid all our valuables under the planks of these platforms so that our minds were at rest, and each one of us remained cautious and vigilant.

MY CHAIR

On April 29, 1948, while we were at the monastery and Jerusalem had become engulfed in terror and danger to an unbearable point, our son-in-law Zuhdi came with Salvo to join us. Zuhdi told me that following a horrifying explosion in the Silberstein Building on Jerusalem's Princess Mary Street and the building's total collapse, my former workplace—the Armenian building known as the Saint Louis Building—was affected and suffered some damage as it was quite old. Mobs attacked the Saraya and looted the furniture.

Zuhdi spotted the chair I had sat on during my thirty years of work, and another chair, being sold to an Arab near the Saraya for thirty piasters. I thought, thank God that I was not sitting on it when it was sold.

MY EMPLOYMENT WITH THE BRITISH MANDATE COMES TO AN END

With the end of the British Mandate for Palestine on May 15, 1948, my employment came to an end. I had started off as a simple clerk and a translator, then moved on to the Revenue Department and worked in the werko and tithe taxation system as set by the Ottomans. Then, when the property tax law came into force in 1929, I worked as the head of an evaluation committee, then in the office management, until after a lot of hard of work I became financial manager for Jerusalem and remained in this post until the end of the mandate period.

I had joined the public service on August 9, 1919, and stayed in it until May 15, 1948. At the end of the mandate, I was exactly fifty-one years and four months old. I had served my country and done my work with integrity, which was acknowledged in an official form that I still keep. With this document, I was able to obtain from the British government my monthly pension that allowed me to make ends meet for the rest of my days.

OUR STAY AT THE MONASTERY

Our first days at the monastery went by in peace, happiness, and bliss. We were full of hope that the Arab armies would enter the Palestinian territory and that this Arab attack would save the stolen land from the Zionists, after which we would return to our homes with our heads held high.

We bought a female donkey. A boy called Ismail, and his brother, would go to Jericho every morning and come back with food and drink from a list that we had given them. We often enjoyed beautiful days in the monastery's orchard at the foot of the mountain, around the pure spring and among the orange, lemon, grapefruit, palm, and banana trees and the vegetables, in the company of friends who used to visit from Jericho. Many of those visitors, such as the families of al-Hazina, al-Halabi, al-Husseini, Abu al-Suud, and Totah, as well as people from the Orthodox community, used to visit us at the monastery and enjoy the breathtaking views from the balconies and the rooftops of the bedrooms.

On hot days, we would place carpets and straw mats on the steps of the monastery's main entrance and sit on them with friends, while each of us busied himself—one played cards, another played backgammon, others discussed politics—which must have been without a doubt a source of nuisance for the head of the monastery and the monks who were not used to this kind of life. But time, the aroma of the grills, and the excellent food which was prepared under the supervision of the excellent Victoria, made them feel anxious and eager to keep us company. For the days we spent with them at the monastery made them feel alive, even though from a religious point of view, Victoria's presence was considered as a sin.[220]

At this time, my brother Khalil was living in Jericho with his wife, and he used to visit us with his family and friends, and share their experience in cooking and the preparation of delicious mezzes with Victoria. On many occasions, hearty mansafs were served to us and to the guests on the big dining table in the monastery's dining room. Those times remain a good memory to this day.

But I should mention what our son George put us through with his thoughtless behavior at the monastery. He was fourteen at the time, bless him, and did not care about anything that went on around him. He was interested only in quarreling with his sister Ayah, whom he subjected to many painful but funny deeds. He would lock her out on one of the monastery's balconies and keep the door closed for long hours while she screamed and cried. But nobody could hear her given the huge size of the monastery and the area of its buildings. Once we learned what she had suffered because of her brother, I would get angry and lose my temper—for I was in such a state at the time—until a political solution was reached, and we could free Ayah from her prison. Thus, we stayed in the Monastery of Quruntal for one hundred and ninety days.

JERICHO, AFTER THE NABKA

On Monday morning, October 25, 1948, we left the monastery at Quruntal and began a life of vagrancy. We went to Jericho, where we stayed in a property belonging to Suud Ereiqat in Mahallat Sabiha, opposite the palace of Musa Bey al-Alami. On the same day, I went to Jerusalem where I received "an honorarium" of six hundred eleven Palestinian pounds from the office in charge of settling the accounts of the British Mandate. We spent the winter in Deir al Su'ud,[221] and on April, 24 1949, we moved to our friend Tawfiq Nasser Meqmar's Bellvue Hotel, where we stayed until May 12 1949.

Jericho was like a battlefield, packed with the people of Palestine who had left the homes of their stolen country. No one seemed to care but about oneself. There was no management, stability, food, or anything of the kind, and everyone tried to get creative in their own way to obtain their daily bread. From the Bellvue Hotel, to the market of the central square, to the mosque on the eastern side, to Ain al-Sultan Street, Jericho was filled with wooden stalls which lined both sides of the main streets. There was no difference between effendis, workers, and farmers. One sold yogurt, another sold cheese, white wall-rocket, mallow, candy, and any type of food, while everyone seemed as though they were at a funeral, thinking about what they had become overnight, cursing the British, the Jewish settlers, the Arabs, the states, and the armies, and crying over the destiny and the future of their children who had lost their country and were now without shelter. They had even lost the graves of their fathers and ancestors, and each one of them began to understand the trickery and conspiracy that had taken place. They now realized that their country had been lost, all of it, in a three-card trick.

Every day I wandered around among the people, the new refugees who were still arriving in Jericho through mischief, coming from various villages and places which had not been included in the partition plan and yet ended up in the hands of Jewish settlers without a fight.

I will never forget the refugees who came to Jericho from al-Ladd and al-Ramla in a horrifying state. They told us that when settlers occupied their areas, they said to those among them who wore the kaffiyeh and the agal, "Scram! Your king has sold you, not even for a piaster per head but for one and a half piasters for two."

We had arrived in Jericho when it was under military rule. Through our brother Nasri Ibrahim Nazzal, who owned the Winter Palace Hotel there, we made the acquaintance of the military governor of Jericho, Mr. Zaouqan al-Hussein, who came from one of the best families of al-Salat and who visited us in the orchard of the Quruntal Monastery. He was educated and had memorized a lot of Arabic poetry.

Since the situation was still chaotic following the dissolution of the British Mandate state, and since public departments had become deserted, Mr. Yaacoub al-Husseini, a pharmacist, was appointed head of the municipal council by the military governor and ordered to issue people identity cards. Thus, I visited Jericho's mayor and obtained an identity card, which I still keep to this day as a keepsake, and another one for our son George. The employee who gave me this identity card wrote, "Eye color, gray." This was the first thing the Arabs did after the mandate, and it made me feel I was a cat rather than a human being.

The Consultative Committee for Refugees in Jericho

When Jericho became the largest refugee destination for Palestinians from all the areas that had been occupied by Jews, the military governor formed a committee in Jericho, including Said Dajani, Jericho's subgovernor as president; and Nafez Muhyiddine al-Husseini, Hajj Jawdat al-Halabi, Ibrahim Ali al-Hazina, Lutfi al-Maghribi, and Atallah al-Tarazi as members.

I was officially asked to become a member of this committee which was considered to be on a mission to help the refugees, without remuneration. So I proudly accepted the job, and together we worked to manage the issues of the refugees with the help of Mr. Melekian for the Lutherans, as well as the Red Cross, and the president.

We worked with integrity and loyalty. We set up offices to assist the refugees, and we recorded their identity details and numbers. Each one was given a card with which they could receive their share of food and clothing that had started coming in as foreign aid. I will never forget the misery and suffering we saw in the refugee tents, and their need for the basics of daily life, food, and clothing.

It was an arduous job that was not safe from the manipulation of traitors. I saw thefts happen in public, but there was no one to act on it. I lost my peace of mind and my sleep, as I was overwhelmed by requests for help at my home at Suud Ereikat's property. The employee who was in charge of the cards at the warehouses of the Maskobiyyeh Building, near the eastern mosque in Jericho, was my school friend and work colleague, Foteh Daadush.

One day I could no longer bear what the traitors were doing, and I tried to draw the attention of those in charge to it. But it was in vain. I submitted my resignation so as to leave Jericho and head for Beirut.

CODA: BEIRUT

VICTORIA'S DEATH

The death of my life partner, Victoria, that ideal wife who won the sympathy and approval of all those who knew her, was the only ordeal to have struck me since I was a youth. Indeed, it was the only blow that I was dealt and suffered from, and it made me forget everything I had been through, even my vagrancy and leaving my beloved Jerusalem. I forgot all this because of the death of my dear Victoria who owned the best part of my heart. May God rest her soul and grant her paradise, and give strength to me, her children, her grandchildren, and all her family.

She died on January 22, 1958, that doomed day, in a first-class room at the hospital of the American University in Beirut. Her funeral took place in the afternoon of that day at Saint Mary's Orthodox Church of Dormition in Ras Beirut, and she was buried in the church's cemetery, for which we were grateful. The funeral was attended by all the family, friends, and acquaintances, some of whom had come from Jordan. The gathered crowd cried bitterly for the loss, for Victoria was so good-natured, humble, loving, and selfless even towards others, and not just towards her own family. So her children Yusra, Layla, George, and Ayah grew up to love one another as her religious guidance to them had taught them to do.

When her funeral proceeded to the Jeanne d'Arc Quarter, all the shop owners closed their shops and joined the funeral, while they talked about her good character and asked God for mercy on the soul of Umm George. We received condolences at Yusra's home on Jeanne d'Arc's Street over many days and nights, and Yusra's neighbors opened their homes to visitors, too. I am forever grateful to them for this gesture.

I Beg You to Stop

On the first night after the funeral, I was at Yusra's home, which was quite large, particularly the hall. A number of visitors had come to express their condolences, when suddenly we saw a stranger whom we had not seen before, standing with a long, wide piece of paper in his hand. In a loud voice, he started reciting a eulogy in a heartbreaking style, praising the deceased with verses of nonsensical poetry. Then he moved on to praise her good husband, and his good progeny, as though he had lived with us and gotten to know us well. All those present looked at me, wondering what sarcastic thoughts must be going through Wasif's mind. A few seconds later, I spoke out because I just had to make a joke in that sad and painful situation. I begged the speaker to stop and handed him some money. But he insisted on giving me the paper with the speech on it. I refused and said, "No, brother, keep it. You need it more than I. You can read it to others." Everyone laughed, even Yusra, Layla, and Ayah, who were barely able to contain themselves at that embarrassing moment. I said to myself, Glory be to God, how he always sends me something to joke about.

The death of my life partner Victoria was a massive blow that I could not cope with in any way.

AN OUD FOR RENT

After coming to Beirut, I regularly visited the home of George Murad. There I felt as though I were in my own home, given the mutual love and loyalty between me and Abu Emile Murad. We had been friends with him for years in Jerusalem, with his late uncle, Abu Abdallah, and with his family who lived inside the wall.

A number of good friends also visited there, such as Munir Abu Fadel Saba, Hanna Hakim, George (who was about to get engaged), and other Jerusalemites. We longed for memories of the past and for oud playing and singing which we missed since the day of the decision to partition Palestine, a day which was a massive blow to all Arabs, that had made us give up the joyous life.

At one happy gathering at brother Abu Emile's home, we unanimously decided to borrow an oud. Abu Michel al-Najjar happened to be with us at the time. He was a friend of Abu Emile's, and of Ibrahim Hamad's, the grocer based in the same building where Abu Emile lived and worked. We all went to a friend of Abu Michel's, whose name was Faddoul Rbeiz and who had a grocery store opposite Saint Mary's Orthodox Church of Dormition. In the shop we were received warmly. Then Hamad and Murad, with Abu Michel's help, began praising Wasif's art, oud playing, and knowledge of old singing, which impressed the grocer, Faddoul Rbeiz. The latter invited us into the backroom of his shop where I saw three ouds hanging on the wall. One seemed to be in good condition, while the other two looked rather deplorable. We sat down, and it turned out that Faddoul Rbeiz could play the oud a little. He handed me the instrument, and we had what was indeed a wonderful time after I had not played the oud for so long. The audience was amazed. Some passersby gathered in the street, and everyone listened to me play on the maqam Rast. My nights playing the oud in the years past all came back to me, particularly the first years of the British Mandate.

I asked Faddoul Rbeiz if I could borrow the other oud for a short time, on the condition that I would have it repaired and fitted with new strings. My friends came to my help—particularly Abu Michel—and begged him to lend me the oud. They assured him that he had nothing to fear, particularly after they had sensed in his looks that he liked my playing and was convinced of my artistry. After a few moments, Faddoul Rbeiz said, "Why not. You're welcome. This oud is yours, provided that you pay me three Lebanese pounds each month." I agreed immediately and paid in advance for the first month. My friends who were with me were quite moved by how he had treated me. As for me, I wondered to myself: Has time been so unfair to me that I now have to rent an oud on a monthly basis, having left back at home in the Jawhariyyeh Collection seventy-two Western and rare Eastern musical instruments? But I guess this must be in order for me to fulfill my role as a refugee. If you looked at the rent, it was extremely cheap at less than ten Lebanese piasters per day, since I paid twenty-five piasters for my shoeshine.

After the Nakba, I was taken far, far back in time. I had held the oud for the first time at Costandi al-Sous's party. How much I suffered as a boy before I was able to acquire one. How I saved for my first oud and got it only with the greatest difficulty from Sabri Abd Rabbuh, the baker. Now, after the Nakba, I was back to where I had been as a child, in dire need of money. But at the same time I remained optimistic and thanked the Lord both for the good times and bad, particularly for having survived, with my children, the battles of Jerusalem. This, for me, was the most important thing.

I took the oud and had it repaired. I also had it dyed so it that it looked brand new, and I fitted it with new strings. I kept it for at least six months. At the end of each month, in order to play my part in this act to perfection, I would go to see the grocer Faddoul Rbeiz with some friends such as Zawaneh George Murad and Qandlaft. After a flowery Jawhariyyeh-style introduction, I would apologize to Rbeiz for the delay and pay him thc amount of three hundred Lebanese piasters, while thanking him for the generosity and compassion he showed towards the stranger I was.

APPENDIX

THE RECORDS OF THE WERKO [an Ottoman urban property tax abolished by the British Mandate government in 1928]—the grading of properties and lands that took place across the country twenty-five years ago. This is known as the werko register and lists properties under individual entries and reference numbers.

THE SUMMARY—a record in which the lands are listed together under their reference number on a separate page for each owner. Each page is dedicated to a particular taxpayer and lists the number of the relevant piece of land against its type, borders, area, and the werko tax due on it. Should the land in question be located in the city, the owner paid a tax at 10/1000 of the land's value, while state-owned arable land located in villages was taxed at 4/1000 of its estimated value.

THE DURKUM—a register of the names of the werko taxpayers, listed by district.

[RECORD OF] DETAILS OF TITHE TAXES DUE FOR BOTH SUMMER AND WINTER, AND GUIDELINES FOR THE EVALUATION OF THESE TAXES IN THE VILLAGES, AS WELL AS RECORDS OF THIS EVALUATION PROCESS—The check register lists the individual account of each taxpayer and the estimated tax, or rather the tax due to be paid in the relevant year. Against these, payments already received from the taxpayer are noted, along with the number and date of their receipt and the number of the notification with which payment had been collected, as well as a note on how the monies had been transferred to the government's coffers.

THE DAILY—a notebook, or special record book, in which the daily revenues of the Revenue Department were entered under the relevant sections. The record is signed after inspection by Jerusalem's financial secretary.

MASTER NOTEBOOK—a rather special record book, in which the types of the payments received were entered on a daily basis. Their total had to tally with that stated in the Daily, and also had to be signed daily by the financial secretary.

As for the forms used, they are many. One of them is a special form used for tapu transactions. No sale, zoning, mortgaging, endowment, or anything of the kind was processed at the Tapu Department unless this form was submitted along with the relevant file to the Revenue Department, following which we would carry out the necessary inspection to find out whether the party or parties concerned had paid their werko and tithe taxes in the previous and current years. Relevant details from the Werko Department summary record are then entered on these forms, where the payment of the tax is confirmed and the form is signed by the Werko officer, Ibrahim Effendi al-Alami, who was the chief official in charge, then by the financial secretary Muhammad Aref al-Costantini and finally by the financial inspector Atallah Mantoura.

On the many occasions where the financial inspector or the financial manager got the impression that the sale price declared by the seller and the buyer on the form was less than the real price of the property, an inspection of the property in question was ordered and carried out by a special committee made up of the land registration officer or someone representing him and the financial secretary or someone representing him.

(from "Moving to the Revenue Department" on pg. 228)

Wasif explains the tax process in detail: "Six grading committees were appointed for the city of Jerusalem. Each committee was made up of a president, a legal surveyor, and two of the city's landlords and notables. The president of the committee got two votes, the surveyor one, and the remaining two members one vote each, making up five votes in total. Whenever opinions diverged, the head of the committee, who was entitled to one vote more than the other three members tipped the balance, in favor of the government.

We began this laborious job according to a map on which the city outside the wall and on all sides of it was divided into 109 blocs. A "bloc" was an area demarcated in relation to the adjoining ones and contained twenty to three hundred units. A "unit" was a private property—either land for construction or a property built on a piece of land.

After assigning a serial number to a unit within a bloc, the engineer would record the details of this unit in a special register. In this register, the area of the land or of each floor of the property was noted in square meters. The engineer also noted the type of building and the materials used in its construction, specifying whether it was built of concrete or stone, if the ceiling or the roof was an ordinary one or brick, the number of rooms and facilities, and information regarding running water, rain water, and similar details which, in my opinion, made a lot more sense to the government than to the landlord himself. At the same time, we would prepare a form to be filled out regarding the rent charged under the contract for every unit of the building, the reference number and date of the contract, the landlords of the adjoining properties, and their real shares.

An official authorization signed by the governor allowed the president of the committee to enter any property at any time for the purpose of grading, along with the other members of the grading committee, in order to undertake a detailed inspection of any of the contents of the house and subsequently to come up with a fair grading. In the case of unlet properties, we used to grade the building taking the neighboring properties into consideration. When the property was rented out through word-of-mouth, we resorted to this same measure.

After grading the units of a bloc, all the property details were recorded in the "grading list." Details of the landowner and the serial number of the land or the unit were recorded in the list, which was displayed on the wall in the hall of the Saraya for thirty days from the date of the grading, next to the landowner's name, with the estimated value of the land or the property indicated. At the same time, the landowner was given a special form with this information and had the right to appeal to the committee within the thirty-day period, should he believe he had been dealt an injustice.

Buildings were graded based either on the real rent, as stated in the contract, or on the committee's estimate. Twenty percent was then deducted for repairs, and the named owner was informed of the remaining amount, known as the net yearly rent. For the grading of land, we would consider the area and grade it by square meter. Should the area of the land total one thousand square meters and the rate be five-hundred fils per square meter, the estimated value of the land would be five-hundred Palestinian pounds. Under the property tax law, six percent of five-hundred pounds was calculated, which would come to thirty pounds. This amount would be the net yearly rent, and the named owner was officially notified to the effect.

The government collected a tax equaling ten to fifteen percent of the net yearly rent of both buildings and lands—three pounds for a piece of land that was a valued at one thousand pounds, and so on. If a building was graded as a house with a rent value of one hundred pounds per year, after twenty percent was deducted, the yearly rent would be set at eighty pounds, and the owner would have to pay ten percent of that amount. So his due tax for a year's period would be eight Palestinian pounds.

Many articles in the law granted tax exemption by means of a certificate issued either by the municipality or by the Jerusalem Planning Department, for lands that were unsuitable for building, as well as to charities, religious, and educational institutes, and so on. Should the owner feel for any reason that he had been wronged, either due to an extortionate grading value, or in terms of the area of the property or the name or the like, he had thirty days from the last day of the publication of the grading announcement to file a complaint with the same committee, which would reconsider the grading in a special meeting and inform him of its decision. The plaintiff then had fifteen days to appeal to the appeal committee, which was formed of a president, a surveyor, and one member, and whose decision was final."

(from "The urban property tax in Jerusalem" on pg. 266)

NOTES

All references to the original manuscript of the written diaries are noted MS.

Hearing Palestine

[1] MS 64, 107.

[2] MS 101.

[3] MS 102.

[4] See A. J. Racy, *Making Music in the Arab World: The Culture and Artistry of Tarab* (Cambridge: Cambridge University Press, 2003).

[5] MS 45.

[6] MS 56.

[7] MS 196.

[8] Danielson has identified the interrelation between Qu'ranic recitation and song in early twentieth-century Egypt. See Virginia Danielson, *The Voice of Egypt: Umm Kulthūm, Arabic Song, and Egyptian Society in the Twentieth Century* (Chicago: University of Chicago Press, 1997), 23–26.

[9] Wasif Jawhariyyeh's Musical Notebook (unpublished, 576 pages) is housed at the Institute of Jerusalem Studies in Ramallah.

[10] These were the Church of the Flagellation, Saint Anne's Church, the Church and Convent of the Sisters of Zion, and the Austrian Hospice. Yehoshua Ben-Arieh, *Jerusalem in the Nineteenth Century: The Old City* (Jerusalem and New York: Yad Izhak Ben Zvi Institute, 1984), 169–180.

[11] MS 71.

[12] MS 166.

[13] MS 130.

[14] Janakis were female singers, often also playing the darbuka.

[15] MS 175.

[16] Issam Nassar and Salim Tamari, eds., *Al-Quds al-intidabiyyeh fi al-mudhakkirat al-Jawhariyyeh: al-kitab al-thani min mudhakkirat al-musiqi Wasif Jawhariyyeh, 1918–1948* [*British Mandate Jerusalem in the Jawhariyyeh Memoirs: Volume II of the Memoirs of the Musician Wasif Jawhariyyeh, 1918–1948*] (Beirut: Institute for Palestine Studies, 2005), 313.

[17] For a detailed study of the radio station, see Andrea Stanton, "A Little Radio Is a Dangerous Thing: State Broadcasting in Mandate Palestine, 1936–

1949" (Columbia University: dissertation, 2007). I discuss the specific place of music in this institution in Chapter 5, "Separation," in *Orientalism and Musical Mission: Palestine and the West* (Cambridge: Cambridge University Press, 2013).

[18] MS 249

[19] MS 216. Khalil Sakakini recorded this in his diary in the early 1930s. See Weldon C. Matthews, *Confronting an Empire, Constructing a Nation: Arab Nationalists and Popular Politics in Mandate Palestine* (London and New York: I. B. Tauris, 2006), 173.

[20] As Elke Kaschl has put it, "[b]y adopting Arab dance practices and making them their own, Zionist dance leaders in historic Palestine [...] emphasized that Israeli-Jewish modernity was to be culturally distinct from European modernity." She argues that "Jewish dance leaders [...] believed that they could recover their own, long-lost authentic traditions from the time of the Bible and 're-enchant' Jewish practices." In essence, then, "the Arab villager came to serve as a stand-in for Jews searching for their authentic cultural roots." *Dance and Authenticity in Israel and Palestine: Performing the Nation* (Leiden and Boston: Brill, 2003), 58–59.

[21] MS 189.

[22] MS 232–233, also footnote 250.

[23] MS 261.

[24] MS 252.

[25] Report for the years 1934–1936, and prospectuses for 1935, 1936, and 1937. Housed in the Archive of the Palestine Conservatoire, National Library of Israel, Mus 54, A6. I discuss the politics of this institution in *Orientalism and Musical Mission*.

[26] MS 223.

[27] He suggested using Roman letter names for certain pitches, upper and lower case for the different registers, and he described and drew a picture of the fingering positions for achieving these. It is worth noting that none of this was new to Europe and other parts of the Middle East, including Tunisia and Turkey (and depending on when he wrote it, perhaps not Cairo and Beirut either). It seems to be a symptom of his pleasure in personal inventiveness, rather than connected to pretensions of having produced a new system. See pp. 9–10 of the Musical Notebook for the relevant sketch. The notebook is housed at the Institute of Jerusalem Studies in Ramallah.

[28] Issam Nassar and Salim Tamari (eds.), *Al-Quds al-'Uthmaniyyah fi al-mudhakkirat al-Jawhariyyeh: al-kitab al-awwal min mudhakkirat al-musiqi Wasif Jawhariyyeh, 1904–1917* [*Ottoman Jerusalem in the Jawhariyyeh Memoirs: Volume I of the Memoirs of the Musician Wasif Jawhariyyeh, 1904–1917*] (Beirut:: Institute for Palestine Studies, 2003), 313.

[29] Ajaj Nuwayhid, *Sittun 'aman ma' al-qafila al-'arabiyya* [*Sixty years in the Arab Caravan*]. Prepared by Bayan Nuwayhid al-Hut. (Beirut: Dar al-Istiqlal, 1993), 280. This translation by Nada Elzeer.

[30] Nuwayhid, *Sittun 'aman ma' al-qafila al-'arabiyya*, 267–268.

[31] Lachmann's primary interests were in comparative musicology, a new discipline that looked beyond musicology's traditionally European remit. He was a founder of the pioneering *Gesellschaft der Musik des Orients* (Society for Oriental Music) and edited the *Zeitschrift für Vergleichende Musikwissenschaft* (*Journal of Comparative Musicology*).

[32] Robert Lachmann, "'Oriental Music,' A Series of Twelve Talks on the Palestine Broadcasting Station (1936–1937) by Lachmann." First lecture, delivered November 18, 1936. Transcribed in "*The Lachmann Problem*": *An Unsung Chapter in Comparative Musicology* (Jerusalem: Magnes Press, 2003), 329–330.

[33] In this critical respect, Lachmann's work falls in line with a Finnish anthropologist of the Palestinians, Hilma Granqvist, who set out in 1925 to research "The Women of the Old Testament," but who rapidly observed what she termed "Biblical dangers." See Hilma Granqvist, *Marriage Conditions in a Palestinian Village* (Helsingfors: Societas Scientarum Fenna, 1931), 1–14.

[34] Lachmann's conflicts with the Hebrew University are documented in Katz, "*The Lachmann Problem.*" On the university's Zionist foundations, see Tom Segev, *One Palestine, Complete: Jews and Arabs Under the British Mandate*, translated by Hain Waterman (London: Abacus, 2001), 73–75.

[35] "Section for the Study of Non-European Music, First Report," dated 14 June 1935, reproduced in Katz, "*The Lachmann Problem,*" 112.

[36] MS 250ff.

[37] For a discussion of these debates in the context of the conference, see A. J. Racy, "Historical Worldviews of Early Ethnomusicologists: An East-West Encounter in Cairo, 1932." In Philip V. Bohlman and Daniel Neuman, eds., *Ethnomusicology and Modern Music History* (Urbana: University of Illinois Press, 1991), 68–91. Some of the surviving recordings from Lachmann's Palestine collection have been digitized and can be heard in the Sound Archive in the National Library of Israel. His much more extensive logbook indicates that many recordings have been lost or destroyed, including those of Wasif.

[38] Letter from Lachmann to the president of the Hebrew University, Judah Leon Magnes, dated November 13, 1935. Published in Katz, "*The Lachmann Problem,*" 129.

[39] The now notorious expression stems from Philip J. Baldensperger, *The Immovable East: Studies of the People and Customs of Palestine.* Edited with a biographical introduction by Frederic Lees. (Boston: Small, Maynard, and Co., 1913).

[40] MS 337.

[41] MS 299.

Wasif Jawhariyyeh's Jerusalem

[1] This introduction is based on two separate essays published as introductions to Volumes I and II of the Jawhariyyeh memoirs in Arabic: *Al-Quds al-'Uthmaniyyah fi al-mudhakkirat al-Jawhariyyeh: al-kitab al-awwal min mudhakkirat al-musiqi Wasif Jawhariyyeh, 1904–1917* (Al-Quds: Mu'assasat al-Dirasatl-Maqdisiyh, 2003); and *Al-Quds al-intidabiyah fi al-mudhakkirat al-Jawhariyyeh: al-kitab al-thani min mudhakkirat al-musiqi Wasif Jawhariyyeh, 1918–1948,* (Al-Quds: Mu'assasat al-Dirasat al-Maqdisisyah, 2005); both volumes edited by Salim Tamari and Issam Nassar. Quoted translations may differ slightly from the English text of this version of the memoir, since they were done by this writer.

[2] Although Wasif was clearly a protégé of the Husseini family, he does not indicate that he was a sympathizer of the Palestine Arab Party, which they led at a later date. When his patron Hussein al-Husseini died, he allied himself with Ragheb al-Nashashibi, the political adversary of Hajj Amin, without identifying himself with the Defense Party. These shifts should not be read as opportunism on Jawhariyyeh's part. Both families viewed Wasif as an artist and musician, and had no political expectations of him.

[3] See Rochelle Davis, "Ottoman Jerusalem," in *Jerusalem 1948: The Arab Neighbourhoods and their Fate in the War* (Jerusalem: Institute of Jerusalem Studies, 1999), 10–29.

[4] Yehoshua Ben-Arieh, *Jerusalem in the Nineteenth Century: Emergence of the New City (*Jerusalem: Yad Izhak Ben-Zvi, 1986), 152–172.

[5] MS 64.

[6] MS 155.

[7] MS 327ff.

[8] Wasif Jawhariyyeh, *Musical Notebook*, undated and unpublished, Institute of Jerusalem Studies, Ramallah. This 576-page handwritten manuscript, dedicated to the Ottoman Sultan and signed "Wasif Jawhariyyeh—Quds Sharif," was most likely written, at least in part, in the Ottoman period. It is divided into five sections: (1) Muwashahhat and Anashid, (2) Madhahib and Adwar, (3) Love Songs, (4) Balads and Quartets, and (5) Taqatiq and Erotic Songs.

[9] Ibid., "*Tarkib al-Nota al-Ifranjiyya 'ala Awtar al-'oud,*" 9–10.

[10] MS 19.

[11] MS 18.

[12] MS 145–146.

[13] Wasif writes, "My master Omar was widely recognized as a grand master in the performance of the muwashah, a genre which is almost extinct today in the Arab world, except perhaps in Aleppo. Omar used to tell me about his teacher, Ali Darwish, who was a world authority in this genre." Wasif Jawhariyyeh MS 221–223.

[14] MS 298.

[15] MS 335.

[16] MS 321.

[17] Edward Said, *Out of Place: A Memoir* (New York: Vintage, 1999), 6.

[18] Rashid Khalidi writes of these contested loyalties in, "Competing and Overlapping Loyalties in Ottoman Jerusalem," in his work *Palestinian Identity: The Construction of Modern National Consciousness* (New York: Columbia University Press, 1997) 63–88. See also James Gevin, *Divided Loyalties: Nationalism and Mass Politics in Syria at the Close of Empire* (Berkeley: University of California Press, 1998), 141–195; and Hasan Kayali's 'revisionist' perspective, *Arabs and Young Turks: Ottomanism, Arabism, and Islamism in the Ottoman Empire, 1908–1918* (Berkeley: University of California Press, 1997), 81–115.

[19] MS 225.

[20] On perceptions of the British Mandate in historical debates, see Bernard Wasserstein, "The British Mandate in Palestine: Mythos and Realities," in *Middle East Lectures*, Vol. 1, (Tel Aviv: The Dayan Center for Middle East and African Studies, 1995), 29–41.

[21] See Tamari and Nassar, eds., *Al-Quds al-'Uthamaniyya fil Mudhakkarat al Jawhariyyeh*, (Beirut: Institute for Palestine Studies, 2002), 253–254.

[22] MS Volume 2, 19.

[23] Izzat Tannous, *The Palestinians: Eyewitness History of Palestine Under the British Mandate* (London and New York: I. G. T. Co., 1988), 35.

[24] Mana', *Tarikh Filasteen*, 249.

[25] Ronald Storrs, *Orientations* (London: Nicholson and Watson, 1937), 272–273.

[26] Bayan Nuwaihid al Hut, *Al Qiyadat wal Mu'assasat al Siyasiyya fi Filasteen, 1917-1948* [Leadership and Political Institutions in Palestine] (Beirut: Mu'assast al Dirasat al Filastiniyyah, 1981) 66.

[27] In Wasif's memoirs, the national movement was already divided on the issue of census boycott, with Fawzi Nashashibi, a cousin of Raghib and a future leader of the opposition (pro-British) faction, already counseling support for the census.

[28] Wasif Jawhariyyeh, MS Vol. 2, 84–85.

From Ottomans to Arabs

[1] Hasan Kayali, *Arabs and Young Turks: Ottomanism, Arabism, and Islamism in the Ottoman Empire, 1908–1918* (Berkeley: University of California Press, 1997).

[2] *Safarbarlik* was the term by which people in Syria and Palestine referred to the Great War. Originally, it referred to the conscription of young men into the Ottoman army. See Najwa al-Qattan, "Safarbarlık: Ottoman Syria and the Great War," in *From the Syrian Land to the States of Syria and Lebanon*, Philipp and Schumann, eds., (2004), 64.

[3] Salim Tamari, *Year of the Locust: A Soldier's Diary and the Erasure of Palestine's Ottoman Past* (Berkeley: University of California Press, 2011).

[4] See N. Naim Turfan, *Rise of the Young Turks: Politics, the Military and Ottoman Collapse* (London and New York: I. B. Tauris, 2000), 3–14.

[5] Kayali, *Arabs and Young Turks*, 20. For a complete list of the names and origins of the grand viziers in the Empire, see http://en.wikipedia.org/wiki/List_of_Ottoman_Grand_Viziers (July 8, 2010).

[6] Ibid, 17–20.

[7] Charles Smith, *Palestine and the Arab-Israeli Conflict: A History with Documents*, seventh edition (Boston: Bedford/St. Martin's, 2009), 49.

[8] The fact that some of these reforms were not successfully implemented in Palestine, or in some cases were employed well before they became laws, as Doumani suggests in regards to the 1858 Ottoman Land Code, does not undermine this point. Doumani argues that sales transactions of the *miri*, or state lands, took place as early as the 1830s. See Beshara Doumani, "Rediscovering Ottoman Palestine: Writing Palestinians into history," *Journal of Palestine Studies,* Vol. 21/2 (winter 1992): 12.

[9] M. Sükrü Hanioglu, *A Brief History of the Late Ottoman Empire* (Princeton: Princeton University Press, 2008), 150.

[10] Zeine N. Zeine, *The Emergence of Arab Nationalism* (Beirut: Khayats, 1966), 83.

[11] Khalil Al-Sakakini, *The Diaries of Khalil Sakakini: Orthodox Renaissance, World War I, Exile to Damascus*, Volume II, edited by Akram Musallam (Jerusalem, 2004), 97 [in Arabic].

[12] Louis Fishman, "The 1911 Haram al-Sharif incident: Palestinian notables versus the Ottoman administration," *Journal of Palestine Studies* Vol. 33/34 (spring 2005): 13–14.

[13] Ibid, 136.

[14] Ibid, 105.

[15] Tamari, *Year of the Locust*, 154.

[16] Hanioğlu, *A Brief History of the Late Ottoman Empire*, 160.

[17] Khalil Al-Sakakini, *Yawmiya Khalil Sakakini, New York, Sultana*, Book One, Jerusalem, (Jerusalem: Institute of Jerusalem Studies and Khalil Sakakini Center, 2003), 308, 320–21.

[18] Cited in Heather Rae, *State Identities and the Homogenization of People* (Cambridge: Cambridge University Press, 2002), 153.

[19] Pan-Turanism was an ideology that aimed at politically uniting the Turkic, Tatar, and Uralic peoples in an Ottoman state stretching from the Altai Mountains in Eastern Asia to the Bosphorus.

[20] Zeine, *The Emergence of Arab Nationalism*, 113.

[21] Iljan Selçuk, *Yüzbaşi Selahttin' in'Romani*, II. Kitap (Istanbul: Remzi Kitabevi, 1975), 15, cited in Ryan Gingeras, *Sorrowful Shores: Violence, Ethnicity, and the End of the Ottoman Empire, 1912–1923* (Oxford: Oxford University Press, 2009), 12.

[22] Ibid, 12–13.

[23] Ussama Makdisi, "Ottoman Orientalism," in *The American Historical Review*, Vol. 107, issue 3, (2002), available online at (http://www.historycooperative.org/journals/ahr/107.3/ah0302000768.html). Makdisi argues in this article that the Ottoman Turks in Istanbul adopted a view of their Asian territories and their peoples similar to that of the Europeans at the time. This was possibly a way to make themselves appear more modern on par with their European counterparts.

[24] Pasha Ahmed Djemal, *Memoirs of a Turkish Statesman, 1913–1919,* (New York: George H. Doran Company, 1922), 127.

[25] Ibid., 197–237.

[26] Jawhariyyeh, *Al-Quds al-'Uthmaniyyah, 160.*

[27] Ibid, 163.

[28] Tamari, *The Year of the Locust*, 153–154 (Arabic edition).

[29] Roberto Mazza, "Antonio de la Cierva Lewita: The Spanish Consul in Jerusalem, 1914–1920," *Jerusalem Quarterly* no. 40 (winter 2009/10): 38.

[30] Abigail Jacobson, "Alternative Voices in Late Ottoman Palestine: A Historical Note," *Jerusalem Quarterly File* no. 21 (August 2004): 47.

[31] *Zikr* is an Islamic mystical ritual of the Sufis. It literally means "remembrance" and "pronouncement" of the names of God.

[32] Jawhariyyeh, *Al-Quds al-'Uthmaniyyah*, 77.

[33] Ibid., 74.

[34] Al-Sakakini, *Yawmiya Khalil Sakakini*, Book One, 347.

[35] James Gelvin, *The Modern Middle East: A History*, 2nd edition (New York and Oxford: Oxford University Press, 2005), 103.

[36] Jawhariyeh, *Al-Quds al-'Uthmaniyyah,* 198.

[37] Abigail Jacobson, "Alternative Voices in Late Ottoman Palestine: A Historical Note," *Jerusalem Quarterly File* no. 21 (August 2004): 47.

[38] Sakakini, *The Diaries of Khalil Sakakini*, vol. 2, 97.

[39] Jawhariyyeh, *Al-Quds al-'Uthmaniyyah*, 280.

THE STORYTELLER OF JERUSALEM

The Ottoman Era, 1904–1917

Covers pages 1 to 96.

[1] Al-Karak is a town in Jordan south of Amman.

[2] Besides being a name, the word *jawhariyyeh* means 'essential.'

[3] Knafeh is a Palestinian sweet made of very fine vermicelli-like pastry, found throughout the Levant and Egypt. It is sometimes known as shredded phyllo. It originated in the city of Nablus north of Jerusalem, as it is often called al-Nablusiya.

[4] Fakhri, Wasif's brother, went on to become a musician with the Jerusalem Radio Arabic Orchestra.

[5] William Assad al-Khayyat was an American citizen who was appointed chancellor of the British Consulate in Jerusalem.

[6] Also known as Mevleviya, Mawlawiyah stands for a Sufi order (or *tariqa*) associated with the teachings of Mawlana Jalalludin Rumi of Konya. The reference here is to a mosque and a *zawiyya*, a building for spiritual retreat, belonging to this religious order.

[7] An argileh, or water pipe, is used to smoke tobacco in the Middle East. In different countries and regions it has different names, such as nargile, shisheh, and hookah.

[8] Jabal al-Mukabbir is the hill on which the headquarters of the mandate government was later built.

[9] The shirwal was a baggy trouser worn by men in Palestine and the Levant.

[10] During Ottoman rule, the werko was a property tax imposed on land and buildings.

[11] *Shathat Sitna Maryam*, Our Lady Mary Picnic, was an annual event at which Orthodox Christians visited the tomb of the Virgin below the Mount of Olives, where they would attend church service and hold a picnic in the olive groves.

[12] Wasif is referring to tin plates coated in glass and then baked.

[13] An abaya is a traditional Arab long cloak.

[14] Wasif is making a wordplay on *deir* ('monastery') and *dar* ('house').

[15] Lahem bi ajeen is a meat pie.

[16] Simat is a dessert made with semolina and milk, topped with sugar syrup.

[17] Labaniyeh is made with yogurt, lemon, and seasoning (often tahini).

[18] The darbuka is a single-head, goblet-shaped drum. The naqqara is a double-head clay drum with contrasting pitches.

[19] Mahallat al-Wad is a neighborhood in the southeast section of the walled Old City, not far from Via Dolorosa and al-Haram al-Sharif.

[20] Khan al-Aqbat (the Inn of the Copts) is an area in the center of the Old City. Suwaiqat Allun is a market in the Old City near the Christian Quarter.

[21] A matlik was an Ottoman brass coin.

[22] The Schneller School was a Christian orphanage school established in Jerusalem in 1860 by Johann Ludwig Schneller. It was also known as the Syrian Orphanage. It was located near the village of Lifta. During the Second World War, the British authorities in Palestine expelled all German citizens, including those at the school and turned the orphanage into a central British army camp. The camp was attacked in March 1948 by Zionist militants from the Lehi (Stern Gang) and Irgun, and then turned over to the Haganah to become the headquarters of its Etzioni Brigade.

[23] The qombaz is a traditional, loose outer garment of the Levant.

[24] The qanun is a zither-type, Near Eastern string instrument of trapezoidal shape.

[25] Hijazi (1852–1917) was a musician, singer, and pioneer of theater in Egypt.

[26] Taqtouqa is a traditional genre of light vocal music, technically less demanding and sung in regional or colloquial Arabic.

[27] Musa Kazem Pasha was head of the Arab Higher Committee, 1922–1934.

[28] The name beit Jeez was not recognized by the editors. It is possible that Wasif meant Beit Ijza which was a village near Jerusalem.

[29] The Jawhariyyeh Collection included antiques, musical instruments, and photographs collected by Wasif in his house in Talbiyah, outside the wall, the majority of which were lost in the Nakba of 1948.

[30] Patriarch Damianos the First was the head of the Greek Orthodox Church in Jerusalem from 1897 until 1931.

[31] *Effendim* is a Turkish term for "sir" that was commonly used throughout the Ottoman homelands.

[32] Deir Amr was a village in the western part of the city, until it was uprooted and destroyed by Israel in 1948.

[33] The village of Suba is one of the villages of West Jerusalem that were occupied in 1948. It was wiped out after Nakba.

[34] The tithe was a tax the Ottomans imposed on agricultural crops.

[35] Kasla was a Palestinian village west of Jerusalem that was ethnically cleansed and destroyed by Zionist forces in 1948. The other two villages also faced the same fate.

[36] The village of Beit Mahsir was twenty-six kilometers west of Jerusalem. After it was ethically cleansed, destroyed, and erased by Israel in May 1948, a park was established in its place. Sarees, another village west of Jerusalem, faced the same fate in 1948.

[37] The nay is an open-ended flute with a breathy tone, made from reed. The arghool and mijwiz are wind instruments of the oboe family, consisting of two pipes, one of which is a drone.

[38] The dabkeh is an Arab folk dance that is native to the Levant.

[39] The oud, or 'ud, is a string instrument similar to the Western lute used in Arabic and Turkish music. The riqq is a tambourine.

[40] Wasif often refers to a close friend or colleague as "my brother."

[41] One of the palaces of the Husseini family, the American Colony's ownership was transferred before the First World War to a number of Swedish American missionaries. It was used as headquarters for missionaries, then turned into a hospital, and then in the 1960s became a hotel.

[42] *Karakoz* is traditional shadow puppet theater. Originating in China, India, Indonesia, and Southeast Asia, it migrated to the Arab region in the tenth century. Muhammad Ibn Daniel, an eye doctor from Musul, helped to popularize this folk art in Cairo during the thirteenth century.

[43] The Austrian Hospice is the Austrian hospital in Jerusalem Old City, at the intersection of the Via Dolorosa and al-Wad Road near the Fifth Station of the Cross.

[44] Latin Christians in Palestine refers to Roman Catholics. The name relates to the fact that during the crusades, the church in Jerusalem was the church of the Latin Kingdom.

[45] Bachelors apartments were flats which young men of means kept in Old Jerusalem for their private entertainment. Special parties were held in them involving music, singing, prostitution, and the consumption of alcohol and cannabis.

[46] Taqasim are solo pieces that are often improvised according to a certain *maqam*, or modal structure, characteristic of Arab music.

[47] Johann Ludwig Schneller, a missionary who lived in Jerusalem, established the Schneller Orphanage in Jerusalem. Its first residents were children from Mount Lebanon who were orphaned as a result of the 1860 conflict between the Druze and the Maronites.

[48] Mea Shearim was one of the first Jewish neighborhoods to be built outside of the walled city in the mid-nineteenth century. It was home to ultra-Orthodox Jews. Najarlia on the other hand appeared to be another Jewish neighborhood.

[49] This is a reference to Doctor Tawfiq Kanaan of Beit Jala, who was a dermatologist and a famous writer of folk literature.

[50] Mahallat al-Namamreh, better known as Hayy or Haret al-Nammamira, and sometimes al-Namariyyeh, was an early Palestinian Arab neighborhood built in the Baq'aa area in 1873 by the Nammari clan in lower Baq'aa. During the same period, or soon after, al-Wa'ri clan built the al-Wairiyyeh neighborhood in upper Baq'aa. Both families originate from the Old City, and they were the first to relocate outside the city walls after Muhammad al-Khalili, who built his mansion in the same area in the mid-eighteenth century, according to Taher al-Nammari.

[51] Faydi al-Alami was a Jerusalem notable who served as mayor of the city from 1906 to 1909.

[52] The Julian calendar lags fourteen days behind the Gregorian calendar.

[53] Mezze is a collection of Middle Eastern salads and appetizers offered in small portions, often with alcoholic drinks.

[54] Swaiqat Alloun is a part of the market linking Jaffa Gate to the market of the Christian Quarter.

[55] The celebrations of Prophet Moses stopped after the 1967 war and the resulting Israeli occupation, but were revived after the Palestinian Authority was established following the Oslo Agreement of 1993.

[56] Sayyardis is Arabic for 'moving,' and more recently for 'car.'

[57] The Status Quo arrangement is a legal document issued in the middle of the nineteenth century, preserving the distribution of religious rights set by the Ottomans for the various Christian communities. The mandate authorities kept the policy.

[58] A shirwal is a pair of baggy, traditional trousers.

[59] Barazek are sesame cookies that are famous in Jerusalem.

[60] Natef is a creamlike topping made with egg white, sugar, orange blossom water, and rose water.

[61] Zalatimo's is a sweetshop that makes a special pastry known as mutabaq, which usually is filled with cheese. The shop is located under the Coptic church in Khan al-Zeit market in the Old City which leads from Damascus Gate to the vicinity of the Church of the Holy Sepulchre.

[62] The Andalusian muwashah is a musical form that originated in medieval Spain and Portugal. The muwashah is often composed using a complex rhythm, ranging from 2/4 to 48/4 and greater. A muwashah may use more than one rhythm, although the norm is a single rhythm throughout. Lyrics in a muwashah are poetry in classical Arabic and must neatly fit the rhythm (every syllable must fall on a beat).

[63] This reference is to the French Dominican Monastery whose building on Nablus Road outside of Damascus Gate of the Old City today houses the École Biblique.

[64] Sanhedria is an ultra-Orthodox neighborhood located in northern Jerusalem, bordering on Ramat Eshkol, established in 1926.

[65] Hassan Beyk al-Turjman, landlord and interpreter at Jerusalem's sharia court, was the father of Ihsan al-Turjman, the soldier-diarist, whose memoirs appear in Salim Tamari's *Year of the Locust* (Beirut: Institute for Palestine Studies, 2009).

[66] Saad-wa-Said became the main restaurant compound in Arab in Jerusalem.

[67] Bir is Arabic for "well."

[68] During Ramadan the firing of a cannon at dawn and dusk marks the start and end of fasting each day.

[69] *Ya sah al-sabr* is a song sang by the Egyptian singer Munira al-Mahdiya (1885–1965). Most likely, Wasif is referring to "Bishraf Tatious," a violin piece based on the Rast maqam played by the violinist Sami al-Shawa.

[70] The region includes Deir Ghassana and nearby villages.

[71] Jerusalem representatives served in the Ottoman Parliament.

[72] These lyrics are part of a form of Islamic religious chanting known in Arabic as "ibtihal." It is often sung during religious festivities and Sufi rituals. It is not known if Hijazi was the first to sing it.

[73] Iskandar Farrah was an actor and an employee of Damascus Customs during the time of Midhat Pasha in 1878–1879.

[74] Marun al-Naqqash is often referred to as the first Arab playwright. He was born in Sidon in 1817 and died in Tartus in 1855. He discovered theater and opera while on a trip to Egypt. Al-Sheikh Ahmad Abu Khalil al-Qabbani was one of the earliest theater actors in Egypt. He was born in Damascus in the 1830s to a Turkish family from Konya. He moved to Egypt where he formed his famous theatrical troupe, from which a number of future stars would emerge. He died in 1902. See Matti Moosa, *The Origins of Modern Arab Fiction* (Boulder, CO: Lynn Rienner Publishers, 1997), 35–40.

[75] The year 1278 Hijra is the year 1861 AD.

[76] The reference is to the play *Horace*, written by French author Pierre Corneille in 1640.

[77] George Abyad (1880–1959) was born in Beirut, moving to Alexandria where he eventually emerged as a pioneer of Egyptian theater and cinema.

[78] The Arabic word for *teacher* (here "Mr.") contains all the letters of the word *uncle*, so the two words could sound similar.

[79] Surat al-Baqarah is the longest chapter in the Quran.

[80] Cinematograph may mean the cinema or movies, but technically it refers to a type of camera that doubled as a projector.

[81] Bishlik was an Ottoman currency unit and a coin.

[82] Amman, the capital of Jordan, is a new city dating back to the late nineteenth century. It was built on the site of the Roman city of Philadelphia,

whose stones were used by the immigrant Circassians and Chechens who arrived from Russia to build the first homes in the city.

83 Abu Zaid al-Hilali was an eleventh-century Arab leader whose fables of heroism are part of the folklore of the Arabic-speaking world.

84 Antara was an Arabian poet from Najd (now Saudi Arabia) from the pre-Islamic period (d. early seventh century). He was famous for his poetry and adventures. He was in love with his cousin Abla, but as a slave he could not marry her. Antara and Abla is one of the celebrated loves stories in early and Medieval Arab culture.

85 Al-Maskobiyyeh was built in the 1850s and 1860s.

86 Ragheb Bey al-Nashashibi became mayor of Jerusalem in 1920.

87 Fesikh is fermented, salted, and dried mullet. Palamida is Atlantic bonito.

88 "Our community" refers to Arab Orthodox Christians.

89 Also known as Lion's Gate, Saint Stephen's Gate is one of the gates of the Old City of Jerusalem.

90 Khan al-Ahmar is an inn located between Jerusalem and Jericho, traditionally described as the site where the biblical parable of the Good Samaritan took place.

91 Aqbat Jaber is located just outside of Jericho to the west. It later became the site of a refugee camp for Palestinians who were expelled in 1948. It is not clear where al-Marazi was. According to Islamic tradition, the Nabi Musa Road leads to the tomb of the prophet Moses.

92 Mawwal is a traditional genre of vocal music that is usually presented before the actual song begins.

93 Although marrying Cypriots, in particular, was common, the relation between marriage and avoiding military service is not clear.

94 Saris Village is situated west of Jerusalem, near Jaffa Road. The Haganah occupied it on April 13, 1948, during Operation Nachshon. It was depopulated, and the settlement Shoresh was built nearby.

95 Beit Mahsir was a village west of Jerusalem that was occupied by the Zionist forces on May 10, 1948 and its people ethnically cleansed. Two Israeli colonies were built on it, Beyt Me'ir and Misillat Tziyyon.

96 Mansaf is a traditional lamb dish prepared in dried yogurt and served with bulgar rice.

97 Qershalleh is a kind of kaak, or street bread, similar to rusk cake.

98 Dawr is an old Arabic music form in which the musician improvises on a theme, always returning to the original scale. Mawwal is vocal music before the actual song.

99 Halabia is the Arabic adjective of Aleppo.

100 The building, which currently houses the Islamic Orphanage, was known as Khasky Sultan and is located in Aqabat al-Mufti in the Old City. The

name relates to the history of the building, for it was named after the wife of Sultan Suleiman the Magnificent, Roxelana. *Khasky Sultan* means "the Sultan's favorite" and was Roxelana's nickname. This building was erected between 1552 and 1556. See Youssef al-Natsha's article in *Jerusalem Quarterly File*, no. 7 (winter 2000), 29–35.

[101] Aqabat al-Takiya referes to the neighborhood in the Old city where the the soup kitchen Khasiki Saltana is located which was established in the 16th century by the wife of sultan Sulieman

[102] Al-Manyalawi was a pioneering nineteenth-century Egyptian singer and musician whose recordings from the first decade of the twentieth century have survived to this day. He died around 1911.

[103] The date given here, July 1914, is likely to be old style, since the real date of the mobilization of Turkey is often said to have been on 2 or 3 August. Neither of these two dates, however, falls on a Friday.

[104] The reference here is to the coup of the Young Turks against the sultan in 1908. The Ottoman Decentralization Society was a political party formed in 1913 in Cairo calling for the decentralization of the Ottoman state.

[105] Photographer Khalil Raad's shop was just outside of Jaffa Gate. He is considered to be the first Arab photographer in Palestine. The Said bookshop was located in the same place, as well. The family of the late Edward Said owned this bookshop.

[106] The Regie Department was a government monopoly based on foreign capital that controlled tobacco production and distribution.

[107] Samakh was a Palestinian village on the southern shore of Lake Tiberias (the Sea of Galilee). It was depopulated in 1948 and its lands were incorporated by Israel into Kibbutz Ma'agan.

[108] Wasif notes: "The plane had indeed landed in Jaffa and was received there by Turkish officers and government officials. Nouri Bey and Ismail Bey were given a hearty reception in Lawrence Hotel. After lunch, photographs were taken in the hotel's garden, and they were given a worthy farewell. Then the catastrophe happened, and they met their death. I keep pictures of the scenes at the hotel in Jaffa."

The Mandate Years, 1917–1948

Covers pages 97 to 258.

[109] From the Quran, Surat Al-Baqarah (verse 216).

[110] A kalpak is a hat made of felt or sheepskin that was commonly worn by men in the Balkans, Turkey, and Iran.

[111] Sheikh Badr is a quarter in West Jerusalem, situated near the village of Lifta.

[112] Romema was a Jewish suburb in western Jerusalem, built on Lifta land.

[113] This seems to be a reference to the YMCA on King David Street in West Jerusalem.

[114] Ard al-Samar is the area known as Wadi al-Joz, immediately to the north of the Old City.

[115] Gabriel Bey Haddad (known as "the Pasha") worked as an advisor to the early British military administration in Palestine and later became the head of security in Prince Faisal's government in Damascus. In his memoir, *Orientations*, Ronald Storrs wrote of him, "as able as he was loyal and charming, whose services in those first days of general ignorance and suspicion I cannot overrate." (London: Nicholson and Watson, 1943), 335.

[116] The Occupied Enemy Territories Administration (OETA) administered Palestine before the onset of the British Mandate Government in 1921–1922.

[117] The Schmidt's Girl School in Jerusalem was a prominent school established in the late nineteenth century by German Catholics near Damascus Gate.

[118] This phrase is a parody of Quranic verse 101:4: "And what should make thee know what the great Calamity is."

[119] Those men belonged to Jerusalem's notable families, some from Nabulsi and Hebronite origins. Fakhri al-Nashshibi (1899–1941) was leader of the Defense Party and later the Peace Bands, organized by the opposition against the 1936 Rebellion. A nephew of Ragheb Bey, al-Nashashibi was assasinated in Baghdad in 1941.

[120] Ragheb Bey al-Nashashibi (1881–1851) studied architecture and urban planning in Istanbul. He was head of Jerusalem's Public Works Department during Ottoman rule. Appointed by Ali Ekrem Bey and the prime minister's office in Istanbul to plan Beersheba in 1910, he served as the elected mayor of Jerusalem during the mandate (1920–1934) and later as head of the oppositional Defense Party (opposition to the Husseini leadership).

[121] Dar Surarahu was most likely his bachelor's apartment where he used to entertain his friends.

[122] The Governorate here refers to the Government House, known as the Saraya in the Ottoman period. It continued to be the headquarters of the colonial mandate authority during British rule.

[123] Meshkinot is Hebrew for "housing scheme." In this period it referred to housing estates established in Jerusalem by Jewish philanthropists such as Montifiore.

[124] Abu Fuad is the *kunya*, or honorific name, of Hamada Afifi.

[125] In the original, Beit al Umma (House of the Nation) was most likely a nickname for a bordello.

[126] The work involved supervising al-Husseini's estates and the village harvest.

127 Montefiore was then a new Jewish housing estate established in 1860 outside the city walls, opposite Jaffa Gate.

128 Aref Pasha al Daudi (Dajani) 1856-1930, served as mayor of Jerusalem immediately after Ottoman withdrawal from southern Palestine. In 1918 he became the regional president of the Muslim-Christian Association.

129 The Literary Club, al-Muntada al-Adabi, was established in Istanbul and had branches in Damascus, Beirut, Jerusalem, and several other provincial towns in Ottoman Syria. Ostensibly it was a cultural association for the propogation of Arabic language and literature, but it became politicized during the war.

130 Estefan Hanna Estafan was a prominent Jerusalem scholar and ethnographer. A member of the Palestine Oriental Society, he was later appointed as head of the Palestine Archeological Museum during the mandate. It is not clear if the reference here is to him or to his father.

131 Since many of these names are transcribed from Arabic, we were not able to establish the accuracy of their English spelling except for well-known mandate officials.

132 Sami Haddawi (1904–2004) later became one of the senior land experts of the mandate government and published a number of studies on the subject. The first director of the Institute for Palestine Studies, he died in Toronto in 2004 at the age of one hundred and one month.

133 Sir Herbert Samuel was the first British high commissioner for Palestine (1920–1925) and one of the architects of the Balfour Declaration.

134 Norman Bentwich was legal secretary and attorney general in the mandate government (1918–1929).

135 Ronald Storrs was a British colonial officer and administrator. He was the first military governor of Jerusalem (1917–1921), after which he became civil administrator of Jerusalem. During the mandate period he set up the Pro Jerusalem Society, that aimed to preserve the architectural heritage of the city. His published memoir is entitled *Orientations*.

136 Wasif is referring to the establishment of the French Mandate in Syria and the separation of Greater Syria from Palestine.

137 This passage is a quote from Qu'ranic verse 8:61.

138 Jaleel Badran was one of the illustrious figures of Ramallah. He became mayor of Ramallah in the fifties and a minister in the Jordanian government in 1957.

139 The reference is to Saint John's Eye Hospital which was located in Baq'aa (West Jerusalem) until the war of 1948. It was later relocated to Sheikh Jarrah (East Jerusalem) where it has continued to function.

140 The London Jews' Society was a missionary group that undertook the conversion of Jews to Christianity.

[141] The Arabic word for Jewish cooperative neighborhoods in Jerusalem is *kompaniyya* (company). Wasif uses the word *ma'zal*, which can be translated as "separate enclosure," or "ghetto."" We have used "commune," since these Jewish areas were often of mixed residencies.

[142] Roza were Syrian striped satins which were imported from Aleppo and Homs.

[143] Wasif's daughter Yusra Arnita, musicologist and author, died in the US in March 2000.

[144] Mutabaq is a sweet pastry for which Zalatimo's café and bakery in the Old City was renowned and which the café has continued to serve.

[145] This reference is to nonmigrant Jews who did not enter the country following the Balfour Declaration.

[146] Herbert Samuel issued a pardon which included Amin al-Husseini and Aref al-Aref, among others.

[147] The reference to Hajj Amin is inaccurate since al-Husseini, too, was appointed by the British as mufti. The title "grand mufti" was created by the mandate authorities for the post. In the Ottoman period, the position was filled by the "Mufti of Jerusalem."

[148] Charles R. Ashbee, an architect and urban planner, was head of the Pro Jeruslem Society and a civic advisor to the mandate government (1918–1923). He was a follower of William Morris.

[149] Faidallah al-Alami was mayor of Jerusalem (1907–1909) and the father of Musa al-Alami.

[150] Both references to Sarufim and Abdul-Wahhab seem to be satirical. Abdul-Wahhab was known for his hybrid music and plagiarism despite his immense popularity.

[151] Wasif was forced to hide the Jawhariyyeh Collection inside a wall in a private home in West Jerusalem before fleeing during the 1948 war. During the 1967 war, he was able to go to this house after twenty years had passed. Unfortunately, the model had been looted, according to information provided by the late Zuhdi Hashwa in 2003.

[152] The Besharats were a prominent Jerusalem family of Transjordanian origins. Their family residence and property were in the Talbieh neighborhood during the mandate.

[153] Hatem al-Ta'i, pronounced colloquially as Hatem Tayy, was a Bedouin Arab who is thought to be the symbol of Arab generosity and hospitality.

[154] Ahmad Sameh Khalidi (1896–1951) was a Jerusalem educator and author. He studied pharmacy at the American University of Beiurt. He became principal of Teacher's College (later Arab College) and inspector of education during the mandate period. He was the author of several literary and historical works.

[155] "Became like one of the al-Khalidis" means that he became a Khalidi protégé. This is an interesting assertion since the Khalidis, the Nashashibis, and the Husseinis competed for the position of mayor of Jerusalem and later had major factional disputes among their followers.

[156] Musa Kazem Pasha al-Husseini was the first mayor of Jerusalem under British rule (1918–1920). Before the war he served as Ottoman governor of Yemen. He was the father of Abdul Qadir al-Husseini.

[157] Bezelel, or Beit Tzelel, was a Jewish cooperative arts and crafts center established in Jerusalem in 1903.

[158] Fawzi al-Nashashibi founded the scouting movement in Palestine.

[159] The intention is clear. Husseini's party and the Defense Party took opposite sides on the question of the census, and support for the mandate government, even at this early stage. The Defense Party was not formed at this time, so Jawhariyyeh was writing in hindsight. This passage provides an eyewitness observation of the factional strife between the two groups as early as 1921, when the census took place.

[160] The results of the census actually came out and were published by the mandate government, although they had limited credibility.

[161] *Al-Karmel* was an anti-Zionist paper, published in Haifa by Najib Nassar.

[162] Is'af al-Nashashibi (1882–1948) was a major literary figure from Jerusalem. He was inspector of education during the mandate and professor of Arabic at Salahiyya College during the Ottoman period.

[163] In 1998 this "palace'" was turned into a cultural center named after Is'af al-Nasashibi, and it currently contains a number of his books and manuscripts. The center has issued a number of publications, including a study about the works of Is'af al-Nashashibi.

[164] Al-Duyuk and al-Nuwaimeh are Bedouin agglomerations north of Jericho and south of al-Jiftlik.

[165] Born in Alexandria, Zaki Murad was a leading Egyptian composer, singer, and actor of Iraqi Jewish origins. He was the father of Layla Murad and composer Munir Murad.

[166] The lyrics are typical of old and traditional Arabic love songs. The theory that the song was written for Ataturk seems far-fetched.

[167] The Jerusalem intellectuals mentioned constituted the inner circle of what was known after the First World War as the Party of the Vagabonds (Hizb al-Sa'aleek) associated with Khalil Sakakini. The group included writers, poets, journalists, and intellectuals who used to meet regularly in the Vagabond Café (Maqha al-Sa'aleek) owned by Issa al-Toubbeh, the mukhtar of the Orthodox community in Jerusalem near Jaffa Gate in the Old City. For details about this group and the café see "The Vagabond Café and the Prince of Idleness" in Salim Tamari's *Mountain against the*

Sea: Essays on Palestinian Society and Culture (Berkeley: University of California Press, 2009).

168 The windmill house belonged to Nicola Abdo, father-in-law of Khalil Sakakini. It was located near the Jerusalem train station. The reference here must be to the period in which the couple moved to Sultana's family property before they had a house of their own.

169 *Ra's Rus* refers to the *Al-Jadid* series on reading Arabic in which al-Sakakini revolutionized the methodology of teaching Arabic to children.

170 This is a reference to the Al-Khalidiya Library, which is one of the most important manuscript libraries in Palestine and was catalogued in 2001.

171 Qays and Yemen were Southern Arabian tribes to whom many tribes in the Ottoman Empire, including the Syrian region, traced their origins. A strong sense of rivalry existed in the early twentieth century between clans that claimed descent from these two groups. See Jane Hataway's *A Tale of Two Factions: Myth, Memory, and Identity in Ottoman Egypt and Yemen* (New York: SUNY Press, 2003), 103–104.

172 Haytaliyeh is a Syrian-Palestinian sweet made of milk and starch. Mawardiyeh is a sweet made of apricot paste, milk, and starch.

173 Saint Barbara's Day is celebrated by Christians throughout the Middle East, but especially in Palestine, Lebanon, and Syria on the fourth of December as the day of martyrdom of an early Christian saint from the village of Abud, near Ramallah. Her holiday is especially celebrated by the Christian Orthodox community, but she is also venerated by Catholics and Muslims. Her holiday is the equivalent of Halloween in the West.

174 Cannon Square is today Martyrs' Square. It came to be known as Cannon Square after the 1773 Russian bombardment of the city during which one particularly massive cannon was stationed in it.

175 Dondurma is the Turkish name for ice cream that was common in the Arab East until the 1950s.

176 General Louis Bols was the first military administrator of Palestine (1917–1919). It was Bols who handed over the military administration to the civilian authority with the famous statement, attributed to Herbert Samuels: "Received from Major-General Sir Louis Bols K.C.B.—One Palestine, complete."

177 "From our community" refers to the Orthodox Christian community.

178 Wasif probably meant to stress from this blessing that the patriarch had intended to give the couple the house and plot, but that he would in the meantime give them a rent-free residence until he was able to dispose of the property in their favor.

179 Cliff Hotel was an Arab hotel in Jaffa privately owned by the Barakat family, according to Fakhri Jdai.

180 Salim is not identified, but most likely was Mrs. Froso's son.

181 Nicoforia is a Greek Orthodox neighborhood of West Jerusalem, currently bounded by King David and Emile Botta Streets.

182 In protected tenancies in Palestine, key money was paid to the departing tenant of the property by the new tenant as compensation for vacating a protected tenancy. In this case the actual term for the money is *khlu ijjir* (literally, "vacating tenancy"), since key money is technically paid in buying and selling property.

183 All of these neighborhoods are located to the southwest of Jerusalem outside the city wall. With the exceptions of Baq'aa and the German Colony, their names were Hebrewized after 1948. Al-Haririyyeh was located near the railway station, and the mansion of al-Khalili was the villa of the al-Khalili family, built in the eighteenth century in Lower Baq'aa.

184 Scottish Memorial Church is a reference to Saint Andrew's Church, which was built as a memorial to the Scottish soldiers who died fighting the Ottoman army during World War I.

185 Ratisbonne Monastery is a Catholic convent in West Jerusalem, established in the nineteenth century by Marie-Alphonse Ratisbonne, a Catholic convert from Judaism. The monastery is known as a center of Catholic-Jewish studies. It is currently run by the Salisian brothers.

186 It is not clear what Jawhariyyeh meant by "the English Talbieh neighborhood." This could be a reference to the area of Jabal al-Mukabbir near Talbieh, which is home to the military rule headquarters and the former British army camp known as the "Allenby Barracks."

187 The Palace Hotel was built in Mamilla by the Islamic Awqaf (religious endowment) of Jerusalem, as a Palestinian equivalent to the King David Hotel. Completed in 1928, it was later converted to office space and leased to the mandate government.

188 The Jawhariyyeh Photographic Collection is preserved in the Institute for Palestine Studies Library in Beirut.

189 Although Wasif gives no exact date, this would have been in the late 1920s or early 1930s.

190 Aouni Bey al-Hadi was one of the leaders of the Palestinian National Movement during the mandate and one of the founders of the Independence Party that called for the independence of Palestine (Southern Syria) within the boundaries of Greater Syria.

191 Wasif writes, "At the time, Cyprus was considered to be a place of exile and detention for political prisoners of the British Empire, such as the late King Hussein I, the grandfather of the Hashemites who had been betrayed by his son Abdullah. This is what Storrs had in mind when he wished his guests to see them in Cyprus. He never stopped joking, even at serious moments, or during work. Thus the curtain came down on Storrs's time in Palestine."

[192] Hasan Sidqi al-Dajani (1890–1938) was a Jerusalem literary and political figure. Founder and editor of *al-Quds al-Sharif* in 1920, his paper opposed the Balfour Declaration and supported the Nashashibi opposition. He was a leading member of the Defense Party. He translated the novel *Beware*, by Namiq Kemal, from Turkish, published in 1922, and published a number of works on Palestinian law. He was assassinated in 1938.

[193] The "museum" refers to the room of the Jawhariyyeh Collection.

[194] Herbert Charles Plumer, also First Viscount Plumer (1857–1932), was a commander in the British Second Army in WWI. He succeeded Herbert Samuel as the High Commissioner for Palestine.

[195] The word *arab* and *'urbaan* is often used in reference to Bedouins in both the Arab East and in Egypt.

[196] The Zionist Congress in Zurich created the Jewish Agency in 1929.

[197] The three prisoners were hanged on Tuesday, June 17, 1930. This day became known as Red Tuesday in Palestinian history and became commemorated as a day of mourning.

[198] The actual paper reads: "British policy in Palestine issued by Mr. Churchill in June 1922."

[199] The Edicule is the chapel that houses the Holy Sepulchre, or tomb of Jesus.

[200] It is not clear which calvary the author means, the Greek or the Latin one, or the rock of Calvary itself.

[201] The Greek Orthodox Calvary is the spot where Christ is believed to have been crucified. It covers the actual Rock of Golgotha, also known as Calvary.

[202] Umm George is Wasif's wife.

[203] Nicola al-Sayigh was a leading icon painter of the Jerusalem school (d. 1930).

[204] Robert Lachmann (1892–1939) was a German ethnomusicologist, linguist (German, English, French), musicologist, orientalist, and library official. He was an expert in the music of the Orient, a member of the Berlin School of Comparative Musicology, and one of its founding fathers. Lachmann arrived in Palestine in April 1935, after he had been dismissed from his position at the Berlin National Library, following the Nazis' rise to power. He came to Jerusalem at the invitation of Judah L. Magnes, chancellor and later president (1935–1948) of Hebrew University to establish a center and archive for Oriental music, according to Ruth Kark.

[205] The Palace Hotel was built by the Husseini family in 1929, opposite the Mamilla Cemetry, on Mamilla Street.

[206] Field Marshal Sir John Greer Dill (1881–1944) was a British commander in World Wars I and II. He was the general commanding officer of the British Military Forces during the Palestine Rebellion in 1936–1937.

[207] Abdul Qader al-Husseini was the foremost Palestinian national and military leader. He led the forces of al-Jihad al-Muqaddas in the 1948 war, until his death in combat in the Qastal area. He was the son of Musa Kazem Pasha al-Husseini, and father of Faisal Husseini. Nuri Pasha al-Said was prime minister of Iraq during the Hashemite monarchy. Despite his Turkish origins, he joined Prince Faisal during the Arab Revolt and served both the Syrian Hashemite regime and the Iraqi monarchy of King Faisal and Ghazi. He was killed during the 1958 republican revolution.

[208] The Broadcasting House was formally called the Palestine Broadcasting Service (PBS). It was launched on March 30, 1936.

[209] It's not clear from Wasif's handwriting if the name was Azzuri or Azzuzi.

[210] The Palestine Royal Commission, known as the Peel Commission, issued its recommendations in 1937.

[211] The etymology seems to be Persian rather than Turkish.

[212] The reference is to the Palestine Arab Party, established in 1935 and headed by Jamal al-Husseini.

[213] Farid al-Atrash was the famous Egyptian singer of Syrian origin and the brother of Asmahan.

[214] This is one of al-Atrash's songs that helped make his fame in his debuts. It is also the only song he sang which was not his own composition.

[215] Umm Kulthum is doing a wordplay. The word *atrash* means "deaf."

[216] Most likely the name 'Ammail is Amiel.

[217] The reference is to the period when his father, and later Wasif, were acting as tax collectors for the Husseinis in Khirbet Deir Amr.

[218] Zuhdi Hashweh was a noted Jerusalem lawyer who represented the interests of Christian Orthodox endowments. He married Wasif's daughter Layla.

[219] Quruntal is the popular name for the Rum Orthodox Monastery of Saint George Gorge south of Jericho.

[220] Wasif is referring to the monastic prohibition of female presence in the monastery.

[221] Deir al-Su'ud could be a reference to the Monastery of the Ascension.

GLOSSARY

abaya: a square cloak, traditionally made from wool

adhan: the call to prayer by a muezzin from the mosque five times a day, traditionally from the minaret

arghool: *also yarghoul*, a traditional Arabic wind instrument consisting of two pipes, one of which is a drone

awqaf: religious endowment

ayaan: local urban notables who were traditionally close to power during the Ottoman centuries; they belonged to certain families of significance within the history of Islam and many of them were landowning gentry who served in some capacity in the *sharia* courts

Balfour Declaration: a 1917 letter by Lord Balfour, which became a vital British policy statement on Palestine and an important declaration of British support for Jewish Zionist aspiration, included the statement that "His Majesty's Government view with favor the establishment in Palestine of a National Home for the Jewish people, and will use their best endeavors to facilitate the achievement of this subject..."

bloc: a basic unit for the delineation of land boundaries in the Tapu, where each bloc contains several parcels of land

British Mandate for Palestine: Britain acquired a mandate over Palestine at the meeting of the Supreme Council of the League of Nations in San Remo, Italy, in April 1920, was approved by the League in July 1922, and went into effect in September 1923

buzuq: a long-necked, fretted lute

Christian Quarter: known as *Haret an-Nasar*ah in Arabic, it is one of the four quarters of the old City of Jerusalem, which contains the Christian holy sites, including the Church of the Holy Sepulchre

Church of the Holy Sepulchre: one of the holiest Christian sites—the place both of the crucifixion and the tomb of Jesus of Nazareth—and a major pilgrimage center for Christians from around the world

city wall: the 2.5 mile-long (approx 4000 m) wall with 8 gates that surrounds the Old City of Jerusalem, built in the 16th century when Jerusalem was part of the Ottoman Empire

Civil Administration of Jerusalem: following the establishment of the British Mandate and after a few years of military administration in the city by the British following its conquest, the British formed a civilian government fully administered by British personnel

cumbus: a Turkish instrument developed in 1930 as a popular alternative to the more costly classical *oud*

dabkeh: an Arab folk, line-dance usually performed at weddings and celebrations

***dakdookah*:** a peasant folk song

darbuka: also known as the *tabla or durbakkeh*, the *darbuka* is a goblet drum, traditionally made out of clay with a fish or goat skin head

***dawr* (pl. *adwar*)**: a genre of Arabic vocal music sung in colloquial Arabic

dhimmi: a member of a protected religious community in the Muslim community, usually a Christian or a Jew

effendi: an Ottoman term for a member of the professional classes

gendarmerie: a military force charged with duties inside the cities and among the civilian population

Governorate, Government House: the center of government offices in district centers and large cities, known as the Serayy or Saraya

Grand Mufti of Jerusalem: the Sunni Muslim cleric in charge of Jerusalem's Islamic holy places, a position which, during the British occupation, was appointed by the British Mandate authorities

Greater Syria: known historically as *Bilad ash-Sham*, Greater Syria was the territory under the Ottoman rule enclosed by Taurus Mountains to the north, the Mediterranean Sea to the west, the Arabian Desert to the south and the Euphrates River to the east

Haganah: a Zionist militia established in 1920 which later emerged as a highly trained army, focused on terrorizing and expelling Arabs from the area about to constitute the Jewish state

hajj: pilgrimage to Mecca (for Muslims) and to Jerusalem (for Muslims, Christians and Jews)

High Commissioner for Palestine: the highest official in Mandate Palestine, appointed by the British Government in London

Jawhariyyeh Collection: artifacts, musical instruments, and photographs collected by Wasif Jawhariyyeh in his Nikforyieh home, of which the photographic collection has survived and is kept today at the Institute of Palestine Studies in Beirut

Jerusalem Governorate: the district of Jerusalem during the British Mandate

Jewish Agency: founded in 1929 as the administration authority of the Jews in Palestine, it ran the affairs of the *Yeshuv* and was recognized by the British mandatory power as the official authority in Palestine for the Jews; it continues to be active now in Israel and deals mostly with recruiting Jewish immigrants from abroad

Jewish National Home: Palestine was seen as the place to establish this national home in the words of the Balfour Declaration of 1917

Karakoz: a Turkish term for shadow puppet theater, means "black eyes"

katholikon: a large and central church in the Orthodox Christian tradition

keffiyeh: also known as *hattah*, it is a cotton headdress fashioned from a square scarf, traditionally worn by Arab men

khaniqah: a religious building belonging to a sufi order of Tariqah

***layali*:** unmetered modal improvisation based on a *maqam*

madaf or madafeh: guest house, mostly in villages and small towns

***maqam* (pl. *maqamaat*)**: a set of notes with specific melodic phrasing and development that conveys a mood and may include microtonal variations such as full tones, half tones, and quarter tones

mawwal: a traditional music genre of vocal improvisation using colloquial poetry

McMahon Agreement: the October 1915 agreement accepted by Palestinians as a promise by the British that Palestine would be returned to its Arabs inhabitants after the war had ended in return for their support to the Allies in the war

mijwiz: a woodwind instrument that consists of two short, equal length reed pipes tied together, played by using a circular breathing technique

military administraton: the British government in Palestine which administered the country before the establishment of the Mandate, between 1917-1921

military governor of Jerusalem: the highest British administrator in Jerusalem during the period of the military administration (1917-1921)

muezzin: is the person appointed at a mosque to lead, and recite, the call to prayer (*adhan*)

muwashah (pl. muwashahat): a composed song of Andalusian origin that uses classical Arabic poetry and complex rhythmic patterns and is sung by a chorus and a soloist

mufti: a Muslim jurist who issues interpretive judgments about the application of Islamic law

mukhtar: the village elder man, often an appointed official who represent the neighborhood before the government

Nakba: the "Catastrophe" in Arabic, refers to the destruction of Palestinian society in 1948 when more than 750,000 Palestinians fled or were forced into exile

nay: an open-ended reed flute

New City: the expanded city outside the city walls of Jerusalem, often the term is used to designate the Westen suburbs of the city

Nicoforia: a neighborhood of Jerusalem located west of Jaffa Gate

Old City: known in Arabic as *al-Balad al-Qadimeh*, it is a walled area of approximately 0.35 sq mi (0.9 sq km), which contained 28 *mahallahs* (neighborhoods) in the Ottoman period, and four quarters during the British Mandate: the Christian Quarter, the Muslim Quarter, the Jewish Quarter, and the Armenian Quarter

oud: a short-necked, fretless lute, which has five pairs of stings and one bass string, and is plucked with an eagle's feather

Palestine Broadcasting Service (PBS): the state-owned radio station which operated from 1936 until the end of the British Mandate

pasha: honorific term for the highest appointed official in the Ottoman administration

patriarchate: a term used for the main religious establishments in the Christian communities, most notably the Orthodox, the Catholic, the Syriac and the Melkite, each with a head known as the Patriarch

***qaim maqam* (sub-governor)**: a title used for the governor of a provincial district or the representative of the sultan during the Ottoman Empire

qanun: a zither-like, trapezoid-shaped, string instrument that is placed flat on the knees of the seated musician and plucked with two plectra on the forefingers

qumbaz: an open wrap-around coat, often in striped fabric, usually clinched with a belt and covered with an *abaya*

rebeck: *rababah* in Arabic, the earliest known bowed instrument, its front covered in a membrane such as sheepskin, has a long neck, and is played upright

Regie Department: the tobacco state monopoly

Registry: *Qism al Tahrirat* in Arabic; the department of records in the Mandate Government

Revenue Department: see Werko

riqq: a small tambourine covered with a fish or goat skin head over its wooden frame with five sets of brass cymbals, each consisting of two pairs

Saadia Quarter: a *mahalla* in the old city located near Herod's Gate

sajat: brass finger cymbals

safarbarlek: Ottoman military conscription during wartime

Saraya, Government House, the Governorate: Ottoman term, also known as the Serail, for the district government bureaucratic compound which housed the main administrative departments of district centers

sharia: Islamic law

sheikh: an elderly man; a Muslim religious cleric

Status Quo: resulted from a sultani decree issued first in the 18th century by which sites within the Church of the Holy Sepulchre in Jerusalem were divided between various religious denominations, which was updated in 1853 in the aftermath of the Crimean war to include a special role for imperial counties in the protection of the agreement and the privileges enjoyed by the different dominations in the Church

Sublime Porte: the Imperial seat of the Sultan and his Government in Istanbul

sultan: during the Ottoman Empire (1299-1922), the sultan was at the apex of the hierarchical Ottoman system

Sykes-Picot Agreement: a 1916 secret pact between Britain and France to divide up the Ottoman Empire among Britain and France after the victory of the Allies in World War I, and whose provisions contradicted previous British promises of independence to the Arab territories

tanboor: an ancient, long-necked string instrument of Persian origin

Tapu Department: department of land registry

***taqsim* (pl. *taqasim*)**: an instrumental improvisation or solo

taqtouqa: a light song with a simple melody

tarab: a state of ecstasy and surrender one encounters while listening to a piece of music

Transjordan: the Emirate of Transjordan, a British protectorate, was the name given in 1922 to the region east of the Jordan River, previously known as southern Syria, which in 1946 became the Hashemite Kingdom of Jordan when it acquired its independence after a 23-year rule by Emir Abdullah bin Hussein al-Hashemi

uhzuja: a celebratory dance normally performed by men

Werko Department: land tax department in the Ottoman and early Mandate period

White Paper: a policy paper issued by the British Authorities in Palestine in 1939 in which a representative government was proposed in response to the rebellion of 1936-39

World Zionist Organization: the Zionist Organization (ZO), established in 1897, became the World Zionist Organization (WZO) in 1960 following the adoption of a new constitution. Its program focused on the creation for the Jewish people a home in Palestine

zawiyya: a religious school for sufi orders and other *tariqas*, usually located inside major mosques, such as al Azhar, Qairawan, Zaitunah, and al Haram al Sharif

LIST OF JOURNAL ENTRIES

LIST OF JOURNAL ENTRIES